THE LAW AND
POLITICS OF WTO WAIVERS

Despite being an important legal instrument in the law of the WTO, the waiver has hitherto been the subject of little scholarly analysis. Isabel Feichtner fills this gap by challenging the conventional view that the WTO's political bodies do not engage in significant law-making. She systematizes the GATT and WTO waiver practice and suggests a typology of waivers as individual exceptions, general exceptions and rule-making instruments. She also presents the procedural and substantive legal requirements for the granting of waivers, deals with questions of judicial review and interpretation of waiver decisions, and clarifies the waiver's potential and limits for addressing the need for flexibility and adaptability in public international law and WTO law in particular. By connecting the analysis of waiver competence and waiver practice to the general stability/flexibility challenge in public international law, the book sheds new light on the WTO, international institutions and international law.

ISABEL FEICHTNER is Assistant Professor of Law and Economics at Goethe University Frankfurt am Main, Germany.

CAMBRIDGE INTERNATIONAL TRADE AND ECONOMIC LAW

As the processes of regionalization and globalization have intensified, there have been accompanying increases in the regulations of international trade and economic law at the levels of international, regional and national laws.

The subject matter of this series is international economic law. Its core is the regulation of international trade, investment and cognate areas such as intellectual property and competition policy. The series publishes books on related regulatory areas, in particular human rights, labour, environment and culture, as well as sustainable development. These areas are vertically linked at the international, regional and national level, and the series extends to the implementation of these rules at these different levels. The series also includes works on governance, dealing with the structure and operation of related international organizations in the field of international economic law, and the way they interact with other subjects of international and national law.

Series editors:

Dr Lorand Bartels, *University of Cambridge*
Professor Thomas Cottier, *University of Berne*
Professor William Davey, *University of Illinois*

Books in the series:

Trade Policy Flexibility and Enforcement in the WTO: A Law and Economics Analysis
Simon A. B. Schropp

The Multilaterization of International Investment Law
Stephan W. Schill

The Law, Economics and Politics of Retaliation in WTO Dispute Settlement
Edited by Chad P. Bown and Joost Pauwelyn

Non-Discrimination in International Trade in Services: 'Likeness' in WTO/GATS
Nicolas Diebold

Processes and Production Methods (PPMs) in WTO Law: Interfacing Trade and Social Goals
Christiane R. Conrad

African Regional Trade Agreements as Legal Regimes
James Thuo Gathii

The Law and Politics of WTO Waivers: Stability and Flexibility in Public International Law
Isabel Feichtner

THE LAW AND
POLITICS OF WTO WAIVERS

Stability and Flexibility in
Public International Law

ISABEL FEICHTNER

CAMBRIDGE UNIVERSITY PRESS
Cambridge, New York, Melbourne, Madrid, Cape Town,
Singapore, São Paulo, Delhi, Tokyo, Mexico City

Cambridge University Press
The Edinburgh Building, Cambridge CB2 8RU, UK

Published in the United States of America by Cambridge University Press, New York

www.cambridge.org
Information on this title: www.cambridge.org/9781107012899

First published 2012

Printed in the United Kingdom at the University Press, Cambridge

A catalogue record for this publication is available from the British Library

Library of Congress Cataloguing in Publication data
Feichtner, Isabel.
The law and politics of WTO waivers : stability and flexibility in public international
law / Isabel Feichtner.
p.   cm. – (Cambridge international trade and economic law ; 7)
Includes bibliographical references and index.
ISBN 978-1-107-01289-9 (hardback)
1. World Trade Organization.   2. Foreign trade regulation.   3. Foreign trade promotion.
4. General Agreement on Tariffs and Trade (1947)   5. Waiver.   I. Title.
K3943.F45   2012
343′.087 – dc23   2011035043

ISBN 978-1-107-01289-9 Hardback

Für Noa

CONTENTS

ACKNOWLEDGEMENTS

This book is the outcome of my Ph.D. research which I conducted from 2005 to 2009 whilst I was a research fellow at the Max Planck Institute for Comparative Public Law and International Law in Heidelberg and teaching assistant to Joseph Weiler and Visiting Doctoral Researcher at NYU. In 2008 and 2009 my work was financially supported by a Schlieben Lange scholarship.

I thank Armin von Bogdandy for supervising this research project and engaging with my thoughts, my colleagues at the Max Planck Institute for discussions and friendship, my friend Jürgen Friedrich for his comments on the manuscript, Joseph Weiler for encouragement, and my family for their patience.

Parts of Chapters 4 and 6 are based on two previously published articles, 'The Administration of the Vocabulary of International Trade: The Adaptation of WTO Schedules to Changes in the Harmonized System', 9 *German Law Journal* (2008) and 'The Waiver Power of the WTO: Opening the WTO for Political Debate on the Reconciliation of Competing Interests', 20 *European Journal of International Law* (2009).

1

Why study the WTO waiver?

International law and institutions increasingly not only deal with trans-actions across the borders of sovereign states, but instead promote and protect transnational societal interests. To give but a few examples: inter-national legal regimes obligate states to limit greenhouse gas emissions by national households and industry, to put into place administrative and judicial procedures for the protection of intellectual property rights, or they restrict domestic governmental powers to adopt policies that encroach upon human rights or impede international trade.

The observation that international law promotes transnationally shared societal interests, such as interests in a clean environment, cross-border trade, property or human rights protection does not implicate a value judgment. It does not follow that such law is beyond criticism and exclu-sively for the good of human kind. Rather it implicates trade-offs – trade-offs between economic and non-economic interests, for example, or trade-offs between individual freedom and public interest policies. The extension of the scope of international law and governance in their subject matters as well as their intrusiveness in domestic administrative, legislative and judicial processes brings to the fore a number of ten-sions. These include the tension between international governance and domestic government, the tension between societies at different stages of economic development and with different forms of government, the tension between international legal regimes that promote overlapping or contradictory objectives, and finally the tension between, on the one hand, the constant flux of societal preferences and realities and, on the other hand, the rigidity of traditional international law-making instruments, in particular international treaties.

In this book I inquire into the potential of the WTO waiver power – i.e. the power of the WTO Ministerial Conference to suspend any legal obligation of the WTO Agreement or the annexed Multilateral Trade Agreements – to address these tensions. My inquiry is based on two assumptions. Firstly, that the formal validity of international law is a value that should not be given up lightly; that law should not be perceived merely as an instrument to achieve objectives outside the law, such as economic development or environmental protection, but that the legal form constitutes a value in itself that merits protection. The second assumption is that international law and governance should be accompanied by a transnational political debate concerning the trade-offs between societal interests which such law and governance entail.

In light of these assumptions the WTO's waiver power appears as a promising instrument. It is promising firstly, because the waiver may be used to flexibilize international law and thus address the tensions identified above; secondly, because the waiver process is a political process which potentially allows for debate about trade-offs between competing societal interests; thirdly, because the waiver procedure is a law-making procedure and the waiver a binding legal act which formally suspends legal obligations and thus allows for non-compliance without putting into question the law's validity.

In light of these characteristics it is surprising that the waiver power and waiver decisions to date have not received much attention in the literature on the WTO and public international law in general, and all the more so since the practice of granting waivers is – compared with the remainder of the decision-making practice of the WTO's political organs – extensive.

This study proceeds as follows: Part I presents what I call the stability/flexibility challenge in international law and develops the thesis that formal international law-making processes are important to flexibilize international law and at the same time maintain its valididity. In this part I also discuss different conceptualizations of WTO law, and defend my view that WTO law should be perceived as a body of public law that aims at securing market conditions and at ensuring legitimate trade governance. From such a perspective a number of flexibility demands may be directed towards WTO law.

Part II addresses the waiver's potential to meet these flexibility demands. It analyses in detail the waiver competence, the drafting history, waiver practice, legal requirements for the adoption of waiver decisions, decision-making process, implementation, interpretation and review. It suggests a typology of waivers as individual exception, general exception and rule-making instrument and presents a doctrinal reconstruction of the waiver according to the general categories of international institutional law.

Part III inquires into the potential of the waiver power as compared to other legal mechanisms to flexibilize international legal regimes: on the one hand to take account of individual parties' needs and preferences and on the other hand to respond to needs and preferences shared transnationally. It will conclude with an assessment of the politics of the waiver process, in particular its potential to allow for an inclusive debate on the reconciliation of competing societal interests.

As Joseph Weiler frequently points out, there are law books and books about the law. This book aims at being both. As a law study it presents, in Part II, a systematic doctrinal analysis of the waiver power and waiver decisions and systematizes the waiver practice in order to distil therefrom a typology of waivers. As a study about the law, the book, in particular Parts I and III, aims to clarify the relationship between law and politics as well as the waiver's potential and limits for addressing the need for flexibility and adaptability in public international law and WTO law in particular.

PART I

The stability/flexibility challenge in public international law and particularly the WTO

In the first part of this book I set out the premises, as well as the research questions, which inform my analysis of the WTO's waiver power. Chapter 2 briefly presents the flexibility challenges that arise if transnational societal interests are protected or promoted through international law in a way that restricts domestic self-government.[1] Such challenges concern, first, the relationship between domestic and international governance, second, the adaptability of legal norms to transnational needs and preferences and, third, the coordination and linkage of different international legal regimes. While these challenges arise from international governance through law, the claim is not to do away with law or to 'soften' it. Instead, it is argued that law performs an important function in legitimate international governance, and that to perform this function its validity needs to be based on formal requirements. Validity and flexibility need to be reconciled through law-making procedures that may take account of the identified flexibility challenges.

After this general exposition of the study's analytical framework, I turn to the WTO. The perception of the flexibility challenges posed by an international legal regime depends on how one interprets its objectives. Chapter 3 first sets out an understanding of the WTO as an organization which is aimed at coordinating potentially conflicting societal interests. It then conceptualizes WTO law as a body of public law that, on the one hand, contributes to the creation of a public good, namely the global market and, on the other hand, places restrictions on domestic public authority. The chapter concludes by setting out the main flexibility challenges posed by WTO law.

---

1 Throughout this study I use the terms 'domestic law' and 'domestic self-government', not only to refer to state law and self-government within states, but also to European Union law and government in the European Union.

The stability/flexibility challenge in public international law

A. INTERNATIONAL LAW AS PUBLIC LAW

International law today aims not only at the delimitation of sovereign spheres of influence, the reconciliation of opposed national interests, or the reciprocal exchange of benefits between states. It increasingly seeks to promote and protect societal interests which are shared across borders – transnational interests, or, to use Wolfgang Friedmann's term, 'common human interests'.[1] Such international law aims at the protection of common goods, as for example the marine environment, the protection of shared values and interests, such as human rights or certainty for transnational business transactions, and the internationalization of common spaces, such as the deep seabed or the moon.[2]

International legal regimes[3] that pursue such aims influence domestic government. They do so in prohibiting certain government measures or by requiring governmental action. Sometimes international institutions themselves exercise governmental functions, by adopting legislative acts, or by engaging in administration or adjudication.[4]

This type of international law which to varying degrees affects and constrains the ability of polities to self-govern can no longer be seen

---

1 Friedmann, *Changing Structure of International Law*, 62 *et seq.*; cf. Weiler and Motoc, 'Taking Democracy Seriously', 47, 63 *et seq.*
2 Feichtner, 'Community Interest'; Weiler, 'The Geology of International Law', 547, 556.
3 The term 'international legal regime' as used throughout this study encompasses international treaties, international organizations and other international institutions, but also instruments giving rise to non-binding norms; the term is thus used to describe a narrower set of institutions than Stephen Krasner's definition of international regime which encompasses 'principles, norms, rules, and decision making procedures around which actor expectations converge in a given issue-area': Krasner, 'Structural Causes and Regime Consequences', 185.
4 Cf. Alvarez, *International Organizations as Law-Makers*; see also the contributions in Bogdandy *et al.* (eds.), *The Exercise of Public Authority by International Institutions*.

as a pure *inter*-national law of co-existence akin to a private law that regulates the interaction between states as equal and unitary subjects of law. Rather, it constitutes an international *public* law.[5] More illustratively, it may be termed a 'world internal law' (*Weltinnenrecht*).[6] Attached to the characterization as public law are certain normative demands: on the one hand regarding the content of the legal norms and, on the other hand, regarding processes of norm creation.[7] These demands are partly reflected in legal doctrine. The concept of *jus cogens*, for example, may be seen to protect the conformity of international law with certain fundamental values.[8] Demands concerning processes of norm creation, such as demands for transparency and participation of actors other than government actors, are as of yet only insufficiently reflected in international legal doctrine. Doctrine still predominately perceives the state as a unitary entity represented by individual government officials.

The impact of international law on domestic government is further accentuated by the increasing legalization and judicialization of international regimes. Legal norms are more and more precise, leaving states less freedom of implementation. Increasingly autonomous bodies, in particular courts and tribunals, are empowered to interpret and apply these norms as well as to make new law.[9]

---

5 Frowein, 'Konstitutionalisierung des Völkerrechts', 427, 428; on the public law approach to international law and institutions see also Bogdandy, Dann and Goldmann, 'Developing the Publicness of Public International Law', 1375.
6 Sir Gerald Fitzmaurice observed that a convention such as the Universal Postal Convention 'although a treaty, was in a way a municipal law of the whole international community': Fitzmaurice, Report on the Law of Treaties, 368th meeting, 218. See also Delbrück, 'Prospects for a "World (Internal) Law?"', 401. According to Joost Delbrück 'World Law may be defined as a body of law that transcends the notion of strictly inter-state law ... World Law encompasses in its scope and application state and non-state actors, transactions and situations of most different kinds beyond the state or national level' (*ibid.*, 403).
7 Kingsbury, 'The Concept of "Law" in Global Administrative Law', 23.
8 Generally on the doctrinal concepts of *jus cogens* and *erga omnes* norms, see Simma, 'From Bilateralism to Community Interest in International Law', 217; Tomuschat, 'International Law. Ensuring the Survival of Mankind', 9; Kadelbach, *Zwingendes Völkerrecht*.
9 Cf. Abbott *et al.* 'Concept of Legalization', 401. Apart from precision and delegation Kenneth Abbott *et al.* identify a third dimension to measure legalization, namely bindingness. However, from an internal perspective bindingness does not seem to be a useful criterion. The legal system distinguishes itself from other social systems by its operative code legal/illegal and thus cannot accommodate different degrees of bindingness without giving up this binary code: cf. Fischer-Lescano and Liste, 'Völkerrechtspolitik', 209, 222; see also section C.III below. On law-making as an exercise of public authority by international courts and tribunals, see Bogdandy and Venzke, *In Whose Name?*

B. THE FLEXIBILITY CHALLENGE

The fact that international legal regimes increasingly restrict and complement domestic government raises several concerns and consequently demands for flexibility. These can be formulated taking three different perspectives: a domestic perspective, an intra-regime perspective and an inter-regime perspective. From each perspective one can distinguish between flexibility demands related to the legitimacy of international governance as well as flexibility demands related to its effectiveness.

I The domestic perspective

International legal rules that promote or protect societal interests are manifestations of political choice. They further certain socio-economic interests to the detriment of others.[10] Thus they are contestable, not only among states as sovereigns, but also within states.[11] However, while legislation in liberal democracies is legitimated through a democratic process and certain constitutional guarantees, law-making at the international level is largely a prerogative of states' executives. The democratic deficit which arises from the empowerment of the executive and the limited influence of domestic parliaments and public opinion on international law-making is exacerbated by the inflexibility of treaty law. While changes in the balance of interests and preferences in the polity domestically can lead to the adoption of new legislation, international law is highly irresponsive to such changes. It continues to bind states and determine their policies even when it is not supported by a parliamentary majority.[12] The legal option to withdraw from an international legal regime often does not represent a practical option due to the dependency of states on international cooperation.[13] Consequently, from the perspective of domestic self-government, it may be claimed that public international law illegitimately restricts the realization of domestic preferences determined in a democratic process or that certain activities of international

10 Kennedy, 'Laws and Developments', 17.
11 Weiler, 'The Geology of International Law', 547, 555–6.
12 For a detailed analysis of legitimacy deficits resulting from international law-making with further references, see Friedrich, 'Nonbinding Instruments' (manuscript on file with the author).
13 Weiler, 'Alternatives to Withdrawal from an International Organization', 282.

institutions violate fundamental principles or values embodied in domestic constitutions.[14]

The rigidity of international law, which is sometimes even greater than that of national constitutions, might not be perceived as a legitimacy deficit if one attributes to international law a constitutional function. The rigidity of international law as constitution is then perceived as a necessary safeguard to protect certain values from intrusion by domestic government or to protect democratic processes from disproportionate influences of special interests.[15] Human rights treaties are frequently conceived as constitutional in this sense.[16] With an increasing judicialization of international human rights regimes the constitutional function is, however, often called into question. Where international courts are called upon to interpret human rights norms, the interpretative choices of domestic polities are reduced. This raises concerns, in particular where such interpretations conflict with interpretations of domestic (constitutional) courts. Arguably, the judicialization of human rights regimes poses the danger of ignoring the contextuality of the concrete application and realization of human rights.[17]

As long as the state constitutes the primary form of political organization that makes democratic self-government possible and as long as there is no consensus as to the concrete realization of 'constitutional' values recognized by international law, international legal regimes need to be responsive to collective choices and cultural context in order to remain legitimate.

The rigidity of international legal instruments not only poses a challenge for the legitimacy of international governance, but also for its effectiveness. From the domestic perspective the rigidity of international legal instruments that restrict domestic governmental freedom may endanger the acceptability by governments of these norms. States may be particularly unwilling to bind themselves in light of the uncertainty as to how norms will be applied in the future by autonomous international organs.

14 Cf. the decision by the ECJ in Cases C-402/05P and C-415/05P, *Kadi and Al Barakaat*, judgment of the Court (Grand Chamber) of 3 September 2008; see also McGinnis and Somin, 'Should International Law Be Part of our Law?', 1175.

15 Tomuschat, 'Der Verfassungsstaat im Geflecht der internationalen Beziehungen', 7; Peters, 'Compensatory Constitutionalism', 579; Keohane, Macedo and Moravcsik, 'Democracy-Enhancing Multilateralism', 1.

16 For a functional comparison of domestic bills of rights and international human rights treaties, see Gardbaum, 'Human Rights as International Constitutional Rights', 749.

17 Lord Hoffmann, 'The Universality of Human Rights'; cf. Helfer, 'Overlegalizing Human Rights', 1832.

It is consequently argued that effectiveness depends on the ability of states to defect within certain limits without incurring excessive costs. Opt-out options, like escape clauses or reservations, are seen as necessary to induce consent to becoming a member of an international institution as well as to maintain acceptance and high levels of overall compliance.[18]

II The intra-regime perspective

The preceding section referred to flexibility demands that may be raised from the perspective of domestic constituencies and governments – demands that international law should yield to domestic preferences. From an intra-regime perspective, the rigidity of international legal instruments – in particular treaties – also poses a flexibility challenge. Since societal needs and preferences, as well as reality, change over time, international legal norms must be adaptable to such changes in order to remain legitimate and effective. In the words of Roscoe Pound: 'Law must be stable and yet cannot stand still.'[19]

Representation of the various societal interests affected by international law is still deficient at the international level and consequently international law often is imbalanced and more representative of certain interests than others – often those which are best able to influence executive officials partaking in international negotiations.[20] Moreover, international legal regimes which are based on the principle of sovereign equality frequently do not take sufficient account of the different stages of development of state parties. To foster acceptance international legal regimes need to be able to address such imbalances through law-making which is more transparent and representative than most of today's international negotiations. The more international law mandates transformations of domestic government and administration, the more the differences in capacity as well as differences in the prioritization of policies resulting from different stages of development must be reflected by the legal norms.[21]

---

18 Bilder, *Managing the Risks of International Agreement*; Downs and Rocke, *Optimal Imperfection?*; Helfer, 'Constitutional Analogies in the International Legal System', 193, 231; Pauwelyn, 'Transformation of World Trade', 1; Pauwelyn, *Optimal Protection of International Law*. Obviously, demands for flexibility to enhance the effectiveness of international agreements presuppose that international law does indeed influence government actions and is not merely epiphenomenal as claimed by Goldsmith and Posner, *Limits of International Law*, and Posner, *Perils of Global Legalism*.

19 Pound, *Interpretations of Legal History*, 1.

20 Benvenisti, 'Exit and Voice in the Age of Globalization', 167.

21 Cullet, *Differential Treatment in International Environmental Law*.

International regimes also need flexibility to cope with regulatory challenges.[22] Changes in reality and knowledge may require the adaptation of legal rules to effectively pursue the objectives of international regulation. Claims for adaptation may be based on the argument that a certain norm does not contribute to the objective of a legal regime or does not do so efficiently. For example, arguments might be made that a certain substance discovered to be a persistent organic pollutant should be included in the Annexes to the Stockholm Convention on Persistent Organic Pollutants, that a substance previously not known for its ozone-depleting effect should be listed in an annex to the Montreal protocol, or that a species listed in one of the appendices to the Convention on International Trade in Endangered Species of Wild Fauna and Flora is no longer endangered and should therefore be de-listed. It might also be claimed that a norm is not efficient since a different norm would achieve the same objective at lesser cost. Finally, it might be argued that further norms should be enacted to pursue the objectives of an international legal regime more intensively, e.g. that CO_2 emissions should be limited further in order to contain the detrimental effects of climate change.

III The inter-regime perspective

Further flexibility needs result from the differentiation of the international legal order into various regimes which pursue diverse, partly overlapping and complementary, partly conflicting objectives. International legal regimes that pursue or protect transnational interests tend to evolve spontaneously; they are often prompted by the formulation of a particular problem, such as climate change or trade in conflict diamonds, which then leads to the formation of an international legal regime, frequently on the basis of an international treaty. Sometimes new regimes are formed since certain actors believe that they may pursue their aims more effectively through a new rather than through an existing institution. The result is a large number of international legal regimes with partly overlapping, partly diverging membership and subject matters and differing institutional structures: a phenomenon often denoted as the fragmentation of international law.[23]

---

22 Chayes and Handler Chayes, *The New Sovereignty*, 226; Tietje, 'Changing Legal Structure of International Treaties', 26.
23 Benvenisti and Downs, 'The Empire's New Clothes', 595 (for an explanation of fragmentation as mainly a function of powerful states' strategies to pursue their interests); Helfer,

Where regimes collide and potentially conflict, there need to be mechanisms to address such conflicts, i.e. to determine which norm shall prevail in a certain situation. As I discuss in more detail in Chapter 6, legal conflict rules do not provide an adequate solution where conflicts of norms result from underlying conflicts of interest. Instead, international legal regimes should allow for such conflicts to be addressed through regime-transcending political processes.[24] Moreover, where regimes do not conflict, but complement each other, flexible linkages between the regimes are required so that the division of labour between regimes can be effective.[25]

C. WAYS TO FLEXIBILIZE INTERNATIONAL LAW: EXCEPTIONALISM, MANAGERIALISM AND TRANSNATIONAL POLITICAL LAW-MAKING

Different reactions to the flexibility demands observed above can be identified. In what follows, three answers are juxtaposed: firstly, exceptionalism – to preserve domestic democratic governance; secondly, managerialism – to ensure effective governance in light of transnational regulatory needs; and thirdly, the quest for transnational politics and legal procedures that frame such politics and legitimate political law-making. To take up the image referenced in the first section of this chapter: the third approach is a quest for 'world internal politics' to complement 'world internal law'.[26]

In the following I shall briefly address exceptionalism and managerialism in order to demonstrate the need for a (supplementary) focus on legally framed transnational politics to legitimate and flexibilize governance through international law.

'Regime Shifting', 1 (explaining regime shifting as a strategy employed by developing countries and NGOs to achieve a change of the norms of the TRIPS Agreement).

24 See Chapter 6 B.I.

25 On coordination of complementary regimes, see Raustiala and Victor, 'The Regime Complex for Plant Genetic Resources', 277; Kaiser, 'Coordination of International Organizations', 315; Young, 'Fragmentation or Interaction', 477.

26 This term was coined by Carl Friedrich von Weizsäcker who saw the transformation of foreign politics as a necessary condition for world peace, see Weizsäcker, 'Bedingungen des Friedens', 8; on Weizsäcker's concept of 'world internal politics', see Bartosch, *Weltinnenpolitik: Zur Theorie des Friedens von Carl Friedrich von Weizsäcker*.

I Exceptionalism

There is a tendency of domestic governmental organs, including courts, to view regional and international law as potentially endangering domestic values and self-government. Such dangers are invoked to justify breaches of international law or to argue against further law-making at the international level.[27] It is true that international governance is characterized by a democratic deficit[28] and that the weakness of international law enforcement and the denial of direct effect to international law may provide important correctives in this regard.[29] The emphasis on the legitimacy deficits of international law is furthermore an important reminder that more international law and more international institutions are not necessarily beneficial and that a delegation of governance functions to the supranational or international level should require some justification along the lines of a subsidiarity argument.[30]

However, it also needs to be acknowledged that in light of pressing transboundary threats, such as climate change or the collapse of global financial markets, as well as the deterritorialization of social activities in need of regulation, the choice is often not between legitimate national governance and illegitimate international governance.[31] Domestic governance is not legitimate if it cannot be effective or if it produces effects for other polities and persons who are excluded from the domestic political process.[32] To give examples: if domestic legislatures can no longer freely decide on the state's tax policy due to the threat of losses in employment should firms move their activities abroad, it is hardly convincing to argue that the taxing power is a core governmental function which may not be delegated to supranational institutions.[33] Furthermore, it is

27 Rabkin, *The Case for Sovereignty*; McGinnis and Somin, 'Should International Law Be Part of our Law?', 1175; for an analysis of American exceptionalism, see the contributions in Ignatieff (ed.), *American Exceptionalism and Human Rights*.
28 Crawford and Marks, 'Global Democracy Deficit', 137.
29 Bogdandy, 'Pluralism, Direct Effect, and the Ultimate Say', 397; Trachtman, 'Bananas, Direct Effect and Compliance', 655.
30 Macedo and Moravsik, 'Democracy-Enhancing Multilateralism', 1, 2 (arguing that democracy-encroaching multilateral institutions should only be accepted when the countervailing benefits outweigh the democratic costs); Feichtner, 'Subsidiarity'.
31 Keohane, Macedo and Moravsik, 'Democracy-Enhancing Multilateralism', 1, 4, 5 (arguing that multilateralism 'expand[s] the scope of democratic choice and improve[s] democratic control over policies that actually affect citizens').
32 Fraser, *Scales of Justice*, 12 *et seq.*
33 For the argument that taxation constitutes a core governmental function which is protected against Europeanization by the German constitution, see the Federal Constitutional

an expression of the hegemonic thinking that underlies the exceptionalist approach that, on the one hand, it is claimed that international obligations unduly restrict governmental autonomy and, on the other hand, no issue is taken with standards that are imposed unilaterally beyond territorial borders, for example to prohibit the import of products produced in a certain way, or with trade preferences that are made conditional upon compliance with unilaterally determined requirements.[34] The exceptionalist approach places strong emphasis on the value of democratic self-government. Often, however, it does not engage seriously with the legitimacy deficit resulting from domestic policy-making that excludes a wide range of persons from the political process and does not inquire into the possibilities for legitimate governance beyond the state.

II Managerialism

While exceptionalism purports to be concerned with democratic government, the answer to the flexibility challenge which I refer to as managerialism stresses effectiveness as the main objective of international governance and the source of legitimacy.[35] Since formal international law-making, predominately in the form of treaty-making, appears too rigid to adapt to rapidly changing cognitive expectations and technological development there is a turn to other, less rigid forms of regulation. These frequently involve expert networks that work out policies in the form of soft-law instruments.[36]

Court of Germany in its decision on the Lisbon Treaty, *Lisbon Case*, BVerfG, 2 BvE/08 of 30 June 2009, para. 252, www.bverfg.de/entscheidungen/es20090630_2bve000208.html (last accessed 11 March 2011).

34 The prohibition of the importation of shrimps not caught in compliance with US standards was at issue in *US – Shrimp* in which the Appellate Body found, inter alia, that international environmental law favoured multilateral over unilateral action: Appellate Body Report, *US – Shrimp*, WT/DS58/AB/R, adopted 6 November 1998, para. 168; for the United States practice of demanding from its trading partners intellectual property protection which goes beyond the obligations of the TRIPS Agreement, see Abbott, 'Intellectual Property Provisions of Bilateral and Regional Trade Agreements'.

35 For the argument that a democratic deficit may be compensated by increased effectiveness, see Scharpf, 'Democratic Policy in Europe', 136; cf. Keohane and Nye, 'Club Model of Multilateral Cooperation', 264, 285 *et seq.*

36 Slaughter, 'Global Government Networks', 1041. Policy formulation or preparation by networks may also take place within international institutions where governmental experts get together to discuss specific policies, see Lang and Scott, 'Hidden World of WTO Governance', 575, 602.

Such a managerialist approach to international governance furthers a deformalization and depoliticization, and potentially deepens the fragmentation of international law. Law is perceived as merely instrumental to achieve certain extralegal aims such as health, prosperity, etc. The value of law becomes a function of its capability to reach these material aims effectively.[37] As a consequence political scientists and lawyers have started to talk about different degrees of 'bindingness' of international law. Joel Trachtman writes:

> [T]he degree of binding effect is a design feature that may be adjusted and combined with the substantive rule to create the optimal set of incentives for conduct.[38]

Fragmentation is increased due to the specialization of persons that create these new instruments. These are more often technical experts than diplomats with a holistic focus. The fact that the instruments they adopt often do not become binding law and need not be ratified further means that there is less pressure for an examination how these policies relate to policies in other areas.

The two developments, exceptionalism and managerialism, are not unconnected. The scepticism of the exceptionalist stance with respect to formal binding international law is frequently not evidenced with respect to the soft managerial version of transnational governance. However, managerialism might undermine exactly the values that exceptionalism purports to protect, namely the ability of constituencies to determine through representative and transparent procedures, accompanied by public debate, how their societies should be ordered in a just way.[39] In what follows it is proposed that formal law as well as representative political debate in international institutions play an important role in protecting this capability for self-government.

III Transnational political law-making

In light of the pluralism of worldviews and values in society (domestic and transnational) the legitimacy of governance can neither be based on

---

37 For criticism of the resulting depoliticization of international law, see Klabbers, 'Two Concepts of International Organization', 277; Koskenniemi, 'Fate of Public International Law', 1.

38 Trachtman, 'Bananas, Direct Effect and Compliance', 655–6; see also Abbott *et al.*, 'Concept of Legalization', 401.

39 For the argument that soft law favours powerful states, see Krisch, 'International Law in Times of Hegemony', 369, 392.

a community of values nor on scientific truth. By contrast, formal law has a specific potential to legitimate government. Depending on the framing of the law-making process, compromise between different interests can be transformed into legal text which forms the basis for governmental action. The legal form provides security and predictability. The legal texts make the bases for governmental action transparent and limit the exercise of legal governmental authority. Law reduces the decisiveness of power in international relations, whether it is military power or the power of knowledge, inter alia by requiring actors to frame their positions in legal terms. An interpretation of the relevant law has to be put forward which is based on the legal text and follows the commonly accepted rules of interpretation.[40] The law constitutes a common good in that every person can refer to it as a standard to judge the behaviour of those who are bound by the law.[41] As formulated by Martti Koskenniemi: law provides 'a platform to evaluate behaviour including behaviour of those in dominant positions'.[42] Legal reasoning requires that similar situations are treated similarly and thus also mitigates power imbalances.[43]

The legal form furthermore links formally separate regimes. While there will always be legal pluralism as long as there is decentralized law-making, the fact that formal law from different legal regimes belongs to the same social system, leads to a certain extent to an integration of the fragmented international legal order. International judges, for example, will not ignore binding legal rules from one regime when interpreting norms from another. If not directly applicable, these rules become relevant through the principles of interpretation.[44]

For law to be able to provide security and predictability and to reduce power imbalances qua the legal form, the concept of validity is essential.[45] Validity, sometimes also referred to as normativity, separates law from non-law. It is based on criteria formulated by legal rules (in municipal contexts the constitution) and not on an evaluation whether the legal norm is meaningful when measured against economic, political or any

---

40 *Ibid.*, at 409.
41 For the view that the existence of a regime as such could be regarded as an international common good, see Abbott, 'Modern Relations Theory', 335, 383.
42 Koskenniemi, 'What Is International Law For?', 57, 65.
43 Abbott *et al.*, 'Concept of Legalization', 401, 419.
44 Howse, 'Adjudicative Legitimacy and Treaty Interpretation', 35, 51 *et seq.*
45 On Kelsen's concept of validity, see Kelsen, *Reine Rechtslehre*, 7 *et seq.*

other extralegal standards.[46] While the results of interpretation and application of a norm may not be fully determined by the legal text,[47] its quality as law, its validity, depends on criteria which distinguish a legal norm from a theorem of economics or morality.[48]

To maintain the concept of validity, law may not be linked to other social systems by making its 'bindingness' dependent on whether it promotes a certain political or economic objective. Instead linkage between the legal system and other social systems must be achieved through law-making procedures. Through formal law-making procedures law can be adapted to changes in social preferences, knowledge or reality. They may ensure the flexibility and adaptability of law without replacing or equating law with power, science or economics.

The legitimacy of the law and in particular its capacity to mitigate power imbalances strongly depends on the framing of these law-making procedures. A representative political debate on the reconciliation of competing and conflicting societal interests bestows legitimacy on the law which substantially differs from that which is frequently sought in functionally delimited law-making processes.

In functionally delimited regimes actors (often including governmental and non-governmental actors) often seek to legitimate the outcomes of law-making processes on the one hand by seeking scientific expertise and on the other hand by allowing affected stakeholders to participate.[49] What is missing in conceptions of governance or theories of transnational law is a conceptualization of politics which allows for different visions of international society to be debated, including the interrelation and prioritization of sectorally separate policies. Policy elaboration within informal networks or international institutions might allow for the expression of different views as to regulatory standards and regulatory means; it hardly permits, however, a debate on sector transcending visions of societal ordering, including the prioritization of policies in light of limited resources.[50]

---

46 These rules are what H. L. A. Hart called rules of recognition: Hart, *Concept of Law*, 79.
47 For a view that law is indeterminate see e.g. Koskenniemi, *From Apology to Utopia*, 36 *et seq.*
48 For the potential of legal formalism as defended by Hans Kelsen to safeguard the legitimacy of international governance, see Bernstorff, *Hans Kelsen's Public International Law Theory*, 233 *et seq.*; cf. Koskenniemi, *The Gentle Civilizer of Nations*, 179–265.
49 Friedrich, 'Nonbinding Instruments'.
50 Kratochwil, 'Politics, Norms, and Peaceful Change', 193.

It is abundantly clear that as of now a 'transnational political space' framed by procedural law which would allow for representative political deliberation has not yet emerged on the international level. Furthermore, the realizability of transnational democratic processes is questionable due to the lack of a global polity.[51] Yet, given the need for governance beyond the state, law-making processes that are regime-transcending and representative of diverse societal interests would be a step towards more legitimate, if not more democratic, international governance.[52]

One further caveat needs to be noted. The question cannot be ignored as to whether law's formality and validity can be maintained in all areas without unduly compromising its functionality. Rather than being merely a political choice, for example by hegemonic states, the deformalization and depoliticization of international law and governance, described above as managerialism, in some areas are owed to the changed function of law in global society. As Niklas Luhmann observed, the fact that in the global society cognitive structures of expectations prevail and changes happen increasingly fast impacts law's normativity. He describes this impact as follows:

> It may be true that under the pressure of this gradual shift in realities and possibilities the central point of legal experience is more strongly based on the material dimension. The material formulation of the content of legal tenets and the conceptual-doctrinal construction of their contexts would then not only be general aids to recognizing that which is seen as legal norm. Law would take the form of normed models of behaviour which have been drafted as solutions of recognized problems, are legislated upon, tried and changed according to the rules of experience. Normativity would then only have the function of securing the constancy of expectation as long and in as far as it appears meaningful. Moral and ideological reasoning would then be replaced by a functional critique.[53]

Thus, there may be areas of governance in which the formal separation of law and other social systems, such as economics, and consequently the independence of law's validity from these other systems, may

---

51 See only Weiler, 'Geology of International Law', 547.
52 For a proposal for democratic governance, see Kreide, 'Ambivalence of Juridification', 18, 24 *et seq*. For a conception of legalization beyond the state that includes international law-making, see Zangl and Zürn, 'Verrechtlichung Jenseits des Staates', 239.
53 Luhmann, *Sociological Theory of Law*, 264.

not be maintained. The generalizations of this section must therefore be viewed with caution. International regimes need to be analysed in depth as to their objectives in order to determine the needs for flexibility as well as the potential of formal law-making for legitimate governance. Such an analysis will be undertaken in the next chapter for the WTO.

3

The WTO – public law of conflict management

To state the obvious: no consensus exists – neither on the WTO's object-ives, nor the role and function of law in the WTO. While some see free trade as the main objective, others propose a conceptualization of the WTO as aiming to render domestic decision-making more inclusive, possibly even more democratic. The function of WTO law is described at one end of the spectrum as securing efficient exchanges between members, at the other as providing for a constitution that protects individual autonomy against members' governments.

In this section I wish to juxtapose different conceptions of WTO law and its objectives and to give reasons for my own view that WTO law should be conceptualized as a body of public law which aims at a legitim-ate balance between competing societal interests, trade interests as well as other socio-economic interests. From the perspective of WTO law as a body of public law with the objective of reconciling competing socio-economic interests, I shall formulate the flexibility demands which may be directed towards WTO law as it currently stands. Once it is acknowledged that the main function of WTO law lies in managing con-flicts between competing societal interests it becomes clear that the law cannot be treated as merely an instrument to achieve certain substantive objectives such as trade liberalization, but that the legal form itself con-stitutes an important value: on the one hand as an authoritative embodi-ment of political compromise among competing interests and, on the other hand, by framing political procedures in which such compromise can be reassessed and new compromises sought.[1]

This exposition will set the ground for an assessment of the waiver practice[2] as well as the potential of the waiver power and process to provide the flexibility that is needed to legitimate WTO law and ensure

---

1 Arendt, *Human Condition*, 194–5.
2 The waiver practice is presented in Chapter 4.

its effectiveness.[3] The waiver power is of particular relevance since it provides the only political law-making procedure in the WTO which is actually used in practice.

A. THE OBJECTIVES OF THE WTO: RECIPROCAL TRADE LIBERALIZATION, PROTECTION OF INDIVIDUAL AUTONOMY OR CONFLICT MANAGEMENT?

I Trade liberalization to enhance welfare

According to a widely held view WTO law aims at enhancing economic welfare through trade liberalization. Trade liberalization has come to be seen as the predominant objective of the WTO.[4] While globalization critics hold economic liberalization responsible for many ills from environmental degradation to the increasing divide between the extremely rich and the extremely poor, the supporters of trade liberalization staunchly defend its merits as a matter of scientific truth.[5] Trade liberalization, according to its advocates, not only leads to economic prosperity but is also conducive to peace and democracy.[6]

Trade lawyers as well as the WTO itself still predominately refer to David Ricardo's theory of comparative advantage as the economic justification for trade liberalization.[7] If trade is not restricted domestic economies specialize in sectors in which they have a comparative advantage over other economies. This leads to an efficient international division of labour.[8] According to this economic theory it will be beneficial for a state to unilaterally dismantle trade barriers even if other states do not follow suit.[9] The WTO accordingly notes on its website:

> [L]iberal trade policies – policies that allow the unrestricted flow of goods and services – sharpen competition, motivate innovation and breed

---

3 For this assessment see in particular Part III of this study.

4 See e.g. Bagwell, Mavroidis and Staiger, 'It's a Question of Market Access', 56, 59.

5 For two opposing views, see Stiglitz, *Globalization and its Discontents*; Bhagwati, *In Defense of Globalization*.

6 Petersmann, 'Time for Integrating Human Rights into the Law of Worldwide Organizations', 35.

7 See e.g. van den Bossche, *Law and Policy of the World Trade Organization*, 16 *et seq.*; WTO, *Understanding the WTO*, 13 *et seq.*

8 Ricardo, *Works*, vol. 1, 133 *et seq.*

9 For more detail on the economic rationale for trade liberalization, see Trebilcock and Howse, *Regulation of International Trade*, 2 *et seq.*

success. They multiply the rewards that result from producing the best products, with the best design, at the best price.[10]

On the basis of such theory it is also generally held that trade liberalization is good for development in that it will lead to growth and consequently poverty reduction. This assumption which underlies most multilateral institutions' development policies ignores, however, economic research which shows that many of the developing countries with high growth rates have been successful in part due to policies which involved some protection of domestic markets.[11] Dani Rodrik concludes that 'there is no convincing evidence that trade liberalization is predictably associated with subsequent economic growth'.[12] In this connection it is pointed out that the industrialized countries of today at the beginning of their industrial development were often highly protectionist towards domestic industry.[13]

According to the conventional economic theory based on comparative advantage, gains from trade do not require reciprocal liberalization. Nonetheless, the WTO's preamble expresses its members' desire to enter 'into reciprocal and mutually advantageous arrangements directed to the substantial reduction of tariffs and other barriers to trade and to the elimination of discriminatory treatment in international trade relations'.[14] This reciprocity is explained by the need to protect trade liberalization against protectionist government measures that are induced by the lobbying efforts of domestic groups. Governments 'tie their hands' by entering into international agreements and at the same time gain support of domestic exporters who benefit from the reciprocal liberalization commitments of the other contracting parties.[15] The main instruments to promote trade liberalization are thus reciprocal market access commitments (reduction of tariffs and admission of services) and the protection of such market access commitments through the prohibition of quantitative

---

10 www.wto.org/english/thewto_e/whatis_e/tif_e/fact3_e.htm (last accessed 11 March 2011).
11 Rodrick, *One Economics, Many Recipes.*
12 Rodrik, *Global Governance of Trade*; cf. also Trachtman, 'Ensuring a Development-Friendly WTO', Trachtman notes the growing consensus that '[t]here is substantial uncertainty in general as to what types of obligations will contribute to development although there is growing consensus that no single prescription is best for all countries'.
13 Rodrik, *Global Governance of Trade,* 7; Chang, *Kicking Away the Ladder.*
14 WTO Agreement, preamble, 3rd recital.
15 Petersmann, *Constitutional Functions and Constitutional Problems,* 113 *et seq.*

restrictions and other barriers to trade, in particular (discriminatory)[16] domestic taxation and regulation.[17] The market access commitments are negotiated bilaterally during multilateral trade negotiation rounds. They are included in schedules of concessions and thus become integral parts of the agreements.[18] The most-favoured-nation obligation ensures that it is not only the members who have negotiated the commitments who benefit from them, but that the commitments are extended to all other members.[19]

Frequently the benefits of trade liberalization through WTO law are perceived from a statist or member-to-member perspective: it is the WTO's objective to increase each member's overall economic welfare. The WTO is not, however, concerned with the internal distribution of the gains from trade. These gains are not equally distributed. Some, in particular consumers and the export industry, will gain and some, import-competing domestic industry operating at a competitive disadvantage, will lose domestically. Economic theory predicts that there will be sufficient gains to compensate the losers. This overall welfare gain is frequently seen as sufficient justification for multilateral trade liberalization in the WTO. The domestic distribution of the gains from trade and compensation of the losers of trade liberalization is a matter to be achieved domestically.

II Trade liberalization to protect individual autonomy

Another perspective concentrates not so much on joint domestic wealth maximization, but instead focuses on the individual. It stresses that trade liberalization is not only welfare enhancing, but necessary to protect individual autonomy and dignity. Ernst-Ulrich Petersmann, the most prominent advocate of this view, argues that individual freedom to engage in transnational economic activities is a human right. It is mandated by

---

16 The SPS and TBT Agreements not only prohibit discrimination, but set out standards that all regulatory measures of a certain type have to meet in order to reduce impediments to trade.

17 The view that trade liberalization through market access commitments and the prohibition of discrimination is the main objective of the WTO is defended for example by McGinnis and Movesian, 'The World Trade Constitution', 511; Bagwell, Mavroidis and Staiger, 'It's a Question of Market Access', 56.

18 Articles II:7 GATT, XX:3 GATS.

19 While this is true with respect to tariff concessions (Art. I GATT) the most-favoured-nation obligation in the GATS is subject to exemptions (Art. II GATS).

human dignity as well as the rational self-interest of all individuals in equal freedom. Petersmann thus sees the justification of WTO law not merely in the efficiency gains from trade liberalization, but predominately in theories of justice as developed by Kant or Rawls.[20]

III Conflict management

The claim that the main objective of the WTO is trade liberalization, either justified by the gains to domestic welfare or the protection of human dignity and autonomy, is not convincing. It is neither supported by the legal texts, the history of the institution, nor the interpretations of the legal norms by the Appellate Body. Most importantly, however, liberalization as the main justification of multilateral cooperation in the WTO is normatively not persuasive.[21]

It is not to be denied that trade liberalization does play a prominent role in the WTO. Even though there are no legal obligations in the agreements to commit to tariff reductions or liberalization in the area of services, regular trade negotiation rounds aim at the progressive reduction of tariffs as well as market access in the area of services.[22] Furthermore, acceding states are asked by members to make substantial liberalization commitments.[23] However, according to the WTO's preamble market access shall merely be instrumental to achieve diverse social objectives.[24] These

---

20 Petersmann, 'Time for Integrating Human Rights'. Petersmann also recognizes the need to address market failures and distributive effects of liberalization and argues for an integration of competition norms as well as social rights into the WTO framework. He suggests a '"new integration paradigm" linking trade liberalization and its adjustment problems to promotion of economic and social human rights and joint financial "burden sharing" (as in European integration)' (*ibid.* at 34).

21 For a most convincing reconstruction and discussion of different conceptualizations of the WTO, see Howse, 'From Politics to Technocracy – and Back Again', 94; Howse, 'Legitimacy of the World Trade Organization', 355. The following draws heavily on the insights formulated in these texts. For a conception of the WTO as aiming at coordinated interdependence, see Bogdandy, 'Law and Politics in the WTO', 609; Krajewski, *Verfassungsperspektiven und Legitimation des Rechts der Welthandelsorganisation.*

22 Cf. WTO Agreement, preamble, 3rd recital.

23 Charnovitz, 'Mapping the Law of WTO Accession', 855; Qin, '"WTO-Plus" Obligations and their Implications for the World Trade Organization Legal System', 483.

24 Wolfgang Benedek distinguishes between economic aims and instrumental aims, and qualifies the market access commitments envisaged by the preamble's 3rd recital as instrumental aims: Benedek, *Rechtsordnung des GATT aus völkerrechtlicher Sicht*, 42; for an interpretation of and commentary on the entire preamble of the WTO Agreement, see Bogdandy, 'Preamble WTO Agreement', 1.

objectives are set out in the first two recitals of the WTO Agreement's[25] preamble:

> Recognizing that their relations in the field of trade and economic endeavour should be conducted with a view to raising standards of living, ensuring full employment and a large and steadily growing volume of real income and effective demand, and expanding the production of and trade in goods and services, while allowing for the optimal use of the world's resources in accordance with the objective of sustainable development, seeking both to protect and preserve the environment and to enhance the means for doing so in a manner consistent with their respective needs and concerns at different levels of economic development,
>
> Recognizing further that there is need for positive efforts designed to ensure that developing countries, and especially the least developed among them, secure a share in the growth in international trade commensurate with the needs of their economic development.

The first recital makes clear that the ultimate aim is not merely economic wealth, but instead economic wealth which leads to a *raising of standards of living* as well as *full employment*. Thus the WTO is not oblivious as to the distribution of the gains of trade. The well-being not of states but of individuals is placed at the centre in this recital. Furthermore, the objectives of sustainable development and environmental protection are fundamental. They shall determine how economic activities are conducted. The second recital finally notes economic development of the poorer WTO members as an objective of the organization.

The first recital reiterates the aims of the GATT 1947, and adds the aims of sustainable development and environmental protection. Progressive trade liberalization with the ultimate aim of free trade was not what the negotiators of an International Trade Organization, of which the GATT was the surviving remnant, had in mind. John Ruggie in his illuminating work on the political bargain which underlay the postwar international economic institutions points to a telling statement by Jacob Viner as representative of the dominant view at that time:

---

25 Throughout this study I shall use the term 'WTO Agreement' when referring to the preamble and Articles I–XVI of the WTO Agreement and the term 'WTO Agreements' when referring to the WTO Agreement and the Multilateral Trade Agreements. With respect to the terminological confusion as to the term 'WTO Agreement', see Bogdandy and Stelzer, 'Article II WTO Agreement', 20, 21 *et seq.*

There are few free traders in the present day world, no one pays any
attention to their views and no person in authority anywhere advocates
free trade.[26]

Instead of unfettered trade, the main aim of trade multilateralism after
World War II was to prevent mutually destructive economic policies,
but at the same time to allow domestic policy interventions to safeguard
domestic stability. States intended to prevent beggar-thy-neighbour practices which had led to the disastrous economic situation that contributed
to the outbreak of World War II.[27] This balance between protection of
multilateral trade and regulatory autonomy is what Ruggie called 'embedded liberalism'.[28] The outcome of negotiations that were to lead to an
International Trade Organization and ultimately resulted in the provisional application of the GATT was a political bargain among diplomats
that agreed on the desirability of multilateralism in trade and domestic
regulatory autonomy with regard to domestic stability, but who disagreed
on many of the specifics of trade regulation and legitimate domestic
intervention. As a result the GATT 1947 did not constitute a coherent
set of rules that could be explained on the basis of economic rationality. The rules constituted compromises between statesmen with different
preferences as to domestic policies, but one common aim: to prevent
destructive protectionism while maintaining a large degree of domestic
regulatory autonomy.[29]

The main GATT rules to prevent protectionism are the prohibition
of quantitative restrictions (Art. XI GATT) and the non-discrimination
principles of national treatment and most-favoured-nation treatment
(Art. III, I GATT). These rules were complemented by various norms
that protected domestic regulatory autonomy. The rules on safeguards
allow for the temporary imposition of protectionist measures in case
liberalization leads to a serious injury to domestic producers (Art. XIX
GATT). The GATT further recognizes that economic freedom potentially
conflicts with the protection of important non-economic interests. Art.
XX GATT permits government measures to protect, inter alia, public

---

26 Viner, 'Conflicts of Principle in Drafting a Trade Charter', cited in: Ruggie, 'International
    Regimes, Transactions, and Change', 379, 396.
27 Wilcox, *A Charter for World Trade*, 3 *et seq*. See also Art. 1 of the Havana Charter that starts
    with the words: 'Recognizing the determination of the United Nations to create conditions
    of stability and well-being which are necessary for peaceful and friendly relations among
    nations.'
28 Ruggie, 'International Regimes, Transactions, and Change', 379, 393.
29 *Ibid.*, 393 *et seq.*; Hudec, 'GATT or GABB?', 1299, 1317.

morals, human, animal or plant life or health, and natural resources even if such action discriminates between like products or consists in a quantitative restriction of imports. Such measures must, however, meet certain requirements, in particular they may not discriminate in an arbitrary and unjustifiable manner between members. Art. XXI GATT contains a broad security exception. The GATT further acknowledges special relationships among contracting parties and thus provides exceptions for discrimination resulting from regional integration or historic preferences (Art. XXIV, I:2 GATT).

These rules had been negotiated by politicians who were united in their aim not to repeat the destructive economic policies of the interwar period, but who were conscious of their respective countries' differences, in particular concerning preferences for government intervention in economic activities.[30] They were applied, interpreted and further developed, however, by an (initially relatively closed) group of trade experts who had a much stronger focus on the economic rationale of trade liberalization than on the grand political bargain that the GATT initially was conceived as. Joseph Weiler observed:

> A very dominant feature of the GATT was its self-referential and even communitarian ethos explicable in constructivist terms. The GATT successfully managed a relative insulation from the 'outside' world of international relations and established among its practitioners a closely knit environment revolving around a certain set of shared normative values (free trade) and shared institutional (and personal) ambitions situated in a matrix of long-term first-name contacts and friendly personal relationships. GATT operatives became a classical 'network'.[31]

Robert Howse impressively demonstrates how this network adhered to the economic theorem that trade liberalization results in efficiency gains, neglected questions of distributive justice, and held the view that the gains from trade needed to be protected against domestic interest group politics. The 'technocratic' outlook of trade practitioners was accompanied and reinforced by an increasing acceptance by political elites of the demands of economic liberalism which called into doubt the value of domestic policies that intervened in the market for adjustment purposes.

---

30 Gardner, *Sterling–Dollar Diplomacy*.
31 Weiler, 'The Rule of Lawyers and the Ethos of Diplomats', 191, 194, 195 (footnote omitted); cf. Robert Hudec who stressed the 'favourable set of community attitudes' during the first decade of the GATT: Hudec, 'GATT or GABB?', 1299, 1339; Keohane and Nye, 'Club Model of Multilateral Cooperation', 264.

The regulatory freedom which the GATT rules afforded to the contracting parties was steadily reduced through the adoption of certain interpretations as well as of additional rules.[32] For example, Art. III GATT on national treatment was interpreted as prohibiting not only de jure discrimination between domestic products and like foreign products, but as also prohibiting de facto discrimination which did not require protectionist intent.[33] Moreover, likeness was determined predominantly on the basis of the physical characteristics of products and their competitive relationship while production methods were considered irrelevant.[34]

That the concept of embedded liberalism lost pertinence was further evidenced by the development of new rules, such as those now contained in the SPS and TBT Agreements. These rules go beyond the prohibition of discrimination, but aim at reducing the impediments to cross-border trade that result from differences in domestic technical and health regulations. During the Uruguay Round further agreements on the liberalization of services and the protection of intellectual property were negotiated, which restrict domestic regulatory autonomy even further.[35]

The new rules make increasingly apparent the interrelatedness of market access and other public interests, concerning, inter alia, the protection of the environment, labour standards, health, food or human security. The obligations to reduce barriers to trade and to protect intellectual property restrict the possibility to regulate in furtherance of such other interests. At the same time it is disputable whether all of these obligations are in fact conducive to economic welfare. While there is indeed little doubt among economists that the dismantling of de jure discriminatory barriers to trade enhances overall economic welfare domestically, what is much more contentious is whether the prohibition of certain non-discriminatory regulation (as through the SPS or TBT Agreements) or the protection of intellectual property rights (as required by the TRIPS Agreement) is equally welfare enhancing. It was noted that many norms cannot be explained on the basis of economic principles, but are rather motivated by mercantilist interests of certain powerful actors in advanced

---

32 Howse, 'From Politics to Technocracy and Back Again', 94, 98 *et seq.*

33 On the development of this interpretation, see Hudec, 'GATT/WTO Constraints on National Regulation', 619.

34 For an analysis and critique of this case law, see Howse and Regan, 'Product/Process Distinction', 249.

35 On the rationale of the TRIPS Agreement which is less concerned with trade than with minimum standards and thus differs from the other trade agreements, see Cooper Dreyfuss and Lowenfeld, 'Two Achievements of the Uruguay Round', 275, 279–80.

industrial economies.[36] Again there will be winners and losers as a result of compliance with these rules. However, it may well be the case that the gains will not be sufficient to compensate the losers.[37] Not only are the losses distributed unequally within domestic societies, they also accrue unequally across members. Thus, in particular, developing country members may not benefit at all from compliance with some of the agreements, such as the GATS or the TRIPS Agreement.[38]

One reaction to the lack of justification for parts of WTO law in terms of economic welfare is the demand to limit its scope to the prohibition of discriminatory restrictions to market access.[39] A restriction of the scope of WTO law would no doubt be desirable in so far as it would mitigate welfare reductions caused by compliance with the law. However, even if by changing or getting rid of certain rules the economic justification, namely the enhancement of domestic economic welfare, may be maintained, it remains questionable whether a justification of trade rules in terms of economic theory is sufficient to legitimate incursions into domestic regulatory autonomy.

Robert Howse convincingly argued that it is not. What is efficient economically might not necessarily be politically feasible or desirable. Howse gives the following examples: as concerns the protection of consumers from the dangers posed by certain products, the argument may be made that labelling is economically more efficient than the prohibition of the products in question. However, not in all contexts would labelling indeed prevent harm, as, for example, where the persons who handle the products cannot read. Educating and retraining workers may be economically more efficient than trade restrictions to protect inefficient domestic

36 These include the rules on antidumping, subsidies, agriculture, trade related investment measures and intellectual property protection: see Rodrik, *Global Governance of Trade*, 27. For the increased ideological content of WTO rules, see also Lamy, *Emergence of Collective Preferences in International Trade*; Cosbey, *Sustainable Development Roadmap for the WTO*, 1.

37 Howse, 'Legitimacy of the World Trade Organization', 355, 365 *et seq.*; Trachtman, 'WTO Cathedral', 127, 132 *et seq.*

38 Trachtman, 'WTO Cathedral', 127, 132–3; Chimni, 'World Trade Organization, Democracy and Development', 5.

39 Bagwell, Mavroidis and Staiger, 'It's a Question of Market Access', 56; McGinnis and Movesian, 'Against Global Governance in the WTO', 353, 364–5; Trachtman suggests in 'The WTO Cathedral' that there should only be an obligation of specific performance with respect to those rules compliance with which is indeed maximizing joint welfare. A different position proposes to integrate non-economic matters such as labour rights and environmental protection into the WTO: Guzman, 'Global Governance and the WTO', 303; Petersmann, 'Time for Integrating Human Rights'.

industries, but states may not always have the fiscal means to do so.[40] What seems irrational to the economist, might nonetheless be preferable to a society and its politicians in a given situation under real world circumstances. Therefore the decision as to which trade measures to allow and which to prohibit is a contingent question. International agreements that provide rules for such decisions consequently require legitimation beyond economic rationality.[41]

The realization that there is no uncontestable truth that justifies trade rules either found in science or natural justice raises anew the question as to the justification, the objectives of trade rules. Howse proposes a conceptualization of the objectives of international trade law which reclaims the idea of embedded liberalism. According to him the justification for international trade law may be seen in 'constraining the externalization of the costs of domestic adjustment to economic and social change and crisis, so as to prevent a protectionist race-to-the-bottom'.[42] It rests on the consensus that excessive protectionism is undesirable and potentially destabilizing. Similarly Dani Rodrik notes: '[T]he WTO should be conceived of not as an institution devoted to harmonization and the reduction of national institutional differences, but as one that manages the interface between different national systems.'[43]

WTO law may and should still be interpreted as mainly aiming at a coordination of competing societal interests. However, this objective differs from the embedded liberalism envisaged by the GATT negotiators. Their aim was primarily to find a balance between, on the one hand, the protection and promotion of transnational trade and, on the other hand, the maintenance of domestic governmental freedom to provide domestic stability, for example through the adoption of social welfare laws or state monopolies. Today the constellation is slightly different. In particular, regulation which potentially impedes trade is increasingly the product of international and transnational processes. Furthermore, such regulation is not merely aimed at domestic stability, but also addresses transnational situations such as environmental degradation or extraterritorial situations such as human security in countries and regions outside the regulating state. Another difference is the increased disparity between members of the international trading regime in their state of economic development.

---

40 Howse, 'Human Rights in the WTO. Whose Rights, What Humanity?'
41 Howse, 'From Politics to Technocracy and Back Again', 94, 104.
42 Howse, 'Human Rights in the WTO. Whose Rights, What Humanity?'
43 Rodrik, *Global Governance of Trade*, 34.

Consequently, WTO law has to address the relationship between trade facilitation and domestic regulation while taking into account different stages of economic development, and also the relationship between trade facilitation and transnational and international regulation.

In light of these changed circumstances WTO law may be conceptualized as containing destructive protectionism and coordinating members' trade policies by demanding that domestic policy-making takes due account of foreign interests.[44] Where policy-making takes place in inclusive transnational or international processes, WTO law shall pay deference to the outcomes of such processes.[45] According to such a view of WTO law its justification may be seen in the substantive value of peace as well as the procedural value of democracy.[46]

B. WTO LAW: CONTRACT OR PUBLIC LAW?

How we define the objectives of WTO law has important implications for its interpretation[47] and the role we attribute to the legal form. I wish to distinguish in this section between two broad conceptions of the function of law in the WTO: on the one hand the conception of WTO law as a contract which secures mutually beneficial bargains between sovereigns; on the other hand the conception of WTO law as public law which firstly shapes global markets as public institutions and secondly restricts exercises of public authority that affect trade.

I WTO law as contract

The WTO Agreements are frequently depicted as contracts between members for the reciprocal and mutually beneficial exchange of benefits.[48] In support of this view the following passage from the Appellate Body report in *Japan – Alcoholic Beverages* is frequently quoted:

44 Bogdandy, 'Legitimacy of International Economic Governance', 103, 120 *et seq.*
45 Howse and Nicolaïdis, 'Enhancing WTO Legitimacy', 73–94.
46 Not because the WTO itself is democratic, but because it may strengthen domestic democratic processes. On this basis Robert Howse has for example proposed an interpretation of the SPS Agreement as promoting inclusive, transparent and informed domestic deliberation on matters such as food safety regulation: Howse, 'Democracy, Science, and Free Trade', 2329; cf. also Joerges and Neyer, 'Politics, Risk Management', 219.
47 Bogdandy, 'Legitimacy of International Economic Governance', 103, 113.
48 For example Petros Mavroidis only writes of 'the WTO contracts': Mavroidis, 'Judicial Supremacy, Judicial Restraint', 583; for a recent contract-theoretic assessment of WTO law, see Schropp, *Trade Policy Flexibility and Enforcement in the WTO*.

> The WTO Agreement is a treaty – the international equivalent of a contract. It is self-evident that in an exercise of their sovereignty, and in pursuit of their own respective *national interests*, the Members of the WTO have made a bargain. In exchange for the benefits they expect to derive as Members of the WTO, they have agreed to exercise their sovereignty according to the commitments they have made in the WTO Agreement.[49]

Based on the view that the aim of the GATT, and today the WTO, is to enable reciprocally beneficial exchanges of market access commitments between sovereigns, it is argued that it is the main function of the legal norms to maintain an overall balance of benefits.[50] Legal norms according to such a view are merely instrumental to the substantive objective of mutually beneficial exchanges among members.

The view of law as merely an instrument to secure bargains is reflected by the pragmatic approach to compliance of the contracting parties under the GATT 1947, as well as by approaches to WTO law that hold that law's function is to secure efficient exchanges between members.

1 Law as fallback option in a community of interests under the GATT 1947

As was noted above, the GATT 1947 had been the outcome of a great political bargain between states who, on the one hand, agreed that they wanted to promote multilateralism and prevent destructive protectionism, but who, on the other hand, fundamentally disagreed on questions such as government interventionism, infant industry protection or trade preferences. Even though compromises on these questions took the form of detailed legal rules, GATT practice in many instances put these rules aside in order to find pragmatic solutions.[51] Where the bargain – as perceived by the governmental officials interacting in the GATT – could be upheld through diplomacy, recourse to 'legalism', i.e. strict insistence on compliance with the substantive rules, was held to be unnecessary. To give an example: with respect to the trade preferences granted by the EEC to

---

49 Appellate Body Report, *Japan – Alcoholic Beverages II*, WT/DS8/AB/R, WT/DS10/AB/R, WT/DS11/AB/R, adopted 1 November 1996, 15 (emphasis added). By comparing an international treaty to a contract under municipal law the Appellate Body brushes over the long-standing discussion among international law scholars on the distinction between *traités lois* and *traités contrats*; on this distinction see for example Brölmann, 'Law-Making Treaties', 383. For criticism of analogizing international treaties to contracts, see Raftopoulos, *Inadequacy of the Contractual Analogy in the Law of Treaties*; Kratochwil, 'Limits of Contract', 456.

50 Hippler Bello, 'WTO Dispute Settlement Understanding', 416, 417–18.

51 Hudec, 'GATT Legal System', 615.

the former colonies of its member states it was agreed – after extensive debate on the legality of these preferences under the GATT – that the contracting parties would no longer focus on compliance with GATT rules, but instead would attempt to find pragmatic solutions should a conflict concerning these preferences arise.[52] Even in formal dispute settlement proceedings, panels sometimes did not base their decisions on the applicable substantive legal rules. An example is the *Citrus Fruit* case. While the United States brought a complaint that preferences granted by the EEC to citrus products from certain Mediterranean countries violated Art. I GATT, the panel report (which remained unadopted) left open the legal question whether the preferences indeed violated Art. I GATT or were justified by Art. XXIV GATT. Instead it considered whether the preferences nullified or impaired benefits accruing to the United States under Art. I:1 GATT.[53]

While in those instances the substantive legal rules were set aside in favour of pragmatic solutions to trade conflicts, in other situations the substantive rules were considered insufficient to protect the benefits from the negotiated concessions. The consideration that legal rules alone might not suffice to protect the reciprocal bargains on tariff concessions led to the procedures known as non-violation complaints (Art. XXIII:1(b) and (c) GATT). Such complaints can be based on the allegation that a certain government measure, even though not in violation of the legal rules, or a certain situation nullifies or impairs benefits accruing under the agreement.[54]

Such an approach to law that subordinates legal rules to the substantive bargain can only count on acceptance if a strong consensus as to the content of this bargain exists. The subjects of the legal rules need to form a community of interests and values. At least for developed contracting parties' trade experts who regularly met in Geneva this was the case in the early GATT years.[55]

Where such consensus did not exist, resort was taken to legal discipline. While developed contracting parties' trade diplomats in relation to each other adopted a pragmatic approach, focusing more on outcomes than

---

52 Intersessional Committee, Report on the Treaty Establishing the European Economic Community, BISD 7S (1959), 69, 70, para. 3; Hudec, *Developing Countries in the GATT Legal System*, 50. On the preferences granted by the EC to products from former colonies of its member states, see Chapter 4 B.I.3.3.
53 Panel Report, *EC – Citrus Fruit*, L/5776 (7 February 1985, not adopted), para. 4.25.
54 For a detailed discussion of the rationale and requirements of non-violation complaints, see Chapter 5 F.II.3.
55 See *supra* note 31.

on legality, they insisted on formal legality with respect to developing countries who did not share the same interests. With balance-of-payments problems, this led to the curious situation that even though the rules on balance-of-payments difficulties were generally regarded as inefficient, developing contracting parties regularly requested waivers of these rules on the insistence of developed contracting parties while the latter violated them without ever requesting a waiver.[56] The disparity is explained by the fact that while developed contracting parties shared a commitment to the objectives of the GATT this commitment was not shared by developing contracting parties. Against this lack of shared commitment the legal relationship between developing and developed contracting parties as the only relationship between them gained in importance.[57]

2 Law as an instrument to ensure efficient compliance

With an increasing number of members and the accompanying pluralism of views, consensus as to objectives and values is hard to achieve even among members at the same level of economic development. Hence legal rules acquire greater importance. In the WTO the shift towards a more rules-based system is reflected by the strengthened and judicialized dispute settlement mechanism. The panels and Appellate Body are called upon 'to preserve the rights and obligations of Members under the covered agreements' (Art. 3:2 DSU). Despite the emphasis on members' legal rights and obligations the Dispute Settlement Understanding can be understood, however, to still reflect the view that the WTO Agreements serve to protect mutually beneficial bargains. Art. 3:3 DSU states:

> The prompt settlement of situations in which a Member considers that any benefits accruing to it directly or indirectly under the covered agreements are being impaired by measures taken by another Member is essential to the effective functioning of the WTO and the *maintenance of a proper balance between rights and obligations of Members.*[58]

Even though the Dispute Settlement Understanding speaks of the balance between rights and obligations this is sometimes taken to mean that the WTO Agreements shall ensure a proper balance of substantive benefits derived from compliance. As was stated above, in the GATT

---

56 On this practice, see Chapter 4 B.I.2.2.a.
57 Hudec, *Developing Countries in the GATT Legal System*, 32.   58 Emphasis added.

this view frequently resulted in a preference for pragmatic solutions to disputes between contracting parties. It was, however, also noted that the pragmatic approach required an underlying consensus as to the substantive aims of the agreement. Where such consensus does not exist, as in an organization with such a diverse membership as the WTO, it is unlikely that diplomacy and pragmatism will result in mutually acceptable solutions.

In spite of the pluralist membership and the concomitant judicialization there persists an approach to WTO law which is similar to that under the GATT in that it perceives the legal norms as instrumental, in this variant instrumental to achieve efficiency in international trade. It is represented by scholars who hold that compliance with legal rules is only desirable when it is efficient. Some go even further and claim that if compliance is not efficient there shall not be a legal duty to comply. According to the latter view efficiency determines when law is binding and when it is not. While under the GATT it was the subjective community of interests that determined the 'bindingness' of legal rules it is now the objective standard of efficiency.

One variant of the economic approach which makes 'bindingness' dependent on efficiency is the application of the efficient breach doctrine to WTO law.[59] According to this doctrine, originally developed for domestic contract law, a party to a contract should not be obliged to perform its contractual obligations, if performance is inefficient, i.e. if the costs of compliance outweigh its benefits. This can be achieved by rules on remedies, but also by rules excusing performance.[60] Starting from the premise that the members of the WTO reciprocally exchange benefits as do private persons, compliance with WTO law should secure the efficiency of these exchanges.[61] If performance is inefficient non-compliance shall be a legal option. Where defection in these cases is not allowed through legal

59 Scholars increasingly apply the doctrine of efficient breach to international agreements. See e.g. Scott and Stephan, *The Limits of Leviathan*; Schwartz and Sykes, 'Economic Structure of Renegotiation and Dispute Resolution', S179; Pauwelyn, *Optimal Protection of International Law.*

60 See Kornhauser, 'Introduction to the Economic Analysis of Contract Remedies', 683, 695, who likens excuse rules to damages rules since 'excuse rules simply impose a damage award of zero on the non-performing party'.

61 For literature that inquires into the capacity of international trade law to achieve efficient outcomes, see Downs and Rocke, *Optimal Imperfection?*; Rosendorff and Milner, 'Optimal Design of International Trade Institutions', 829; Sykes, 'Protectionism as a "Safeguard"', 255; Schwartz and Sykes, 'Economic Structure of Renegotiation and Dispute Resolution', S179; Trachtman, 'WTO Cathedral', 127.

exceptions, this approach constitutes a departure from general international law which demands specific performance, i.e. requires compliance and does not allow non-compliance for the sole reason that compliance would lead to inefficient results.

In the international law literature the application of this doctrine varies. The application of the efficient breach doctrine to international treaties requires clarification on how the costs and benefits of compliance and non-compliance are to be determined. Warren Schwartz and Allan Sykes are explicit in this respect. According to them, breach of the WTO Agreements is efficient when the political welfare benefits of non-compliance to the promisor outweigh the political welfare costs of non-compliance to the promisee, and the promisee is compensated for his loss. Political welfare here is understood as the political welfare of public officials that can be measured in campaign contributions, votes or graft.[62]

This conception leads, however, to an absurd result. It not only postulates that the WTO Agreements are to be seen as contracts for the mutual exchange of benefits, but moreover claims that the law is and should be designed to protect the welfare of political elites.[63] While public choice theory is a useful explanatory tool to predict the behaviour of politicians and consequently their disposition to defect from international obligations, it is a wholly different matter to derive from such theory the normative claim that non-compliance should be allowed if it maximizes the gains of individual politicians.[64] This is undesirable, since usually what is beneficial from the viewpoint of the individual politician's welfare – as measured for example in votes – will not be equally beneficial for the general public.[65]

More convincing then is a suggestion put forward by Joel Trachtman. He starts from the observation that the WTO Agreements contain several rules that raise doubts whether compliance with them would indeed enhance social welfare within the compliant WTO member. As was discussed above, economic theory suggests that trade liberalization is indeed

---

62 Schwartz and Sykes, 'Economic Structure of Renegotiation and Dispute Resolution', 179, 184.
63 See Trachtman, 'WTO Cathedral', 127 (stating that Schwartz and Sykes put forward a theory of politically efficient breach and not of efficient breach).
64 Lewis Kornhauser makes the general observation that public choice theory is an explanatory rather than a normative project: Kornhauser, 'Economic Analysis of Law'.
65 For the critique that government preferences may diverge from societal preferences, see Jackson, 'International Law Status of WTO Dispute Settlement Reports', 109, 118.

welfare enhancing. It is generally held to be Pareto-efficient in the sense that no single state will lose from trade liberalization.[66] These assumptions are usually not contended with respect to tariff reductions and the prohibition of discriminatory trade barriers. However, with respect to the prohibitions of certain domestic regulatory measures which do not de jure discriminate between domestic and foreign goods or services it is not at all clear whether compliance with these prohibitions will indeed enhance social welfare domestically.[67] Consequently, Trachtman proposes that with respect to these rules there should be no duty of strict performance.[68]

While social welfare appears as a more useful determinant of the authority of legal rules than political welfare, this approach, too, is subject to criticism in so far as it directly links the validity of law, in the sense of its bindingness, to law's welfare enhancing qualities. To make WTO law's bindingness dependent on the outcome of economic analysis, ignores that law is more than an instrument to pursue rational preferences.[69] Frequently, it is a compromise of competing preferences of a variety of actors which taken together would not meet the requirements established by economic analysis for rationality.[70] This is also true for international agreements. Even though legal doctrine adheres to the fiction that the parties to such agreements are unitary entities, international agreements cannot be compared to contracts between individual persons with a single will. Just like national legislation they are the outcome of battles between competing factions, such as consumer groups, environmentalists, exporters etc., structured by the respective political processes domestically and internationally. It would not only be fictitious to assume that states pursue rational preferences when they enter into international agreements and to take these preferences as a standard against which to evaluate the law, it would also be undemocratic. Ideally the conclusion of an international agreement for democratic states represents a democratic choice.[71] This

---

66 With respect to the domestic gains trade liberalization is to result in Kaldor-Hicks efficiency, meaning that the gains (for example to consumers) will be sufficient to compensate the losers (such as domestic import-competing industries).

67 Trachtman, 'WTO Cathedral', 127, 132–3. 68 Ibid.

69 See discussion in Chapter 2 above.

70 On these requirements, see Kornhauser, 'Introduction to the Economic Analysis of Contract Remedies', 683.

71 Admittedly, the democratic quality of international law is an ideal which is not nearly realized, as will be discussed throughout this study. And indeed due to the democratic deficit, arguments that law should be rational or efficient, or in other terms should be legitimated by its output, gain in weight.

choice should not be substituted by considerations of efficiency.[72] As I shall argue in the following section a public law conception of WTO law better takes account of WTO norms not only as instruments to achieve economic goals, but predominantly as expressions of political compromise and as instruments of trade governance.

II WTO law as public law

The conception of WTO law as a contract between members largely focuses on the material benefits which accrue to each member as a whole from trade liberalization. To recall, the Appellate Body in *Japan – Alcoholic Beverages* spoke of bargains among members 'in pursuit of their own respective *national interests*'.[73] This conception conceals that trade law has important effects not only on the global distribution of economic benefits between states, but also for individuals and domestic policy-making. This was already discussed in section A of this chapter which I concluded with the proposal that the main objective of WTO law should be seen as the management of conflicting societal interests. In this section I would like to build on this conception and elaborate on the particular role of the legal form in relation to this objective.

With respect to the objective of the WTO to manage conflicting societal interests, WTO law should not be regarded as constituting contractual relationships between WTO members, but rather as a public law which performs two functions. Firstly, it protects market conditions and thus, in shaping global markets, exercises a governance function. Secondly, WTO law sets out requirements to ensure that domestic policy-making that affects trade takes due account of trade interests. It thus frames and restricts the exercise of public authority. Consequently WTO law performs two public law functions: it is constitutive in that it protects (together with other bodies of law) market conditions and thus shapes global markets (section 1 below), and it is restrictive in that it limits the exercise of public

---

72 This criticism of the law and economics approach to WTO law is not to deny the benefits of a vigorous economic analysis of legal rules. Economic analysis may serve as a very valuable tool to clarify the costs and benefits of compliance given certain rational preferences. The results of such analysis may constitute weighty arguments in discussions about legal reform. Thus, if it can be shown that the Uruguay Round indeed did lead to an imbalanced outcome in the sense that the WTO Agreements depreciate overall social welfare within developing countries this would place a considerable justificatory burden on industrialized countries who 'sold' the bargain as one beneficial to all.

73 Appellate Body Report, *Japan – Alcoholic Beverages II*, WT/DS8/AB/R, WT/DS10/AB/R, WT/DS11/AB/R, adopted 1 November 1996, 15 (emphasis added).

authority (section 2). While I advocate a public law approach to WTO law, I argue that it should not be attributed a constitutional function (section 3).

1 WTO law's constitutive function

Certain features of WTO law allow it to be read and interpreted as not only protecting reciprocal exchanges of market access commitments between WTO members, but further as aiming at the protection of individual economic activities through the establishment and protection of certain market conditions. The legal form and judicial dispute settlement play an important role in this respect. They protect legal expectations and thus promote security and predictability for economic operators. At the same time, the legal form allows for the reconciliation of competing societal interests. By sharing the legal form with other norms of international law that promote or protect transnational societal interests, WTO norms do not form a separate regime, but are to a certain extent integrated into the larger body of international law.

1.1 From the protection of actual trade flows to the protection of market conditions

The legal texts as well as case law support the argument that it is indeed one function of WTO law (and not merely a side effect of contractual exchanges between states) to secure market conditions and thus to contribute to shaping global markets.

This function was explicitly addressed by the panel in *US – Section 301*. It considered that:

> Many of the benefits to Members which are meant to flow as a result of the acceptance of various disciplines under the GATT/WTO depend on the activity of individual economic operators in the national and global market places. The purpose of many of these disciplines, indeed one of the primary objects of the GATT/WTO as a whole, is to produce certain market conditions which would allow this individual activity to flourish.[74]

Several characteristics of WTO law support the conclusion that the protection of market conditions for the benefit of individuals rather than the reciprocal exchange of market access benefits is one central purpose of the legal norms. In a famous departure from international legal practice

---

74 Panel Report, *US – Section 301*, WT/DS152/R, adopted 27 January 2000, para. 7.73.

Art. XVI:4 WTO Agreement demands that '[e]ach Member shall ensure the conformity of its laws, regulations and administrative procedures with its obligations as provided in the annexed Agreements'. This means that the mere existence of the named governmental acts may constitute a violation whether they are indeed applied or not.[75] The obligation to ensure that government action conforms to WTO law even if it does not affect actual trade is explained by the aim to protect individual economic operators from the competitive disadvantages and chilling effects that may result from the mere prospect that discriminatory trade restrictions may be applied in the future.[76]

A further interpretation developed by GATT case law supports the understanding that WTO law aims at constituting and protecting market conditions and not only at protecting concrete individual transactions. It is the interpretation of the notion 'nullification or impairment of benefits'. A finding of nullification or impairment of benefits is a requirement for a legal complaint to be successful (Art. XXIII GATT). In the determination whether a violation of legal norms resulted in a nullification or impairment of benefits accruing under the agreements the focus shifted away from actual trade flows. Case law established that a nullification and impairment of benefits occurs if conditions of competition are negatively affected.[77] Such negative impact on market conditions is usually seen to exist as soon as legal obligations that protect these market conditions are violated. Consequently, Art. 3.8 DSU establishes a legal presumption of nullification and impairment of benefits in case a legal obligation is violated.

Finally, the fact that no demanding requirements of standing have been established[78] can be taken as a further sign that WTO law promotes a common interest in the stability of market conditions as established by the legal rules that goes beyond the 'private' interests of individual WTO members in concrete market access.

---

75 That governmental acts, independent of their application, may result in a violation was already established by GATT practice, see e.g. Panel Report, *EEC – Parts and Components*, adopted 16 May 1990, BISD 37S/132, paras. 5.25–5.26; Panel Report, *Thailand – Cigarettes*, adopted 7 November 1990, BISD 37S/200, para. 84; Panel Report, *US – Tobacco*, adopted 4 October 1994, BISD 41S/131, para. 118.

76 Panel Report, *US – Section 301*, WT/DS152/R, adopted 27 January 2000, para. 7.81.

77 See e.g. Panel Report, *US – Superfund*, adopted 17 June 1987, BISD 34S/136, para. 5.1.9.

78 In *EC – Bananas III* the Appellate Body confirmed the panel's finding that a member need not have a legal interest in a dispute in order to bring a claim, WT/DS27/AB/R, adopted 25 September 1997, paras. 132 *et seq.*; Bustamante, 'Need for a GATT Doctrine of Locus Standi', 533.

1.2 Security and predictability for economic operators

Security and predictability are key if the law is to achieve the objective of constituting and protecting market conditions.[79] This objective is expressed in Art. 3.2 DSU which states that the 'dispute settlement system of the WTO is a central element in providing security and predictability to the multilateral trading system'.

The significant strengthening of the dispute settlement system as compared with the GATT 1947 promotes certainty, in particular for economic operators. If a case is not settled voluntarily, formal dispute settlement proceedings in the WTO may no longer be blocked by an opposing member, nor can the authorization of retaliatory measures be blocked in case the losing party does not, within a reasonable period of time, comply with the recommendations of the Dispute Settlement Body.[80] The institution of appellate review by a standing Appellate Body further promotes predictability through the establishment of a coherent body of case law.[81] Once dispute settlement reports have been adopted by the Dispute Settlement Body there is an obligation of the defendant party to comply.[82]

Nonetheless, it has to be acknowledged that the protection of the public or common interest in the stability of market conditions as established by the legal norms still mainly lies with governments and depends on their willingness to bring claims against each other. If a conflict arises, the Dispute Settlement Understanding encourages voluntary settlements between members. It does, however, impose the obligation that settlements be consistent with the agreements and notified to the organization.[83] One step beyond the enforcement of legal rules through state to state dispute settlement may be seen in the WTO's Trade Policy Review Mechanism which subjects domestic trade policies to regular review. WTO organs, however, have no power to instigate any enforcement actions in case such review reveals a deviation from the law. Nonetheless,

---

79 Panel Report, *US – Section 301*, WT/DS152/R, adopted 27 January 2000, para. 7.75.
80 Art. 6.1 DSU; 22.6 DSU.
81 Howse, 'Adjudicative Legitimacy and Treaty Interpretation in International Trade Law', 35, 51 *et seq.*; Trachtman, 'Domain of WTO Dispute Resolution', 333; Mavroidis, 'Remedies in the WTO Legal System', 763.
82 Jackson, 'WTO Dispute Settlement Understanding', 60; Jackson, 'International Law Status of WTO Dispute Settlement Reports', 109; Charnovitz, 'Recent Developments and Scholarship on WTO Enforcement Remedies', 151, 161; Steger, 'WTO Dispute Settlement', 243, 245 *et seq.*; for a different view, see Schwartz and Sykes, 'Economic Structure of Renegotiation and Dispute Resolution', S179.
83 Arts 3.5, 3.6 DSU.

Kenneth Abbott called the Trade Policy Review Mechanism 'the clearest example of public interest thinking to emerge from the [Uruguay] Round'.[84]

1.3 Legitimating compromise between competing interests

The substantive rules of the WTO Agreements that secure certain market conditions, such as the rules on national treatment, most-favoured-nation treatment, anti-dumping, subsidies or safeguards, are not undisputed. They embody compromises between competing interests and have distributional consequences within and across societies. Take, for example, the rules on safeguards: they attempt to achieve a compromise between the interests of foreign exporters in market access and the interests of domestic industry in protection from foreign competition. Or take the SPS rules with respect to which the Appellate Body stated the following:

> The requirements of a risk assessment under Article 5.1, as well as of 'sufficient scientific evidence' under Article 2.2, are essential for the maintenance of the delicate and carefully negotiated balance in the SPS Agreement between the shared, but sometimes competing, interests of promoting international trade and of protecting the life and health of human beings.[85]

The legal form performs several functions in this respect. Firstly, it potentially legitimates the compromises which are represented by the legal norms. It does so, if the legal norms are the outcome of representative procedures. To date this is not usually the case with respect to WTO law as will be discussed below (section C). Secondly, the transparency of the law allows everyone to assess the distributional effects of the international trading system[86] and on this basis to formulate criticism and proposals for legal reform. Thirdly, the law provides a normative standard against which government action may be assessed and critiqued.

1.4 Integration with other legal regimes

WTO law is not the only body of law which defines the space and limits of economic behaviour. So do, for example, investment law, as well as human rights and environmental law. While the multitude of international legal

---

84 Abbott, 'GATT as a Public Institution', 31, 68.
85 Appellate Body Report, *EC – Hormones*, WT/DS26/AB/R, WT/DS48/AB/R, adopted 13 February 1998, para. 177.
86 Goldstein and Martin, 'Legalization, Trade Liberalization, and Domestic Politics', 603, 604 *et seq.*

regimes poses obstacles to the integration of these bodies of law, the fact that all these norms share the legal form and thus belong to the legal system facilitates their integration. The commonality of the legal form allows, for example, for some degree of integration by way of systemic interpretation according to Art. 31:3 (c) VCLT.[87] Interpretation of the law by panels and Appellate Body according to the customary rules of treaty interpretation means, inter alia, that the legal rules are interpreted not only in light of certain substantive objectives of the WTO, but that account is taken of legal norms of other international regimes which might pursue diverging objectives.[88]

2 WTO law as restriction on the exercise of public authority

Apart from establishing and potentially legitimating market conditions, WTO law restricts governmental authority. It does so by obliging governments to meet certain requirements when they adopt certain measures – legislation, administrative procedures or other governmental action – that affect trade. These include requirements of nondiscrimination,[89] of consultation[90] and rationality[91] in policy-making. They may be interpreted as making domestic governance more responsive to foreign interests, but also potentially more democratic with respect to the domestic constituency through the introduction of rationality requirements which may serve to enhance transparency.[92] WTO norms further restrict governmental freedom and enhance transparency by requiring that members notify certain measures to other members and the organization.[93]

3 WTO law as constitution?

Some of the scholars who subscribe to the view that WTO law aims at the stabilization of market conditions primarily for the benefit of private

---

87 International Law Commission, *Fragmentation of International Law.*
88 Howse, 'Legitimacy of the World Trade Organization', 355, 387.
89 See e.g. Art. III GATT.
90 Appellate Body Report, *US – Shrimp*, WT/DS58/AB/R, adopted 6 November 1998, para. 166 (in this case the Appellate Body arguably established a duty to negotiate before adopting unilateral restrictions on imports produced with harmful effects abroad).
91 One example for a rationality requirement is the least-restrictive measures test used by the Appellate Body when applying Art. XX GATT. See also Howse, 'Democracy, Science, and Free Trade', 2329 (on the rationality requirements of the SPS Agreement).
92 *Ibid.*
93 See e.g. Art. 7, Annex B SPS Agreement; Art. 2.9.2, Art. 2.10.1 TBT Agreement.

persons argue for attributing a constitutional function to WTO law.[94] Seen as constitution it would be WTO law's function to protect individual transnational economic activity as a matter of human rights from government intrusion.[95] The elevation of transnational economic activity to a human right supports the claim that any governmental restriction has to meet a high burden of justification. Thus, Ernst-Ulrich Petersmann argued that government policies, to be admissible under Art. XX GATT, would need to be justified on the basis that they are needed not only to protect certain public interests, but other *human rights values*.[96] Moreover, the claim is made that WTO law should be accorded direct effect in domestic legal orders so that individuals could challenge governmental policies on the basis that they violate WTO law.[97]

A constitutionalization of WTO law entails, however, the danger that other interests, such as regulatory environmental or social policy objectives, which potentially conflict with economic activity, might be subordinated to individual economic rights.[98] It was further pointed out, in particular by Robert Howse and Kalypso Nicolaïdis, that the Appellate Body would not be the most suitable organ to adjudicate conflicts between economic interests and competing interests in the protection of the environment, food or human security. If, however, WTO law were constitutionalized in the sense that it was the main objective of the WTO law to strike a balance between such interests, such would be its role.[99]

Talking about WTO law as a constitution is furthermore not desirable since it gives it the appearance of superiority. In light of the many concerns that relate to WTO law's legitimacy such an appearance is not warranted. Rather it should be stressed that like any legislation WTO law should be responsive to societal demands for change. One procedure which might

---

94 For different conceptions of constitutional functions performed by WTO law, see Cass, *Constitutionalization of the World Trade Organization*.
95 See Petersmann, *supra* note 20.
96 Petersmann, 'Time for Integrating Human Rights into the Law of Worldwide Organizations', 39.
97 *Ibid*. Cottier, 'A Theory of Direct Effect in Global Law', 106. For a discussion of direct effect of WTO law in the EC legal order that distinguishes between treaty norms and adopted dispute settlement reports, see Bogdandy, 'Legal Effects of World Trade Organization Decisions within European Union Law', 45; Panel Report, *US – Section 301*, WT/DS152/R, adopted 27 January 2000, para. 7.72 (stating that WTO law is not interpreted by WTO organs as having direct effect).
98 For a convincing critique of a constitutional reading of WTO law, Howse and Nicolaïdis, 'Legitimacy and Global Governance', 227; Bogdandy, 'Law and Politics in the WTO', 609.
99 Howse and Nicolaïdis, 'Legitimacy and Global Governance', 227, 228.

ensure such responsiveness and enable such change, the waiver power, is the object of this study.

III Conclusion

WTO law not only affects the external relations of states, but has a strong impact on the regulatory autonomy of states and on individuals. It aims at the establishment of market conditions and at the same time the reconciliation of competing interests and values. It is thus not only an instrument to secure substantive gains from trade, but to ensure legitimate governance. To perform this function, the validity of law, its 'bindingness', may not depend on the consensus of trade officials nor on some extralegal standard like efficiency. At the same time it may not be interpreted as attributing to economic rights a hierarchical rank above other societal interests.

This said, it has to be acknowledged that WTO law as it stands has not entirely abandoned the paradigm of a contractual, inter-state law. This is most obvious with respect to the norms that concern market access commitments. These are negotiated bilaterally and may also be renegotiated without the participation of all members. Thus, one might indeed see these commitments as bilateral bargains between members, as contracts. By contrast the general legal rules of the agreements are to be seen as legislation, which protects not only national interests, but diverse transnationally shared societal interests.

C. FLEXIBILITY CHALLENGES

In the preceding sections I developed the argument that from the perspective of democratic liberalism the objectives of the WTO should neither be perceived merely in terms of economic welfare nor of individual autonomy. Rather a conceptualization of the WTO's objectives needs to take into account the contingency of any division between admissible and inadmissible restrictions of trade.

In light of this contingency the determination of trade restrictions that are admissible and those that are inadmissible may not be set in stone, e.g. by attributing to WTO law the status of a constitution. On the other hand, the responsibility of drawing a dividing line should not be handed over either to diplomats who decide what is acceptable, or to technocrats who decide what is efficient. In order not to foreclose the option of democratic contestation and the possibility of legitimate change through law-making procedures that approximate democratic representativeness, it must be legal rules that determine the proper balance.

In what follows I indicate demands for flexibility of WTO law that relate to the proper balance between the promotion of transnational economic activity and the freedom to restrict trade. The flexibility demands will be identified from the three perspectives introduced in Chapter 2, namely the domestic, the intra-regime and the inter-regime perspectives.

I Domestic preferences

There is a clear tension between WTO law and the regulatory autonomy of domestic polities. That international law may conflict with domestic law-making is nothing new in international law and international legal rules take account of such conflicts. According to Article 27 of the Vienna Convention on the Law of Treaties a party to a treaty 'may not invoke the provisions of its internal law as justification for its failure to perform a treaty'. Together with the basic principle *pacta sunt servanda* (Article 26 VCLT) this principle seeks to ensure the effectiveness of international law.

These principles, where they restrict domestic regulatory autonomy, require justification. One justification is found in the normative judgment that stability and legality in international relations are preferable to disorder and war.[100] From the need for justification it follows that international scholars cannot repeat like a mantra that if states consent to a treaty they are bound due to the principle of *pacta sunt servanda*, regardless of whether the populations of such states express a preference for non-compliance. For the normative judgment to hold, good reasons must be found to justify the principle *pacta sunt servanda* and the rule that domestic law may not be invoked as an excuse for non-compliance. In the domestic setting the situation is not much different. It is true that due to the monopoly of power of the state many citizens do not have the choice whether to comply with legal norms or not. In liberal democracies, however, the democratic process together with constitutional guarantees provide individuals with good reasons to comply with the laws that are the outcome of such processes and with other governmental action based on these laws. The more attenuated the link between the domestic democratic process and international law, the greater the need either to fathom independent reasons for adherence to international law

---

100 Howse, 'Legitimacy of the World Trade Organization', 355, 360.

(such as the democratic legitimacy of international law itself), or to allow for exceptions from compliance if strong domestic preferences militate against compliance. This is particularly pertinent for WTO law, which – compared to other international legal regimes – is both relatively more restrictive on regulatory autonomy and created in a process comparatively far removed from domestic democratic processes.

Some of the rules which restrict domestic regulatory autonomy have already been mentioned and will not be reiterated here.[101] WTO law mandates members to ensure that their laws, regulations and administrative procedures are in conformity with WTO law (Art. XVI WTO Agreement). The effect of this rule is clearly detectable. Today there is almost no public debate on proposed regulation, in particular in the domain of environmental protection, be it related to climate change, GMOs or biofuel, in which the question is not raised as to the compatibility of regulation with the norms of the WTO.[102]

While the strongest contenders for possible conflict with WTO norms in the advanced economies are governmental measures on consumer safety, environmental protection or protection of labour standards, there might also be a strong preference domestically for measures to protect a certain industry against competition. Such protectionism might be motivated by fears of 'social dumping', i.e. fears that domestic industry may not be able to compete with imports which have been produced under significantly lower social or environmental standards. Apart from the fear that domestic standards may be endangered, there may be a desire to protect domestic workers from unemployment. While the provisions on safeguards allow some temporary protection of industry to facilitate domestic adjustments, such as retraining of workers, members might further wish to protect a certain industry to avoid losses that may not be easily addressed through policies of redistribution. For example, a society might have an interest in maintaining a farming industry due to the cultural, ecological or communal values attributed to it.[103]

---

101 For a list of non-protectionist domestic measures that may be in violation of WTO rules, see Charnovitz, 'An Analysis of Pascal Lamy's Proposal on Collective Preferences', 449, 466.

102 As a reaction to such debates concerning domestic climate change regulation the WTO and UNEP secretariats published the joint study, 'Trade and Climate Change', 2009, www.wto.org/english/res_e/publications_e/trade_climate_change_e.htm (last accessed 11 March 2011).

103 Robert Howse gives the example of textile workers in Quebec and considers that their losing their occupation might result in injury to human dignity and community that

There might be good economic arguments against measures to protect industries that are not competitive. However, if such measures are the outcome of a transparent and representative democratic process, they cannot easily be dismissed as beggar-thy-neighbour protectionism, to be attributed to the special influence on government by powerful interest groups. The avoidance of such protectionism was, however, identified as one of the main objectives and substantive justifications of WTO law. The fact that there might be preferences for domestic regulation that does not endanger this objective supports the argument that WTO law should react to such preferences by providing for some form of exception that could apply in such cases.[104]

The case for such exceptions becomes even stronger if one looks at negotiations during the Uruguay Round and subsequent multilateral trade negotiation rounds. Several imbalances can be noted: firstly, there is a clear imbalance between advanced countries who pursue a certain agenda and developing countries who are often badly informed about the content of the negotiating proposals and at the same time put under considerable pressure either to agree to such proposals or to face unilateral action by developed countries.[105] Furthermore, there are strong allegations that developing countries only agreed to the TRIPS Agreement since they were promised concessions in other areas, in particular trade in goods,[106] promises which have remained largely unfulfilled. Due to the package deal solution as well as the termination of the old GATT, countries could not choose between the old GATT and the new WTO, but instead had to accept the WTO Agreements as a whole if they did not want to be excluded from international trade cooperation entirely.[107]

Secondly, there was (and is) in trade negotiations an imbalance between national executives and parliaments. Since the negotiation of

---

could not easily be compensated by the creation of jobs in other sectors, retraining programmes or unemployment benefits: Howse, 'Legitimacy of the World Trade Organization', 355, 364.

104 Rodrik, 'One Economics, Many Recipes', 230 et seq.; Lamy, Emergence of Collective Preferences in International Trade, 11 et seq.

105 Jawara and Kwa, 'Behind the Scenes at the WTO'; Howse, 'Legitimacy of the World Trade Organization', 355, 360.

106 Or merely the prospect that the US would lift unilateral trade sanctions imposed under section 301 of the Trade Act of 1974 for the refusal to grant patent protection not mandated by international law: see Hestermeyer, Human Rights and the WTO, 39–41.

107 For a critique of this 'package deal' approach, see e.g. Howse, 'For a Citizen's Task Force', 877, 881.

the agreements is the prerogative of the executive, parliaments as of right frequently only participate at the ratification stage. Ratification, however, does not afford an opportunity to influence the content of the agreements. The relationship between the executive and parliaments has to be reconsidered with respect to treaties that strongly intrude into the regulatory autonomy of states.[108] An example where the rights of national parliaments to participate in the negotiating process have been considerably strengthened due to this impact is the European Union. The German Constitutional Court, for example, interpreted the constitution of the Federal Republic of Germany as mandating participation rights, not only in processes of treaty amendment, but also when the European Union makes use of its implied powers.[109] When the WTO agreements were negotiated during the Uruguay Round this was done in a non-transparent way that did not allow parliamentary oversight or debate. Frequently, not even the diplomats at Geneva had insight into negotiations conducted among a few powerful states in so-called green room proceedings.[110]

A third imbalance concerns the large influence in negotiations of certain powerful private interests of industry, for instance represented by the pharmaceutical lobby, or of labour if compared to other societal interests.[111] It is one observation that in general organized interests have a greater impact on policy-making than diffused interests such as those of consumers. Another, more critical one, is that the executive is sometimes more responsive to these interests than are parliaments. Thus international law-making may be particularly strongly influenced by organized special interests.[112] This finding contradicts the constitutionalist claim that WTO law's main value lies in tying the hands of governments so they do not fall prey to special interests.[113]

---

108 Cf. Krajewski, 'Legitimizing Global Economic Governance through Transnational Parliamentarization'.

109 *Lisbon Case*, BVerfG, 2 BvE/08 from 30 June 2009, www.bverfg.de/entscheidungen/es20090630_2bve000208.html (last accessed 11 March 2011).

110 Charnovitz, 'Emergence of Democratic Participation in Global Governance', 49, fn. 16; Marco Bronckers demands that citizens and parliaments should be able to verify beforehand what the rules may be: 'Bronckers, Better Rules for a New Millennium', 547, 566; Robert Howse suggests that referenda should be held within members on outcomes of the Doha Round: Howse, 'Human Rights in the WTO'.

111 Rodrik, *Global Governance of Trade*. On corporate influence on rule-making during the Uruguay Round, see Braithwaite and Drahos, *Global Business Regulation*.

112 Benvenisti, 'Exit and Voice in the Age of Globalization', 167.

113 Cf. also Krajewski, 'Democratic Legitimacy and Constitutional Perspectives of WTO Law', 167, 178 *et seq.*

Consequently, if the demand is voiced for exceptions from compliance to mitigate the restrictions that WTO law imposes on domestic democratic government, it has to be recognized that these restrictions not only become problematic if democratic preferences change or rules result in unforeseen consequences. Such restrictions are also problematic because democratic preferences were only insufficiently taken into account at the negotiation phase. Obviously international rules cannot equally reflect the preferences of all parties (otherwise they would hardly be needed), but societal preferences should at least have the chance to impact international law-making. This can be achieved by strengthening the participation of domestic parliaments, governmental agencies (other than the one directly responsible) and national publics in international negotiations.[114]

As a last point it should be noted that during accession negotiations countries that wish to accede to the WTO are often asked to accept obligations and make market access commitments which go beyond the obligations of existing members.[115] Countries that wish to become members often stand little chance against the combined bargaining power of the existing membership. The accession process is, thus, frequently taken as a way to demand reforms in the acceding member that are not necessarily related to the objectives of the organization. While the EU's demands in accession proceedings for rule of law reforms in potentially new EU member states are justified by its own commitment to the rule of law and human rights, demands of the WTO membership for economic reform that goes beyond what is demanded by the general rules can hardly be justified on the basis of WTO objectives.[116]

II Claims of inadequacy and injustice

Flexibility claims may not only be raised from a domestic, but also from an intra-regime perspective, that relates the legal rules to the institution's objectives as well as transnational and membership preferences.

Claims of inadequacy relate to the unsuitability or inefficiency of legal rules to achieve certain objectives. An example for such a claim was made

---

114 For a good overview on the various ways to make international negotiations more representative, see Friedrich, 'Nonbinding Instruments' (manuscript on file with the author).

115 Charnovitz, 'Mapping the Law of WTO Accession', 855, Qin, '"WTO-Plus" Obligations', 483.

116 On the process of accession to the European Union, see Rötting, *Das verfassungsrechtliche Beitrittsverfahren zur Europäischen Union*; on WTO accession, see Williams, *A Handbook on Accession to the WTO*.

in the GATT 1947 with respect to the balance-of-payments provisions. Under the GATT 1947 a consensus developed as to the inefficiency of the legal rules to address balance-of-payments problems. This has been one of the rare instances in which on the basis of economic theory members agreed that measures prohibited under the GATT (tariff surcharges) were economically the better choice than the measures foreseen by the agreement in such situations (quotas). This situation was addressed, inter alia, by suspending the inefficient rules through waiver decisions.[117]

By contrast, claims of injustice are claims that relate to questions of participation in the organization as well as the distributional consequences of the rules. Thus, such claims may entail arguments that certain interests are not represented in the organization even though they are affected by it, or that the distributional effects of the rules are unjust.[118]

Claims of injustice levelled against the WTO include the claim that WTO law insufficiently takes account of differences in economic development among WTO members and that it neglects important values and interests which are shared transnationally. These problems originate in the deficient negotiation process in terms of effective representation of developing countries, domestic constituencies and transnational interests.

Two allegations are made particularly forcefully: firstly, that WTO law impedes the economic development of poor countries even though this is one of the organization's objectives as formulated in its preamble and, secondly, that the TRIPS Agreement not only impedes development, but unduly favours interests of industry over interests of the general public to benefit from innovation.[119]

Turning to the first allegation: a common statement that decries the injustice of the WTO Agreements vis-à-vis developing countries refers to the imbalance in market access for products of interest to developing country members as compared to market access for products from developed country members. Industries in which developing countries have a comparative advantage such as the textile or agricultural industries are still heavily protected in developed economies, be it through tariffs or subsidies.[120]

---

117 For a more detailed discussion, see Chapter 4 B.I.2.2.a.
118 Fraser, *Scales of Justice*, 12 *et seq.*
119 See e.g. Cosbey, *Sustainable Development Roadmap for the WTO*; Aaronson and Zimmermann, *Trade Imbalance*, 32 *et seq.*; Salomon, *Global Responsibility for Human Rights*, 139 *et seq*; Stiglitz, *Globalization and its Discontents*, 244 *et seq.*
120 Stiglitz and Charlton, *Fair Trade for All*, 12 *et seq.*

Another argument holds that market access might not be as essential to development as it is usually made out to be. More important, it is argued, is regulatory freedom to adopt innovative policies which in the respective societal and political context promise to spur domestic investment and consequently lead to growth. This policy space, however, is restricted through demands on developing countries to further open their markets, the prohibition of trade-related investment measures such as local content rules, the prohibition of export subsidies, as well as the obligation to grant intellectual property rights. Consequently, it is proposed that in order to promote development, the restrictions that these rules impose should be loosened under certain circumstances such as, for example, a substantiated demonstration of an economic policy that requires the imposition of measures in violation of WTO rules.[121]

Moreover, the costs of implementation for developing countries might divert resources from other policies which, for the purpose of poverty reduction, should receive higher priority.[122] It is thus demanded that transitional periods should be prolonged or exemptions granted and that there should be greater transparency as regards the likely costs of implementation.[123]

The second and most vehemently voiced claim of injustice concerns the TRIPS Agreement.[124] Developing countries' governments, international institutions such as the WHO, and NGOs defend the view that the TRIPS Agreement does not achieve a just balance between, on the one hand, intellectual property protection to spur research and development and, on the other hand, the public availability of benefits from innovation.[125] Indeed, the pharmaceutical lobby strongly influenced the negotiations of the TRIPS Agreement with the result that exceptions to the obligation to protect patent rights and the option to issue compulsory licences are very limited.[126] Consequently, these rules impede the access of poor populations to affordable medicines and arguably violate the human right to health.[127] Moreover, public health care in industrialized members may

---

121 Rodrik, *One Economics, Many Recipes*, 230 *et seq.*; Trachtman, 'Ensuring a Development-Friendly WTO'; see discussion in Chapter 6 A.III.4.1.

122 Rodrik, *Global Governance of Trade*.

123 *Ibid.*; Ostry, 'Uruguay Round North–South Grand Bargain', 285, 288.

124 See only Salomon, *Global Responsibility for Human Rights*, 139 *et seq.*; Pogge, 'Montréal Statement on the Human Right to Essential Medicines', 97.

125 Petersmann, 'Time for Integrating Human Rights into the Law of Worldwide Organizations'.

126 Sell, 'Industry Strategies for Intellectual Property and Trade', 79.

127 For a detailed analysis of the relationship, Hestermeyer, *Human Rights and the WTO*.

also suffer, for example where pandemics require the prompt supply of large amounts of pharmaceutical products which exceed national production capacities.

As a further injustice it is pointed out that the TRIPS rules impede development by prohibiting practices such as reverse engineering of patented technology. These may be an important factor in development as is demonstrated by the history of advanced countries who in the early stages of their development themselves had purposefully weak protection of intellectual property.[128]

Another criticism of the TRIPS Agreement points out that while the agreement protects forms of knowledge predominant in Western societies, it does not similarly protect traditional knowledge, or even counteracts such protection. Enterprises might use traditional knowledge to develop products for which they claim patent protection without sharing the benefits with the societies who originally possessed the traditional knowledge.[129] The principles of the Convention on Biological Diversity (CBD) on prior consent and benefit-sharing that address this situation are not reflected in the TRIPS Agreement.[130]

III Regime coordination

As a consequence of decentralized law-making at the international level two situations arise which raise demands for flexibility from an

128 Rodrik, *Global Governance of Trade*; Hestermeyer, *Human Rights and the WTO*.
129 Dutfield, 'TRIPS-Related Aspects of Traditional Knowledge', 133.
130 The TRIPS Council is currently discussing – as mandated by paragraph 19 of the Doha Declaration – the relationship between the TRIPS Agreement and the Convention on Biological Diversity (CBD) and more specifically the question how the provisions of the CBD on prior informed consent and benefit-sharing with respect to traditional knowledge can be accommodated by the TRIPS Agreement. One proposal to address this question foresees that the TRIPS Agreement is changed so as to require patent applicants to disclose the origin of genetic resources and traditional knowledge in the invention for which they seek the patent. This, it is argued, would make the CBD provisions on prior informed consent and benefit-sharing more effective and would be one step towards implementing Art. 16.5 CBD which calls on the contracting parties to cooperate in order to ensure that intellectual property rights support and do not counteract the objectives of the CBD: see Communication from Norway, Amending the TRIPS Agreement to introduce an obligation to disclose the origin of genetic resources and traditional knowledge in patent applications, IP/C/W/473 (14 June 2006). Amendment of the TRIPS Agreement to include a disclosure obligation is advocated by a group represented by Brazil and India that includes Bolivia, Colombia, Cuba, Dominican Republic, Ecuador, Peru, Thailand, the African Group and some other developing countries: see information by the WTO at www.wto.org/english/tratop_e/trips_e/art27_3b_background_e.htm.

inter-regime perspective. On the one hand, values which are pursued and protected in one regime are neglected in another, leading to ever more situations of potential conflict. On the other hand, different regimes may pursue the same objectives, but be lacking formal linkage for the coordination of their activities.

With respect to the World Trade Organization (WTO) the first scenario has materialized in the following ways: on the one hand, international regimes which foresee measures which affect trade are faced with claims that such measures are inconsistent with WTO law; on the other hand, the narrow focus of WTO law on trade and intellectual property protection neglects the negative effects which this law – and in particular the TRIPS Agreement – has on other internationally protected interests and values, such as the human right to health care or indigenous traditional knowledge. Since the WTO has – due to mandatory dispute settlement – a relatively strong enforcement mechanism, WTO law, in case of conflict, is likely to prevail.[131]

Different ways have been proposed to address this situation, including claims for the interpretation of WTO law in light of other international norms,[132] the application of non-WTO law by the WTO dispute settlement organs,[133] as well as institutional reforms, such as the inclusion of non-trade experts in WTO panels.[134]

The second scenario resulting from the division of the international legal order into a number of largely unconnected legal regimes can be illustrated by the relationship of the WTO and the World Customs Organization (WCO). Both aim at trade facilitation and may be seen as engaged in a division of labour to this effect. The WCO administers, for example, the Harmonized System nomenclature for the classification of goods which is an important tool in the negotiation and implementation of tariff commitments.[135] Despite this substantive overlap and the resulting need for coordination between the two organizations neither of the two

---

131 Holger Hestermeyer refers to this as the 'factual hierarchy of regimes': Hestermeyer, *Human Rights and the WTO*, 193 *et seq.*; Trachtman, *Economic Structure of International Law*, 201.

132 See e.g. Marceau, 'Conflicts of Norms and Conflicts of Jurisdictions', 1081.

133 See e.g. Pauwelyn, 'Role of Public International Law in the WTO', 535.

134 See e.g. Graber, 'New UNESCO Convention on Cultural Diversity', 553, at 571 *et seq.* (proposing to include non-trade experts, such as for example cultural experts, in panels which adjudicate on cases in which cultural interests are at stake); for suggestions on institutional solutions to conflicts between the TRIPS Agreement and human rights, see Hestermeyer, *Human Rights and the WTO*, 287 *et seq.*

135 Feichtner, 'Administration of the Vocabulary of International Trade', 1481.

organizations provides rules or procedures which might structure such coordination effectively.

D. THE POTENTIAL OF THE WAIVER POWER TO ACHIEVE FLEXIBILITY

The main flexibility challenges result from claims that WTO law is too restrictive and does not take sufficient account of domestic preferences and policies agreed upon in other international or transnational frameworks. Obviously the above account is not comprehensive. There are also demands for more WTO law, such as further obligations to afford technical assistance, as well as for further specification of norms that are deliberately vague and explicitly call for concretization.[136]

However, from a perspective that sees the WTO's objective mainly in more inclusive policy-making at the domestic level as well as in coordinating domestic and international policies that affect trade, the main claim is that there is too much rather than too little law: too much emphasis on further liberalization as well as harmonization of domestic policies.[137] From this perspective an instrument that allows for relaxing the rules appears to bear a specific potential.

The desirability of political processes to debate such relaxation that are open to a variety of societal perspectives including perspectives from other international institutions becomes apparent if it is acknowledged that many situations of norm conflict or frictions between international legal regimes are an expression of underlying interest conflicts in society. The waiver power provides a procedure to decide in a political process upon the relaxation of the law. How it was used in the past and its potential to address the identified flexibility challenges in the future will be addressed in the next chapters.

136 Bronckers, 'Better Rules for a New Millennium', 547.
137 See also Krajewski, 'Democratic Legitimacy and Constitutional Perspectives of WTO Law', 167.

PART II

The practice and law of waivers

In the next chapter I first introduce the waiver power and its history. I proceed to analyse the waiver practice under the GATT 1947 and in the WTO in order to determine which flexibility demands have in fact been addressed by the waiver power (Chapter 4). The subsequent chapter presents an account of the law of waivers as it is laid down in legal instruments and as it emerged from the institutional practice (Chapter 5). Both chapters form the basis for the analysis in Part III as to the potential of the waiver to provide flexibility in order to meet individual and collective needs and preferences.

4

The waiver power and practice of the GATT 1947 and the WTO

A. THE WAIVER POWER OF THE GATT 1947 AND THE WTO

The WTO's waiver power is found in Art. IX:3 of the Agreement Establishing the WTO (WTO Agreement). It allows the Ministerial Conference '[i]n exceptional circumstances . . . to waive an obligation imposed on a Member by this Agreement or any of the Multilateral Trade Agreements, provided that any such decision shall be taken by three-fourths of the Members'. The waiver power in Art. IX:3 WTO Agreement supersedes the waiver power in Art. XXV:5 GATT. Under the GATT 1947 this power enabled the contracting parties, acting jointly, to suspend GATT obligations by a two-thirds majority which comprised more than half of the contracting parties.

The waiver power of the GATT 1947 goes back to the United States 'Suggested Charter for an International Trade Organization' (1946).[1] This draft charter provided for a waiver power in Art. 55:2. According to this provision the Conference – the plenary organ of the organization – was to be granted the competence to waive obligations in Chapter IV of the draft charter, i.e. tariffs and customs obligations. During the Preparatory Conference in London it was agreed, upon a proposal of the French delegate,[2] to extend this waiver power to all obligations under the charter.[3] From the *travaux préparatoires* of the London Conference it appears that the waiver power was intended as an emergency exception to allow for a temporary

---

1 *Suggested Charter for an International Trade Organization*, Publication No. 2598, Commercial Policy Series No. 98 (Washington: United States Department of State, 1946).
2 Preparatory Committee of the International Conference on Trade and Employment, Committee V, Ninth Meeting on 7 November 1946, E/PC/T/C.V/25 (11 November 1946), 2–4.
3 London Report, 22, para. D. 2. Subsequently the waiver power was included in Art. 66:2 of the London Draft Charter and was kept as Art. 66:2 in the New York Draft Charter, see WTO, *Analytical Index of the GATT*, vol. II, Article XXV, 890.

suspension of obligations if none of the other escape clauses applied.[4] The general waiver power became Art. 77:3 of the Havana Charter.[5] In the GATT the waiver power was included in Art. XXV:5 GATT.[6]

Art. XXV:5 GATT 1947 authorized the CONTRACTING PARTIES[7] 'in exceptional circumstances not elsewhere provided for' to waive any obligation under the GATT 1947. A waiver decision could be taken by a two-thirds majority of votes cast which had to comprise more than half of the contracting parties (Art. XXV:5 cl. 2 GATT). Such a decision did not have to include a termination date, nor did it have to provide for an annual review of the waiver. The issue whether waivers could be terminated was a matter of contention in GATT 1947.[8]

This waiver power has been called '[p]erhaps the most important single power of the CONTRACTING PARTIES'[9] and a working party considering a waiver requested by the member states of the European Coal and Steel Community stated:

> [T]he text of paragraph 5 (a) of Art. XXV is general in character; it allows the CONTRACTING PARTIES to waive any obligation imposed upon the contracting parties by the Agreement in exceptional circumstances not provided for in the Agreement, and places no limitations on the exercise of that right.[10]

---

4 The delegate from the United States, Mr Kellogg, stated that the proposed waiver power was meant to 'cover cases which were exceptional and caused particular hardship to any particular member', E/PC/T/C.V/PV/9, 8, see also E/PC/T/C.V/25, 3. The French delegate at the same meeting stated that the waiver power should allow the suspension of obligations if they 'would impose some economic hardship on some countries, those hardships . . . being of a temporary character', E/PC/T/C.V/PV/9, 9.

5 Art. 77:3 Havana Charter for an International Trade Organization, 24 March 1948, Canadian Treaties Series No. 32, 3; UN Doc. E/CONF. 2/78 (1948). Art. 77:3 reads: 'In exceptional circumstances not elsewhere provided for in this Charter, the Conference may waive an obligation imposed upon a Member by the Charter; *Provided* that any such decision shall be approved by a two-thirds majority of the votes cast and that such majority shall comprise more than half of the Members. The Conference may also by such a vote define certain categories of exceptional circumstances to which other voting requirements shall apply for the waiver of obligations.'

6 The present text of Art. XXV:5 GATT is identical to that which was agreed upon on 30 October 1947. For the provisions which were added during the first session of the CONTRACTING PARTIES and then deleted again at the Review Session in 1954–55, see WTO, *Analytical Index of the GATT*, vol. II, Article XXV, 890.

7 Under the GATT 1947 the contracting parties acting jointly were designated as the CONTRACTING PARTIES (Art. XXV:1 GATT). This designation will be used throughout this study where it refers to the Conference of the Parties as an organ of the GATT.

8 Jackson, Davey and Sykes, *Legal Problems of International Economic Relations*, 226.

9 Jackson, *World Trade and the Law of GATT*, 541.

10 CONTRACTING PARTIES, The European Coal and Steel Community, report adopted 10 November 1952 (G/35), BISD 1S/85.

During the Uruguay Round the waiver power was reviewed. From the beginning of negotiations the European Economic Community (EEC) had suggested a reconsideration of Art. XXV:5 GATT 1947.[11] With its proposal the EEC claimed to be pursuing the aim 'to prevent the perpetuation of, or to forestall virtually permanent privileged situations'.[12] The proposal was perceived as a response to the US Agricultural Waiver granted in 1955.[13] This waiver[14] allowed the United States to take measures in violation of its obligations under Art. II and Art. XI GATT 1947 in respect of agricultural products and is said to have led to a general deterioration of the GATT disciplines in the agricultural sector.[15] The EEC's proposal was widely supported.[16] It provided, inter alia, for specific time limits to be set when a waiver is granted, an annual review of waivers and the termination or replacement of existing waivers. On the basis of this proposal the GATT Secretariat prepared a draft decision which was included in the 1990 Brussels Draft Final Act.[17] This draft decision did not contain an agreement on when existing waivers had to be terminated. On this point the negotiating group had not been able to agree since the US had linked this issue to the outcome of negotiations in other areas, especially in agriculture.[18]

Eventually, the following requirements were incorporated into Art. IX:4 of the WTO Agreement: waiver decisions must state the exceptional circumstances justifying the waiver, the terms and conditions governing the application of the waiver, and the date on which the waiver will terminate. Waivers shall be reviewed on an annual basis.

The Understanding in Respect of Waivers of Obligations under the General Agreement on Tariffs and Trade 1994 ('the Understanding') which

---

11 Stewart (ed.), *GATT Uruguay Round*, vol. II, 1845.
12 Communication from the European Economic Community, MTN.GNG/NG7/W/4 (18 May 1987), 2.
13 Stewart (ed.), *GATT Uruguay Round*, vol. II, 1845.
14 Waiver Granted to the United States in Connection with Import Restrictions Imposed under Section 22 of the United States Agricultural Adjustment Act of 1933, As Amended (hereinafter referred to as 'Agricultural Waiver'), 5 March 1955, BISD 3S/32 (1955).
15 Jackson, *World Trade and the Law of GATT*, 718; Dam, *GATT: Law and International Economic Organization*, 262; Lowenfeld, *International Economic Law*, 42. This waiver will be discussed in more detail in section B.I.2.2(a) below.
16 Stewart (ed.), *GATT Uruguay Round*, vol. II, 1851; Croome, *Reshaping the World Trading System*, 189.
17 Trade Negotiations Committee, Draft Final Act Embodying the Results of the Uruguay Round of Multilateral Trade Negotiations, Revision, MTN.TNC/W/35/Rev.1 (3 December 1990), 311 *et seq.* ('Understanding on the Interpretation of Article XXV').
18 Croome, *Reshaping the World Trading System*, 189.

constitutes part of the GATT 1994[19] includes further requirements for requests of waivers of GATT obligations.[20] With respect to waivers granted under the GATT 1947 and still in force on the date of entry into force of the WTO Agreement,[21] para. 2 of the Understanding states that these waiver decisions automatically expired at the latest two years from the date of entry into force of the WTO Agreement unless extended according to the procedures set out in the Understanding and Art. IX WTO Agreement. Thus, since the beginning of 1997 all existing waivers of GATT obligations have been governed by the rules set out in the Understanding and Art. IX:3 and 4 WTO Agreement. The Understanding further clarifies that the invocation of the GATT dispute settlement provision (Art. XXIII GATT) is not precluded by a waiver decision.

Art. IX:3 WTO Agreement now constitutes the WTO's general waiver competence.[22] It authorizes the Ministerial Conference in exceptional circumstances to waive an obligation of the WTO Agreement or any of the Multilateral Trade Agreements.[23] A waiver decision, according to this provision, needs to be adopted by three-fourths of the members. Art. IX:3 WTO Agreement thus imposes stricter voting requirements than Art. XXV:5 GATT, which required a two-thirds majority of votes cast comprising more than half of the contracting parties. Obligations that are subject to a transitional period or a period for staged implementation may only be waived by consensus decisions.[24] In practice all waiver decisions are taken by consensus[25] and usually by the General Council which acts on behalf of the Ministerial Conference when the Ministerial Conference is not in session.[26]

19 Section 1 lit. c no. v Introductory Note to GATT 1994.

20 For a discussion of these requirements see Chapter 5 C.I.

21 According to Section 1 lit. b no. iii Introductory Note to GATT 1994 waivers granted under Art. XXV:5 GATT 1947 and still in force on the date of entry into force of the WTO Agreement formed part of the GATT 1994.

22 Apart from this general waiver competence there are a number of specific waiver competences in the WTO Agreements. These include Art. VI:6(b) GATT; Art. XVIII:18 GATT; Art. XXIV:10 GATT; Art. 12.8 TBT Agreement; Art. 10.3 SPS Agreement; Art. 63.2 TRIPS Agreement; Art. 66.1 TRIPS Agreement; Art. 27.4 Subsidies and Countervailing Measures (SCM) Agreement; Art. 29.4 SCM Agreement; Art. 5.3 TRIMs Agreement.

23 The Multilateral Trade Agreements are the agreements and associated legal instruments included in Annexes 1, 2 and 3 of the WTO Agreement (Art. II:2 WTO Agreement); these are the Multilateral Agreements on Trade in Goods (Annex 1A), the General Agreement on Trade in Services (Annex 1B), the Agreement on Trade-Related Aspects of Intellectual Property Rights (Annex 1C), the Understanding on Rules and Procedures Governing the Settlement of Disputes (Annex 2) and the Trade Policy Review Mechanism (Annex 3).

24 Footnote 4 to Art. IX:3 WTO Agreement.

25 On decision-making on waiver requests see Chapter 5 C.III.

26 Waivers of obligations in the Plurilateral Trade Agreements shall be governed by the provisions of the respective plurilateral agreement (Art. IX:5 WTO Agreement).

The stricter requirements of the WTO Agreement for the granting of waivers have been evaluated as an important element of the increased legalization of the WTO as compared to the GATT.[27] A closer look at the waiver process reveals, however, that the codification of procedural requirements during the Uruguay Round has not in all instances led to a closer scrutiny of waiver requests or the operation of waivers once granted. As will be seen in Chapter 5, even though the GATT 1947 did not prescribe a specific procedure for the granting of waivers, waiver requests under the GATT 1947 were carefully scrutinized by working parties, a practice which was not continued in the WTO. Furthermore, while the GATT 1947 did not prescribe the annual review of waiver decisions, many waivers included such a requirement and reviews were indeed conducted by the CONTRACTING PARTIES. By contrast, the annual reviews of waivers which are prescribed by Art. IX:4 WTO Agreement to date have remained a mere formality. They do not amount to more than the General Council taking note of existing waivers. It is thus premature to infer from a mere look at the treaty provisions that the waiver process is more legalized in the WTO than it was under the GATT 1947. This said, it is certainly true that the changed voting requirements have led to a change in the waiver practice. In particular, waivers are no longer granted to developed country members to allow them to adopt protectionist measures. Together with the requirement that waivers have to be of limited duration this change in the law helps to prevent waivers that permanently legalize privileges of powerful members as did the Agricultural Waiver under the GATT with respect to certain protectionist measures taken by the United States.

The next section will examine in more detail the waiver practice and in particular the various situations which prompted the request and granting of waiver decisions under the GATT 1947 and in the WTO.

B. THE WAIVER PRACTICE OF THE GATT 1947 AND THE WTO

Under the GATT 1947 the CONTRACTING PARTIES adopted about 115 waiver decisions. If one includes the frequent decisions to amend or extend waivers this number rises to over 400.[28] Waiver decisions under

27 See e.g. Bogdandy, 'Law and Politics in the WTO', 609, 629 *et seq.*; cf. Opinion Advocate General Tesauro delivered on 13 November 1997, *Hermès International (a partnership limited by shares) v FHT Marketing Choice BV*, C-53/96, [1998] ECR I-03603, para. 29.

28 For a list of waiver decisions (including amendment and extension decisions) of the CONTRACTING PARTIES under Art. XXV:5 GATT 1947, see WTO, *Analytical Index of the GATT*, vol. II, Article XXV, 892–905.

the GATT were taken by vote. While there were never many votes cast against the adoption of a waiver decision it is also true that most waiver decisions were not taken unanimously.[29]

The waiver power under the GATT was the object of some criticism. Thus it was said that in practice the prerequisite that a waiver be justified by 'exceptional circumstances not elsewhere provided for' (Art. XXV:5 GATT) did not place a substantive restriction on the waiver power.[30] The fact that the power to grant waivers was not subject to any substantive requirements and could be exercised without having to impose time limits gave rise to the further criticism that the waiver power could be, and indeed was, used to circumvent the amendment procedure laid down in Art. XXX GATT 1947.[31] However, after the granting of the very broad Agricultural Waiver to the United States in 1955,[32] in practice most waiver decisions included time limits and were subject to annual reviews. Despite the critique the waiver power under the GATT 1947 overall was evaluated positively. It was acknowledged that it had provided the GATT with the necessary flexibility to survive in spite of the strong opposition to the GATT within some contracting parties.[33]

While the WTO Agreement did not introduce any additional substantive requirements for the exercise of the waiver power, the consensus practice, that was established in the WTO for waivers, constitutes a considerable limitation on the exercise of the power. Nonetheless, a good number of waiver decisions have been adopted to date. From the entry into force of the WTO Agreement in 1995 until the end of 2010 202 waiver decisions (including extension decisions) were granted.[34]

---

29 Even if no votes were cast against the adoption of a waiver decision there were usually a few contracting parties who abstained.
30 Jackson, *World Trade and the Law of GATT*, 544. For an analysis of this requirement, see Chapter 5 B.III.1 and 2.
31 Jackson, *World Trade and the Law of GATT*, 138, 139; Long, *Law and its Limitations in the GATT Multilateral Trade System*, 18, 19; on the relationship between Art. XXV:5 GATT 1947 and Art. XXX:1 GATT 1947, see Chapter 5 B.II.
32 On this waiver see section B.I.2.2(a) below.
33 Jackson, *World Trade and the Law of GATT*, 30; Jackson, *The Jurisprudence of GATT and the WTO*, 189; Lowenfeld, *International Economic Law*, 41, 42; see also Benedek, *Die Rechtsordnung des GATT aus völkerrechtlicher Sicht*, 162.
34 This number is derived from a note by the WTO Secretariat, Paragraph 6 of the Doha Declaration on the TRIPS Agreement and Public Health. Information on Waivers, IP/C/W/387 (24 October 2002) (this note includes in its Annex I a list of all waiver decisions granted in the WTO until 15 October 2002) and the Annual Reports of the WTO which are available on the WTO's website at www.wto.org/english/res_e/reser_e/annual_report_e.htm (last accessed 11 March 2011).

The waiver power is commonly depicted as a safety valve, an escape clause to allow for non-compliance when individual members find themselves in situations of economic hardship, though not to accommodate policy choices that entail non-compliance with WTO obligations.[35] This statement alone raises a number of questions. In particular it can be asked when non-compliance is due to a lack of capacity to comply and when it is to be attributed to a policy choice. The *travaux préparatoires* suggest that the waiver power may be exercised to address temporary situations that are beyond the control of a state such as economic crises caused by floods or droughts.[36] Not unforeseen and mostly not as temporary as natural disasters, but also impeding compliance, are deficits in administrative capacity necessary to implement obligations. Such capacity problems were also addressed by waivers in the past.[37] More difficult becomes the distinction between inability and unwillingness to comply when a member encounters unforeseen costs of compliance. A member might be obliged to reduce tariffs, but finds itself in a situation of financial crisis. It might argue that it is unable to comply since it depends on the revenue from customs duties. Here one might say that it constitutes a deliberate policy choice not to reduce tariffs in times of financial crisis instead of cutting expenditure or relying on other sources of revenue.[38] Even more clearly the result of a policy choice appears to be the maintenance of export subsidies on agricultural products in order to protect the domestic agricultural sector.[39]

All of the instances mentioned in the previous paragraph in the past have given rise to the adoption of waiver decisions which suspended obligations of individual members. Even though there is no sharp dividing line between non-compliance due to lack of capacity and non-compliance due to competing policy choices this distinction will structure the following presentation of the practice with regard to waiver decisions that suspend obligations of individual members. While the following presentation of WTO practice in this regard is comprehensive, that of GATT practice is not. I shall refer to the practice under the GATT 1947 in particular to illustrate a substantial difference between GATT and WTO practice, namely

---

35 See statements made during the London Conference *supra* note 4.

36 *Ibid.*; for a detailed discussion see Chapter 5 B.III.1.1.

37 Cf. the waiver decisions suspending obligations of the Customs Valuation Agreement and the Harmonized System waiver decisions discussed in sections B.I.1.1. and B.I.1.2. below.

38 Cf. the waiver decisions granted to Albania and Cape Verde discussed in section B.I.2.1(b) below.

39 Cf. the waiver granted to Hungary discussed in section B.I.2.1(b) below.

that under the GATT several important waivers were granted to allow developed countries to adopt or maintain openly protectionist measures.

Apart from individual waiver decisions, there is a practice – under the GATT 1947 as well as in the WTO – of so-called collective waivers: decisions that waive obligations for groups of members or potentially all members. Most of these decisions conform even less to the picture of a safety valve than many of the individual waiver decisions. Broadly speaking, collective waivers have performed three different functions: firstly, collective waivers have deferred compliance to address capacity problems; secondly, collective waivers have modified legal rules and thus been used as instruments of legislation; and thirdly, collective waivers have achieved regime linkage by way of providing exceptions from WTO law for measures mandated by another international legal regime. Due to the importance of collective waivers with respect to fundamental questions, such as the legislative capacity of the WTO and coordination of the WTO with other international institutions, the WTO and GATT practice in this respect will be presented in its entirety.

I Individual waiver decisions

Most waiver decisions under the GATT 1947 and in the WTO waive obligations of individual members. An individual waiver decision suspends an obligation – often with respect to a specific measure which otherwise would violate this obligation.[40] In the following I attempt a distinction between, on the one hand, non-compliance which is due to capacity problems in complying and, on the other hand, non-compliance due to policy conflicts. In the first constellation the member requesting the waiver does not question the policy objectives of the suspended obligation. In the second constellation there is a policy conflict: the member requesting the waiver wishes to adopt or maintain a measure for reasons which contradict the objectives of WTO/GATT law. Such a measure may be part of an openly protectionist policy or a market integration project which is not justified by the exceptions for regional market integration, in particular Art. XXIV GATT. A distinct group of waivers that falls within this second constellation encompasses waivers that legalize tariff preferences which developed countries accord to products from developing countries. These

---

40 A number of individual waiver decisions suspend obligations in general and not with respect to specific measures; others are granted for reasons of legal certainty without a preceding determination of illegality.

waivers will be presented in a separate section because they differ from the rest of this practice. Firstly, they legalize preferences which predominately pursue foreign policy objectives while the other waivers legalize measures of domestic/regional policy. Secondly, they form a particularly large and, economically as well as politically, significant group and thus merit a separate treatment in its historical context.

1 Waivers to account for capacity problems

1.1 Waivers that extend transitional periods to implement obligations under the Customs Valuation Agreement

The WTO Agreements provide in several ways for special and differential treatment of developing and least-developed country members.[41] One important aspect of the differential treatment of developing country members is that they benefited from longer transitional periods for compliance with obligations in most of the agreements.[42]

Some of the provisions on transitional periods provide for the possibility of an extension of the transitional period. They do not, however, specify procedures for the extension; a fact which has led to some insecurity and debate among WTO members.[43] In a few instances the transitional periods under the Agreement on the Implementation of Art. VII of GATT 1994 (Customs Valuation Agreement/CVA) and the Agreement on Trade-Related Investment Measures (TRIMs Agreement) have been extended not by decisions of the Council for Trade in Goods or the Customs Valuation Committee, as provided for by the respective provisions on transitional periods in these agreements, but instead by the General Council on the basis of the waiver power in Article IX:3 WTO

---

41 On the different types of special and differential treatment provisions in the WTO Agreements, see Kessie, 'Legal Status of Special and Differential Treatment Provisions', 12, 23–34.

42 Provisions on transitional periods are included in the Agreement on Agriculture, the SPS Agreement, the TBT Agreement, the Agreement on Trade-Related Investment Measures, the Agreement on the Implementation of Art. VII of GATT 1994, the Agreement on Import Licensing Procedures, the Agreement on Subsidies and Countervailing Measures and the Agreement on Safeguards: see Committee on Trade and Development, Note by the Secretariat, Implementation of Special and Differential Treatment Provisions in WTO Agreements and Decisions, WT/COMTD/W/77 (25 October 2000), paras. 13, 14.

43 More generally transitional periods have been criticized as arbitrary as they were not based on an assessment of the problems which developing countries would encounter with the implementation of the new legal obligations: see, e.g. Ostry, 'Uruguay Round North–South Grand Bargain', 285, 288.

Agreement. The waiver procedure in Art. IX:3 WTO Agreement in these instances complemented the provisions on transitional periods in the TRIMs Agreement and the Customs Valuation Agreement.

There are, however, noteworthy differences between both agreements with respect to the cause for implementation deficits. In the case of the TRIMs Agreement compliance can be achieved relatively easily through an adaptation of legislation.[44] Implementation deficits here often result from a choice by developing country members to employ trade-related investment measures as part of a particular development policy. The waiver decisions that suspended obligations of the TRIMs Agreement will therefore be dealt with in the section on waivers granted to accommodate policy preferences of individual members.

By contrast, obstacles to compliance with the Customs Valuation Agreement result not so much from conflicting policy choices, but are rather due to a lack of technical and administrative capacity.[45] While there is no disagreement among the WTO membership as to the desirability of a 'fair, neutral and uniform system for the valuation of goods'[46] the rules of the Customs Valuation Agreement only insufficiently take account of the economic situation of many developing countries, in particular their limited technical and administrative capacities for implementing them.[47] To address implementation problems the Customs Valuation Agreement provides for transitional periods for developing countries and allows developing countries to make reservations, once these transitional periods have expired.[48] The provisions on the extension of transitional

---

44 Bora, 'Trade-Related Investment Measures', 171, 173.
45 Hudec, *Developing Countries in the GATT Legal System*, 99, fn. 37 (noting that all derogations for developing countries in the Customs Valuation Code 'rested on problems of administrative capacity and not on a policy of allowing developing countries to use trade-distorting valuation standards for development purposes').
46 Preamble to the Customs Valuation Agreement, 4th recital.
47 On the problems that developing country members encounter in implementing the Customs Valuation Agreement, see Shin, 'Implementation of the WTO Customs Valuation Agreement', 125; Rege, 'Customs Valuation and Customs Reform', 128, 130–6. In general on the rules of customs valuation including the special and differential treatment provisions of the CVA, see Forrester and Odara, 'Agreement on Customs Valuation', 531.
48 For an overview of these special and differential treatment provisions, *ibid.*, 531, 567 *et seq.* While it is generally acknowledged that transitional periods are required to allow developing countries to adopt the necessary reforms in their customs administration, to ensure full implementation it is arguably more important to provide them with technical assistance and to engage in administrative cooperation. On the need for technical assistance in connection with measures to further ownership of the rules by developing countries, see Rege, 'Customs Valuation and Customs Reform', 128, 134 *et seq.* For

periods as well as on reservations to the prohibition to determine customs value on the basis of official minimum values have been complemented by the waiver procedure as is elaborated in what follows.

Art. VII GATT sets out principles for the valuation of goods for customs purposes. The main principle states that value for customs purposes should be based on the actual value of the imported product and not on arbitrary or fictitious values (Art. VII:2 (a) GATT). The principles of Art. VII GATT are strengthened and concretized by the valuation rules of the Customs Valuation Agreement – one of the plurilateral agreements that were negotiated during the Tokyo Round and adopted in 1979.[49] According to Art. 1:1 of the Customs Valuation Agreement '[t]he customs value of imported goods shall be the transaction value, that is the price actually paid or payable for the goods when sold for export to the country of importation'. The agreement further sets out rules for the determination of the transaction value as well as a hierarchy of methods for the determination of the customs value if the transaction value cannot be determined. It explicitly prohibits the determination of the customs value on the basis of officially established minimum customs values (Art. 7:2 (f) CVA).

The principle that the customs value shall be determined on the basis of the transaction value raises difficulties for many developing countries since it entails the risk that customs revenue is forgone due to fraudulent declaration practices of importers. This risk is particularly serious for developing countries who frequently rely on customs duties as a major source of government revenue and is increased by a lack of computerized systems and databases that are required for price comparison to detect customs fraud.[50]

more general demands for more effective implementation assistance, see e.g. Finger and Winters, 'What Can the WTO Do for Developing Countries?', 71, 92, 93; Finger, 'Trade and Development', 75, 91, 92.

49 The CVA was originally negotiated during the Tokyo Round and adopted as a plurilateral agreement in 1979. On the negotiation of this agreement and the turn from the concept of 'notional price' to determine customs value as employed by the EC and most other countries to the concept of 'transaction value' as favoured by, among others, the United States, see Rege, 'Customs Valuation and Customs Reform', 128 *et seq.*

50 *Ibid.* The Decision Regarding Cases Where Customs Have Reasons to Doubt Truth or Accuracy of the Declared Value (LT/UR/D-4/2), which was adopted during the Uruguay Round and forms part of the agreements, addresses to a certain extent developing countries' concerns with respect to fraudulent declarations of transaction value. It allows customs authorities to ask importers to establish that 'the declared value represents the total amount actually paid or payable for the imported goods'. If customs authorities maintain reasonable doubts as to the accuracy of the declared value they may determine customs value by an alternative method as laid out in the CVA.

With adoption of the WTO Agreement the Customs Valuation Agreement was included in Annex 1A of the WTO Agreement and thus became mandatory for all WTO members. Art. 20:1 CVA provides that developing country members that were not a party to the Tokyo Round Agreement may delay the application of the provisions of the CVA for five years.[51] Annex III para. 1 to the Customs Valuation Agreement recognized that these five years might be insufficient for certain developing country members to implement the obligations of the agreement. Therefore, a developing country could request an extension of the transitional period. Such a request had to be submitted before the expiry of the transitional period (Annex III para. 1). The Committee on Customs Valuation was the organ competent to grant extensions. A request for extension of the transitional period was to be given sympathetic consideration in cases where the requesting developing country member showed good cause (Annex III para. 1 cl. 2).[52]

Once the transitional period had expired developing countries who valued goods on the basis of officially established minimum values according to Annex III para. 2 'may wish to make a reservation to enable them to retain such values on a limited and transitional basis under such terms and conditions as may be agreed to by the Members'. Members who wished to make such a reservation had to submit a request to the Committee on Customs Valuation which could grant a waiver of the obligation not to determine customs value according to minimum values. Requests for reservations were to be given sympathetic consideration if the requesting member showed good cause.[53]

While most requests for extensions of the transitional period for implementation of the CVA under Annex III para. 1 and reservations under Annex III para. 2 were granted by the Committee on Customs Valuation, twelve waiver decisions were adopted by the General Council on the basis of Art. IX:3 WTO Agreement. They either extended the transitional period of individual members to implement their obligations

---

51 According to the WTO's Analytical Index fifty-eight developing country members made use of this provision, WTO, *Analytical Index: Guide to WTO Law and Practice*, Customs Valuation Agreement, Article 20.1, para. 27.

52 According to the WTO's Analytical Index twenty-two members made use of this possibility to request additional extensions, WTO, *Analytical Index*, Customs Valuation Agreement, Article 20.1, fn. 22.

53 See Committee on Customs Valuation, Decision adopted 12 May 1995, pursuant to the Ministerial Decision at Marrakesh, section I, G/VAL/1 (27 April 1995). According to the WTO's Analytical Index thirty-eight developing countries submitted requests for such reservations, *ibid.*, Customs Valuation Agreement, Interpretation of Annex III, para. 39.

under the Customs Valuation Agreement[54] or allowed members to use minimum values for the valuation of certain goods for customs purposes.[55] These waiver decisions were adopted (instead of extension or reservation decisions as foreseen in the CVA) because it was the prevailing view in the Committee on Customs Valuation that requests for waivers under Art. IX:3 WTO Agreement had to be submitted when a decision on the extension of the transitional period or a reservation was to be taken after the expiry of the transitional period.[56]

The last waiver decision with respect to the Customs Valuation Agreement which allowed Senegal to use officially established minimum values for the valuation of certain goods for customs purposes expired on 30 June 2009. The waiver decision stated: 'This request is a single and last request to maintain minimum values.'[57] It thus precluded a request for a further extension. The extension decisions under the CVA emphasize the beneficiaries' commitments and efforts to implement the Customs Valuation Agreement.[58]

1.2 Individual Harmonized System waiver decisions

A relatively large number of individual waiver decisions, namely 132 out of the 202 decisions granted in the WTO from 1995 until the end of 2010, suspended (or still suspend) Art. II GATT to enable WTO members to implement the Harmonized Commodity Description and Coding System (Harmonized System/HS) or changes to the Harmonized System in their domestic tariffs, i.e. their structured lists of product descriptions.

The Harmonized System is maintained by the World Customs Organization (WCO) and provides a common vocabulary for international trade by classifying all traded goods according to a nomenclature. WTO members' goods schedules and domestic tariffs are based on

---

54 WT/L/307, WT/L/396, WT/L/439, WT/L/453.

55 WT/L/354, WT/L/408, WT/L/442, WT/L/475, WT/L/476, WT/L/571, WT/L//655, WT/L/735.

56 Cf. Committee on Customs Valuation, Decision Concerning the Interpretation and Administration of the Agreement on Implementation of Article VII of the GATT 1994 adopted 12 May 1995, section B, paras. 3 and 4. This decision was originally adopted by the Tokyo Round Committee on Customs Valuation. See also Committee on Customs Valuation, Minutes of the Meeting on 12, 28 April and 10, 31 May 2000, G/VAL/M14 (22 June 2000), para. 1.8 (statement by the chairman of the committee). This position was disputed by India, *ibid.*, para. 1.9.

57 General Council, Senegal – Waiver on Minimum Values in Regard to the Agreement on the Implementation of Article VII of the General Agreement on Tariffs and Trade 1994, Decision of 31 July 2008, WT/L/735 (6 August 2008).

58 See e.g. WT/L/307, preamble.

the Harmonized System. When changes to the Harmonized System are agreed upon in the WCO these changes need to be implemented. This means that domestic tariffs as well as goods schedules need to be adapted to these changes. When this adaptation negatively affects tariff concessions, members need to engage in renegotiations of concessions according to Art. XXVIII GATT. In these cases waivers of Art. II GATT are granted to the extent necessary to enable WTO members to adapt their domestic tariffs to HS changes and to subsequently engage in the necessary renegotiations to adapt their schedules to these changes.[59]

Under the GATT 1947 Harmonized System waivers were granted on a case-by-case basis to individual contracting parties. Waiver decisions were frequently extended, in particular for developing countries who often encountered difficulties in the adaptation process. This waiver practice led to the criticism that waivers were granted and extended quasi-automatically. As assistance for developing countries was gradually increased in the WTO,[60] a practice was adopted with respect to the Harmonized System changes of 1996, 2002 and 2007 to grant collective HS waivers to all members that met certain conditions.[61] These collective waivers are regularly extended to enable members to complete renegotiations of affected tariff commitments according to Art. XXVIII GATT. Individual waiver decisions continued to be granted to WTO members which were still in the process of introducing for the first time the Harmonized System nomenclature into their schedules of tariff concessions. The last of these waivers were granted in 2003.[62]

Members also needed to request individual waivers when they had implemented the 1996 Harmonized System changes (HS1996 changes) domestically, but had not completed the adaptation of their schedules by the time the last collective HS1996 Waiver expired in April 2002. The beneficiaries of these individual waiver decisions were all developing country members who encountered administrative problems with the adaptation exercise. As an answer to these difficulties the procedures for the

59 On the administration of the Harmonized System in the World Customs Organization, its relevance for WTO law and the procedures for adapting WTO members' goods schedules to changes in the Harmonized System, see Feichtner, 'Administration of the Vocabulary of International Trade', 1481; in more detail on the methodology for adapting goods schedules, see Yu, 'Harmonized System', 12, 13.
60 Feichtner, 'Administration of the Vocabulary of International Trade', 1481, 1497 et seq.
61 On these collective waiver decisions, see below section II.3.1.
62 For references to the WTO documents which contain these waiver decisions, see WTO, Annual Report 2004, 36.

introduction of Harmonized System changes to schedules of concessions substantially increased the technical assistance for developing country members. Thus the current procedures concerning the introduction of HS2002 and HS2007 changes foresee that the Secretariat will introduce such changes into developing countries' schedules.[63] This technical assistance by the WTO Secretariat addresses many of the problems which resulted before in long delays in the adaptation of schedules to the Harmonized System. As a consequence it also reduces the need for additional individual waivers beyond those which are granted on a collective basis.

1.3 Waivers of Cuba's obligation under Art. XV:6 GATT

Already under the GATT 1947 Cuba was regularly granted waivers from its obligation in Art. XV:6 GATT and this practice is continued in the WTO.[64] Art. XV:6 GATT requires members either to become a member of the International Monetary Fund (IMF) or to enter into a special exchange agreement with the WTO in order to ensure that the objectives of the GATT will not be frustrated as a result of exchange action.

Under the GATT 1947 Sri Lanka (Ceylon), Haiti, Indonesia and the Federal Republic of Germany entered into special exchange agreements with the CONTRACTING PARTIES between 1950 and 1952. Subsequently these contracting parties became members of the IMF. Other contracting parties which were not IMF members were granted waivers of their obligations under Art. XV:6 GATT or were freed of this obligation by way of reservations in their accession protocols.[65]

Today most members of the WTO are IMF members. WTO members who are not members of the IMF, but who use solely the currency of another member are excepted from the obligation in Art. XV:6 GATT.[66]

---

63 General Council, A Procedure for the introduction of Harmonized System 2002 Changes to Schedules of Concessions Using the Consolidated Tariff Schedules, Decision of 15 February 2005, WT/L/605 (2 March 2005); General Council, A Procedure for the Introduction of Harmonized System 2007 Changes to Schedules of Concessions Using the Consolidated Tariff Schedules, Decision of 15 December 2006, WT/L/673 (18 December 2006).

64 The waiver decisions which were granted in the WTO by the General Council each suspended this obligation for a period of five years. The last such decision was granted by the General Council on 15 December 2006 and waives Art. XV:6 GATT until 31 December 2011, WT/L/678 (19 December 2006).

65 On this practice under the GATT, see WTO, *Analytical Index of the GATT*, vol. II, Article XV, 437, 438.

66 CONTRACTING PARTIES, A Special Exchange Agreement Between the Contracting Parties and a Government Which Uses Solely the Currency of Another Contracting Party, Resolution of 20 June 1949, BISD II, 18.

This is not the case for Cuba and Taiwan who are not IMF members.[67] While Taiwan concluded a special exchange agreement with the WTO as part of its accession to the WTO,[68] Cuba is regularly granted waivers of its obligations under Art. XV:6 GATT.[69]

Cuba receives these waivers on the one hand because it cannot become an IMF member due to the opposition to Cuban membership by the United States and on the other hand because its planned economy would make it difficult as well as unnecessary to apply a special exchange agreement.[70]

2 Waivers to accommodate policy preferences

Members not only request waivers due to capacity problems in complying with the law. In some instances members also request a waiver if they choose to pursue a policy objective in a way that is in conflict with WTO law. These requests encounter much more resistance than those presented in the previous section. Objections are the stronger the more the intended policy affects the commercial interests of other members.

The restrictive practice in the WTO with respect to these waivers is contrasted with a number of waiver decisions under the GATT 1947 which allowed developed countries to adopt openly protectionist measures and engage in integration projects in clear violation of the provisions of the General Agreement. Furthermore the GATT practice of granting waivers to developing countries for the adoption of tariff surcharges is presented. In these cases waivers were used to address a widely accepted economic inefficiency of GATT rules.

2.1 WTO practice

(a) **Waivers legalizing trade-related investment measures** The waiver procedure was used not only to extend transitional periods under the Customs Valuation Agreement as discussed above,[71] but also to extend transitional periods under the Agreement on Trade-Related Investment Measures. Even though in both cases the waiver decisions in effect

---

67 Cuba withdrew from the IMF in 1964.
68 See Charnovitz, 'Mapping the Law of WTO Accession', 855, 873.
69 See for example General Council, Cuba – Article XV:6 of the General Agreement on Tariffs and Trade 1994, Decision of 15 December 2006, WT/L/678 (19 December 2006).
70 Cf. Request by Cuba for a waiver, Article XV:6, dated 25 May 1964, C/42 (27 May 1964).
71 Section B.I.1.1.

extended transitional periods, there is one important difference between these two groups of waivers. While countries in principle agree on the objectives of the Customs Valuation Agreement there exists disagreement as to the desirability of the prohibition of trade-related investment measures by the TRIMs Agreement and the GATT from the perspective of development economics.[72] Even though compliance with the obligation to dismantle certain trade-related investment measures does not require much technical expertise and frequently does not involve administrative complexity, several developing countries had not even begun abolishing the prohibited trade-related investment measures when the transitional periods expired. Due to the differences in opinion as to whether trade-related investment measures should be prohibited or not, the debate on the extension of transitional periods under the TRIMs Agreement was much more contentious than the debate on the extension of transitional periods under the Customs Valuation Agreement, which was granted mainly to accommodate developing country members' capacity problems.[73]

The TRIMs Agreement was negotiated during the Uruguay Round. It elaborates on the application to investment measures of the national treatment obligation in Art. III:4 GATT and the prohibition of quantitative restrictions in Art. IX:1 GATT.[74] Art. 2.1 TRIMs Agreement imposes an obligation on WTO members not to apply investment measures related to trade in goods that are inconsistent with the provisions of Art. III and Art. XI GATT; an annex to the agreement includes an illustrative list of such TRIMs.[75] According to Art. 5.1 TRIMs Agreement members had to notify the Council for Trade in Goods, within ninety days of the date of entry into force of the WTO Agreement, of all trade-related investment

---

72 UNDP, *Human Development Report 2005. International Cooperation at a Crossroads*, 2005, 134 (criticizing the TRIMs Agreement for prohibiting trade-related investment measures which played an important role in the economic development in particular of countries in Asia); Lee, *Reclaiming Development in the World Trading System*, 117 *et seq.* (arguing that trade-related investment measures may optimize investment to serve development needs).

73 See *supra* section B.I.1.1.

74 Trebilcock and Howse, *Regulation of International Trade*, 457; in detail on the negotiation of and obligations under the TRIMs Agreement, de Sterlini, 'Agreement on Trade-Related Investment Measures', 437.

75 The Agreement does not define the term 'trade-related investment measure'. For definitions in the literature see the overview in: Joint Study by the WTO and UNCTAD Secretariats, *Trade-Related Investment Measures and Other Performance Requirements, Part I, Scope and Definition; Provisions in International Agreements*, G/C/W/307 (1 October 2001), paras. 3 *et seq.*

measures that they were applying and which were not in conformity with the TRIMs Agreement.[76] The transitional period for the elimination of these TRIMs was two years for developed country members, five years for developing country members and seven years for least-developed country members (Art. 5.2). Art. 5.3 TRIMs Agreement allowed developing country members (including least-developed country members) to request an extension of the transitional period. The request had to demonstrate particular difficulties of the requesting member with the implementation of the TRIMS Agreement (Art. 5.3, cl. 1). The Council for Trade in Goods, when deciding on these requests, was to take into account the individual development, financial and trade needs of the member requesting the extension (Art. 5.3, cl. 2).

Shortly before the transitional period ended for developing country members on 31 December 1999, a number of developing countries sought to obtain a decision by the Ministerial Conference in Seattle that would have extended the transitional period for all developing countries.[77] This attempt failed, however, and consequently ten developing countries submitted individual extension requests to the Council for Trade in Goods. Since the TRIMs Agreement did not specify a procedure for the handling of extension requests – e.g. it did not set out criteria for assessing 'the individual development, financial and trade needs' (Art. 5.3) that would justify an extension – a discussion ensued in the Council for Trade in Goods on the correct procedure. One of the contentious issues was whether the requests should be treated collectively or rather each individually on its own merits.[78] On 8 May 2000 the General Council adopted a decision in which it directed the Council for Trade in Goods to give positive consideration to individual requests for the extension of transitional periods presented in accordance with Art. 5.3 TRIMs Agreement.[79] This decision did not, however, end discussions in the Council for Trade in Goods. It also did not hinder the United States from requesting the establishment of a panel in a dispute with the Philippines concerning trade-related

---

76 Notifications were made by twenty-six WTO members. Of these twenty-five were developing country members and one was a least-developed country member: see de Sterlini, 'Agreement on Trade-Related Investment Measures', 437, 448.

77 *Ibid.*, 437, 455.

78 Council for Trade in Goods, Minutes of the Meeting on 15 October 1999, G/C/M/41 (22 November 1999), paras. 6.1–6.18; see also de Sterlini, 'Agreement on Trade-Related Investment Measures', 437, 456.

79 General Council, Minutes of the Meeting on 3 and 8 May 2000, WT/GC/M/55 (16 June 2000), para. 190; the text of the decision is contained in Annex II to these minutes.

investment measures in the Philippines' Motor Vehicle Development Programme which the Philippines had notified under the TRIMs Agreement and for which it had requested an extension.[80] The United States held the view that with the expiration of the transitional period the measures were illegal and thus could be challenged in dispute settlement proceedings.[81] Discussions in the Council for Trade in Goods continued and informal bilateral and plurilateral consultations between requesting and interested members were held, as well as informal meetings of the Council for Trade in Goods, until it eventually adopted, on 31 July 2001, seven extension decisions.[82]

The request by Thailand was treated differently from the others for the reason that it was submitted after the transitional period had expired on 31 December 1999.[83] Even though the TRIMs Agreement is – contrary to the Customs Valuation Agreement – silent on the question as to when an extension request has to be submitted, several developed country members were of the view that the transitional period should only be extended on the basis of Art. 5.3 TRIMs Agreement if a request was submitted before the expiry of the transitional period.[84] Consequently, they insisted that an extension of Thailand's transitional period could only be achieved through the waiver procedure and a decision by the General Council on the basis of Art. IX:3 WTO Agreement. Therefore Thailand's request was submitted to the General Council as a request for a waiver under Art. IX:3 WTO Agreement.[85] The General Council

---

80 United States, Request for the Establishment of a Panel, WT/DS195/3 (13 October 2000). The panel was established, the United States did not, however, proceed with the selection of panelists, Dispute Settlement Body, Minutes of the Meeting on 17 November 2000, WT/DSB/M/92 (15 January 2001), paras. 89–92.

81 Dispute Settlement Body, Minutes of the Meeting on 23 October 2000, WT/DSB/M/91 (30 November 2000), Statement by the representative of the United States, para. 88; Dispute Settlement Body, Minutes of the Meeting on 17 November 2000, WT/DSB/M/92 (15 January 2001), Statement by the representative of the United States, para. 81.

82 The Council for Trade in Goods adopted extension decisions for Argentina (G/L/460), Colombia (G/L/461), Malaysia (G/L/462), Mexico (G/L/463), Pakistan (G/L/466), the Philippines (G/L/464) and Romania (G/L/465), see Council for Trade in Goods, Minutes of the Meeting on 27 and 31 July 2001, G/C/M/50 (17 September 2001), 2, 3. There was no decision on the request by Chile. Since Chile had requested an extension merely for one year its request had become moot by the time the Council on Trade in Goods adopted the extension decisions: see de Sterlini, 'Agreement on Trade-Related Investment Measures', 437, 455.

83 Thailand had submitted its extension request on 2 May 2000 (G/C/W/203).

84 de Sterlini, 'Agreement on Trade-Related Investment Measures', 437, 457, fn. 71.

85 Council for Trade in Goods, Minutes of the Meeting on 27 and 31 July 2001, G/C/M/50 (17 September 2001), 2, 3.

adopted the waiver decision on the same day as the Council for Trade in Goods adopted the extension decisions.[86]

The extension decisions by the Council for Trade in Goods as well as the waiver decision adopted by the General Council formed a package deal which extended the transitional period for all benefiting developing country members for two years until 31 December 2001.[87] Moreover, the extension decisions provided for the possibility of a further extension for a maximum of two years until 31 December 2003. A request for such a further extension had to be submitted by 31 August 2001. It had to be accompanied by a description of the steps taken and foreseen for the elimination of the remaining TRIMs, a phase-out plan and a commitment to submit periodic progress reports to the Council for Trade in Goods.[88] All eight members that had been granted an extension requested a further extension. These extensions were granted by the Council for Trade in Goods on 5 November 2001.[89] Since Colombia intended to apply certain TRIMs to a number of bean products which it had not notified under Art. 5.1 TRIMs Agreement it had to request a waiver under Art. IX:3 WTO Agreement in addition to an extension of the transitional period.[90] The General Council granted the waiver on 20 December 2001[91] upon a recommendation to this effect by the Council for Trade in Goods.[92]

86 General Council, Thailand – Extension of the Transition Period for the Elimination of Trade-Related Investment Measures Notified Under Article 5.1 of the Agreement on Trade-Related Investment Measures, Decision of 31 July 2001, WT/L/410 (7 August 2001).

87 The request by Egypt was not considered as part of the package deal since it was submitted after the General Council Decision on 8 May 2000; G/C/W/249 (Request by Egypt, dated 23 February 2001); see also de Sterlini, 'Agreement on Trade-Related Investment Measures', 437, 457.

88 See e.g. General Council, Thailand – Extension of the Transition Period for the Elimination of Trade-Related Investment Measures Notified Under Article 5.1 of the Agreement on Trade-Related Investment Measures, Decision of 31 July 2001, WT/L/410 (7 August 2001), para. 3.

89 Council for Trade in Goods, Minutes of the Meeting on 5 October and 5 November 2001, G/C/M/53 (14 November 2001), para. 1.7. The extension decisions are contained in documents G/L/497–504.

90 Colombia, Request for Waiver Concerning the Implementation of Article 5.2 of the Agreement on Trade-Related Investment Measures, dated 5 November 2001, G/C/W/340 (6 November 2001); de Sterlini, 'Agreement on Trade-Related Investment Measures', 437, 457, fn. 73.

91 General Council, Colombia – Extension of the Application of Article 5.2 of the Agreement on Trade-Related Investment Measures, Decision of 20 December 2001, WT/L/441 (10 January 2002).

92 Council for Trade in Goods, Minutes of the Meeting on 4 December 2001, G/C/M/58 (27 March 2002), 2. A further extension request by Pakistan (G/C/W/478) submitted by the end of 2003 was formally withdrawn by Pakistan in 2006 (G/C/M/83).

All of the extension and waiver decisions stress the commitments of the beneficiaries to eliminate their TRIMs[93] as well as their 'particular difficulties in implementing the provisions of the TRIMs Agreement'.[94] Nonetheless, it needs to be stressed that the motivations of developing countries in requesting these decisions differed. While some developing countries justified their requests by pointing to legal or economic impediments (such as financial crises) to the elimination of the TRIMs in question, other developing countries argued that the TRIMs were required to achieve certain development objectives (such as the replacement of illegal crops).[95] These differing justifications reflect a division among the WTO membership as to the desirability of a prohibition of trade-related investment measures as contained in the TRIMs Agreement. Some developing countries are of the view that certain TRIMs currently prohibited by the GATT and the TRIMs Agreement should in fact be permitted if developing countries adopt them to pursue development policies. The lack of consensus as to what the law should be on TRIMs is partly due to a lack of consensus among scholars as to the effects of trade-related investment measures such as local content requirements[96] and other performance requirements on economic development, as well as to their trade distorting effects.[97] At the same time it is undisputed that the developed country members which today are the main advocates of legal restrictions on the use of trade-related investment measures freely employed such measures themselves on their own paths to economic development.[98]

During the Doha Round negotiations several developing countries suggested including further flexibilities in the TRIMs Agreement in order

---

93 See e.g. WT/L/410, preamble, recital 8; WT/L/441, preamble, recital 3.

94 See WT/L/410, preamble, recital 7. The demonstration of such difficulties is a requirement for the extension of the transitional period according to Art. 5.3 TRIMs Agreement.

95 On the differing justifications of the extension requests, see de Sterlini, 'Agreement on Trade-Related Investment Measures', 437, 455 *et seq.*; Bora, 'Trade-Related Investment Measures', 171, 173.

96 A local content requirement demands the purchase or use by an enterprise of products of domestic origin or from any domestic source, whether specified in terms of particular products, in terms of volume or value of products, or in terms of a proportion of volume or value of its local production, see TRIMs Agreement, Annex, para. 1 (a).

97 For an overview on the debate see de Sterlini, 'Agreement on Trade-Related Investment Measures', 437, 440–3, see also Joint Study by the WTO and UNCTAD Secretariats, *Trade-Related Investment Measures and Other Performance Requirements, Part II, Evidence on the Use, the Policy Objectives, and the Impact of Trade-Related Investment Measures and Other Performance Requirements*, G/C/W/307 Add. 1 (8 February 2002); and *supra* fn. 72.

98 Chang, '*Kicking Away the Ladder*'; Lee, *Reclaiming Development in the World Trading System*, 115.

to allow developing countries to temporarily adopt or maintain trade-related investment measures, in particular local content requirements, under certain circumstances for development purposes.[99] Developed countries are, however, strictly opposed to such proposals that would loosen the restrictions currently imposed by the TRIMs Agreement. They favour instead a case-by-case approach. The waiver procedure allows for such an approach. Upon submission of a waiver request by a developing country member that wishes to maintain a trade-related investment measure in violation of the GATT and the TRIMs Agreement, the individual situation of the respective developing country can be assessed. Moreover, not all developing country members support suggestions to loosen the legal restrictions on the adoption and maintenance of trade-related investment measures.[100]

(b) Waivers of the obligation to comply with specific commitments The other group of waivers that allow WTO members to maintain measures in violation of WTO law for policy reasons consist of decisions that waive certain specific commitments which differ from one member to the other. To date five waiver decisions have been adopted to relieve individual members of specific commitments which they undertook when becoming members of the WTO.

The first of these waiver decisions was granted to Hungary in 1997. It waived the obligations in Articles 3.3, 8 and 9.2 of the Agreement on Agriculture in order to allow Hungary to maintain certain export subsidies for agricultural products.[101] The waiver was granted after the initiation of dispute settlement proceedings by several WTO members against Hungary in 1996. These members claimed that Hungary violated the Agreement on Agriculture by providing export subsidies to certain agricultural

---

99 See Communication from Brazil and India, dated 8 October 2002, G/C/W/428 (9 October 2002); for a scholarly view in favour of allowing TRIMs currently prohibited by the TRIMs Agreement when applied to facilitate economic development, see Lee, *Reclaiming Development in the World Trading System*, 119 *et seq*. The transitional periods of the TRIMs Agreement also remain on the agenda of the ongoing multilateral trade negotiations: one of the LDC agreement-specific proposals that is being discussed during the Doha Round is the proposal for a new transitional period for least-developed country members that would allow them to maintain TRIMs for a further seven years with the possibility to request an extension: see Ministerial Conference, Doha Work Programme, Ministerial Declaration, adopted 18 December 2005, WT/MIN(05)/DEC (22 December 2005).

100 de Sterlini, 'Agreement on Trade-Related Investment Measures', 437, 472 *et seq*.

101 General Council, Hungary – Agreement on Agriculture, Decision of 22 December 1997, WT/L/238 (29 October 1997).

products which it had not listed in its schedule and by providing export subsidies in excess of its commitment levels.[102] After the establishment of a panel on 25 February 1997,[103] however, the complainants and Hungary reached a mutually agreed solution in accordance with Art. 3:6 DSU.[104] On 8 September 1997 Hungary requested, as foreseen by the mutually agreed solution, a waiver which would waive Art. 3:3, 8 and 9:2 of the Agreement on Agriculture until 31 December 2001 and thus permit it to maintain export subsidies for certain agricultural products until this date. In support of its waiver request Hungary argued that it was due to an error of its trade officials that Hungary's schedule only covered a small fraction of products and subsidies and that consequently it was obliged to eliminate practically all of its export subsidies.[105] It further argued that some export subsidization was required so that Hungary could maintain its market share of agricultural exports.[106]

Here it needs to be noted that when becoming a WTO member Hungary had the legal option of maintaining the subsidies in question by listing them in its schedule. Since, however, it failed to do so, Hungary was obliged by the Agreement on Agriculture to dismantle them. After discussion of the waiver request in the Council for Trade in Goods,[107] the General Council adopted the waiver decision on 22 October 1997. The decision waived the respective obligations as requested until 31 December 2001.[108]

In 2004 and 2005 two waiver decisions suspended specific commitments which Albania had undertaken with respect to trade in services and trade in goods. The first decision relieved Albania until 31 December 2004 from its market access commitments undertaken under

---

102 Argentina, Australia, Canada, New Zealand, Thailand and the United States, Hungary – Export Subsidies in Respect of Agricultural Products, Request for Consultations of 27 March 1996, WT/DS35/1 (2 April 1996); for the requests for the establishment of a panel by Australia, New Zealand, the United States and Argentina on 9 January 1997, see WT/DS35/4, 5, 6 and 7.

103 Dispute Settlement Body, Minutes of the Meeting on 25 February 1997, WT/DSB/M/29 (26 March 1997).

104 Cf. Council for Trade in Goods, Minutes of the Meeting on 6 October 1997, G/C/M/23 (6 November 1997), para. 4.4.

105 Hungary – Agricultural Export Subsidies, Request for a waiver from Hungary, dated 8 September 1997, G/L/183 (17 September 1997), para. 4.

106 *Ibid.* para. 3.

107 Council for Trade in Goods, Minutes of the Meeting on 6 October 1997, G/C/M/23 (6 November 1997), paras. 4.1–4.25.

108 General Council, Minutes of the Meeting on 22 October 1997, WT/GC/M/23 (28 November 1997), 18.

Art. XVI GATS with respect to public voice telephone services.[109] Albania had requested the waiver because its economic situation following the war in Kosovo and the September 11 attacks in New York City seriously impeded its ability to privatize the telephone sector as planned by January 2003.[110] The second waiver, granted to Albania in 2005, suspended its obligation to implement certain tariff concessions according to the commitments undertaken in its GATT schedule.[111] To support its request for a waiver Albania had referred to a loss in customs revenue if the tariff concessions were implemented according to the implementation plan to which Albania had committed when it acceded to the WTO Agreement. This loss in revenue would be a strain on its budget and endanger macroeconomic stability. Albania had also pointed to the need for infant industry protection.[112] The waiver decision which was granted upon this request did not affect the tariff rates as bound in Albania's schedule, but merely extended the time limits for the staging of implementation of certain tariff concessions.[113] It set different dates for the implementation of interim and final bound tariff rates. In the decision to grant the waiver an important factor was that Albania had committed to – and in fact already applied – very low tariff rates.[114]

A similar waiver was granted in 2009 to Cape Verde. It suspended Cape Verde's obligation concerning the first implementation stage of its tariff concessions. The waiver extended this first stage which would otherwise have ended on 1 January 2009 until 1 January 2010.[115] The reasons for the request as well as the adoption of the waiver decision were concerns for Cape Verde's macroeconomic stability in light of the worldwide financial

---

109 General Council, Albania – Implementation of Specific Commitments in Telecommunications Services, Decision of 17 May 2004, WT/L/567 (7 June 2004).

110 Implementation of Specific Commitments in Telecommunications Services, Request for a Waiver from Albania, dated 20 November 2003, S/L/148 (21 November 2003). In the request Albania refers to the war as well as to the terrorist attacks on 11 September 2001 as exceptional circumstances justifying a waiver (para. 3). The waiver decision itself, however, only refers to the war in Kosovo (preamble, recital 5).

111 General Council, Albania – Implementation of Specific Concessions, Decision of 26 May 2005, WT/L/610 (30 May 2005).

112 Request for a WTO Waiver from Albania, dated 19 November 2004, G/C/W/504 (24 November 2004), 4.

113 *Ibid.*, preamble, recitals 4, 5.

114 General Council, Albania – Implementation of Specific Concessions, Decision of 26 May 2005, WT/L/610 (30 May 2005), preamble, recitals 7, 8.

115 General Council, Cape Verde – Implementation of the Schedule of Concessions, Decision of 28 July 2009, WT/L/768 (31 July 2009).

crisis.[116] The waiver neither affected the final implementation date nor the final rate at which tariffs became bound.

Finally, a decision adopted in 2007 waives Mongolia's commitment to phase out and eliminate its export duty on raw cashmere for a period of an additional five years until 29 January 2012.[117] In its protocol of accession Mongolia had committed to phase out and eliminate this duty within ten years of its accession to the WTO Agreement, i.e. by 29 January 2007.[118] According to Mongolia's waiver request the maintenance of export duties is part of a larger development policy which, inter alia, aims at the sustainable growth of Mongolia's cashmere industry. It is intended to prevent the outflow of raw cashmere to the detriment of national processing businesses. Moreover, export duties, by reducing the demand for raw cashmere, will contribute to the regulation of goat herds as part of efforts to fight desertification and other environmental damage that result from an unsustainable use of pasture lands.[119] It is noteworthy that by contrast to all other waiver decisions discussed in this section the waiver decision granted to Mongolia explicitly mentions the non-economic policy objectives that Mongolia pursues with its export duties on raw cashmere. The waiver decision acknowledges that in addition to improving industrial competitiveness Mongolia seeks to promote social and environmental objectives including 'creating employment; improving livestock health and quality of raw materials; enforcing internationally compatible standards; ensuring equitable utilization of pasture land; and providing social welfare services to herders'.[120]

All of these five waiver decisions waive commitments which go beyond the general obligations of the WTO Agreements.[121] Under the Agricultural Agreement developed countries have to incrementally reduce their export subsidies on agricultural products. They are not obliged, however, to eliminate all subsidies at once, but may maintain those listed in their schedules, subject to certain parameters and reduction commitments.

---

116 *Ibid.*, preamble, recital 5; Communication from Cape Verde, Request for a WTO Waiver, dated 6 April 2009, G/C/W/618 (20 April 2009).
117 General Council, Mongolia – Export Duties on Raw Cashmere, Decision of 27 July 2007, WT/L/695 (1 August 2007).
118 Report of the Working Party on the Accession of Mongolia, WT/ACC/MNG/9 (27 June 1996), para. 24.
119 Request for a Waiver from Mongolia, dated 22 January 2007, G/C/W/571 (26 January 2007).
120 General Council, Mongolia – Export Duties on Raw Cashmere, Decision of 27 July 2007, WT/L/695 (1 August 2007), preamble, recital 5.
121 On the variable degrees of commitment in the WTO, see below Chapter 6 A.II.

The waiver which was granted to Hungary for the maintenance of certain export subsidies thus does not go beyond what Hungary could have achieved by listing the export subsidies in question in its schedule. Likewise, the waiver granted to Mongolia allows it to impose export duties that are not prohibited under the WTO Agreements. A waiver was required to legalize the export duties because Mongolia had agreed to the elimination of such duties during accession negotiations. Finally, the waivers granted to Albania and Cape Verde also waived liberalization commitments with respect to trade in goods and services which these countries were not obliged to undertake according to the WTO Agreements, but which they agreed to during accession negotiations.

This is not to say that Mongolia, Albania or Cape Verde would have been free not to assume these commitments. Accession commitments are part of a deal struck during accession negotiations. In particular, market access commitments can be seen as consideration by the acceding country for the benefits that it derives upon accession from other members' existing liberalization commitments.[122] However, the fact that the waivers granted to Hungary, Albania, Cape Verde and Mongolia do not suspend general obligations which impose similar burdens on all members, but that they suspend specific liberalization commitments which differ from one WTO member to the other,[123] is important to explain why consensus could be reached on these waiver decisions.

2.2 GATT 1947 practice

The previous section showed that in the WTO only a few waivers are granted to accommodate domestic policy preferences.[124] To date such waivers have exclusively been granted either where the agreement in question already provided for a delay in implementation by way of transitional periods or where the waiver request concerned specific liberalization commitments. In addition these waivers are usually justified by reference to an

---

122 WTO members agreed to exercise restraint with respect to seeking commitments and concessions from least-developed countries acceding to the WTO: General Council, Accession of Least-Developed Countries, Decision of 10 December 2002, WT/L/508 (20 January 2003).

123 Commitments assumed during accession negotiations not only differ from member to member: moreover, they frequently exceed the obligations of existing members; for a discussion of accession commitments, see Charnovitz, 'Mapping the Law of WTO Accession', 855; see also Qin, '"WTO-Plus" Obligations and their Implications', 483.

124 Waivers that legalize special preferences granted by developed country members to developing country members constitute a particular group which will be discussed below in section B.I.3.

exceptional situation such as an economic crisis or a negotiating error. With one exception (the waiver granted to Hungary for the maintenance of agricultural subsidies) all of these waivers were granted to developing country members. By contrast, under the GATT 1947 a number of waivers were granted to individual developed contracting parties for measures with which they pursued internal economic policies some of which seriously affected commercial interests in other contracting parties. Such policies were directed at the protection of domestic industries, mainly the agricultural industry, or market integration. Several of these waiver decisions were not justified by reference to situations of economic crisis or the excessive costs that compliance would entail. Instead they were justified by the strong domestic political support for the measures in question, the economic and political benefits that would be derived from them, or the lack of detrimental effects to the objectives of the GATT.

Apart from a discussion of waiver decisions that legalized developed contracting parties' policy choices, this section presents the waiver practice of allowing developing contracting parties to impose tariff surcharges to address balance-of-payments difficulties. These waivers can be interpreted as remedies to the inefficiency of the GATT rules on balance-of-payments problems. They are furthermore of interest in that they reveal a difference in the attitude towards compliance by, on the one hand, developing and, on the other hand, developed countries under the GATT 1947. While developed contracting parties imposed tariff surcharges without prior authorization by waivers, developing contracting parties regularly requested waivers as justification for such measures.

(a) Waivers to legalize protectionist measures

(i) US Agricultural Waiver   One of the most far-reaching waivers for an individual contracting party, the United States, was the so-called Agricultural Waiver (also called Section 22 Waiver) which the CONTRACTING PARTIES adopted in 1955.[125] This waiver decision suspended the United States' obligations under Art. II and Art. XI GATT 'to the extent necessary to prevent a conflict with such provisions of the General Agreement in the case of action required to be taken by the Government of the United States under Section 22' of the Agricultural Adjustment Act.[126]

---

125 CONTRACTING PARTIES, Waiver Granted to the United States in Connection With Import Restrictions Imposed Under Section 22 of the United States Agricultural Adjustment Act (of 1933), As Amended, Decision of 5 March 1955, BISD 3S (1955), 32.
126 *Ibid.*, 34.

At the time the GATT was negotiated the United States were main-taining protectionist legislation with respect to trade in agricultural commodities and they took care to ensure that this legislation was accommodated by GATT rules, in particular Art. XI GATT.[127] However, a 1951 amendment of Section 22 of the Agricultural Amendment Act required the imposition of certain trade restrictions which would have violated Art. II and Art. XI GATT. Thus, Section 22, as amended, authorized the President of the United States to impose fees or quantitative limitations on agricultural imports upon a finding that agricultural imports would materially interfere with domestic agricultural programmes, including loan, purchase or price support programmes.[128] Section 22 further included a provision which stated:

> No trade agreement or other international agreement heretofore or here-after entered into by the United States shall be applied in a manner incon-sistent with the requirements of this section.[129]

The US Congress recognized that Section 22 might cause the United States to breach its obligations under the GATT and in 1955 it submitted a request for a waiver.[130] Since the US President would have to comply with the congressional mandate laid down in Section 22, and due to the weak congressional support for the GATT in general, the CONTRACTING PARTIES had not much choice but to grant a waiver in order to maintain legality and US support for the GATT. In the words of John Jackson:

> Should the US be forced to carry out the congressional enactment without a waiver, damage to the legal principles of GATT could, it was thought, ensue and indeed one result might be the withdrawal of the United States from GATT.[131]

The waiver was approved with a vote of twenty-three in favour and five against.[132]

---

127 Jackson, *World Trade and the Law of GATT*, 733; Dam, *GATT: Law and International Economic Organization*, 260.
128 For the text of Section 22, see annex to the waiver decision (*supra* note 125). For a description of the operation of Section 22, see United States, Request for a Waiver in Connection With Section 22 of the Agricultural Adjustment Act, L/315 (28 January 1955), 3 *et seq.*; Panel Report, *US – Sugar Waiver*, adopted 7 November 1990, L/6631, BISD 37S/228, paras. 2.1, 2.2.
129 Section 22 (f), 7 U.S.C. 624.
130 United States, Request for a Waiver in Connection With Section 22 of the Agricultural Adjustment Act, L/315 (28 January 1955).
131 Jackson, *World Trade and the Law of GATT*, 735.
132 CONTRACTING PARTIES, Ninth Session, Summary Report of 44th Meeting on 5 March 1955, SR. 9/44 (15 March 1955), 17.

The waiver decision was very broad in that it waived Arts. II and IX GATT to the extent necessary to prevent conflict with Section 22. It was unlimited in time and did not provide for a reconsideration of the waiver. At the annual reviews of the decision contracting parties regularly pointed to the unfairness of the waiver.[133]

(ii) Hard-core Waiver and other waivers to legalize residual quantitative restrictions   The United States was not the only country that imposed restrictions on agricultural imports in violation of obligations under the GATT. Several European countries imposed quantitative restrictions on imports to deal with balance-of-payments crises as a result of World War II. As long as these difficulties persisted the restrictions were justified under Art. XII GATT. Contracting parties were, however, obliged to dismantle the restrictions once the IMF had decided that they were no longer necessary (Art. XV:2 GATT).[134] When the IMF adopted such decisions for a number of European countries, these countries eliminated their quantitative restrictions on most industrial trade.[135] However, some quantitative restrictions, which came to be known as residual restrictions, were maintained in particular with respect to trade in agricultural commodities.[136] Already in 1955 it had been argued by European contracting parties that some restrictions were necessary to protect the weakest sectors in order to avoid economic and social hardship.[137]

In 1955, on the same day the CONTRACTING PARTIES adopted the Section 22 Waiver, they also approved the so-called Hard-core Waiver decision.[138] Its objective was to allow contracting parties, which at the date of the granting of the waiver maintained import restrictions for balance-of-payments reasons, to maintain such restrictions for a limited period of time.[139] According to this decision any contracting party could

---

133   Kenneth Dam noted: 'The breadth of the waiver, coupled with the fact that the waiver was granted to the contracting party that was at one and the same time the world's largest trading nation and the most vocal proponent of freer international trade, constituted a grave blow to GATT's prestige': Dam, *GATT: Law and International Economic Organization*, 260. By contrast Jackson pointed to the limited use which the United States in fact made of Section 22: Jackson, *World Trade and the Law of GATT*, 736.

134   Hudec, *GATT Legal System and World Trade Diplomacy*, 265.   135 *Ibid.*, 266.

136   Dam, *GATT: Law and International Economic Organization*, 261.

137   Hudec, *GATT Legal System and World Trade Diplomacy*, 266.

138   CONTRACTING PARTIES, Problems Raised for Contracting Parties in Eliminating Import Restrictions Maintained During a Period of Balance-of-Payment Difficulties, Decision of 5 March 1955, BISD 3S, 38–41.

139   Since only the closed group of contracting parties, which had quantitative restrictions in place when the waiver was granted, could avail themselves of the decision I deal with this waiver here and not below in the section on collective waivers.

request an individual waiver of its obligations under Art. XI GATT to maintain quantitative restrictions, if certain requirements were met.

As justification for the waiver the decision recognized in its preamble

> that in certain cases restrictions have been maintained during a period of persistent balance-of-payments difficulties spreading over a number of years, and that some transitional measure of protection by means of quantitative restrictions may be required for a limited period to enable an industry having received incidental protection from those restrictions which were maintained during the period of balance-of-payments diffi-culties to adjust itself to the situation which would be created by removal of those restrictions.[140]

The Hard-core Waiver decision waived Art. XI GATT to allow individ-ual contracting parties the temporary maintenance of import restrictions subject to a further majority decision of the CONTRACTING PARTIES. This decision was only to be taken if the contracting party that requested such a decision satisfied the CONTRACTING PARTIES that the removal of the quantitative restriction for which the decision was sought would result in serious injury to a domestic industry.[141] The requesting con-tracting party further had to commit to a plan for the removal of the restriction over a short period of time.[142]

The Hard-core Waiver decision thus attempted to establish strict crite-ria for the temporary maintenance of existing quantitative restrictions and to keep them under the surveillance of the CONTRACTING PARTIES. However, it did not succeed in providing a framework for the gradual dismantling of the residual restrictions. Belgium was the only country to seek a waiver under the Hard-core Waiver decision.[143] Two other contract-ing parties, Luxembourg and the Federal Republic of Germany, who also maintained residual restrictions, did not meet the conditions of the Hard-core Waiver decision. Instead, they were granted separate waivers of Art. XI GATT in order to avoid the strictures of the Hard-core decision.[144] Other contracting parties maintained residual restrictions without any

---

140 Note 138 *supra*, preamble, 4th recital.   141 *Ibid.*, para. 2 (a).

142 *Ibid.*, para. 3 (a).

143 CONTRACTING PARTIES, Waiver Granted to Belgium in Connexion With Import Restrictions on Certain Agricultural Products, Decision of 3 December 1955, BISD 4S (1956), 22.

144 CONTRACTING PARTIES, Waiver Granted to Luxemburg in Connexion With Import Restrictions on Certain Agricultural Products, Decision of 3 December 1956, BISD 4S (1956), 27; CONTRACTING PARTIES, German Import Restrictions, Decision of 30 May 1959, BISD 8S (1960), 31.

legalizing decision.[145] After a few extensions[146] the Hard-core Waiver decision expired, without the problem of residual restrictions being resolved.[147]

In 1967, after a number of other attempts to find a solution to the residual restrictions problem had failed,[148] New Zealand submitted a proposal that provided that governments who maintained residual restrictions should either submit a commitment to eliminate the restrictions or formally request a waiver.[149] New Zealand supported its proposal by arguing that it was unfair to require the rigorous supervision of balance-of-payments restrictions while not imposing similar disciplines with respect to residual restrictions. Even though there was no doubt that the proposed waivers, if requested, would be granted, the contracting parties that maintained residual restrictions opposed the proposal as legalistic. For Robert Hudec this opposition to the waiver proposal demonstrated the general breakdown of consensus with respect to the substantive legal rules.[150]

(iii) UK Margins of Preferences Waiver   The UK Margins of Preferences Waiver, adopted in 1953, suspended Art. I:4 (b) GATT in order to allow the United Kingdom to raise tariffs on imports for which tariffs were unbound without at the same time having to impose a customs duty on Commonwealth products which were imported into the UK free of duty.[151]

Art. I:2 GATT contains an exception from the most-favoured-nation obligation for historical preferences.[152] However, Art. I:4 (b) GATT

---

145 Dam, *GATT: Law and International Economic Organization*, 261, 262; Jackson, *World Trade and the Law of GATT*, 709.

146 For a list of extensions, see BISD 14S (1966), 225.

147 On the issue of residual restrictions in general and the attempts to dismantle them which succeeded the hard-core waiver decision, see Hudec, *GATT Legal System and World Trade Diplomacy*, 265 et seq.

148 Hudec, *GATT Legal System and World Trade Diplomacy*, 265 et seq.

149 CONTRACTING PARTIES, Summary Record of the Tenth Meeting, 16 November 1967, SR.24/10 (24 November 1967), 117.

150 Hudec, 'GATT or GABB?', 1299, 1345, 1346; Hudec, *GATT Legal System and World Trade Diplomacy*, 280, 281.

151 CONTRACTING PARTIES, Waiver Granted to the United Kingdom in Connection With Items Not Bound in Schedule XIX and Traditionally Admitted Free of Duty From Countries of the Commonwealth, Decision of 24 October 1953, BISD 2S (1954), 20. In 1955 the waiver decision was amended to also apply to items for which the tariff binding was withdrawn subsequent to the waiver decision, CONTRACTING PARTIES, Amendment of the Waiver Granted to the United Kingdom in Connection With Items Traditionally Admitted Free of Duty From Countries of the Commonwealth, Decision of 5 March 1955, BISD 3S (1955), 25.

152 On this exception see below B.I.3.1.

requires that the margin of preference, i.e. the absolute difference between the most-favoured-nation rate of duty and the preferential rate of duty,[153] over time remains the same as it was on 10 April 1947. To give an example: if the MFN duty rate on a certain product is 10 per cent *ad valorem* and the preferential duty rate is 3 per cent *ad valorem*, the margin of preference is seven percentage points. This margin shall not be increased, for example, by increasing the MFN duty rate without at the same time increasing the preferential duty rate. This provision had the effect that contracting parties which maintained preferences under Art. I:2 GATT could raise MFN duty rates only if they also raised the preferential duty rate for these products. An increase of the most-favoured-nation duty rate alone would have increased the margin of preference and thus resulted in a violation of Art. I:4 (b) GATT.

Since the UK wished to increase duties on goods for which tariffs were unbound, without having to impose corresponding duties on Commonwealth imports which under traditional arrangements were free of duty,[154] it requested a waiver of Art. I:4 (b) GATT.[155] It openly admitted that the purpose of the envisaged increase in tariff duties was greater protection for domestic industry. The UK further stressed that the purpose was not an increase of advantages enjoyed by Commonwealth products.[156] The UK justified its request by pointing to the fact that it merely wished to increase duty rates on unbound items, something any contracting party was permitted to do under GATT law. The waiver was only required because the increase in duties would also increase the margins of preferences. Where this increase did not cause trade diversion from foreign importers to Commonwealth importers, the waiver – in view of the UK – only addressed a technical matter.[157] It remedied, in the opinion of the UK, a situation in which the strict application of the legal rules was contrary to the spirit of the General Agreement.[158]

---

153 See interpretative note *ad* Article I:4 GATT.
154 On the UK traditional system of duty-free imports from Commonwealth countries, particularly of foodstuffs, see Dam, *GATT: Law and International Economic Organization*, 45.
155 Memorandum by the United Kingdom Government, Difficulties Arising out of the Application of Article I, L/115 (28 August 1953).
156 *Ibid.* Even though the purpose was not to advantage Commonwealth products, the UK argued that it could not impose duties on the same products from Commonwealth countries without a modification of existing tariff legislation for which parliamentary approval could not be secured (*ibid.*).
157 See CONTRACTING PARTIES, Eighth Session, Summary Record of 5th Meeting on 21 September 1953, SR.8/5 (26 September 1953), 5, 13 (statement by the UK delegate).
158 *Ibid.*, 13.

The waiver request was approved and a waiver decision adopted by twenty-six votes in favour, none against and seven abstentions.[159] In order to ensure that the increase in margins of preferences did not result in trade diversion from foreign importers to Commonwealth importers, the waiver decision provided for special consultation and arbitration procedures.[160]

(iv) Waivers legalizing tariff surcharges – a special case of waivers to address the inefficiency of legal rules   Under the GATT 1947 several developing countries requested and were granted waivers of Art. II:1 GATT for the imposition of tariff surcharges to address balance-of-payments difficulties.[161] The GATT allowed, if certain conditions were met, the adoption of quotas to counter balance of payments difficulties (Arts. XII, XVIII:B GATT). By contrast, the imposition of tariff surcharges, i.e. the imposition of additional duties across the board on all imported products, violated Art. II GATT when such duties were imposed on products for which the tariff rates were bound. Tariff surcharges are, however, often more practicable than quotas and economically preferable.[162] Therefore contracting parties resorted to the imposition of tariff surcharges to address balance-of-payments problems.[163] While developing countries regularly requested waivers prior to the imposition of tariff surcharges, developed countries imposed tariff surcharges without requesting waivers.[164]

Even though surcharges had become almost a de facto part of the GATT,[165] a proposal for a formal amendment by a developing country

159 CONTRACTING PARTIES, Eighth Session, Summary Record of 21st Meeting on 24 October 1953, SR.8/21 (31 October 1953), 7.

160 CONTRACTING PARTIES, Waiver Granted to the United Kingdom in Connection With Items Not Bound in Schedule XIX and Traditionally Admitted Free of Duty From Countries of the Commonwealth, Decision of 24 October 1953, BISD 2S (1954), 21. On these procedures see Chapter 5 D.III.2.4.

161 On GATT law and practice with respect to balance-of-payments problems, see Jackson, *World Trade and the Law of GATT*, 673–716, specifically on tariff surcharges, 711–14; Jackson, *World Trading System*, 241–4.

162 Cf. Note by the Secretariat, The Use of Import Surcharges by Contracting Parties, COM.TD/F/W/3 (25 May 1965), 1, 2; Hudec, *GATT Legal System and World Trade Diplomacy*, 227, fn. 54; Jackson, *World Trading System*, 242.

163 For a list of countries which had notified the CONTRACTING PARTIES of their use of tariff surcharges by May 1965 and the action taken, see Note by the Secretariat, The Use of Import Surcharges by Contracting Parties, COM.TD/F/W/3 (25 May 1965), 4, 5.

164 Hudec, *GATT Legal System and World Trade Diplomacy*, 227. Waivers from Art. II GATT for the imposition of tariff surcharges were granted to Chile, Nicaragua, Peru, Sri Lanka (Ceylon) and Uruguay: see WTO, *Analytical Index of the GATT*, vol. I, 892 *et seq.*

165 Jackson, *Law of World Trade*, 714.

that would have generally legalized tariff surcharges was never adopted, but ended up in a negotiating impasse.[166] As an explanation for why the GATT was not amended it was suggested that the status quo allowed contracting parties to point to the formal illegality of surcharges in order to exert pressure on the country imposing the surcharge.[167]

This practice demonstrates, on the one hand, that waiver decisions have been used to address the economic inefficiency of certain GATT rules. On the other hand, it shows the inequality between developing and developed countries. Developed contracting parties openly disregarded GATT rules while developing countries complied with the legal procedures and ensured legality of their actions by obtaining waiver decisions.

The imposition of price-based measures, including tariff surcharges, to address balance-of-payments difficulties was eventually permitted under the 1979 Declaration on Trade Measures Taken for Balance-of-Payments Purposes[168] which in the Uruguay Round was clarified and supplemented by the Understanding on the Balance-of-Payments Provisions of the GATT 1994.[169]

(b) Waivers to legalize market integration   Under the GATT 1947 two waiver decisions were adopted to allow developed contracting parties to integrate their markets even though the integration arrangements did not meet the requirements of Art. XXIV GATT.[170] These waivers were the waiver granted to the member states of the European Coal and Steel Community (ECSC Waiver) and the waiver granted to the United States in connection with the US–Canadian agreement on automotive products (US Automotive Products Waiver).

(i) ECSC Waiver   In 1952 the six member states (France, Germany, Italy, the Netherlands, Belgium and Luxembourg) of the European Coal and Steel Community (ECSC), founded in 1951, were granted a waiver of unlimited duration of their obligations under Articles I, II, XI and XIII

---

166 See Report of the Ad Hoc Group on Legal Amendments to the General Agreement, COM.TD/F/4 (4 March 1966); see also, Hudec, *GATT Legal System and World Trade Diplomacy*, 227, note 54; Jackson, *Law of World Trade*, 714.

167 Jackson, *Law of World Trade*, 714.   168 BISD 26S (1979), 205.

169 On these legal instruments, Jackson, *World Trading System*, 243 *et seq.*

170 There were a number of other integration arrangements which also did not meet the requirements of Art. XXIV GATT for which, however, no waivers were requested. For a critical review of early GATT practice, see Dam, 'Regional Economic Arrangements and the GATT', 615.

GATT in order to allow them to participate in the ECSC without violating their obligations under the GATT.[171]

A waiver was required to ensure the legality of the integration of the market in coal and steel products under the GATT but also under the ECSC Treaty. Similarly to Section 22 of the US Agricultural Adjustment Act, Art. 71 ECSC Treaty stipulated that 'the powers granted . . . concerning commercial policy toward third countries shall not exceed the powers which the member states are free to exercise under the international agreements to which they are parties'.

The measures covered by the waiver were not justified under Art. XXIV GATT – the exception for regional trade agreements – since the ECSC only aimed at integration in the coal and steel sector and not with respect to substantially all trade as required by Art. XXIV:8 GATT. This, merely partial, integration of economies was also the reason why a waiver under Art. XXIV:10 GATT was not considered to be an option to bring the measures into conformity with the GATT. According to Art. XXIV:10 GATT the CONTRACTING PARTIES could approve, by a two-thirds majority, proposals for regional integration that did not fully comply with the requirements of Art. XXIV:5–9 GATT. Such proposals, however, had to 'lead to the formation of a customs union or free trade area' in the sense of Art. XXIV:8 GATT.

The CONTRACTING PARTIES acknowledged that the objectives of the ECSC were broadly consistent with GATT objectives[172] and that the integration pursued by the ECSC could result in economic advantages also for other contracting parties.[173] One country, Czechoslovakia, was, however, strongly opposed to this waiver and held that Art. XXV:5 GATT was not intended to justify a deliberate violation of the GATT which was not caused by a situation of hardship and not of a temporary nature.[174] Czechoslovakia accused the CONTRACTING PARTIES of double standards as evidenced by the following statement of the Czech delegate in the Working Party examining the waiver request:

---

171 CONTRACTING PARTIES, Waiver Granted in Connection with the European Coal and Steel Community, decision of 10 November 1952, BISD 1S (1953), 17.

172 The European Coal and Steel Community, Working Party Report, adopted by the CONTRACTING PARTIES on 10 November 1952 (G/35), BISD 1S (1953), 85, para. 3; cf. CONTRACTING PARTIES, Waiver Granted in Connection with the European Coal and Steel Community, decision of 10 November 1952, BISD 1S (1953), 17, preamble, recital 4.

173 Ibid., preamble, recital 4.

174 Statement by Czechoslovak Delegation at 10th meeting of the 7th session, Working Party 4 on the European Coal and Steel Community, W.7/47 (29 October 1952), 4.

> We must not establish, Mr Chairman, a different procedure for big nations and for small ones. Tomorrow or after-tomorrow we shall deal for example with the item: Nicaragua–El Salvador Free Trade Area and we shall very strictly examine and review – as we have already done last year – whether all the conditions of Art. XXIV are fulfilled. And we will be right in doing so. Cannot we apply at least the same attitude in the case of the Schuman Plan which is far more dangerous to the principles of our General Agreement?[175]

In the end, however, it is not surprising that the waiver request for a project of such high political significance as the ECSC was approved by the CONTRACTING PARTIES.[176] The ceremony which was held for the presentation of the waiver demonstrates the acknowledgement of the political significance of the ECSC by the CONTRACTING PARTIES.[177] The waiver was adopted with twenty-seven votes in favour, one against (Czechoslovakia) and two abstentions (Cuba, Indonesia).[178]

(ii) US Automotive Products Waiver   A further market integration project, albeit of lesser political weight, for which a waiver was granted, was the United States–Canada Automotive Pact of 1965. On 16 January 1965 the US and Canada had concluded this agreement which provided for duty-free treatment for automotive products (original parts as well as vehicles) traded between the US and Canada.[179] The same year the United States was granted a waiver of the most-favoured-nation obligation in Art. I:1 GATT in order to allow it to import automotive parts as well as automotive vehicles from Canada free of duty while maintaining its duties on the imports of like products from other contracting parties.[180] Canada did not require a waiver since it accorded the duty-free treatment on a most-favoured-nation basis to all, not only US, importers.

---

175 *Ibid.*, 5.
176 CONTRACTING PARTIES, Seventh Session, Summary Record of the Seventeenth Meeting, held on 10 November 1952, SR.7/17 (12 November 1952), 8.
177 For the speeches made on this occasion, see European Coal and Steel Community, Presentation of Waiver, L/66 (18 November 1952).
178 CONTRACTING PARTIES, Seventh Session, Summary Record of the Seventeenth Meeting, held on 10 November 1952, SR.7/17 (12 November 1952), 8.
179 The Agreement Concerning Automotive Products Between the Government of the United States of America and the Government of Canada, concluded on 16 January 1965, was circulated by the Executive Secretary of the GATT to the contracting parties in L/2339 (27 January 1965). For a discussion of this agreement and its compatibility with the GATT, see Metzger, 'United States–Canada Automotive Products Agreement of 1965', 103.
180 CONTRACTING PARTIES, United States Imports of Automotive Products, Decision of 20 December 1965, L/2528 (28 December 1965).

The objective of the agreement between the US and Canada was the integration of the automotive industry of the two countries in order to permit efficient production. In view of Canada and the US the North American automotive industry in fact constituted one single great industry due to the geographical proximity of the US and Canadian automotive industry, the close corporate relationships, the interchangeability of products and identical consumer demands in Canada and the US. This single industry was held to be arbitrarily and uneconomically divided by tariffs and other barriers of trade and the removal of these barriers was to facilitate the efficient integration of production operations.[181]

The United States submitted the Automotive Pact on the removal of trade barriers between the US and Canada to the GATT for consideration. It did not, however, submit a waiver request at the same time. The United States argued that the duty-free treatment provided for in the agreement would not affect the economic interests of other contracting parties. As concerned automotive parts the US maintained that there were no significant imports from third countries into the United States of original parts and that the few imports that did occur were not affected. With regard to imports of vehicles the US held that North American cars had to be considered different products from foreign cars. They were, it was argued, not in a relationship of price competition since they supplied different segments of the market.[182] Thus, in the view of the United States, the trade preferences granted to Canadian original automotive parts as well as vehicles did not create any trade diversion. While the US admitted that the implementation of the agreement would give rise to a 'technical inconsistency with Art. I of the GATT' they believed that this was 'more with the letter of the General Agreement than with its spirit'[183] – an argument reminiscent of that of the UK in support of the Margins of Preferences Waiver.

The GATT working party which had been established to examine the agreement came to the conclusion that, if the United States implemented the agreement, its action would be 'clearly inconsistent with Art. I and it would be necessary for the United States Government to seek a waiver from its GATT obligations'.[184] Consequently, on 15 October 1965, the

---

181 See Opening Statement Made by the Representative of the United States to the Working Party on Canada/United States Agreement on Automotive Products, L/2409 (25 March 1965), Annex A.

182 *Ibid.*, 11, 12.   183 *Ibid.*, 12.

184 Report of the Working Party on Canada/United States Agreement on Automotive Products, L/2409 (25 March 1965), para. 17. Hudec notes that during negotiations of the

United States submitted a waiver request.[185] This was only a few days before the implementing legislation, the Automotive Products Trade Act of 1965, was signed by the US President and the proclamation by the President by which he exercised his authority under the act to remove US duties on automotive products.[186]

After consideration of the waiver request by a working party, the majority of which shared the view that the tariff preferences would not result in trade diversion, the CONTRACTING PARTIES adopted a waiver decision with forty-one votes in favour and none against.[187] To counter the fear of some contracting parties that, contrary to the assurances by the US, the preferential treatment of Canadian automotive products might result in trade diversion, certain safeguards were included in the waiver. Thus, the waiver would terminate if the US and an allegedly injured contracting party agreed after consultations, or if the CONTRACTING PARTIES decided, that there was substantial trade diversion or an imminent threat thereof.[188]

During the discussions several contracting parties pointed to an alleged inconsistency in the attitude of the United States who, on the one hand, requested a waiver to be able to grant trade preferences to another developed country, but who was, on the other hand, vehemently opposed to the granting of new trade preferences to developing countries.[189] The United States defended itself against this accusation of double standards by stressing the exceptional situation in this case, as well as its conviction that its measures with respect to automotive products from Canada

agreement the issue of GATT compatibility had been put aside since the US had not anticipated any opposition by other contracting parties. It had believed that the commercial effects would not trouble other contracting parties and that there would be no opposition to a waiver in light of other deviations, in particular by the EEC, from Art. I GATT: Hudec, 'GATT or GABB?', 1299, 1319, fn. 47.

185 Request for Waiver by the Government of the United States, Canada/United States Agreement on Automotive Products, C/62 (15 October 1965).

186 Cf. Report of Working Party on United States Automotive Products Waiver Request, L/2509 (15 November 1965), para. 8.

187 CONTRACTING PARTIES, United States Imports of Automotive Products, Decision of 20 December 1965, L/2528 (28 December 1965).

188 Ibid., paras. 4, 5.

189 General Council, Minutes of Meeting held on 19 November 1965, C/M/31 (30 November 1965), 2, 3; cf. Report of Working Party on United States Automotive Products Waiver Request, L/2509 (15 November 1965), para. 16. Uruguay in transmitting its vote in favour of the waiver submitted a statement pointing out 'its support for the establishment of a general system of preferences for the benefit of less-developed countries, a policy which is being supported both in GATT and in UNCTAD': Statement by Uruguay in Voting for the Waiver, L/2530 (4 January 1966).

would not result in trade diversion. By contrast, trade diversion was one of the main objectives of the trade preferences demanded by developing countries.[190]

In November 1996 the WTO General Council extended the waiver decision until 1 January 1998[191] since otherwise it would have expired on 31 December 1996 according to the Understanding in Respect of Waivers of Obligations under the GATT 1994 which had been negotiated during the Uruguay Round. The United States had requested an extension for only one year since as of 1 January 1998 tariffs on all products covered by the waiver would be eliminated as part of the tariff elimination schedule of the US–Canada Free Trade Agreement, which had been incorporated into NAFTA, and which is justified under Art. XXIV GATT.[192] In light of the changed world market in automobiles it is questionable whether the waiver would have been extended had the preferential treatment not been integrated into the framework of NAFTA.[193]

(c) **Conclusion**   A number of waiver decisions were adopted under the GATT 1947 which allowed for clear violations of the GATT legal rules. Some of the measures legalized by these waivers were not only formally inconsistent with the legal rules, but resulted in adverse effects on trade. Nonetheless, this practice should not be overestimated and taken as evidence that the waiver power was used more sweepingly under the GATT 1947 than in the WTO or endangered the effectiveness of the legal order.

---

190 Cf. Working Party Report on United States Automotive Products Waiver Request, L/2509 (15 November 1965), paras. 6, 7, 14. Kenneth Dam pointed out that although the arrangement would not be trade diverting in the sense of replacing third-country production by production within Canada and the United States, it would create trade only in a very limited sense. While trade between the two states might increase and while this trade might involve some rationalization of production, the arrangement – so Dam said – was not expected to lead to lower prices, which are the justification of international trade. He therefore concluded that while the case against the waiver was very weak the case for the waiver was also weak: Dam, *GATT: Law and International Economic Organization*, 50.

191 General Council, United States – Imports of Automotive Products, Decision adopted by the General Council at its meeting on 7, 8 and 13 November, WT/L/198 (18 November 1996).

192 See statement by the representative of the United States in the Council for Trade in Goods, Minutes of Meeting held on 19 September 1996, G/C/M/13 (9 October 1996), para. 4.11.

193 See the critical statement in the Council for Trade in Goods by the representative of Japan who stressed that the situation had changed and that today automotive products were being supplied and in competition throughout the world, Minutes of Meeting held on 15 October 1996, G/C/M/14 (30 October 1996), paras. 1.4, 1.5.

Rather, the use of the waiver power in these instances might be interpreted as an attempt to strengthen the GATT legal order.[194]

Thus the Agricultural Waiver, as noted above, can be interpreted as ensuring the United States' continued membership in the GATT; the Hard-core Waiver was a (vain) attempt to discipline and submit to multilateral surveillance quantitative restrictions imposed by European states; and the ECSC Waiver legalized a project of such political significance that it would have been pursued even without a legalizing waiver. By contrast, when in the 1960s and 1970s major contracting parties openly violated the GATT and ignored the waiver process this was much more a sign of the breakdown of consensus with respect to the legal rules.[195] While at that time the developed contracting parties turned to adopt the famous 'pragmatic approach', developing countries continued to seek waivers when they intended to impose measures, such as tariff surcharges, in deviation from the legal rules.[196]

3 Preferences – waivers to pursue external policy objectives

In the WTO a number of decisions have been adopted that waive individual members' obligations under Art. I:1 GATT (in a few cases also under Art. XIII:1, 2 GATT) in order to enable them to grant non-reciprocal tariff preferences to products from selected developing countries without extending the same preferences to like products from other members.[197] These tariff preferences are neither justified under the Enabling Clause[198] (because they discriminate between developing countries) nor under Art. XXIV GATT (because preferences are often only granted to selected products and not on a reciprocal basis).

Waiver decisions that legalize tariff preferences afforded by developed country members to products from developing countries differ from the

---

194 Robert Hudec noted that the practice of contracting parties during the first decade of the GATT to request waivers in instances of non-compliance constituted an implicit recognition of the respective obligation. This was evidenced not only by the request of waiver decisions, but also the requesting parties' willingness to accept the sometimes cumbersome control procedures which usually accompanied waivers: Hudec, 'GATT or GABB?', 1299, 1338.

195 *Ibid.*, 1303–4, 1343–6.

196 Hudec, *GATT Legal System and World Trade Diplomacy*, 227.

197 Until May 2009 twenty-two such waiver decisions (including extension decisions) have been granted by the WTO General Council/Ministerial Conference.

198 CONTRACTING PARTIES, Decision on Differential and More Favourable Treatment, Reciprocity and Fuller Participation of Developing Countries, adopted 28 November 1979, L/4903.

waiver decisions discussed above in two important respects. Firstly, the requesting members refer not primarily to their own domestic situation in order to support their requests for a waiver, but to the exceptional situations in the developing countries which will benefit from the tariff preferences.[199] It is argued that preferences are needed in order to increase export earnings and investment opportunities and, more generally, economic development in the preference-receiving countries. Secondly, waiver requests and waiver decisions for tariff preferences stress that the preferences are compatible with and in fact further the objectives of the WTO as described in the preamble to the WTO Agreement, in particular the aim 'to ensure that developing countries, and especially the least-developed among them, secure a share in the growth in international trade commensurate with the needs of their economic development'.[200] Trade preferences are presented as positive efforts to integrate developing countries into the global economy as called for in Art. XXXVI:3 GATT. Compared to other waivers adopted in the WTO these waivers are granted for relatively long periods of time (up to ten years) and are frequently extended.

The practice of granting waivers for trade preferences dates back to the early years of the GATT 1947. To better understand this practice it is useful to distinguish three phases: the early GATT years, the time when the Generalized System of Preferences (GSP) was negotiated and the period after adoption of the GSP. When the GATT was drafted the most-favoured-nation principle was already not without exceptions as concerns preferential tariff treatment. It allowed for certain historical tariff preferences to be accorded by contracting parties to products from their dependent territories (Art. I:2 GATT). Nonetheless CONTRACTING PARTIES were relatively strict in their attitude towards further exceptions. A number of waivers were granted for further tariff preferences, but these were only granted after careful examination, were narrow in scope and subject to reporting requirements.

With decolonization developing countries increasingly demanded non-reciprocal tariff preferences as a matter of international solidarity and justice. In particular Latin American countries pushed for general

---

199 I write 'not primarily' since in some instances domestic interests of the requesting member are directly implicated. Thus, the United States grants trade preferences to Andean countries under the Andean Trade Preference Act with the ultimate objective of reducing cocaine imports into the United States, see below section B.I.3.3(b).
200 WTO Agreement, preamble, 3rd recital.

preferences to be accorded to products from all developing countries independent of any historical colonial ties between the preference-granting and the preference-receiving country. On their initiative the Generalized System of Preferences (GSP) was negotiated, outside the GATT, mainly in the United Nations Conference on Trade and Development (UNCTAD) and the Organisation for Economic Co-operation and Development (OECD). In 1966, while negotiations on a GSP were still ongoing, Australia, as the first country to adopt a general preference scheme for products from developing countries, was granted a waiver from Art. I:1 GATT. Eventually agreement was reached in UNCTAD on the parameters of a Generalized System of Preferences and in 1971 the CONTRACTING PARTIES adopted a ten-year collective waiver (1971 GSP Waiver) that suspended Art. I:1 GATT to the extent necessary for the implementation of GSP schemes by contracting parties. Further reform efforts by developing countries concerned preferences to be accorded among developing countries. Before agreement could be reached on a general exception from Art. I:1 GATT for such preferences, the CONTRACTING PARTIES in 1968 adopted a decision which legalized preferences granted under an agreement between India, the United Arab Republic and Yugoslavia. In 1971, the same year the GSP Waiver was adopted, the CONTRACTING PARTIES adopted a further collective waiver to generally legalize preferences granted between developing countries.[201]

Even after the 1971 GSP Waiver (succeeded in 1979 by the Enabling Clause) had introduced into GATT law a general exception from the most-favoured-nation obligation for tariff preferences to products from developing countries, GATT contracting parties – and later WTO members – continued to request individual waivers for preference schemes. These waivers are required to legalize preference schemes that are adopted outside the Generalized System of Preferences and benefit only selected developing countries.

3.1 Selected tariff preferences before the Generalized System of Preferences

The practice of waiving the most-favoured-nation obligation to enable contracting parties to grant trade preferences had already started in 1948. Several waivers were adopted to cover trade preferences that did not fall within the scope of the exception in Art. I:2 GATT. This exception to the

---

201 The two collective waiver decisions of 1971 will be discussed in more detail in section B.2.1(a) below.

most-favoured-nation obligation was included in the GATT for so-called historical preferences.[202] It is mainly owed to the United Kingdom's and France's desire to retain existing tariff preferences with respect to colonies and former colonies and compromised the United States' aim of eliminating all preferences.[203] The excepted preferences were specifically listed in annexes to the GATT. They covered most preferences granted by developed contracting parties to their dependent territories. Art. I:4 GATT prescribes that the margin of preference, i.e. the absolute difference between the most-favoured-nation rate of duty and the preferential rate of duty,[204] shall not be increased.[205]

Several waiver decisions were granted under the GATT 1947 for preference arrangements not covered by the exception in Art. I:2 GATT or to allow for increases in the margin of preference contrary to Art. I:4 GATT. The former were granted for preference arrangements which were similar to those covered by Art. I:2 GATT in that they were based on specific relationships between the preference-granting and the preference-receiving territory or country. These ties were either of a historic (preferences granted to former dependent territories), a geographical (proximity) or a legal (preferences granted due to a trusteeship agreement with the United Nations) nature.

The first request for a waiver to suspend Art. I:1 GATT in order to legalize non-reciprocal tariff preferences was made by the United States in 1948 when it took over the administration of certain islands in the Pacific from Japan under a trusteeship agreement with the United Nations.[206] To support its request the US referred to its obligation under the trusteeship agreement to promote the best interests of the inhabitants of the trust territories. The US further argued that exports of other territories trading in the same products would not be negatively affected since the US

---

202 The provision of the Havana Charter which permitted new preferences (Art. 15) was not included in the GATT 1947 due to the refusal by the United States, see Hudec, *Developing Countries in the GATT Legal System*, 14. On the exception for historical preferences in Art. I:2 GATT, see WTO, *Analytical Index of the GATT*, vol. I, Article I, 40–3; Jackson, *World Trade and the Law of GATT*, 264–70.

203 On the negotiating history see Gardner, *Sterling–Dollar Diplomacy*, 348 *et seq.*

204 See interpretative Note *ad* Article I:4.

205 See *supra* B.I.2.2(a) (UK Margins of Preferences Waiver).

206 Request of the United States for a Waiver under Article XXV of the GATT in Respect of Preferential Treatment for the Trust Territory of the Pacific, GATT/CP.2/WP3/6 (1 September 1948).

merely replaced preferences formerly granted by Japan and since the volume of exports from the Pacific Island territories was insignificant.[207] The waiver was granted for an unlimited period of time and included a general authorization for duty-free treatment of imports from the trust territories applicable to all products.[208] Similar waivers were granted in 1953 to Australia to allow it to grant duty-free treatment to products from Papua (Australian possession) and New Guinea (trust territory)[209] and in 1973 to New Zealand for handicraft products from its South Pacific island neighbours Fiji, Tonga, Nauru, Papua/New Guinea and Western Samoa.[210]

Waivers were also requested for preferences granted by European countries to their dependent and formerly dependent territories. The first such waiver was requested by Italy in 1951 to legalize duty-free market access granted to certain products from Libya.[211] Italy sought the waiver to continue the preferential treatment afforded to certain products since World War II beyond Libya's independence which was to be obtained on 1 January 1952. Italy pointed to its obligations under international and in particular United Nations law to help the economic development of its former colony as well as to the unlikelihood that the preferences would result in damage to the trade of other contracting parties.[212] The waiver at first

---

207 *Ibid.*; see also Report of the Working Party No. 3 on the Request of the United States for a Waiver under Article XXV of the GATT in Respect of Preferential Treatment for the Trust Territory of the Pacific, GATT/CP.2/36 (7 September 1948).

208 CONTRACTING PARTIES, Decision of 8 September 1948, BISD II, 9. The speed of the waiver process in this case is noteworthy and testifies to the lack of contestation in this case. The waiver was first requested by the US on 23 August 1948 (GATT/CP.2/W.6) and the waiver decision was adopted 8 September 1948.

209 CONTRACTING PARTIES, Australian Treatment of Products of Papua-New Guinea, Decision of 24 October 1953, BISD 2S (1954), 18. The waiver was adopted with twenty-eight votes in favour and none against and granted for an unlimited period of time. The waiver decision was amended a few times, mainly to extend its product coverage. This at first only included primary products and was later extended to forestry products and products substantially derived from primary products: see BISD 4S, 14, BISD 5S, 34, BISD 8S, 28. The tariff preferences legalized by the waiver were later granted within the framework of the Papua New Guinea/Australia Trade and Commercial Relations Agreement, which entered into force on 1 February and was notified under Article XXIV (L/5138).

210 CONTRACTING PARTIES, New Zealand – Tariff-Free Quotas for Handicraft Products from South Pacific Islands, Decision of 13 November 1973, BISD 20S (1974), 29.

211 Request by the Government of Italy for a Waiver under Article XXV of the GATT to permit the Continued Free Entry into Italy of Products Originating in Libya, GATT/CP.6/35 (19 October 1951).

212 *Ibid.*; see also Note by the Executive Secretary, G/21 (28 August 1952).

was granted only for one year and thereafter was extended several times.[213] Another waiver was granted to Italy for continued special tariff treatment to certain products from Somalia after Somalia's independence.[214] France was granted a waiver to extend preferences which it accorded to goods originating in the former French Zone of Morocco – and which were justified under Art. I:2 GATT – to imports from any part of the Kingdom of Morocco.[215]

An example for a waiver of Art. I:4 GATT is the waiver granted to the UK to allow it, if a certain procedure was followed and specific conditions were met, to grant preferential tariff treatment to products from its dependent overseas territories beyond the limits of Art. I:4 GATT.[216]

All of these waiver decisions were narrow in geographical and often product scope. The preference-granting contracting parties went to great length in justifying their waiver requests by pointing to their responsibilities deriving from either their legal status as administrative authority, their historic status as a colonial power or their responsibility as neighbouring country. The narrow scope of most preference schemes guaranteed that they would not lead to significant trade diversion.

In the WTO some of these waivers were extended. A waiver decision still legalizes US preferential treatment to products from the former trust territory of the Pacific Islands.[217] France's waiver for preferential treatment to products from Morocco was extended four times and eventually expired on 1 March 2006 with the entry into force of the Euro Mediterranean Agreement that established an association between the EC and the EC member states on the one side and the Kingdom of Morocco on the other.[218]

---

213 BISD II, 10, for the extension decisions, see WTO, *Analytical Index of the GATT*, vol. II, Article XXV, 897.
214 CONTRACTING PARTIES, Italian Customs Treatment for Certain Products of Somalia, Decision of 19 November 1960, BISD 9S (1961), at 40; for the decisions to extend this waiver, see WTO, *Analytical Index of the GATT*, vol. II, Article XXV, 897.
215 CONTRACTING PARTIES, French Trading Arrangements with Morocco, Decision of 19 November 1960, BISD 9S (1961), 39.
216 CONTRACTING PARTIES, Special Problems of Dependent Overseas Territories of the United Kingdom, Decision of 5 March 1955, BISD 3S (1955), 21.
217 General Council, United States – Former Trust Territory of the Pacific Islands, Decision of 27 July 2007, WT/L/694 (1 August 2007). This decision waives Art. I:1 GATT until 31 December 2016.
218 Under the GATT 1947 the waiver had been granted for an unlimited period of time. The WTO extension decisions are contained in documents WT/L/187, WT/L/250, WT/L/294 and WT/L/361. In the WTO the waivers were requested by and granted to the EC.

An exception to these narrow preference schemes were the trade preferences granted by the European Economic Community founded in 1957. Part IV of the Treaty of Rome granted duty-free market access to the dependent African territories of Belgium, France, Italy and the Netherlands. After these territories had become independent by 1962 duty-free market access was granted on the basis of international agreements, namely the two successive Yaoundé Conventions, thereafter the four successive Lomé Conventions and, since 2000, the Cotonou Agreement. The geographical scope of the conventions broadened over time. Most importantly, with accession of the UK to the EEC in 1973, African, Caribbean and Pacific Commonwealth countries were added. While the two Yaoundé Conventions had adopted the principle of reciprocal trade liberalization, the first Lomé Convention of 1975 abandoned reciprocity in favour of unilateral trade-preferences.[219] The preferences were not covered by the exception in Art. I:2 GATT since they were accorded not only by the former colonial powers, but by the European Community. Even though most contracting parties held the view that these preferences were not justified under the GATT, the EC member states did not request a waiver until 1994.[220]

Further tariff preferences were granted between developing countries within the framework of regional integration agreements. These were neither justified by the exception in Art. I:2 GATT, nor the exceptions for free trade areas and customs unions (Art. XXIV GATT), nor waiver decisions. Nonetheless these preferences were tolerated by the other contracting parties to the GATT.[221]

3.2 Towards a general exception from the most-favoured-nation principle for preferences

While the Havana Charter in its Art. 15 had allowed for new tariff preferences[222] no similar provision was included in the GATT 1947 due

---

219 On the history of the trade preferences granted by the EC, see Bartels, 'Trade and Development Policy of the European Union', 715.

220 See section B.I.3.3(a) below.

221 Hudec, *Developing Countries in the GATT Legal System*, 51. Dam, 'Regional Economic Arrangements and the GATT', 615.

222 Art. 15 para. 1 of the Havana Charter reads: 'The Members recognize that special circumstances, including the need for economic development or reconstruction, may justify new preferential agreements between two or more countries in the interest of the programmes of economic development or reconstruction of one or more of them.'

to resistance by the United States.[223] Consequently, under the GATT 1947 tariff preferences were initially only legal if falling within the exception for historic preferences under Art. I:2 GATT, if granted within a customs union or free trade area that met the requirements of Art. XXIV GATT, or if legalized by a waiver decision.

In the 1960s developing countries, however, began to call for tariff preferences from developed contracting parties to be afforded on a non-reciprocal basis to industrial products from developing countries. They argued that preferences would promote economic development by increasing their export earnings. The focus of developing countries on increased export earnings followed a previous concentration on import substitution by way of fencing of domestic markets through trade barriers.[224] More export opportunities to the markets of developed countries, in particular for manufactured products, would promote the establishment of manufacturing industries and diversification in production in the exporting developing country. Preferences would create such export opportunities, on the one hand by allowing imports from developing countries to compete with domestic production in the importing country and, on the other hand, by allowing them to compete with other imports from industrialized countries not benefiting from a preference.[225] Developing countries not only demanded preferences from developed countries, they also advocated an exception from the most-favoured-nation obligation for preferential trade among themselves.

In 1958 an expert report commissioned by the CONTRACTING PARTIES, the so-called Haberler Report, had confirmed the need to open the markets of developed countries to products from developing countries in order to promote economic development.[226] As a consequence the

---

223 Hudec, *Developing Countries in the GATT Legal System*, 14. On the negotiations of developing countries' privileges in the International Trade Organization and eventually the GATT 1947, *ibid.*, 3 *et seq.*

224 On this shift, *ibid.* 40 *et seq.* Developing countries demanded more freedom to adopt trade barriers to protect domestic infant industries and to adopt quantitative restrictions to limit imports to counter balance-of-payments disequilibria. For how these claims were addressed during the 1945–55 Review Session resulting in amendments to the GATT, *ibid.*, 26 *et seq.*

225 See Report of the then Secretary-General of UNCTAD Raúl Prebisch to the first United Nations Conference on Trade and Development: Prebisch, *Towards a New Trade Policy for Development*, at 21.

226 Haberler *et al.*, *Trends in International Trade: Report by a Panel of Experts*. The Haberler Report was a report by trade experts commissioned by the contracting parties to study trends in international trade, 'in particular the failure of the trade of less developed countries to develop as rapidly as that of industrialized countries, excessive short-term fluctuations in prices of primary products, and widespread resort to agricultural

expansion of export earnings of developing countries became one of the objectives of an action plan adopted by the CONTRACTING PARTIES.[227] While this action plan did not yet mention the issue of new preferences, in 1963 a working group was established to study preferences.[228]

Work in the GATT on the issue of trade preferences in derogation of the most-favoured-nation obligation did not yield any results in the form of binding obligations on the part of developed countries. Part IV on Trade and Development which was added to the GATT in 1964 did not introduce any binding legal obligations.[229] Despite the efforts of developing countries no provision was included in this part which would have authorized preferences.[230] At that time the United States continued to be the main opponent to a derogation from the most-favoured-nation principle for new preferences.[231]

Since no consensus could be achieved within the GATT on a general rule on preferences, developing countries shifted their efforts to the United Nations.[232] In 1964 ECOSOC convened the first United Nations Conference on Trade and Development (UNCTAD).[233] This conference adopted a general principle on preferences (General Principle Eight) according to which developed countries should grant tariff and non-tariff preferences to all developing countries without extending them to developed countries. It further stated that special preferences enjoyed by selected developing countries should be regarded as transitional and eventually be eliminated when substituted by international measures guaranteeing at

protection', CONTRACTING PARTIES, Decision of 29 November 1957, BISD 6S (1958) 18.

227 CONTRACTING PARTIES, Programme of Action Directed Towards an Expansion of Trade, Decision of 17 November 1958, BISD 7S (1959) 27.

228 BISD 12S (1964), 44.

229 On the history of Part IV of the GATT, see Supachai, 'Introduction to Part IV GATT', 766.

230 Hudec, *Developing Countries in the GATT Legal System*, 58. After the negotiation of Part IV was completed, trade preferences continued to be discussed in the newly established Committee on Trade and Development, BISD 13 S (1965) 75.

231 On the differing views of contracting parties on preferences, see Hudec, *Developing Countries in the GATT Legal System*, 51, 52.

232 On the bargaining power which developing countries gained by threatening to leave the GATT and instead to cooperate in a rival UN organization, see *ibid.*, 39 *et seq.*; Nye, 'Review of *The United Nations Conference on Trade and Development of 1964*', 230, 233.

233 The 1964 conference voted to transform itself into an international organization (UNCTAD, Final Act, UN Doc. E/CONF.46/141, vol. I (1964)) which was subsequently established by a General Assembly resolution (UN GA Res 1995 (XIX) December 30, 1964). On the first UNCTAD 1964, see Friedeberg, *The United Nations Conference on Trade and Development of 1964; The History of UNCTAD 1964–1984*, UN Doc. UNCTAD/OSG/186 (1985).

least equivalent advantages.[234] This principle was, however, not supported by developed countries who either voted against it or abstained.[235]

The United States' position changed after the conclusion of the Kennedy Round in 1967 which developing countries as well as UNCTAD viewed as a failure.[236] Developing countries were of the opinion that the traditional multilateral trade negotiations had not resulted in meaningful market access for their products and therefore expected progress on preferences.[237] The change in the US position from opposition towards support for a system of worldwide preferences for manufactured products from developing countries was attributed mainly to the pressure from Latin American countries who did not – like other developing countries – benefit from special preference schemes as well as, indirectly, to UNCTAD pressure.[238] In 1968 the second UNCTAD agreed on the early establishment of a Generalized System of Preferences (GSP) according to which non-discriminatory tariff preferences should be granted to all (or almost all) products from all (or almost all) developing countries without requiring reciprocity.[239]

States were, however, not able to agree on the details of such a preference scheme, in large part due to differences among the prospective beneficiaries of the GSP.[240] To work out these details they established a Special Committee on Preferences.[241] In 1970 this committee adopted 'Agreed Conclusions' on the GSP which were subsequently approved by UNCTAD's Trade and Development Board.[242] These Agreed Conclusions related inter alia to the issues of reverse preferences (i.e. preferences to be granted by developing to developed countries) and special preferences, safeguard mechanisms and beneficiaries, but left many contentious questions, such as the exact list of beneficiaries, open. With respect to the legal status of the GSP, the Agreed Conclusions noted that GATT contracting parties intended to seek a waiver or waivers. Moreover, they

---

234 UNCTAD, Final Act, UN Doc. E/Conf.46/141, vol. I (1964), 10, 11.
235 On the different positions with regard to preferences, see Krishnamurti, 'Tariff Preferences in Favour of the Developing Countries', 643.
236 Hudec, *Developing Countries in the GATT Legal System*, 63.   237 *Ibid.*
238 Nye, 'Review of *The United Nations Conference on Trade and Development of 1964*', 230, 232.
239 UN Doc. UNCTAD, Resolution 21 (II) (26 March 1968).
240 Nye, 'Review of *The United Nations Conference on Trade and Development of 1964*', 230, 232.
241 UN Doc. UNCTAD, Resolution 21 (II) (26 March 1968), para. 2.
242 On the details, see Krishnamurti, 'The Agreement on Preferences', 45.

took note of the preference-giving countries' statements that the granting of preferences did not constitute a binding commitment and was conditional upon the necessary waiver or waivers of GATT obligations.[243]

The change of the GATT contracting parties' positions towards preferences for products from developing countries is reflected in GATT practice. A practice which eventually in 1971 led to the adoption of two collective waivers which suspended Art. I:1 GATT to justify, firstly, preferences under the Generalized System of Preferences agreed upon in UNCTAD and, secondly, preferences granted between developing countries.[244]

Over the years GATT practice had evidenced an erosion of the most-favoured-nation principle due to the division of opinions among contracting parties as to the desirability of preferences. After a protracted debate on the legality of preferences to former colonies of EC member states the contracting parties agreed in 1958 to no longer challenge the EC preferences on legal grounds, but instead to deal with any arising problems pragmatically.[245] Furthermore, contracting parties tolerated tariff preferences that developing countries accorded among themselves in the framework of regional trade agreements even though these agreements did not meet the requirements of Art. XXIV GATT.[246] As Robert Hudec notes in his study of developing countries in the GATT:

> [T]he GATT's review of these developing-country arrangements was gentle and supportive. The agreements were simply passed over with a wait-and-see attitude. The developed-country members of the GATT were reluctant to be seen as discouraging this supposedly effective tool of development, even when it was being used illegally.[247]

In particular two legal decisions by the CONTRACTING PARTIES on individual preference schemes played a significant role in paving the way for the more permanent and general legalization of preferences through the two collective waiver decisions in 1971 and subsequently the Enabling Clause in 1979. One of these decisions is a waiver adopted in 1966 that legalized the unilateral extension of preferences by a developed contracting party, Australia, to developing countries. The other is a decision

---

243 UNCTAD UN Doc. Agreed Conclusions of the Special Committee on Preferences, Section IX. Legal Status, paras. 1 and 2(c).
244 On these waiver decisions, see section B.II.2.1(a) below.
245 BISD 7S (1959), 70, para. 3. On this practice, see Hudec, *Developing Countries in the GATT Legal System*, 50.
246 Dam, 'Regional Economic Arrangements and the GATT', 615.
247 Hudec, *Developing Countries in the GATT Legal System*, 51 (footnote omitted).

adopted by the CONTRACTING PARTIES in 1968 concerning an agreement on preferences among three developing countries, India, the United Arab Republic and Yugoslavia.

In 1966 the CONTRACTING PARTIES waived the most-favoured-nation obligation of Art. I:1 GATT for an unlimited period of time for tariff preferences by Australia on a range of products from developing countries.[248] The decision is explicitly based on Art. XXV:5 GATT and thus does not raise any doubts as to its qualification as a waiver decision. It acknowledges that the Australian preferences are designed to facilitate economic development and thus pursue one of the objectives of the GATT.[249] The decision differed from previous waiver decisions for tariff preferences granted by developed countries to products from developing countries and was an important step towards agreement on the Generalized System of Preferences.[250] It legalized preferential treatment by Australia which was granted indiscriminately to a list of goods from a generally described group of developing countries and not only from individual countries with a special relationship with the donor country. The United States who at that time still opposed generalized preference schemes voted against the adoption of the waiver.

Two years later, in 1968, the CONTRACTING PARTIES adopted a decision which legalized a preference agreement between India, the United Arab Republic and Yugoslavia, open to participation by all other developing countries.[251] The three parties to this agreement presented it as part of wider efforts among developing countries in the field of economic cooperation, as previously called for by the contracting parties.[252] Indeed

---

248 CONTRACTING PARTIES, Australia – Tariff Preferences for Less-Developed Countries, Decision of 28 March 1966, BISD 14 S (1966), 23.

249 *Ibid.*, preamble, recitals 3 and 4. The negotiations of the waiver centred on several contentious issues, including the countries and territories which were to benefit from the preferences, the products to which preferences were to be granted, as well as safeguards against trade diversion and the possibility to withdraw preferences from products if they had become competitive and thus there no longer was a need for a preference, see Australia – Tariff Preferences for Less-Developed Countries, Report of the Working Party, adopted 28 March 1966 (L/2527), BISD 14 S (1966), 162.

250 While the waiver in this respect was an important decision, the preferences it legalized were criticized on economic grounds as cynical and not being of any benefit to the eligible developing countries: Dam, *GATT: Law and International Economic Organization*, 53.

251 CONTRACTING PARTIES, Trade Arrangement Between India, The United Arab Republic and Yugoslavia, Decision of 14 November 1968 (L/3132), BISD 16S (1969), 17.

252 Trade Arrangement Between India, The United Arab Republic and Yugoslavia, Report of the Working Party, adopted 14 November 1968 (L/3032), BISD 16 S (1969), 83, para. 2.

there had been broad support among the contracting parties for preferential arrangements among developing countries.[253] And even though the contracting parties had not been able to agree on the scope of preferences between developing countries to be exempted from the most-favoured-nation obligation,[254] the Trade and Development Committee in 1966 had recommended that developing countries should proceed with the negotiation of preferential arrangements.[255] Consequently, in face of the India–United Arab Republic–Yugoslavia Agreement, contracting parties had not much choice but to 'welcome the initiative of the three countries in endeavoring to work out new techniques of co-operation among developing countries in the interests of trade expansion'.[256] Even though several contracting parties expressed the view that the agreement violated Art. I GATT[257] the decision was not formally adopted as a waiver decision on the basis of Art. XXV:5 GATT.[258]

253 Dam, *GATT: Law and International Economic Organization*, 251; a report of the Working Party on Preferences noted: 'There was general recognition that there was no disagreement on the principle involved in the granting of preferences between less-developed countries, at least in so far as this was on a regional basis.' The delegation of Japan reserved its position on this sentence. Report of the Working Party on Preferences submitted to the CONTRACTING PARTIES on 25 November 1964 (L/2282) BISD 13 S (1965), 100, para. 16.

254 On this debate in the GATT and in particular the restrictions on such preferences demanded by the United States, see Dam, *GATT: Law and International Economic Organization*, 251 *et seq.*

255 Committee on Trade and Development, Report adopted 5 April 1966 (L/2614), BISD 14S (1966), 129, para. 33.

256 Trade Arrangement Between India, The United Arab Republic and Yugoslavia, Report of the Working Party, adopted 14 November 1968 (L/3032), BISD 16 S (1969), 83, para. 6. Discussions in the working party centred mainly on the developing countries which would be allowed to accede to the agreement as well as the economic effects, *ibid.*

257 See CONTRACTING PARTIES, 25th Session, Summary Record of the Third Meeting held on 14 November 1968, SR.25/3, 40 (statement of the representative of the United States). The representative of Uruguay, Hector Gros Espiell, by contrast, defended the view that the agreement did not violate Art. I GATT which had to be interpreted taking into account the principles of the new Part IV (at 39).

258 Not only does the decision not refer to Art. XXV:5 GATT, nor to 'exceptional circumstances' justifying the decision, it was also adopted by consensus and not by a vote as was common for waiver decisions under the GATT and was not included in the Basic Documents Supplement in the section entitled 'Waivers granted under Art. XXV:5 GATT'. The Report of the Working Party notes, however, the view of the United States government that the decision was intended to meet the requirements of Art. XXV:5 GATT, Trade Arrangement Between India, The United Arab Republic and Yugoslavia, Report of the Working Party, adopted 14 November 1968 (L/3032), BISD 16 S (1969), 83, para. 16.

3.3 Special trade preferences after negotiation of the Generalized System of Preferences

While the United States had hoped that agreeing to the Generalized System of Preferences might lead the EC to abandon its policy of granting selected preferences to certain developing countries – a hope which was shared by a number of developing countries – this expectation was not met.[259] Even though the EC adopted a GSP scheme, it continued to grant special preferences outside the GSP to countries with which its member states had special ties. While for a long time it was alone in granting special preferences on a large scale, the United States and Canada followed suit in the 1980s and also instituted special preference schemes on a larger scale. Special preferences beyond those foreseen in the GSP are granted to selected countries due to special historical and geographical relationships. Moreover, such preferences are granted to pursue policy objectives which go beyond economic development, such as political stabilization or reduction of illicit drug production and trafficking.[260]

These special preference schemes encounter twofold opposition. On the one hand they are criticized for the reason that they might impede multilateral tariff negotiations. Preference-granting and preference-receiving countries might be opposed to reductions of most-favoured-nation tariffs since such reductions decrease the value of preferences. On the other hand special preferences are opposed by countries (mainly developing countries which do not benefit from special preferences themselves) who are of the view that preferential treatment should exclusively be afforded within the framework of the GSP. Nonetheless, a practice emerged according to which waiver requests for special preference schemes in general were approved. In recent years, however, several requests by the EC and the United States have encountered strong opposition by a few developing countries which fear that their trade interests are compromised by discriminatory preference schemes. In a few cases this opposition led to a substantial delay in the waiver process and concessions were offered by the requesting member so that the opponents would not veto a waiver decision. In one case opposition by a powerful developing country, namely

---

259 The EC did, however, abandon its policy to demand reverse preferences from beneficiaries of the preference schemes, see Hudec, *Developing Countries in the GATT Legal System*, 63. On the EC's general policy on preferences up to the negotiation of the European Partnership Agreements to replace the Cotonou Agreement, see Bartels, 'Trade and Development Policy of the European Union', 715.

260 Such policy objectives are also frequently pursued through GSP conditionality, see below section B.II.2.1(a).

India, to a special preference scheme by the EC even resulted in formal dispute settlement. As a consequence the preferences in question were found illegal and subsequently modified by the EC to adjust them to the requirements of the Enabling Clause.[261]

(a) GATT practice on special preference schemes outside the GSP

In 1983 the United States, who until 1967 had opposed all new preferences and then had joined agreement on the GSP with the hope of containing selected preferences, itself adopted a special preference scheme. The Caribbean Basin Economic Recovery Act (CBERA), which was enacted on 5 August 1983 and entered into force on 1 January 1984, provided for duty-free treatment of certain products from selected countries in the Caribbean Basin.[262] The Act was part of the Caribbean Basin Initiative which aimed at promoting trade and economic stability of countries in the Caribbean Basin.[263]

To legalize these preferences the CONTRACTING PARTIES waived Art. I:1 GATT for the term of the Caribbean Basin Economic Recovery Act, i.e. from 1 January 1984 until 30 September 1995.[264] The US had supported its waiver request not only by pointing to the objective of economic development, but also by stressing that the impact on trade with other countries not benefiting from the Act would be minimal.[265] Nonetheless, the working party which had been established to examine the waiver request had been divided as to the question whether a waiver should be granted to legalize the preferential scheme.[266] Opposition was mainly voiced by Caribbean states, namely Cuba and Nicaragua, who were not to benefit from the preferences.[267]

Less contentious was the United States' request in 1992 for a waiver of Art I:1 GATT to legalize preferential tariff treatment to products from four

---

261 On this case see below section B.I.3.3(b)(iii).

262 The Caribbean Basin Economic Recovery Act, Public Law No. 98-67 of 5 August 1983 is contained in GATT document L/5577 (14 November 1983).

263 United States Request for a Waiver, Caribbean Basin Economic Recovery Act, L/5573 (1 November 1983).

264 CONTRACTING PARTIES, The Caribbean Basin Economic Recovery Act, Decision of 15 February 1985, L/5779 (20 February 1985).

265 United States Request for a Waiver, Caribbean Basin Economic Recovery Act, L/5573 (1 November 1983), 3.

266 Working Party on United States Caribbean Basin Economic Recovery Act (CBERA), Report, L/5708 (26 October 1984), paras. 58–62.

267 General Council, Minutes of the Meeting on 6–8 and 20 November 1984, C/M/183 (10 December 1984), 58, 59, 60 (statements by the Cuban and Nicaraguan delegates). The waiver was adopted by postal ballot with fifty-two votes in favour, two abstentions, and two negative votes, L/5779, fn. 1.

Andean nations, namely Bolivia, Colombia, Ecuador and Peru. With these preferences, to be granted on the basis of the Andean Trade Preferences Act (ATPA),[268] the US intended to increase opportunities for trade in legitimate products and thus to help the Andean countries to reduce the production and trafficking of illicit drugs. The objectives behind the ATPA were thus directly linked to internal concerns of the US, namely the economic and social consequences of trade in and consumption of cocaine within the US.[269] Again the US stressed that these preferences would not create new barriers or other impediments to trade with other contracting parties due to the small share in trade affected, the limited country scope (four preference-receiving countries) and limited duration (ten years) of the preferences.[270] The waiver was granted in March 1993 for a term of ten years.[271]

In 1986 Canada also had requested a waiver to allow it to grant duty-free treatment to imports from the Commonwealth Caribbean nations with which it had a special relationship due to shared history and close cultural links. The preferences were part of a larger legislative package of trade, development assistance and double taxation measures called CARIBCAN.[272] As was the case with respect to the US request for a waiver for its Caribbean Basin Initiative the GATT contracting parties supported CARIBCAN's objective of economic development. Nonetheless, some contracting parties were concerned about trade diversion and others stressed that a strengthening of the GSP was preferable to special preference programmes.[273] Nonetheless the waiver, which had been requested for an indeterminate period of time,[274] was granted for a term of twelve years.[275]

---

268 The Andean Trade Preferences Act which was signed into law on 4 December 1991 is contained in GATT Document L/6980 Add. 1 (31 January 1992).

269 United States Request for a Waiver, US–Andean Trade Preferences Act, dated 22 January 1992, L/6980 (22 January 1992), 2, 3.

270 *Ibid.*, 3.

271 CONTRACTING PARTIES, US–Andean Trade Preferences Act, Decision of 19 March 1992, L/6991 (20 March 1992). The waiver decision was adopted without a dissenting vote.

272 The CARIBCAN draft legislation was contained in GATT Document L/6008 (25 June 1986).

273 GATT, Working Party Report on CARIBCAN, L/6090 (26 November 1986), paras. 24, 25.

274 GATT, CARIBCAN, Questions and Replies, L/6008 (25 June 1986), 2.

275 The waiver decision was adopted with fifty-two votes in favour and none against. CONTRACTING PARTIES, CARIBCAN, Decision of 28 November, L/6102 (17 December 1986).

The most extensive preference scheme outside the GSP is maintained by the European Communities. The EC grants trade preferences to the so-called ACP states, African, Caribbean and Pacific countries, former colonies of the EC member states.[276] Under the GATT 1947 it was disputed whether the trade preferences granted to the ACP countries were in conformity with GATT law.[277] While the EC maintained that they were justified under the exception for free trade areas in Art. XXIV GATT, other contracting parties were of the view that they violated Art. I:1 GATT. Even though the CONTRACTING PARTIES did not concede the legality of the preferences they decided in 1958 to no longer challenge the EC preferences on legal grounds, but instead to deal with any problems that should arise pragmatically.[278]

The situation changed with the growing opposition by developing countries who competed with ACP states for access to the European market. In particular Latin American exporters of bananas argued that they were negatively affected and discriminated against by the import regimes for bananas of several EC member states. These import regimes not only consisted of preferential import duties for bananas from ACP countries, but also differential quota and import licensing regimes.[279]

In 1993 and 1994 two GATT panels examined, inter alia, the claims of several Latin American contracting parties that the EC's preferences for bananas from ACP countries violated Art. I:1 GATT. In these disputes the EC reiterated its view that the preferences were justified under Art. XXIV GATT. In particular, it argued that the requirement of Art. XXIV:8(b) GATT, that trade restrictions in a free trade area must be eliminated on substantially all trade, had to be interpreted in light of Art. XXXVI:8 GATT which demands of developed contracting parties not to expect reciprocal concessions from developing contracting parties in trade negotiations. Thus, according to the EC, the Lomé Convention gave rise to a free trade

---

276 See above B.I.3.3(b).
277 See, for example, the GATT working party reports on the four successive Lomé Conventions, Report of the Working Party on the ACP–EEC Convention of Lomé, L/4369 (5 July 1976); Report of the Working Party on the Second ACP–EEC Convention of Lomé, L/5292 (5 March 1982); Report on the Working Party on the Third ACP–EEC Convention of Lomé, L/6382 (2 September 1988); Report of the Working Party on the Fourth ACP–EEC Convention of Lomé, L/7502 (19 July 1994).
278 BISD 7S (1959), 70, para. 3. On this practice, see Hudec, *Developing Countries in the GATT Legal System*, 50.
279 For an overview of the EC Banana regime as well as the *Bananas* disputes in the GATT and the WTO until 2001, see Vranes, 'From Bananas I to the 2001 Bananas Settlement', 1–37.

area even though duty-free and preferential tariff treatment was only granted by the EC to products originating in ACP countries, but not vice versa.[280] Both panels rejected this interpretation for the reason that Art. XXXVI:8 GATT was not applicable to negotiations of a free trade area. The panels held that the preferences granted to bananas from ACP countries violated Art. I:1 GATT and were not justified under Art. XXIV GATT since the Lomé Convention did not liberalize substantially all trade between the EC and the ACP countries as required by Art. XXIV:8 GATT.[281] The Panel Report in *Bananas I* recommended that the EC request a waiver since the adoption of a waiver

> would enable the CONTRACTING PARTIES to provide both the parties to [the Lomé IV Convention] and any contracting party affected by the tariff preference with the benefit of legal certainty for planning investments and conducting trade in bananas.[282]

The EC opposed the panels' findings and the reports were never adopted. However, on 10 October 1994 the parties to the Fourth Lomé Convention submitted a waiver request in order to settle the bananas dispute.[283] The Lomé Waiver, which was granted on 9 December 1994, waived Art. I:1 GATT 'to the extent necessary to permit the European Communities to provide preferential treatment for products originating in ACP states as required by the relevant provisions of the Fourth Lomé Convention' until 29 February 2000.[284]

(b) **WTO practice on special preferences outside the GSP**   After the WTO Agreement had entered into force all waivers which had a term exceeding 31 December 1996 needed to be extended. Otherwise they

---

280 Panel Report, *EEC–Bananas I*, DS/32R (3 June 1993, not adopted), paras. 217, 226–228; Report of the Panel, *EEC – Bananas II*, DS/38R (11 February 1994, not adopted), para. 32.

281 DS/32R, paras. 368–72; DS/38R, paras. 155, 159–62.   282 DS/32R, para. 372.

283 ACP Countries–European Communities, Fourth Lomé Convention, Request for a Waiver, L/7539 (10 October 1994).

284 CONTRACTING PARTIES, The Fourth ACP–EEC Convention of Lomé, Decision of 9 December 1994, L/7604 (19 December 1994), para. 1. The waiver decision was adopted by 105 votes in favour, none against, and one abstention, CONTRACTING PARTIES, Fiftieth Session, Summary Record of the First Meeting on 8 December 1994, SR. 50/1 (8 February 1995). The waiver did not, however, settle the *Bananas* dispute since it merely waived Art. I:1 GATT. In the *Bananas III* dispute it was found that aspects of the import regime for bananas also violated Art. III:4, Art. XIII GATT and Art. II, Art. XVII GATS, see Appellate Body Report, *EC–Bananas III*, WT/DS27/AB/R, adopted 25 September 1997.

would have expired on 31 December 1996 according to the Understanding in Respect of Waivers of Obligations under the General Agreement on Tariffs and Trade (para. 2). The waivers granted for preferences under the ATPA, CARIBCAN and Lomé IV were extended on 14 October 1996 until 4 December 2001, 31 December 2006 and 29 February 2000 respectively.[285] Already on 15 November 1995 the waiver for preferences under the CBERA, which in 1990 had been made a permanent part of US law,[286] had been renewed until 31 December 2005.[287]

Shortly before the waiver for Canadian tariff preferences under the CARIBCAN initiative expired, it was extended in 2006 for another five years without much discussion in the Council for Trade in Goods.[288] Several other waivers for preferences granted by the EC and other WTO members were also not contentious. Thus, in 2000 and 2001 the General Council adopted three waivers of Art. I:1 GATT to enable the EC,[289] Turkey[290] and Switzerland[291] to grant tariff preferences to countries of the Western Balkans. The objectives of the preference schemes went beyond market access and included the contribution to peace and security through the social and economic reconstruction in these countries.[292] In 2008

---

285 General Council, United States – Andean Trade Preference Act, Decision of 14 October 1996, WT/L/184 (18 October 1996); General Council, Canada – CARIBCAN, Decision of 14 October 1996, WT/L/185 (18 October 1996); General Council, EC – The Fourth ACP–EC Convention of Lomé, Decision of 14 October 1996, WT/L/186 (18 October 1996).

286 Caribbean Basin Economic Recovery Expansion Act of 1990, Public Law 101-418.

287 General Council, Caribbean Basin Economic Recovery Act, Decision of 15 November 1995, WT/L/104 (24 November 1995).

288 General Council, CARIBCAN, Decision of 15 December 2006, WT/L/677 (19 December 2006).

289 General Council, European Community Preferences for Albania, Bosnia–Herzegovina, Croatia, The Federal Republic of Yugoslavia, and the former Yugoslav Republic of Macedonia, Decision of 8 December 2000, WT/L/380 (13 December 2000); on 28 July 2006 this waiver was extended until 31 December 2011, its scope was broadened to also include preferences granted to products originating in Kosovo, WT/L/654 (2 August 2006).

290 General Council, Turkey – Preferential Treatment for Bosnia–Herzegovina, Decision of 8 December 2000; WT/L/381 (13 December 2000). The General Council decided to terminate this waiver, which was originally granted until 31 December 2006, in 2003 in course of the annual review because Turkey had signed a Free Trade Agreement with Bosnia–Herzegovina, which had entered into force on 1 July 2003 and which now covered these preferences.

291 General Council, Switzerland – Preferences for Albania and Bosnia–Herzegovina, Decision of 18 July 2001, WT/L/406 (26 July 2001). This waiver expired on 31 March 2004.

292 See statement by the delegate of the EC, Council for Trade in Goods, Minutes of the Meeting on 5 April and 18 May 2000, G/C/M/43 (13 June 2000), para. 5.2.

the EC was granted a further waiver to accord preferential treatment to products from Moldova to foster the economic development of Moldova, the poorest European country.[293]

The situation was very different with respect to a request by the EC for a waiver for tariff preferences to be granted on the basis of the Cotonou Agreement, the successor agreement to Lomé IV, as well as with respect to requests by the United States for waivers for preferences on the basis of the amended Caribbean Basin Economic Recovery Act, the Andean Trade Preferences Act, as well as the newly enacted African Growth and Opportunities Act. These requests encountered strong opposition by a few members who saw their trade interests impaired by the US and EC preference schemes. In case of a GSP + arrangement of the EC, for which the EC had requested a waiver, such opposition by India led to formal dispute settlement proceedings between the EC and India on the conformity of the preferences with WTO law. Eventually no waiver was granted, but the EC – after a finding of illegality by the Appellate Body – reformed the preference arrangement in question. These situations are looked at in more detail in what follows.

(i) The Cotonou and Bananas Waivers   On 29 February 2000, the day on which the Lomé Waiver expired, the EC requested[294] a waiver for preferences under the ACP–EC Partnership Agreement (the Cotonou Agreement).[295] The Cotonou Agreement not only regulates trade relations between the EC and the ACP states, it also contains provisions on the political dimension of their relations, on development cooperation strategies and financial cooperation. Its main objective is 'poverty eradication, sustainable development and the gradual integration of the ACP countries into the world economy'.[296] Today seventy-eight ACP states are party to the Cotonou Agreement.[297] With respect to trade relations

---

293 See statement by the delegate of the EC, Council for Trade in Goods, Minutes of the Meeting on 11 March 2008, G/C/M/92 (14 April 2008), para. 4.2; for the waiver decision see General Council, European Communities – Application of Autonomous Preferential Treatment to Moldova, Decision of 7 May 2008, WT/L/722 (15 May 2008).

294 Request for a WTO Waiver from the EC and from Tanzania and Jamaica on behalf of the ACP countries, New ACP–EC Partnership Agreement, dated 29 February 2000, G/C/W/187 (2 March 2000).

295 Partnership Agreement between the members of the African, Caribbean and Pacific Group of States on the one part, and the European Community and its Members on the other part, signed in Cotonou on 23 June 2000, OJ L 317 (15 December 2000), 3–353.

296 Preamble, 2nd recital.

297 See overview of the EC Commission of the Cotonou Agreement, http://ec.europa.eu/europeaid/where/acp/overview/cotonou-agreement/index_en.htm (last accessed 12 March 2011).

the Cotonou Agreement only provides for a transitional arrangement. According to Art. 36:1 the parties to the agreement agreed to conclude, by the end of 2007, WTO-compatible trading arrangements, so-called European Partnership Agreements. These were to progressively remove barriers to trade reciprocally between the parties to these agreements.[298]

During the preparatory period of eight years (from 2000 until the end of 2007) the EC was to provide non-reciprocal preferential treatment to imports from ACP countries substantially equivalent to those granted under the Fourth Lomé Convention (Art. 36:3 Cotonou Agreement). Since this preferential treatment, which was not extended on a most-favoured-nation basis to all other WTO members, violates Art. I:1 GATT, the EC requested the waiver.

A further waiver of Art. XIII GATT was required to legalize the preferential tariff quota for bananas from ACP states under the EC's banana import regime. In *Bananas III* the Appellate Body had found that the EC tariff quotas for bananas were not legalized by the Lomé Waiver of Art. I GATT, since they not only were inconsistent with Art. I GATT but also with Art. XIII GATT which had not been waived.[299]

The waiver process extended over almost two years, mainly due to opposition of Latin American WTO members as well as the US to the new banana import regime proposed by the EC which still favoured ACP bananas.[300] Eventually, at the Doha Ministerial Conference, two waiver decisions were adopted. One waived Art. XIII GATT until 31 December 2005 for a transitional regime of EC autonomous tariff rate quotas on imports of bananas.[301] The other waived Art. I GATT until 31 December 2007 for preferential tariff treatment under the Cotonou Agreement.[302] After that date the tariff preferences were to be replaced by reciprocal preferences to be granted under the Economic Partnership Agreements between the EC and ACP states. Since these Economic Partnership

---

298 On the state of negotiations see http://ec.europa.eu/trade/wider-agenda/development/economic-partnerships/ (last accessed 12 March 2011). Since 1 January 2008 the EU granted tariff preferences to ACP states with whom it had concluded the interim Economic Partnership Agreement under the Economic Partnership Agreement Regulation, Council Reg. (EC) 1528/2007 OJ 2007 L 348/1.

299 Appellate Body Report, *EC – Bananas III*, WT/DS27/AB/R, adopted 25 September 1997, paras. 159 *et seq.*

300 On the negotiation process, see Chapter 7 A.II.

301 Ministerial Conference, European Communities – Transitional Regime for the EC Autonomous Tariff Rate Quotas on Imports of Bananas, Decision of 14 November 2001, WT/L/437 (7 December 2001).

302 Ministerial Conference, European Communities – The ACP–EC Partnership Agreement, Decision of 14 November 2001, WT/L/436 (7 December 2001).

Agreements were to meet the requirements of Art. XXIV GATT further waivers would be unnecessary to legalize preferences.

Decisive for the consensus on the waiver decisions was a compromise between the US, Ecuador and the EC with respect to the bananas issue, a compromise which met some of the demands of Ecuador and the US. The EC, the US and Ecuador had concluded two understandings, one between the EC and the US and one between the EC and Ecuador, which put a preliminary end to the bananas dispute and lifted these countries' opposition to the waiver request.[303] According to these understandings the EC would maintain transitional tariff quotas for bananas, but implement a tariff-only import regime by the end of 2005. Under the tariff-only regime the EC would still be able to grant preferential access to ACP bananas as long as it maintained total market access for Latin American most-favoured-nation producers. As a further concession to non-ACP banana exporters, the waiver of Art. I GATT provided for a right of WTO members to seek arbitration before the future EC bananas tariff takes effect.[304]

Both waivers terminated without the *Bananas III* dispute being settled.[305] When it became clear that the EC would not be able to institute a tariff-only import regime by the end of 2005, it submitted, on 7 October 2005, a request for an extension of the Art. XIII waiver until a negotiated solution could be found which satisfied ACP banana suppliers as well as US banana exporting firms and Latin American exporting countries.[306] Latin American countries were, however, not willing to

---

303 Understanding on Bananas between the European Communities and the United States signed on 11 April 2001, WT/DS27/59, G/C/W/270 (2 July 2001); Understanding on Bananas between the European Communities and Ecuador signed on 30 April 2001, WT/DS27/60, G/C/W/274 (9 July 2001). On this compromise and the two understandings, see Vranes, 'From Bananas I to the 2001 Bananas Settlement', 1, 29 *et seq.*

304 WT/L/436, Annex I.

305 The Cotonou Waiver terminated with respect to bananas even before its expiry date. This was due to the fact that the EC did not comply with arbitration reports which found that its new tariffs for bananas would not maintain total market access for Latin American bananas suppliers, Panel Report, *EC – Bananas III*, WT/DS27/RW2/ECU (7 April 2008), para. 7.200.

306 EC Request for Extension of a Waiver under GATT Article XIII – Tariff Rate Quota for Bananas of ACP Origin, dated 7 October 2005, G/C/W/529 (11 October 2005). The EC submitted that it requested the waiver merely for reasons of legal certainty since it was of the view that its remaining duty-free tariff rate quota exclusively for bananas originating in ACP countries was not in violation of Art. XIII: see Council for Trade in Goods, Minutes of the Meeting of 19 March 2007, Statement by the Representative of the EC, G/C/M/88 (26 April 2007), para. 3.2.

examine the waiver request.[307] Instead Ecuador and the United States initiated formal compliance proceedings in which the Appellate Body found that the EC had failed to comply with earlier rulings on the illegality of the banana import regime.[308] During the proceedings the EU had adopted Council Regulation 1528/2007.[309] This regulation repealed the preferential quotas for ACP bananas and finally instituted the tariff-only import regime for bananas.[310] This regulation also constitutes the (temporary) legal basis for tariff preferences for other goods from ACP countries which until the end of 2007 were granted under the Cotonou Agreement and which are eventually to be replaced by reciprocal preferences agreed upon in Economic Partnership Agreements between the EU and ACP countries. These preferences are not justified by a WTO waiver.

(ii) The CBERA, ATPA and AGOA Waivers   The United States also encountered difficulties when it requested extensions of the CBERA and ATPA Waivers as well as a new waiver to legalize trade preferences under the African Growth and Opportunities Act (AGOA).[311] The United States waited until 24 February 2005 before it submitted requests for waivers to legalize preferences under the amended CBERA and ATPA, as well as the AGOA even though the ATPA Waiver had expired already on 4 December 2001 and preferences under the AGOA had been granted since 2000.[312]

A number of developing countries objected to these requests. China and Pakistan, for example, were opposed to specific content requirements included in the legislation with respect to preferences for textiles and apparel. These requirements made the preferences for textiles and

---

307 Council for Trade in Goods, Minutes of the Meeting of 19 March 2007, Statement by the Representative of the EC, G/C/M/88 (26 April 2007), para. 3.2.

308 Appellate Body Reports, *EC–Bananas III (Article 21.5 ECU II, US)*, WT/DS27/AB/RW2/ECU, adopted 11 December 2008, and WT/DS27/AB/RW/USA, adopted 22 December 2008. For a legal and economic analysis of this report see Schropp and Palmeter, 'Commentary on the Appellate Body Report in EC – Bananas III', 7.

309 Council Reg. (EC) 1528/2007 OJ 2007 L 348/1.

310 For a chronological overview of the different contentious EU import regimes for bananas see Schropp and Palmeter, 'Commentary on the Appellate Body Report in EC – Bananas III', 7, 8–11.

311 Council for Trade in Goods, Request for a Waiver – Caribbean Basin Economic Recovery Act (CBERA as amended), G/C/W/508 (1 March 2005); Council for Trade in Goods, Request for a Waiver – Andean Trade Preference Act (ATPA as amended), G/C/W/510 (1 March 2005); Council for Trade in Goods, Request for a Waiver – African Growth and Opportunity Act (AGOA), G/C/W/509 (1 March 2005).

312 The CBERA Waiver had been granted until 31 December 2005; a new waiver was required, however, due to amendments made in 2000, 2002 and 2004.

apparel dependent on the use of US goods in the production process. China and Pakistan, having a strong interest in trade in textiles, argued that these provisions would benefit US producers of yarn and fabric and that this advantage would be detrimental to the beneficiaries of the preferences.[313] The latter would not be able to make use of the most competitive products. This opposition was overcome by including in the operative part of the waiver decisions a provision stating that 'duty-free treatment [under the respective legislation] shall be designed to facilitate and promote the trade of beneficiary countries and not to raise barriers to or create undue difficulties for the trade of any other Members'.[314] This language is usually included merely in the preambles to waivers legalizing trade preferences.[315] Moreover, the United States had made amendments to the AGOA rules of origin which modified the requirements that apparel made from third-country fabric only benefited from the preferences if the fabric originated in the United States.[316]

Paraguay was more persistent in its opposition to the waiver requests. Already since 2002 Paraguay had been requesting to be included in the preference arrangement under the ATPA or at least to receive the same treatment as the four Andean countries benefiting from the ATPA. Paraguay claimed that it was in a similar situation to them in terms of its fight against illicit drug trafficking as well as its development needs and therefore was discriminated against by exclusion from the preference scheme. Thus Paraguay refused to join in a consensus on the waiver requests.[317] It kept up its opposition until on 24 March 2009 it joined in a consensus of the Council for Trade in Goods which paved the way for the adoption on 29 May 2009 by the General Council of three separate waivers for the ATPA, CBERA and AGOA trade preferences which suspended Art. I:1 and Art. XIII:1 and 2 GATT until 30 September 2015.[318] All this

313 See e.g. Council for Trade in Goods, Minutes of the Meeting of 10 March 2006, G/C/M/83 (1 May 2006), paras. 3.3; 3.8.

314 See e.g. General Council, United States – African Growth and Opportunity Act, Decision of 27 May 2009, WT/L/754 (29 May 2009), para. 3.

315 See Chapter 5 D.III.2.1.

316 See Council for Trade in Goods, Minutes of the Meeting of 19 March 2007, G/C/M/88 (26 April 2007), para. 2.2.

317 See statements by the representative of Paraguay in the Council for Trade in Goods, G/C/M/84, para. 4.25; G/C/M/89, para. 3.3; G/C/M/92, para. 2.3.

318 General Council, United States – African Growth and Opportunity Act, Decision of 27 May 2009, WT/L/754 (29 May 2009); General Council, United States – Caribbean Basin Economic Recovery Act, Renewal of Waiver, Decision of 27 May 2009, WT/L/753

while the United States had granted preferences under these schemes in violation of WTO law.

(iii) EC GSP+ preferences   In one instance the opposition of a WTO member, India, to a preference scheme led to formal dispute settlement and eventually the reform of the preferences legislation. In October 2001 the EC had submitted a request to the Council for Trade in Goods for a waiver of Art. I:1 GATT for certain preferences granted under its revised GSP scheme which entered into force on 1 January 2002.[319] As a part of its so-called GSP + scheme the EC intended to grant additional tariff prefer-ences to products from twelve developing countries that were combating drug production and trafficking.[320] The objective of these preferences, according to the EC, was to 'favour sustainable development and pro-mote shared responsibility, so as to improve the conditions under which countries dependent on trade in narcotics are able to develop alternative legitimate crops and new industries capable of competing in the world market'.[321] This preference scheme thus was very similar to that provided in the Andean Trade Preferences Act and for which the US had been granted a waiver. It merely differed in the coverage of countries.

However, this waiver request was unsuccessful.[322] It was met with resistance by a few developing countries which were not included as bene-ficiaries in the drug arrangements, but were competing with beneficiaries for access to the EC market. In particular India was opposed to the grant-ing of the waiver since it was not included as a beneficiary while Pakistan was. Pakistan had been included in the scheme, allegedly to reward it for its cooperation in the fight against terrorism. Due to the preferences awarded to textiles, India feared that Pakistani exporters of textiles might gain an advantage over their Indian competitors.[323] Discussions of the waiver

(29 May 2007); General Council, United States – Andean Trade Preference Act, Renewal of Waiver, Decision of 27 May 2009, WT/L/755 (29 May 2009).

319 EC Request for a Waiver, New EC Special Tariff Arrangements to Combat Drug Produc-tion and Trafficking, dated 23 October 2001, G/C/W/328 (24 October 2001).

320 Bolivia, Colombia, Costa Rica, Ecuador, El Salvador, Guatemala, Honduras, Nicaragua, Pakistan, Panama, Peru and Venezuela, *ibid.* para. 2.

321 *Ibid.*, para. 1.

322 After the Cotonou Waiver had been granted the ACP countries had assured their support for this waiver: see Council for Trade in Goods, Minutes of the Meeting on 14 November 2001, statement of the representative of Kenya on behalf of the ACP states, G/C/M/57 (6 December 2001), para. 8.

323 Panel Report, *EC – Tariff Preferences*, WT/DS246/R (1 December 2003), paras. 4.38, 4.111.

request remained fruitless[324] and after unsuccessful consultations[325] India requested the establishment of a panel on 6 December 2002.[326] The panel which was consequently established found that the preferences for which the EC had requested the waiver, but which it argued before the panel were justified under the Enabling Clause, violated Art. I:1 GATT.[327] This finding was, albeit with different reasoning, upheld by the Appellate Body.[328]

4 Conclusion

In the WTO most individual waiver decisions are adopted to address capacity problems of developing country members and to allow developed country members to maintain selected preference schemes outside their Generalized System of Preferences legislation. Few waiver decisions have been adopted to free contracting parties from specific commitments to allow them to pursue certain economic and non-economic policy objectives. With the exception of Hungary the beneficiaries of these decisions were all developing countries.

Waivers to address capacity problems are an instrument to maintain legality in a situation where law enforcement through dispute settlement would not be able to reach the desired result of compliance. Deferral of the obligation to comply in most cases must, however, be coupled with technical assistance to be effective. In the case of the adaptation of goods schedules to changes in the Harmonized System substantial technical assistance is afforded by the WTO Secretariat. In this constellation assistance in the adaptation of schedules to the Harmonized System made individual waivers, beyond the waivers granted to all members on a collective basis,[329] largely unnecessary.

Waivers which allow members to pursue domestic policy objectives in violation of WTO law to date have only been granted in very specific circumstances. On the one hand, the waiver procedure in Art. IX:3 WTO Agreement complemented the provisions on the extension of

---

324 See G/C/M/55, paras. 2.1–2.15; G/C/M/58, 2–3; G/C/M/61, para. 10.2; G/C/M/62, 19; G/C/M/65, para. 6.1.

325 Request for Consultations by India, *EC – Tariff Preferences*, dated 5 March 2002, WT/DS246/1 (12 March 2002).

326 Request for the Establishment of a Panel by India, *EC – Tariff Preferences*, dated 6 December 2002, WT/DS246/4 (9 December 2002).

327 Panel Report, *EC – Tariff Preferences*, WT/DS246/R (1 December 2003).

328 Appellate Body Report, *EC – Tariff Preferences*, WT/DS246/AB/R, adopted 20 April 2004.

329 On collective HS waivers see section B.II.3.1. below.

transitional periods in the TRIMs Agreement. Here the waiver proced-ure was used in cases in which the formal procedural requirements of the TRIMs Agreement were not met or where there was disagreement as to the exact procedure. Recourse to the general waiver procedure enabled mem-bers to positively decide on the requests by developing country members while at the same time insisting that the requirements for an extension under the agreement were not met. Consequently, no precedents were created which could bind members with a view to future requests. On the other hand, the waiver power was used to free individual members from specific commitments which they had assumed when becoming WTO members. These waiver decisions stress the exceptional circumstances, such as economic hardship, which would result from compliance. More-over, in these cases it was never called into question that compliance would be desirable and a suspension of obligations was never granted for more than a few years. The restrictiveness of this practice is well explained by the commercial interests of other members in expedient compliance with the negotiated commitments.

By contrast, the relatively numerous waivers which legalize special pref-erence schemes adopted by developed country members present these schemes as pursuing the WTO objective of economic development. Even though from the standpoint of development economics the desirability of such schemes is questionable,[330] resistance to waivers legalizing prefer-ences, although increasing in recent years, has been weak.[331] Developed country members wish to be able to adopt such schemes since they use them to pursue specific foreign policy objectives. Developing country members also generally support them – even though they might suffer from these schemes' trade diverting effects – since they hope to benefit from one of these schemes themselves.

It can thus be stated that the waiver power in the WTO is only used to a very limited extent to allow for the pursuit of policy objectives by WTO members in violation of WTO law. This was different under the GATT, where a number of waivers were adopted to legalize measures adopted by developed countries to pursue certain domestic or regional economic policy objectives. Some of these waiver decisions, it can be said, played an important role in stabilizing the GATT and ensuring acceptance of the GATT by the constituencies of important contracting parties. Thus

---

330 See, for example, Özden and Reinhardt, 'The Perversity of Preferences'; Borchert, 'Trade
     Diversion under Selective Preferential Market Access', 1390.
331 On the reasons for this, see Chapter 7 A.II.

the Agricultural Waiver might have ensured that the United States did not leave the GATT and similarly the UK Margins of Preferences Waiver appeased domestic protectionist forces, which without the waiver might have demanded the United Kingdom's denouncement of the General Agreement. The fact that these countries demanded waivers can be read as evidencing their interest (in the early years of the GATT) in the functioning and strengthening of the legal order. Later, when legal discipline started to deteriorate and an attitude of pragmatism prevailed among developed contracting parties, they openly violated GATT rules while still insisting that developing country members requested waivers when they wished to deviate from the law, such as when they wished to impose tariff surcharges.

Apart from ensuring acceptance and stability of the legal order, individual waiver decisions have been the forerunners of more general norm change either by amendment or the adoption of collective waiver decisions. Thus the tariff surcharges waivers have addressed a generally perceived efficiency deficit of the norms on balance-of-payments problems which was later generally acknowledged by a Tokyo Round Declaration. Similarly the 1966 Australian Preferences Waiver and the 1968 decision on the India–United Arab Republic–Yugoslavia trade agreement have laid the ground for a general legal change on the issue of preferences. While the tariff surcharges remedied inefficiencies of the law, the preferences decisions – at least in view of developing countries – addressed the illegitimacy of the most-favoured-nation clause in view of their development needs. General norm change in these cases was eventually achieved with the adoption of two collective waiver decisions on preferences in 1971 and subsequently of the Enabling Clause in 1979.

II Collective waiver decisions

Waivers are not only adopted for the benefit of individual members. Despite the formulation in Art. IX:3 WTO Agreement that the Ministerial Conference 'may decide to waive an obligation imposed on *a* Member',[332] waiver decisions are adopted that suspend obligations for (potentially) all members or abstractly defined groups of members. These shall be termed 'collective waivers'.[333] Collective waivers broadly speaking have performed three functions.

---

332 Emphasis added.
333 This terminology is also used by the WTO Secretariat: see WTO Secretariat, Paragraph 6 of the Doha Declaration on the TRIPS Agreement and Public Health. Information on Waivers, IP/C/W/387 (24 October 2002).

Firstly, collective waivers were adopted to generally defer the obligation to comply. This deferral of compliance was justified by reference to the burdens that immediate compliance would entail. Secondly, collective waivers abstractly modified legal rules. Thirdly, collective waivers suspended WTO norms in order to allow compliance with norms of another regime and thus achieved regime linkage. Such linkage aimed at coordinated cooperation on the one hand and the avoidance of norm conflict on the other.

1 Deferral of the obligation to comply

While a number of waiver decisions have been granted in the WTO to extend transitional periods on an individual basis,[334] so far only two collective waiver decisions have extended transitional periods. One was adopted under the GATT 1947 for the benefit of all contracting parties (1.1. below) and another was adopted in the WTO for the benefit of least-developed country members as part of the implementation of the Doha Declaration on the TRIPS Agreement and Public Health (1.2. below).

1.1 Art. XX Part II GATT 1947

In 1950 the CONTRACTING PARTIES granted a waiver to all contracting parties of the GATT 1947 that extended time limits of the original Part II of Art. XX GATT. Part II of Art. XX GATT had allowed contracting parties during a transitional post-war period to adopt certain measures, inter alia related to price control or the distribution of goods in short supply, in order to address the detrimental economic effects of the war.[335] These measures were to be removed by 1 January 1951 unless a contracting party requested an extension for a particular measure and the request was approved by the CONTRACTING PARTIES. In 1950, before the transitional period expired, the CONTRACTING PARTIES adopted a waiver decision which suspended the obligation to discontinue measures and to seek special permission for the institution and maintenance of such measures.[336] The waiver decision was extended twice and expired on 1 July 1955.[337] At the Review Session 1954–55 the CONTRACTING PARTIES adopted an amendment provision which retained the exception

---

334 These were discussed above in sections B.I.1.1. and B.I.2.1(a).
335 On Art. XX Part II GATT 1947 see WTO, *Analytical Index of the GATT*, vol. I, 592–4.
336 GATT/CP/94 (18 January 1951), 5.   337 BISD II, 28 and BISD 2S (1954), 27.

for measures to address local short supply in Art. XX:j GATT and deleted the remainder of Part II.[338]

1.2 Art. 70.9 TRIPS Agreement

In 2002 the WTO General Council adopted a waiver decision which suspended the obligations under Art. 70.9 TRIPS Agreement of least-developed-country members with respect to pharmaceutical products until 1 January 2016.[339] Art. 70.9 TRIPS Agreement obliges a WTO member to grant exclusive marketing rights to products for which patent applications have been filed according to Art. 70.8 TRIPS Agreement, for which a patent was granted in another member, and for which market approval was attained. This provision intends to preserve the rights of persons who hold patents for pharmaceutical and agricultural chemical products for the time that patent protection according to Art 27 TRIPS Agreement is not yet granted due to the transitional period for implementation under Art. 65 TRIPS Agreement.[340] The waiver of this obligation is part of a package of measures to mitigate the burdens which the obligations of the TRIPS Agreement impose on developing countries and which affect their capabilities to ensure affordable health care for their populations.

Since the entry into force of the WTO Agreements, the TRIPS Agreement has increasingly come under attack. There are serious contentions within the membership as to the illegitimacy of the TRIPS Agreement in light of values and interests recognized and protected in other international legal regimes, such as human rights treaties, the World Health Organization, or the Convention on Biological Diversity.[341] The limitations that the TRIPS Agreement poses on access to essential medicines received particular attention in light of the expiry of the transitional period on 1 January 2005 for developing countries, such as Brazil, South Africa, India and Thailand, which were important producers of generic medicines. It was argued, inter alia, that the TRIPS Agreement's restrictions on access to affordable (generic) medicines impede the fulfilment

---

338 L/334, and Addendum, adopted 3 March 1955, BISD 3S (1955), 222, 230, para. 41.

339 General Council, Least-Developed Country Members – Obligations Under Article 70.9 of the TRIPS Agreement With Respect to Pharmaceutical Products, Decision of 8 July 2002, WT/L/478 (12 July 2002).

340 On the interpretation of Art. 70 paras. 8 and 9 TRIPS Agreement, see Elfring, 'Article 70', 842, paras. 15–19.

341 See, for example, the contributions in Govaere and Ullrich, *Intellectual Property, Public Policy, and International Trade.*

of human rights, such as the right to life (Art. 6 of the International Covenant on Civil and Political Rights) and the right to the enjoyment of the highest attainable standard of physical and mental health (Art. 12 of the International Covenant on Economic, Social and Cultural Rights).[342] The tension between the promotion of public health through affordable access to essential medicines on the one hand and the protection of intellectual property rights to provide incentives for research and development on the other hand was the subject of intensive debate outside[343] and eventually also within the WTO.

In 2001 the debate on the proper balance between exceptions to patents and patentability to protect public health and the effective protection of intellectual property rights was for the first time officially acknowledged and conducted within the WTO. In June 2001 the TRIPS Council – following a request by Zimbabwe on behalf of the African Group – held a full-day special discussion on intellectual property and access to medicine.[344] Two specific items were discussed, namely the flexibility which members are entitled to under the TRIPS Agreement and the relationship between the TRIPS Agreement and affordable access to medicines.[345]

Subsequently, on 14 November 2001, the Ministerial Conference at Doha adopted the Declaration on the TRIPS Agreement and Public Health.[346] The Declaration acknowledges the serious health problems which many developing and least-developed countries face especially due to HIV/AIDS, tuberculosis, malaria and other epidemics and states that the TRIPS Agreement should not prevent WTO members from taking measures to protect public health. It recognizes the flexibilities which the TRIPS Agreement provides for members to protect public health and promote access to medicine for all.[347] In paragraph 6 the

---

342 For a detailed analysis of whether international law gives rise to a human right to access to medicines and how the TRIPS Agreement interferes with this right, see Hestermeyer, *Human Rights and the WTO*, Chapters 3 and 4; see also Howse and Teitel, 'Beyond the Divide', 10.

343 On the debate outside the WTO in other international institutions such as the WHO, the UN General Assembly, or the Human Rights Commission, see Hestermeyer, *Human Rights and the WTO*, 76 *et seq.*

344 For the minutes of the special discussion on intellectual property and access to medicines, held during the meeting of the TRIPS Council from 18–22 June 2001, see IP/C/M/31 (10 July 2001).

345 *Ibid.*, para. 1.

346 Ministerial Conference, Doha Declaration on the TRIPS Agreement and Public Health, adopted 14 November 2001, WT/MIN(01)/DEC/2 (20 November 2001).

347 *Ibid.* paras. 4, 5.

Declaration calls upon the TRIPS Council to find a solution to the problem that countries with insufficient or no manufacturing capacities in the pharmaceutical sector could face difficulties in making effective use of compulsory licensing under the TRIPS Agreement.[348] It further reaffirms, in paragraph 7, developed-country members' commitments to provide incentives to enterprises and institutions for the promotion and encouragement of technology transfer to least-developed country members pursuant to Art. 66.2 TRIPS Agreement.[349] Finally, the Declaration expresses the agreement that least-developed members will be exempted until 2016 from their obligations to grant patent protection to pharmaceutical products. It calls on the TRIPS Council to give effect to this agreement by extending the transitional period of least-developed country members pursuant to Art. 66.1 of the TRIPS Agreement.[350]

Two decisions were adopted to implement the last part of the Declaration. Firstly, in June 2002 the TRIPS Council extended – pursuant to Art. 66.1 TRIPS Agreement – the transitional period for least-developed countries with respect to their obligations to protect pharmaceutical products and test data until 1 January 2016.[351] Secondly, in July 2002 the General Council adopted the waiver, which has been described above, of least-developed country members' obligations under Art. 70.9 TRIPS Agreement to grant exclusive marketing rights to pharmaceutical products.[352]

348 *Ibid.*, para. 6 (on the implementation of paragraph 6 see B.II.2.2. below).
349 *Ibid.*, para. 7 cl. 1. The obligation of developed-country members under Art. 66.2 TRIPS Agreement with respect to technology transfer is taken up in paragraph 11.2 of the Decision on Implementation Issues and Related Concerns which mandates the TRIPS Council to 'put in place a mechanism for ensuring the monitoring and full implementation of the obligation', Ministerial Conference, Implementation-Related Issues and Concerns, Decision of 14 November 2001, WT/Min(01)/17 (20 November 2001), para. 11.2.
350 *Ibid.*, para. 7 cl. 2, 3.
351 TRIPS Council, Extension of the Transition Period under Article 66:1 of the TRIPS Agreement for Least-Developed Country Members of Certain Obligations With Respect to Pharmaceutical Products, Decision of 27 June 2002, IP/C/25 (1 July 2002). The decision to extend the transition period clarifies that it does not affect the rights of least-developed-country members to seek other extensions of the transition period according to Art. 66:1 TRIPS Agreement, i.e. extensions with respect to obligations not covered by the decision or further extensions of the covered obligations after 1 January 2016. The obligations under the TRIPS Agreement not covered by this decision are suspended for least-developed country members until 1 July 2013, see Council for TRIPS, Extension of the Transition Period under Article 66.1 for Least-Developed Country Members, Decision of 29 November 2005, IP/C/40 (30 November 2005).
352 General Council, Least-Developed Country Members – Obligations Under Article 70.9 of the TRIPS Agreement With Respect to Pharmaceutical Products, Decision of 8 July 2002, WT/L/478 (12 July 2002).

This waiver decision was adopted in addition to the decision to extend the transitional period pursuant to Art. 66.1 TRIPS Agreement since members of the TRIPS Council had been of the view that Art. 66.1 TRIPS Agreement did not authorize the TRIPS Council to apply the extended transitional period also to Art. 70 TRIPS Agreement. The TRIPS Council therefore submitted the draft of a separate waiver decision for adoption to the General Council.[353]

The draft waiver decision, which had been prepared by the Secretariat upon request of the TRIPS Council, had foreseen not only a suspension of obligations to grant exclusive marketing rights, but also a suspension of the so-called mailbox provision in Art. 70.8 TRIPS Agreement.[354] This provision obliges members to enable the filing of patent applications for pharmaceutical and agricultural chemical products even if they are not yet granting patent protection due to the application of a transitional period. Once these applications are processed (upon expiry of the transitional period) the criteria for patentability will be applied as if they were being applied on the date of the filing. Thus it is ensured that the passage of time from the entry into force of the TRIPS Agreement until the examination of the patent application has no detrimental effect for the applicant. If the patent is granted patent protection will be afforded for the remainder of the patent term as calculated from the filing date. While least-developed country members favoured the additional suspension of Art. 70.8 TRIPS Agreement it was opposed by Switzerland, the US and the EC.[355] Consequently, the waiver decision only suspended Art. 70.9 TRIPS Agreement and not the mailbox provision of Art. 70.8 TRIPS Agreement.

The two decisions, the waiver as well as the extension of the transitional period under Art. 66.1 TRIPS Agreement, differ significantly from extension decisions taken under the TRIMs Agreement and the Customs Valuation Agreement.[356] Firstly, they are granted for a significantly longer period (until 2016). Secondly, they benefit all least-developed country members and are not granted on an individual case-by-case basis. And thirdly, it was explicitly noted with respect to the waiver decision that 'it

---

353 Cf. Chairman's statement, Minutes of Meeting of the TRIPS Council held on 25–27 June 2002, IP/C/M/36 (18 July 2002), para. 193.

354 Cf. Chairman's statement, Minutes of Meeting of the TRIPS Council held on 25–27 June 2002, IP/C/M/36 (18 July 2002), paras. 193, 194.

355 Cf. Statements by the representatives of Switzerland, the EC and the United States, Minutes of Meeting of the TRIPS Council held on 25–27 June 2002, IP/C/M/36 (18 July 2002), paras. 195, 202, 204.

356 See *supra* B.I.1.1., B.I.2.1(a).

was understood, in regard to the [annual review of the waiver] that the exceptional circumstances justifying this waiver would continue to exist for least-developed country Members until its expiry date of 2016'.[357] This last statement was made to assure least-developed countries that the waiver decision will not be terminated before its expiry date on the ground that it is no longer necessary to meet their needs. These characteristics demonstrate the acknowledgement by the WTO membership that the difficulties that least-developed country members encounter with the implementation of the obligations of the TRIPS Agreement with respect to pharmaceutical products are of a systemic nature and shared by all least-developed country members.

Despite these difficulties, the two decisions merely defer the obligation of least-developed country members to implement the TRIPS Agreement. They do not formally register doubts – even though serious concerns exist in this respect – that compliance with rules of the TRIPS Agreement also by least-developed countries is generally desirable. As stated by the representative of Senegal on behalf of least-developed countries, the transitional period is perceived as a 'period for building institutional, administrative and other capabilities to enable least-developed countries both to fulfill their obligations and commitments as well as take advantage of their rights'.[358]

2 Modification of legal rules

By contrast to waiver decisions which merely defer the obligation to fully comply with the law, several collective waiver decisions have been adopted under the GATT 1947 and in the WTO that legislate in the sense that they abstractly modify existing legal rules for either all or abstractly defined groups of members. As compared to the waiver decisions discussed in the previous section these waivers do not merely suspend legal obligations. By defining measures or situations in general terms to which a certain obligation shall not apply they create in fact general exceptions to the waived obligation and thus modify it. These waiver decisions are

---

357 See Chairman's statement, Minutes of Meeting of the TRIPS Council held on 25–27 June 2002, IP/C/M (18 July 2002), para. 215.

358 Statement by the Representative of Senegal, speaking on behalf of least-developed countries, Minutes of Meeting of the TRIPS Council held on 25–27 June 2002, IP/C/M (18 July 2002), para. 197. The Senegalese representative stressed in this connection the obligation of developed country members in Art. 66.2 TRIPS Agreement to give incentives to their enterprises and institutions for technology transfer to least-developed country members.

usually presented as furthering the objectives of the organization. Thus these waiver decisions are not to be perceived as merely tolerating non-compliant action but as legal instruments to change the law in accordance with the interests of the membership. This is evidenced by the fact that (with one exception) all of the waivers discussed in this section have been or are intended to be transformed into primary treaty law.

A waiver decision which modifies legal rules for the general membership can be understood as the assertion of a conceptualization of WTO objectives which differs from the conceptualization which was hitherto expressed by the dominant interpretation of the waived obligation. Already Jackson has observed with respect to the waiver practice under the GATT 1947 that the waiver power was used to add new objectives to the GATT.[359]

To date, all collective waiver decisions that modified legal rules have been adopted to address claims that the existing rules did not take sufficient account of the interests and needs of developing country members. The first two of these waiver decisions were adopted in 1971 in order to legalize preferential tariff treatment in accordance with the General System of Preferences as agreed upon in UNCTAD[360] as well as to legalize preferential trade arrangements among developing countries (2.1.a. below).[361] Both of these waiver decisions were replaced in 1979 by the Enabling Clause[362] which – since the entry into force of the WTO Agreement – now forms a permanent part of the GATT 1994.[363] In 1999 the General Council filled an alleged gap in the Enabling Clause's authorization for tariff preferences for developing country products by adopting a waiver decision which allows developing country members to extend non-reciprocal tariff preferences to products from least-developed countries (2.1.b. below).[364] Finally, in 2003, a waiver decision was adopted to implement paragraph 6 of the Doha Declaration on the

---

359 Jackson, *World Trade and the Law of GATT*, 31.
360 CONTRACTING PARTIES, Generalized System of Preferences, Decision of 25 June 1971, L/3545 (28 June 1971).
361 CONTRACTING PARTIES, Trade Negotiations Among Developing Countries, Decision of 26 November 1971, L/3636 (30 November 1971).
362 Differential and More Favourable Treatment, Reciprocity and Fuller Participation of Developing Countries, Decision of 28 November 1979, L/4903 (3 December 1979).
363 It is incorporated into the GATT 1994 through Section 1 lit. b no. iv Introductory Note to GATT 1994.
364 General Council, Preferential Tariff Treatment for Least-Developed Countries, Decision of 15 June 1999, WT/L/304 (17 June 1999). On 27 May 2009 this waiver was extended until 30 June 2019, General Council, Preferential Tariff Treatment for Least-Developed Countries, Decision of 27 May 2009, WT/L/759 (29 May 2009).

TRIPS Agreement and Public Health (2.2 below).[365] In 2005 the General Council adopted an amendment decision with the same content as the waiver decision which upon its entry into force will replace the waiver decision.[366]

2.1 GATT and WTO waivers to legalize trade preferences under the Generalized System of Preferences and among developing countries

In 1971 the CONTRACTING PARTIES adopted two waiver decisions to legalize trade preferences intended to increase export opportunities for products from developing countries and territories. Firstly, they approved a waiver of Art. I:1 GATT to legalize non-reciprocal preferential tariff treatment for products from developing countries that is afforded in accordance with the Generalized System of Preferences (GSP Waiver).[367] Secondly the CONTRACTING PARTIES adopted a waiver of Art. I:1 GATT to legalize tariff preferences among developing countries.[368] A third waiver to legalize trade preferences was adopted in 1999 by the WTO General Council. This waiver decision suspends Art. I:1 GATT to allow developing country members to grant tariff preferences to products from least-developed countries.

(a) 1971 waivers to legalize preferences under GSP and between developing countries   The 1971 GSP Waiver decision[369] suspended Art. I:1 GATT for a period of ten years to the extent necessary to allow contracting parties to adopt GSP legislation. As was discussed above, states had agreed upon a Generalized System of Preferences at the second United Nations Conference on Trade and Development in 1968.[370] It was also agreed that contracting parties to the GATT would ensure the legality of

---

365 General Council, Implementation of Paragraph 6 of the Doha Declaration on the TRIPS Agreement and Public Health, Decision of 30 August 2003, WT/L/540 (2 September 2003) and WT/L/540/Corr. 1 (29 July 2005).

366 General Council, Amendment of the TRIPS Agreement, Decision of 6 December 2005, WT/L/641 (8 December 2005).

367 CONTRACTING PARTIES, Generalized System of Preferences, Decision of 25 June 1971, L/3545 (28 June 1971).

368 CONTRACTING PARTIES, Trade Negotiations Among Developing Countries, Decision of 26 November 1971, L/3636 (30 November 1971).

369 CONTRACTING PARTIES, Generalized System of Preferences, Decision of 25 June 1971, L/3545 (28 June 1971).

370 See *supra* B.I.3.2.

GSP under the GATT.[371] Legality was secured by the 1971 GSP Waiver. The ten-year duration of the waiver is explained by the fact that according to the UNCTAD Agreed Conclusions the GSP was to be initiated for a period of ten years.[372]

The process leading to the adoption of the 1971 GSP Waiver differed from usual waiver practice in that the waiver was not examined by a special working group. Instead prospective donor countries held informal consultations among themselves and drafted a decision which was then submitted to the other contracting parties.[373] The draft decision met with substantial criticism from developing countries. Some of this criticism concerned the form that the legalization of GSP preferences was to take. Héctor Gros Espiell, at the time the representative of Uruguay to the GATT, stressed that it would have been preferable to adopt an interpretative statement based on Part IV on Trade and Development of the GATT which would have made clear that the GATT did not prevent the implementation of GSP by developed countries. In his view the objectives of the GSP were – since the introduction of Part IV – objectives of the GATT. Therefore the waiver power which allowed for the suspension of obligations in *exceptional circumstances* did not seem to him the appropriate instrument.[374] Like several other delegates representing developing countries he stressed that strict adherence to the most-favoured-nation clause resulted in unfairness and inequalities in respect of developing countries and presented the issue of GSP as a matter of justice.[375]

The main substantive criticism related to the fact that the waiver decision left open the question as to which countries were to benefit from the GSP. In particular, European countries which considered themselves developing countries, but had comparatively advanced economies, such as Spain, Greece or Portugal, or communist countries, like Cuba or Poland,

---

371 *Ibid.*

372 UNCTAD UN Doc. Agreed Conclusions of the Special Committee on Preferences, Section VI. Duration.

373 Generalized System of Preferences, Request for a waiver, dated 19 April 1971, submitted by the delegation of Norway on behalf of the prospective donor countries Austria, Canada, Denmark, Finland, Ireland, Japan, New Zealand, Norway, Sweden, Switzerland, the United Kingdom, the United States, and the European Communities and its Member States, C/W/178 (19 May 1971).

374 GATT Council, Minutes of the Meeting on 25 May 1971, C/M/69 (28 May 1971), 8; for more detail on the question of how preferences under GSP should be legalized in the GATT, see Gros Espiell, 'GATT: Accommodating Generalized Preferences', 341.

375 GATT Council, Minutes of the Meeting on 25 May 1971, C/M/69 (28 May 1971) (see statements of the delegates from Peru, Uruguay and Israel).

feared that they would be excluded from some donors' GSP schemes. They were of the view that the waiver should refer to the principle of self-election with respect to developing country status, with the consequence that GSP preferences, which were to be non-discriminatory, had to be extended to all countries which declared themselves to be developing countries.[376] A reference to the principle of self-election was, however, not included. In this point the waiver decision mirrored the state of negotiations in UNCTAD where countries had not been able to agree on a definition of beneficiaries and consequently had left the issue unresolved.[377]

Despite this criticism the waiver was adopted as drafted by the prospective preference-giving contracting parties with forty-five votes in favour and none against.[378] The only concession made to the views of developing countries was the omission of a reference to Art. XXV:5 GATT.[379] The decision did not refer to Part IV on Trade and Development as demanded by developing contracting parties. However, by stating in its preamble that 'a principle aim of the CONTRACTING PARTIES is promotion of the trade and export earnings of developing countries in the furtherance of their economic development'[380] it referenced Part IV implicitly. The preamble further noted, like the UNCTAD Agreed Conclusions, 'the statement of developing countries that the grant of tariff preferences does not constitute a binding commitment and that they are temporary in nature'.[381]

Due to the fact that it had not been possible to agree in UNCTAD on the specifics of the GSP, such as a list of beneficiaries or the scope of preferences, and because only a few prospective donor countries had already drafted GSP legislation, the waiver decision remained vague. It waived Art. I GATT to the extent necessary to permit prospective donor countries to accord preferential tariff treatment to products from developing countries without according such treatment to like products from other contracting parties.[382] The preferential tariff treatment was

---

376 GATT Council, Minutes of the Meeting on 25 May 1971, C/M/69 (28 May 1971) (see statements of the delegates from Spain, Portugal, Cuba, Greece, Turkey and Poland).
377 UNCTAD UN Doc. Agreed Conclusions of the Special Committee on Preferences, Section IV Beneficiaries.
378 CONTRACTING PARTIES, Generalized System of Preferences, Decision of 25 June 1971, L/3545 (28 June 1971), fn. 1.
379 A prior text proposed by donor countries had invoked Article XXV:5 GATT, see Gros Espiell, 'GATT: Accommodating Generalized Preferences', 341, 360. The decision does not refer either to the existence of 'exceptional circumstances'.
380 CONTRACTING PARTIES, Decision of 25 June 1971, L/3545 (28 June 1971), preamble, first recital.
381 *Ibid.*, preamble, recital 5.   382 *Ibid.*, para. (a).

specified by reference to the preamble which itself referred to the 'mutually acceptable system of generalized, non-reciprocal and non-discriminatory preferences' agreed at UNCTAD.[383]

When the waiver was adopted it was clear that some donor countries wished to exclude certain countries from the benefit of preferences even though these countries considered themselves to be developing countries and therefore entitled to preferences. On the other hand there seemed to be agreement when the waiver was adopted that donor countries should not be entirely free in the design of their preference schemes. If a country decided to adopt GSP legislation, preferences had to be generalized, non-discriminatory and non-reciprocal, as stated in the waiver and designed to facilitate trade from developing countries.

While the extent of the legal limitations on donors' freedom to devise GSP schemes is a matter of interpretation, it is important here to note the following: the waiver's description of the preference schemes covered by the waiver was made in abstract terms. The waiver neither legalized specific GSP legislation of individual contracting parties nor did it include a flexible reference to UNCTAD, i.e. it did not refer to UNCTAD for a further definition of permissible GSP schemes. Thus the waiver established a new general rule which could be formulated as follows: Art. I:1 GATT shall not prevent contracting parties from according generalized, non-reciprocal and non-discriminatory preferential tariff treatment to products from developing countries.[384]

In practice GSP arrangements differ very much both in respect of the beneficiaries and the scope of preferences. GSP legislation is often used as an instrument of foreign policy to promote national interests of the donor. This is done through so-called conditionality according to which the extension of preferences is either made conditional on compliance with certain requirements or preferences can be withdrawn if requirements are not met. Such conditions include, for example, the protection of international property rights, minimum labour and environmental standards or cooperation in the fight against terrorism.[385] The economic

383 *Ibid.*, preamble, recital 3. The waiver further included provisions on the review of the waiver, notification of GSP schemes, consultation and dispute settlement (paras. (b)–(e)).

384 On the subsequent GSP practice which did not conform to these requirements, see Howse, 'India's WTO Challenge to Drug Enforcement Conditions', 385.

385 *Ibid.*; Bartels, *Human Rights Conditionality in the EU's International Agreements*; on conditionality in the US GSP up to the GSP law of 1984, Hudec, *Developing Countries in the GATT Legal System*, 112–16. The Appellate Body report in *EC – Tariff Preferences* set

benefits for the preference-receiving countries of tariff preferences are disputed.[386]

In November 1971, a few months after the adoption of the GSP Waiver, the CONTRACTING PARTIES adopted a second waiver decision which suspended Art. I:1 GATT to permit developing contracting parties to grant preferential treatment to products from one another's markets.[387]

The waiver decision, just like the GSP Waiver, did not refer to Art. XXV:5 GATT.[388] It was adopted without a time limit and suspended the application of Art. I:1 GATT for trade preferences to be accorded under the Protocol Relating to Trade Negotiations among Developing Countries.[389] Robert Hudec referred to the Protocol as a 'mini-GATT between developing countries'. It had schedules of tariff concessions and GATT-like rules providing a legal framework for concessions to be negotiated among developing countries.[390] This Protocol was the basis for the subsequent Agreement on a Global System of Trade Preferences among Developing Countries (GSTP) which was negotiated in UNCTAD and entered into force in 1989.[391]

Despite the often limited benefits that developing countries derive from preference schemes, the two waiver decisions fundamentally affected the legal relationship between developing and developed countries in the GATT. In the words of Hudec:

> out some limits on conditionality in that it interpreted the Enabling Clause to require that differential treatment among beneficiaries shall respond to development concerns (WT/DS246/AB/R, adopted 20 April 2004). For an analysis of the consequences of this report for conditionality, see Bartels, 'WTO Enabling Clause and Positive Conditionality', 507. For a proposal to increase legal security for preference-receiving developing countries see Bartels and Häberli, 'Binding Tariff Preferences for Developing Countries', 969.

386 Hudec, *Developing Countries in the GATT Legal System*; 'Dunoff, Dysfunction, Diversion, and the Debate over Preferences', 45, 50 *et seq.* (noting that much of the literature on the economic effects of preferences is deeply sceptical about their value to promote development (at 51)); Hoekman and Özden, 'Trade Preferences and Differential Treatment of Developing Countries'.

387 CONTRACTING PARTIES, Trade Negotiations Among Developing Countries, Decision of 26 November 1971, L/3636 (30 November 1971).

388 It did, however, contrary to the 1971 GSP Waiver, refer to Part IV GATT.

389 BISD 18S (1972), 11.

390 Hudec, *GATT Legal System and World Trade Diplomacy*, 108 *et seq.*

391 On the GSTP, see *Ibid.*, 108 *et seq*; R. E. Hudec, 'Structure of South–South Trade Preferences in the 1988 GSTP Agreement', 210.

The two waivers of Article I in 1971 can be viewed as the end of the period of upheaval that began with the 1957 ministers resolution which called for the Haberler Report. By 1971, the GATT's new relationship with developing countries had been redefined.[392]

Some authors even took the decisions as support for the emergence of a general and binding principle in international law of preferential and non-reciprocal treatment in trade affairs, one of the principles of the New International Economic Order.[393]

Following the demand by developing countries that the exception from most-favoured-nation treatment for GSP preferences be made permanent, CONTRACTING PARTIES adopted the so-called Enabling Clause during the Tokyo Round.[394] The Enabling Clause inter alia authorizes GSP preferences and preferences among developing countries and was meant to be a de facto amendment to the most-favoured-nation obligation in Art. I GATT.[395]

(b) 1999 waiver for preferential tariff treatment for least-developed countries In line with the practice commenced with the 1971 waivers the General Council in 1999 adopted a further decision which initially waived Art. I:1 GATT for a period of ten years, this time 'to the extent necessary to allow developing country Members to provide preferential tariff treatment to products of least-developed countries, designated as such by the United Nations, without being required to extend the same tariff rates to like products of any other Member'.[396] The decision further requires that preferential tariff treatment shall be provided

---

392 Hudec, *GATT Legal System and World Trade Diplomacy*, 65.

393 Yusuf, *Legal Aspects of Trade Preferences for Developing States*, 168; cf. Onyejekwe, 'International Law of Trade Preferences', 425, 435 (stating that the right to development entails an obligation on the side of developed countries to grant tariff preferences to products from developing countries).

394 CONTRACTING PARTIES, Differential and More Favourable Treatment, Reciprocity and Fuller Participation of Developing Countries, Decision of 28 November 1979 (L/4903), BISD 26S (1980), 203.

395 Hudec, *GATT Legal System and World Trade Diplomacy*, 85. The Enabling Clause furthermore authorizes preferential treatment of developing countries with respect to GATT rules dealing with non-tariff trade barriers and special preferences for least-developed countries. On the differences between the Enabling Clause and the 1971 GSP waiver with respect to the authorization of GSP preferences, see Howse, 'India's WTO Challenge to Drug Enforcement Conditions', 385, 387 *et seq.*

396 General Council, Preferential Tariff Treatment for Least-Developed Countries, Decision of 15 June 1999, WT/L/304 (17 June 1999), para. 1.

'on a generalized, non-reciprocal and non-discriminatory basis'.[397] On 12 May 2009 the General Council approved a ten-year extension of this waiver.[398]

The 1999 Preferences Waiver closes a gap in the Enabling Clause with respect to preferential tariff treatment among developing countries. Para. 2 (c) of the Enabling Clause allows for reciprocal tariff preferences granted within regional or global arrangements among developing country members and para. 2 (d) allows for special treatment of least-developed countries in the context of such arrangements. WTO members were, however, of the view that the Enabling Clause did not exempt from the application of Art. I:1 GATT non-reciprocal tariff preferences granted by developing country members to least-developed countries outside regional arrangements or the Global System of Trade Preferences.[399] Footnote 2 to para. 2 of the Enabling Clause states that it remains 'open for the CONTRACTING PARTIES to consider on an *ad hoc* basis under the GATT provisions for joint action any proposals for differential and more favourable treatment not falling within the scope of this paragraph'. This footnote has been interpreted as referring to the possibility that waiver decisions are adopted to legalize preferential treatment not covered by the Enabling Clause.[400]

Preferences by developing country members to products from least-developed countries are seen as suitable measures to further the objectives of the WTO and to better integrate least-developed countries into the world trading system as demanded by the 1994 Ministerial Decision on Measures in Favour of Least-Developed Countries as well as the Comprehensive and Integrated WTO Plan of Action for the Least-Developed Countries adopted at the Singapore Ministerial

---

397 *Ibid.*, para. 2. Curiously this obligation is hidden in the formulation of the requirement to notify the Council on Trade in Goods of the scope of preferential tariff treatment to be afforded.

398 General Council, Preferential Tariff Treatment for Least-Developed Countries, Decision of 27 May 2009, WT/L/759 (29 May 2009).

399 See Statement by the Deputy Director-General in the Committee on Trade and Development, Note on the Meeting of 2 March 1999, WT/COMTD/M/24 (27 April 1999), para. 32. For the view that these preferences are covered by para. 2 (d) of the Enabling Clause, see Bartels and Häberli, 'Binding Tariff Preferences for Developing Countries', 969, 973.

400 Statement by the Deputy Director-General in the Committee on Trade and Development, Note on the Meeting of 2 March 1999, WT/COMTD/M/24 (27 April 1999), para. 35.

Conference on 13 December 1996[401] and the Ministerial Declaration of 20 May 1998.[402]

The waiver has the effect of adding a further general exception to the most-favoured-nation obligation which may be formulated as follows: Art. I:1 GATT shall not prevent developing country members from providing preferential tariff treatment to products from least-developed countries that is granted on a generalized, non-reciprocal and non-discriminatory basis.

2.2 The TRIPS Waiver

The 2003 TRIPS Waiver has to date been the last collective waiver decision that generally modifies legal norms. It releases the requirements for compulsory licensing with respect to pharmaceutical products and thus addresses one particularly contentious issue in the debate on the proper balance between patent protection and access to affordable medicines: the question under which conditions WTO members are allowed under the TRIPS Agreement to permit the production and export of patented medicines without the permission of the patent holder in order to address a health crisis on the territory of another WTO member that itself lacks manufacturing capacity.

Some members were of the opinion that production and export of patented medicines without permission of the patent holder was allowed under Art. 30 of the TRIPS Agreement, which provides limited exceptions to the exclusive rights conferred by a patent.[403] This view was, however, not shared by developed country members.[404] Another avenue to produce and sell patented medicines without permission of the patent

---

401 Ministerial Conference, Singapore Ministerial Declaration, adopted 13 December 1996, WT/MIN(96)/DEC (18 December 1996), para. 14.

402 Ministerial Conference, Ministerial Declaration, adopted 20 May 1998, WT/MIN(98)/DEC1 (25 May 1998). Pieter Jan Kuijper criticized the long time that it took to adopt this waiver and noted 'the callousness with which a crucial waiver for dirt-poor countries can be held hostage for years in the Council for Trade in Goods and at lower levels': Kuijper, 'Sutherland Report and the WTO's Institutional Law', 191, 194.

403 See Communication of Brazil on behalf of the delegations of Bolivia, Brazil, Cuba, China, Dominican Republic, Ecuador, India, Indonesia, Pakistan, Peru, Sri Lanka, Thailand, and Venezuela, dated 21 June 2002, IP/C/W/355 (24 June 2002).

404 See Statement of the Representative of the United States, Minutes of the Meeting of the TRIPS Council on 5–7 March 2002, IP/C/M/35 (22 March 2002), para. 84. In the only panel report which to date has interpreted Art. 30, the provision was interpreted narrowly, see Panel Report, *Canada – Pharmaceutical Patents*, WT/DS114/R, adopted 7 April 2000, paras. 7.39 *et seq.*; Howse, 'Canadian Generic Medicines Panel', 493, 506

holder is provided for in Art. 31 TRIPS Agreement. This provision allows members under certain conditions to grant compulsory licences which authorize the use of the subject matter of a patent, e.g. the production or sale of the patented product, without the consent of the patent holder. However, Art. 31(f) TRIPS Agreement imposes the limitation that a compulsory licence shall authorize the use 'predominantly for the market of the member authorizing such use'. Since many of the developing countries in urgent need of essential medicines do not themselves have the manufacturing capacity to produce these medicines, they depend on imports from other members. These other members are, however, due to Art. 31(f) TRIPS Agreement, not allowed to grant compulsory licences for the production of medicines predominately destined for foreign markets. These restrictions of the TRIPS Agreement's norms on compulsory licensing are recognized in paragraph 6 of the 2001 Doha Declaration on the TRIPS Agreement and Public Health,[405] which instructs the TRIPS Council 'to find an expeditious solution to this problem and to report to the General Council before the end of 2002'.

In August 2003, after long and controversial discussions in the TRIPS Council, paragraph 6 of the Doha Declaration on the TRIPS Agreement and Public Health was eventually implemented by a waiver decision which modifies the rules on compulsory licensing.[406] The debates centered on substantive questions as to which products or processes should benefit from the solution, which WTO members should be the beneficiaries, which the supplying countries, on conditions such as safeguards against trade diversion, on notification requirements, and on the question of remuneration of the patent holders. The legal mechanism to be chosen was also extensively discussed. While some developing countries initially favoured an authoritative interpretation of Art. 30,[407] most industrialized countries supported a modification of Art. 31(f). Some wanted to achieve this modification through an amendment coupled with an interim

---

(criticizing the report for unduly curbing the regulatory autonomy of members and potentially undermining the legitimacy of the WTO).

405   Ministerial Conference, Doha Declaration on the TRIPS Agreement and Public Health, adopted 14 November 2001, WT/MIN(01)/DEC/2 (20 Nov. 2001). On the content of the declaration see *supra* section B.II.1.2.

406   On the process which eventually led to the adoption of the waiver decision, see Abbott, 'WTO Medicines Decision', 317.

407   See Communication of Brazil on behalf of the delegations of Bolivia, Brazil, Cuba, China, Dominican Republic, Ecuador, India, Indonesia, Pakistan, Peru, Sri Lanka, Thailand, and Venezuela, dated 21 June 2002, IP/C/W/355 (24 June 2002).

solution of a waiver or moratorium on dispute settlement;[408] others believed that a waiver would be a suitable final solution.[409]

In December 2002 a consensus on a draft text of a waiver decision – the so-called Motta Draft named after the then chairman of the TRIPS Council Ambassador Motta – failed due to opposition by the US to the scope of application. While the draft referred to paragraph 1 of the Doha Declaration on the TRIPS Agreement and Public Health which mentions HIV/AIDS, tuberculosis, malaria, *and other epidemics*, the US had wished to restrict the application of the decision to HIV/Aids, malaria, and tuberculosis.[410] Subsequently, discussions continued and the issue was at last resolved in August 2003 when the TRIPS Council approved a draft decision – which was identical to the Motta Draft – to be forwarded to the General Council for adoption.[411]

The General Council adopted the waiver decision on 30 August 2003.[412] It waives the requirement that a compulsory licence shall authorize use of a patent predominantly for the supply of the domestic market (Art. 31(f) of the TRIPS Agreement) and the obligation to pay adequate remuneration to the right holder when a compulsory licence is issued (Art. 31(h) of the TRIPS Agreement) if certain conditions are met. The products covered are all pharmaceutical sector patented products, or products manufactured under a patented process, needed to address public health problems as recognized in paragraph 1 of the Doha Declaration.[413] Eligible importing

---

408 See TRIPS Council, Minutes of the Meeting on 17–19 September 2002, IP/C/M/37 (11 October 2002), e.g. at para. 67 (statement of the representative of the EC), para. 65 (statement of the representative of Norway).

409 *Ibid.*, para. 63 (statement of the representative of the United States), para. 66 (statement of the representative of Australia), para. 69 (statement of the representative of Canada). The US had initially proposed to address the problem with a moratorium on dispute settlement, see Communication of the United States, dated 8 March 2002, IP/C/W/340 (14 March 2002).

410 See TRIPS Council, Minutes of the Meeting on 25–27, 29 November 2002 and 20 December 2002, IP/C/M/38 (5 Feb. 2003), at para. 34 (statement by the representative of the United States). On 20 December 2002 the US declared a moratorium on dispute settlement: Communication by the United States to the TRIPS Council, Moratorium to Address Needs of Developing and Least-Developed Members with No or Insufficient Manufacturing Capacities in the Pharmaceutical Sector, IP/C/W/396 (14 January 2003).

411 TRIPS Council, Minutes of the Meeting on 28 August 2003, IP/C/M/41 (7 November 2003), para. 3.

412 General Council, Minutes of the Meeting on 30 August 2003, WT/GC/M/82 (13 November 2003), para. 31. The waiver decision was accompanied by a statement of the chairman (*ibid.*, at para. 29) which, however, does not form part of the waiver decision.

413 General Council, Implementation of Paragraph 6 of the Doha Declaration on the TRIPS Agreement and Public Health, Decision of 30 August 2003, WT/L/540 (2 September

members are any least-developed country member and any other WTO member which has notified the TRIPS Council of its intention to use the system as an importer.[414]

Art. 31(f) of the TRIPS Agreement is waived for the exporting country member on the condition that an eligible importing member notifies the TRIPS Council that it has insufficient or no manufacturing capacity in the pharmaceutical sector for the product in question,[415] and has itself granted a compulsory licence or intends to do so if the product is also patented within its territory.[416] With respect to the compulsory licence granted by the importing country the obligation in Art. 31(h) to remunerate the right holder is waived.[417] The decision further includes terms to ensure transparency and prevent trade diversion[418] and a special provision which waives Art. 31(f) for exports from developing country members and least-developed country members that are party to a Regional Trade Agreement to other developing or least-developed parties to this agreement.[419]

The waiver decision does not specify a termination date as required by Art. IX:4 WTO Agreement; instead it states that it will terminate for each member when the amendment replacing the decision takes effect for that member.[420] On 6 December 2005 the General Council adopted an amendment decision based on a proposal by the TRIPS Council.[421] This amendment will enter into force for the accepting members upon

---

2003), para. 1(a). The scope of diseases was thus not limited as had been proposed by the US.

414 *Ibid.*, para. 1(b). A number of developed country members are mentioned in footnote 3 to para. 1(b) that will not use the system set out in the decision.

415 *Ibid.*, para. 2(a)(ii). This requirement does not apply to LDC members.

416 *Ibid.*, para. 2(a).

417 *Ibid.*, para. 3; the decision states in para. 3(1) that the exporting member when paying remuneration in accordance with Art. 31(h) shall take into account the economic value to the importing member of the use which was authorized by the exporting member.

418 *Ibid.*, paras. 2, 4, 5.

419 *Ibid.*, para. 6. In addition the decision imposes certain obligations on all members. These are the obligation on all developed members to provide technical and financial cooperation in order to facilitate implementation of the provision on the prevention of re-exportation and the obligation on all members to prevent the importation of diverted products produced under the system set out in the decision (para. 4).

420 *Ibid.*, para. 11. A second deviation from Art. IX:4 is the stipulation in para. 8 that an annual review by the TRIPS Council fulfils the review requirements of Art. IX:4 which provides for the annual review of waivers by the General Council.

421 General Council, Amendment of the TRIPS Agreement, Decision of 6 December 2005, WT/L/641 (8 December 2005). On the negotiating history, see Hestermeyer, *Human Rights and the WTO*, 272–4.

acceptance by two-thirds of the members (Art. X:3 WTO Agreement) and formally incorporate the August 2003 decision into the TRIPS Agreement. The deadline for acceptance of the amendment, which was originally set for 1 December 2007, so far has been extended twice by decisions of the General Council and presently ends on 31 December 2011.[422]

The system established by the waiver was harshly criticized, in particular by non-governmental organizations such as Médecins sans Frontières, for being overly burdensome and inefficient.[423] Indeed, only in 2007 did the first WTO members, namely Canada and Rwanda, notify the TRIPS Council that they intended to make use of the decision. Rwanda gave notice that it wished to import a certain amount of an AIDS medication from Canada, and Canada notified the TRIPS Council that it had issued a compulsory licence to produce and export this medication.[424] It is true that an interpretation of Art. 30 of the TRIPS Agreement would have been preferable from a human rights and development perspective.[425] In light of the extremely divergent interests on this issue it has to be welcomed, however, that some norm change in favour of public health in developing countries was achieved within the WTO.[426] While the 1971 waivers can be seen as the legal codification of a successful redefinition of the legal relationship between developing and developed countries in the GATT, the TRIPS Waiver readjusts the balance of economic and competing non-economic values within the TRIPS Agreement.

3 Regime linkage

Apart from suspension and general modification of WTO obligations, collective waiver decisions have also been used to coordinate WTO law with the law of other international legal regimes. Such coordination is

---

422 General Council, Decision of 18 December 2007, WT/L/711 (21 December 2007); General Council, Decision of 17 December 2009, WT/L/785 (21 December 2009). On the acceptance by the European Union and the probability of further acceptances, see Kennedy, 'When Will the Protocol Amending the TRIPS Agreement Enter into Force?', 459.

423 On the amendment decision, see ICTSD, 'Members Strike Deal on TRIPS and Public Health'.

424 On these notifications, see Hestermeyer, 'Canadian-Made Drugs for Rwanda'.

425 Cf. Correa, *Implications of the Doha Declaration*, 28–30, www.who.int/medicines/areas/policy/WHO_EDM_PAR_2002.3.pdf (last accessed 11 March 2011).

426 For a positive view on the TRIPS Waiver, see e.g. Abbott, 'WTO Medicines Decision', 317. On the practice of the United States of seeking a higher level of intellectual property protection through the inclusion of TRIPS plus obligations in bilateral free trade agreements, see Oxfam, 'All Costs, No Benefits'.

important in an international legal order which is characterized not only by sectoral fragmentation, but also by a division of work within sectors between different institutions.

Waiver decisions have achieved linkage between the WTO and another international legal regime in two constellations. Firstly, collective Harmonized System (HS) waivers coordinate WTO law and the law of the World Customs Organization in the area of product classification (3.1 below). These waiver decisions are a device to link these two regimes which pursue the overlapping objective of trade facilitation. They can be understood as contributing to the effective pursuit of the objective of trade facilitation in a regime complex constituted of WTO and World Customs Organization (WCO) law.[427]

Secondly, a collective waiver decision was adopted to legalize trade measures foreseen by another international legal regime, namely the Kimberley Process Certification Scheme for Rough Diamonds (3.2 below). A waiver such as this one, that suspends WTO norms to allow for the adoption of measures mandated by another legal regime with potentially competing objectives, can be understood as an acknowledgement by the WTO of the importance of another regime's objectives and the latter's greater expertise and legitimacy with respect to their attainment. The waiver avoids norm conflict by limiting the WTO's jurisdiction in favour of the other regime.

3.1 Collective Harmonized System waivers: effective cooperation in a regime complex

Harmonized System waivers suspend Art. II GATT for WTO members that have implemented changes to the Harmonized Commodity Description and Coding System (the Harmonized System/HS) in their domestic tariffs, but need more time to adapt their GATT schedules of concessions accordingly.[428] While under the GATT 1947 Harmonized System waivers were adopted individually on a case-by-case basis,[429] in the WTO most

---

427 On the concept of regime complex see Raustiala and Victor, 'Regime Complex for Plant Genetic Resources', 277 (defining regime complex as 'an array of partially overlapping and nonhierarchical institutions governing a particular issue-area', at 279).

428 On the need of WTO members for a waiver when they are implementing HS2002 changes domestically, but have not yet completed the procedures to introduce these changes into their schedules, see Committee on Market Access, Minutes of the Meeting of 15 March 2002 and the resumed Meeting of 12 June 2002, G/MA/M/31 (26 June 2002), para. 4.1.

429 On the practice of the adoption of individual HS waiver decisions, see *supra* section B.I.1.2.

Harmonized System waivers are granted on a collective basis, i.e. one decision is granted to all members who request to be covered by the waiver and who fulfil certain conditions. Up to the end of 2010, twenty-six collective Harmonized System waivers (including extension decisions) have been adopted by the WTO General Council.[430] These waivers, together with the procedures for the introduction of Harmonized System changes to schedules of concessions,[431] ensure the effectiveness and legality of the adaptation of domestic tariffs and schedules of concessions to changes in the Harmonized System.

The waiver decisions recognize that the Harmonized System facilitates international trade and plays an important role for the monitoring and protection of tariff concessions.[432] By enabling the implementation of Harmonized System changes the Harmonized System waivers and procedures provide a linkage between two regimes which pursue the shared objective of trade facilitation. They enable the use by WTO members of a trade tool – the Harmonized System – which is administered by another international institution, the World Customs Organization (WCO).

To understand the relevance and function of HS waivers some information on the Harmonized System and its significance for international trade is required. The Harmonized System provides a common vocabulary by classifying all traded goods according to a nomenclature.[433] This common vocabulary facilitates, and avoids misunderstandings in, communications about products. It thus reduces transaction costs and consequently is of eminent economic importance for today's globalized trade relations. Take for example WTO tariff negotiations with respect to chocolate: while one party might assume that the product commonly referred to as white chocolate is included in the negotiations on chocolate, the other trading partner might assume that it is excluded for the reason that it does not

---

430 For the collective waivers granted by the General Council for the HS1996, HS2002 and HS2007 transposition exercises, see Note by the Secretariat, Committee on Market Access, Situation of Schedules of WTO Members, G/MA/W/23/Rev. 6 (19 March 2009).

431 General Council, A Procedure for the Introduction of Harmonized System 2007 Changes to Schedules of Concessions Using the Consolidated Tariff Schedules (CTS) Database, Decision of 15 December 2006, WT/L/673 (18 December 2006) (concerning the implementation of HS2007 changes).

432 See, for example, General Council, Introduction of Harmonized System 2007 Changes into WTO Schedules of Tariff Concessions, Decision of 15 December 2006, WT/L/675 (19 December 2006) preamble, recital 2.

433 The following paragraphs are based on Feichtner, 'Administration of the Vocabulary of International Trade', 1481.

contain cocoa and thus does not qualify as chocolate. Reference during the negotiations to specific positions of the HS nomenclature reduces the probability of such misunderstandings. If during the exemplary tariff negotiations parties would refer to the HS heading 'Chocolate' no party could later claim that the negotiated tariff should also apply to white chocolate since the HS classifies the product which is commonly referred to as white chocolate not under the heading 'Chocolate', but under the heading 'Sugar Confectionery'.[434]

The Harmonized System is annexed to, and forms an integral part of, the International Convention on the Harmonized Commodity Description and Coding System (HS Convention) which was established under the auspices of the Customs Cooperation Council, now the World Customs Organization. The HS Convention entered into force on 1 January 1988 and replaced the Brussels Convention on Nomenclature for the Classification of Goods in Customs Tariffs of 1950.[435] By the end of 2010, 138 countries and customs/economic unions were parties to the convention. While only parties to the convention are obliged to use the HS nomenclature for their customs tariff and statistical nomenclatures, all in all, more than 200 countries and economies use the HS nomenclature as the basis for their customs tariffs and trade statistics.[436]

The HS is relevant for various international institutions,[437] not only in the economic sector. However, its relevance is greatest within the WTO which shares with the WCO the objective of facilitation of international trade.[438] Several WTO agreements, such as the Agricultural Agreement and the Information Technology Agreement refer for their product

---

434 To be sure, even when the HS is used, classification of products will frequently be contentious. See, for example, the dispute between the European Communities on one side and Brazil and Thailand on the other concerning the classification of salted frozen boneless chicken cuts, Appellate Body Report, *EC – Chicken Classification*, WT/DS269, 286/AB/R, adopted 27 September 2005.

435 The Brussels Convention had replaced the so-called Geneva Nomenclature of 1937.

436 See www.wcoomd.org/home_wco_topics_hsoverviewboxes_hsharmonizedsystem.htm. WCO members are not obliged to become parties to the HS Convention and at the same time parties to the HS Convention do not necessarily have to be members of the WCO (Art. 11(c) HS Convention).

437 Examples are the Convention on International Trade in Endangered Species of Wild Fauna and Flora (CITES), the Basel Convention, the United Nations Food and Agricultural Organization, or the Montreal Protocol. The trade statistical systems of the UN (e.g. the Standard International Trade Classification (SITC) and Central Product Classification (CPC)) are also based on the HS nomenclature.

438 Cf. WTO Agreement, preamble, 1st recital.

coverage to the Harmonized System. The draft rules of non-preferential origin have also been based on the HS.[439] Most importantly, WTO schedules of concessions for goods are based on the HS nomenclature. Today, practically all WTO members base their national tariffs, i.e. their structured lists of product descriptions[440] according to which customs duties are imposed and administered, on the HS nomenclature and have schedules which are based on the HS even though not all WTO members are parties to the HS Convention.[441] During the Uruguay Round tariff negotiations were based on the Harmonized System nomenclature,[442] and on 1 August 2004 WTO members agreed to finalize the results of the currently ongoing non-agricultural market access negotiations of the Doha Round in the HS2002 nomenclature.[443]

The HS, including the notes and general rules of interpretation, as well as explanatory notes and WCO classification decisions of the HS Committee, help WTO members to interpret and determine the content of concessions and to monitor compliance with the obligation in Art. II GATT to grant the negotiated concessions.[444] The HS is also relevant for the interpretation of other WTO obligations relating to goods. Most importantly the HS classification of a product can be one factor in the determination of the 'likeness' of products, a requirement for the application of the most-favoured-nation (Art. I GATT) or national treatment obligation (Art. III GATT).[445]

---

439 The Technical Committee on Rules of Origin which carries out the main technical work of harmonizing non-preferential rules of origin was established by the WTO and is a WTO body, but operates under the auspices of the WCO with the WCO Council exercising supervision over it (Art. 4:2 Agreement on Rules of Origin).

440 Bossche, *Law and Policy of the World Trade Organization*, 379.

441 As of 31 March 2006, seventy-eight WTO members (counting the EC-25 as one) were contracting parties to the HS Convention, www.wto.org/English/thewto_e/coher_e/wto_wco_e.htm (last accessed 12 March 2011).

442 Bossche, *Law and Policy of the World Trade Organization*, 401, 419.

443 General Council, Doha Work Programme, Decision adopted 1 August 2004, WT/L/579 (2 August 2004), Annex B, paragraph 5. That tariff negotiations are conducted on the basis of the HS does not mean that WTO members are limited by the product differentiations which the HS provides. They may further differentiate and negotiate tariff cuts with respect to only a subgroup of a product group subsumed under a subposition of the HS.

444 The relevance of the HS for the interpretation of concessions has been confirmed by the Appellate Body in *EC – Computer Equipment*, WT/DS62, 67, 68/AB/R, adopted 22 June 1998, para. 89 and *EC – Chicken Classification*, WT/DS269, 286/AB/R, adopted 27 September 2005, para. 199.

445 Appellate Body Report, *Japan – Alcoholic Beverages II*, WT/DS8/AB/R, WT/DS10/AB/R, WT/DS11/AB/R, adopted 1 November 1996, 21, 22.

For it to remain viable as a common vocabulary, the HS has to be regularly adapted to changes in reality, such as the development of new products and changing trade patterns, as well as to changes in the needs of its users.[446] The HS is revised – and the HS Convention amended accordingly – every four to six years.[447] The amendments are referred to as Harmonized System changes: the amendments, for example, which entered into force on 1 January 1996 are termed Harmonized System 1996 changes or HS1996 changes.

The contracting parties to the HS Convention are obliged to implement these changes by the time they enter into force.[448] Implementation requires the transposition of HS changes into national tariffs. In turn WTO schedules also need to be adapted to the HS in order to match national tariffs. The adaptation of schedules follows legal procedures adopted under the GATT and in the WTO for each set of HS changes.[449] With respect to the adaptation of schedules to Harmonized System changes, these legal procedures serve three purposes. First, they formally legalize modifications of the treaty which result from modifications of schedules of concessions; second, they are intended to increase the efficiency of the adaptation exercise; and third, the procedures ensure transparency in order to enable members to detect whether concessions in which they have an interest are affected by the implementation exercise. If possible, existing tariff bindings shall remain unaffected by the adaptation of schedules to the HS.[450] If, however, the value of concessions is negatively affected by the adaptation exercise, the respective concessions have to be renegotiated according to Art. XXVIII GATT, with the aim

---

446 The HS Convention recognizes in its preamble the 'importance of ensuring that the Harmonized System is kept up to date in the light of changes in technology or in patterns of international trade' (recital 11).

447 In 1988 the WCO Council endorsed a conclusion by the HS Committee to review the HS at regular intervals of three to four years. So far revisions to the HS have entered into force in 1992, 1996, 2002 and 2007, they are referred to as the HS1992, HS1996, HS2002 and HS2007 changes.

448 A developing contracting party may, according to Art. 4:1 HS Convention, delay the application of all or some subheadings.

449 L/5470/Rev. 1 (30 June 1983) (for the adaptation of schedules of concessions to the Harmonized System); L/6905 (20 September 1991) (aimed at the incorporation of HS1992 changes into GATT schedules as well as any future changes and used for the incorporation of HS1992 and HS1996 changes); WT/L/407 (26 July 2001) and WT/L/605 (2 March 2005) (for HS2002 changes); WT/L/673 (18 December 2006) (for HS2007 changes).

450 See, for example, WT/L/673, para. 4.

of maintaining a general level of reciprocal and mutually advantageous concessions.[451]

Due to the administrative complexity of the transposition exercise and the need for tariff renegotiations, most WTO members cannot complete the adaptation of their schedules of concessions to HS changes before the Harmonized System changes take effect. To legalize the domestic implementation of HS changes in the interim, i.e. until the schedules have been adapted to these changes as well, Harmonized System waivers are granted. These waivers are discussed in the Committee on Market Access which is mandated 'to ensure that GATT Schedules are kept up-to-date, and that modifications, including those resulting from changes in tariff nomenclature, are reflected'.[452] They suspend Art. II GATT to avoid violations where the application of a changed domestic tariff negatively affects tariff reduction commitments.

Under the GATT 1947, when these waivers were adopted on an individual basis, it was a recurrent criticism by developed contracting parties in the Committee on Tariff Concessions that these waivers were granted and extended almost automatically.[453] They were granted in particular to developing contracting parties who, mainly due to capacity problems, encountered difficulties in the process of adapting their schedules to the HS.

In the WTO, HS waivers are now mostly granted on a collective basis. The practice of adopting collective waiver decisions instead of individual waivers was instituted in 1995 with respect to the HS1996 changes.[454] At first the collective HS1996 Waiver was granted to members that requested to be included in an annex to the decision. Later extension decisions not only covered members listed in an annex, but provided that further members would be covered if they notified the Committee on Market Access of their wish to benefit from the waiver.[455] Until 2001 the

---

451 L/5470/Rev. 1 (30 June 1983), Annex 1, para. 1.

452 General Council, WTO Committee on Market Access, Decision adopted on 31 January 1995, WT/L/47 (17 February 1995), para. C.

453 See, for example, Proposal by Sweden, Requests for Extensions of [HS] Waivers, TAR/W/88 (23 September 1993).

454 The first collective waiver decision was General Council, Introduction of Harmonized System Changes into WTO Schedules of Tariff Concessions on 1 January 1996, Decision of 13 December 1995, WT/L/124 (16 January 1996).

455 This practice was instituted with General Council, Introduction of Harmonized System 2002 Changes into WTO Schedules of Tariff Concessions, Decision of 12 December 2002, WT/L/511 (20 January 2003), para. (b).

collective HS1996 Waiver was only granted and extended for periods of six months;[456] in May 2001 it was extended for one last time for the period of one year.[457] Collective HS2002 and collective HS2007 Waiver decisions have been granted for periods of up to one year.[458]

Collective HS1996 and HS2002 Waivers were granted on the condition that members submit the documentation required by the respective implementation procedures.[459] The required documentation mainly consists of that part of the schedule which is affected by HS changes and which is transposed into the newest version of the HS nomenclature and the indication of any changes in the scope of concessions.[460] This requirement posed particular administrative problems for developing countries which consequently often failed to submit the required documentation, or only did so very belatedly. These capacity problems of developing countries were acknowledged by the Committee on Market Access and addressed by the implementation procedures. While the first HS procedures merely stated that the Secretariat would be available to assist governments in negotiations and consultations and that special account would be taken of the needs of developing countries consistent with Part IV of the GATT,[461] this assistance has increasingly been specified and substantiated. The first HS2002 procedures foresaw that developing countries could request technical assistance from the Secretariat for the preparation of the relevant documentation.[462] The amended HS2002

---

456 WT/L/124 (16 January 1996); WT/L/173 (25 July 1996); WT/L/216 (20 May 1997); WT/L/243 (28 October 1997); WT/L/264 (29 April 1998) WT/L/281 (20 October 1998); WT/L/303 (17 June 1999); WT/L/338 (8 November 1999); WT/L/351 (8 May 2000); WT/L/379 (13 December 2000).

457 General Council, Introduction of Harmonized System Changes into WTO Schedules of Tariff Concessions on 1 January 1996, Decision of 8 May 2001, WT/L/400 (10 May 2001).

458 HS2002: WT/L/469 (17 May 2002); WT/L/511 (20 January 2003); WT/L/562 (13 February 2004); WT/L/598 (14 December 2004); WT/L/638 (16 December 2005); WT/L/674 (19 December 2006); WT/L/712 (21 December 2007); WT/L/744 (22 December 2008); WT/L/786 (21 December 2009); WT/L/808 (16 December 2010); HS2007: WT/L/675 (19 December 2006); WT/L/713 (21 December 2007); WT/L/745 (22 December 2008); WT/L/787 (21 December 2009); WT/L/809 (16 December 2010).

459 The collective HS1996 Waiver also covered members which had not submitted documentation. With the extension of 24 April 1997 the collective HS1996 Waiver stated in the provision on documentation: 'if special circumstances apply, the Member concerned shall have requested technical assistance from the Secretariat for the completion of such documentation': WT/L/216 (20 May 1997), para. (i).

460 WT/L/673(18 December 2006), para. 4 and Annex 1.

461 L/5470/Rev. 1 (30 June 1983), Annex 1, para. 4.5.

462 WT/L/407 (26 July 2001), Attachment B, para. 8.

procedures as well as the HS2007 procedures, which are based on the former, now entrust the Secretariat with the preparation of the entire documentation for developing country members.[463] Developing country members are expected to examine the draft files prepared by the Secretariat. When they approve the draft files they are submitted for multilateral review.[464]

The increasing technical assistance afforded to developing countries was reflected by the collective waiver decisions. The collective HS1996 Waiver stated in the provision on documentation that 'if special circumstances apply, the Member concerned shall have requested technical assistance from the Secretariat for the completion of such documentation'.[465] With the adoption of the modified HS2002 procedures collective HS2002 Waivers provided that members could be covered by the waiver not only if they had submitted the required documentation, but also if they had approved draft files prepared by the Secretariat and released them for multilateral review.[466]

While collective waiver decisions with respect to the HS2002 and the latest HS2007 changes are still in effect at the time of writing, the last collective HS1996 Waiver extension expired on 30 April 2002.[467] By that time developed country members had completed the transposition and

---

463 WT/L/605 (2 March 2005), para. 1; WT/L/673(18 December 2006), para. 2 (these HS 2007 procedures foresee that developing country members may opt for preparing their draft files themselves). The Secretariat prepares this documentation by incorporating HS changes into the schedules in the Consolidated Tariff Schedules Database, an electronic database which is not legally binding (WT/L/673, preamble, recital 5). Regarding the transposition the Secretariat has to follow a methodology laid out in an annex to the procedures, WT/L/673, para. 5 and Annex 2.

464 When a developing country member remains passive the draft file can nonetheless be submitted for multilateral review. It can, however, only be certified once the developing country in question has approved it: WT/L/673 (18 December 2006), paras. 8–12, 16.

465 This provision was included starting with the extension of the collective HS1996 Waiver on 24 April 1997, WT/L/216 (20 May 1997), para. (i).

466 The first collective HS2002 Waiver extension which included such a provisions was WT/L/638.

467 The implementation of HS1996 changes took such a long time that it required the extension of the collective waiver decision until 30 April 2002 due to so-called general reservations. According to an institutional practice members could submit unspecified reservations to secure their rights to participate in Article XXVIII GATT negotiations. These general reservations created a problem when a member did not specify the reservation after it had studied the submitted documentation in order to identify whether it really had a claim of interest allowing it to participate in negotiations under Art. XXVIII GATT. In such a case neither bilateral renegotiations of concessions with the reserving member nor the certification of the adapted schedules could take place.

had certified schedules of tariff concessions. The remaining developing countries who had implemented the HS1996 changes domestically, but still had no certified schedules in HS1996 format from that time on, had to request individual waivers.

It may be summarized that the collective waiver decisions address a need for a suspension of Art. II GATT for the time that domestic tariffs and schedules of concessions diverge. This is a need shared by most WTO members that are obliged under the HS Convention to implement HS changes domestically by the time these changes take effect. Together with the implementation procedures the waivers can be seen as representing a managerial approach aimed at the effective transposition of HS changes into schedules of concessions. Collective waivers cease to be granted when the delay in this exercise is no longer seen to be caused by factors affecting all or most members that need to transpose their schedules and renegotiate concessions. At that point in time the Committee on Market Access reverts to the examination of waiver requests on a case-by-case basis. This enables the committee to impose conditions adjusted to the specific situation of the respective member requesting the waiver or even to refuse the granting of further waivers as a way to exert pressure on members that lag behind with the adaptation of their schedules.

3.2 The Kimberley Waiver: deference to another international legal regime to avoid norm conflict

The Kimberley Waiver[468] was adopted in 2003 in order to coordinate the WTO legal order with another international legal regime – the Kimberley Process Certification Scheme for Rough Diamonds (KPCS).[469] It suspends GATT norms until the end of 2012 in order to allow WTO members to implement the KPCS. It thus avoids potential norm conflict by limiting the WTO's jurisdiction with respect to trade measures mandated by the KPCS.

The Kimberley Process Certification Scheme for Rough Diamonds aims at the suppression of trade in so-called conflict or blood diamonds.[470] Conflict diamonds are defined as 'rough diamonds used by rebel

---

468 General Council, Waiver Concerning Kimberley Process Certification Scheme for Rough Diamonds, Decision of 15 May 2003, WT/L/518 (27 May 2003); General Council, Decision of 15 December 2006, WT/L/676 (19 December 2006) (extension decision).

469 The KPCS Document is available at www.kimberleyprocess.com/documents/basic_core_documents_en.html (last accessed 11 March 2011).

470 For a detailed account of the connection between diamond-mining and trading and violent conflicts and of how public awareness was raised by NGOs such as Global Witness and Canada Africa Partnership and led to action of the international community, including the diamond industry, see Nadakavukaren Schefer, 'Stopping Trade in Conflict Diamonds', 391–416. A connection was also made between the diamond trade and the

movements or their allies to finance conflict aimed at undermining legitimate governments'.[471] The aim of the KPCS is to prevent rebels financing their weapons through the diamond trade, and thus to contribute to the larger objective of maintaining and restoring peace and security and to prevent gross human rights violations perpetrated in armed conflicts between governments and rebel movements.[472] After non-governmental organizations had drawn public attention to the role of the diamond trade in these conflicts, African diamond-producing countries in 2000 initiated the Kimberley Process, a multi-stakeholder initiative in which governments, industry, and civil society representatives participate.[473] The KPCS was adopted by a ministerial declaration, the Interlaken Declaration of 5 November 2002 on the Kimberley Process Certification Scheme for Rough Diamonds (Interlaken Declaration).[474]

The Kimberley Process is closely linked to the United Nations. Before the Kimberley Process started, the Security Council, acting under Chapter VII of the UN Charter, had decided upon embargoes on the importation of diamonds from Angola and Sierra Leone.[475] In 2000, the unanimously adopted General Assembly Resolution 55/56 on the role of diamonds in fuelling conflict called upon UN members to devise effective and pragmatic measures to address the problem of trade in conflict diamonds.[476] After the Interlaken Declaration had given effect to the KPCS, it was endorsed in General Assembly and Security Council resolutions.[477]

The KPCS is not an international treaty, but a non-binding instrument.[478] The main requirements are: participants *should* ensure

---

financing of international terrorism, see references in Pauwelyn, 'WTO Compassion or Superiority Complex?', 1177, 1186, fn. 38.

471 KPCS, Section I. The definition of conflict diamonds refers to relevant SC resolutions and the definition in GA Res 55/56, recital 2.

472 Interlaken Declaration of 5 November 2002 on the Kimberley Process Certification Scheme for Rough Diamonds, recital 1, available at www.kimberleyprocess.com/documents/basic_core_documents_en.html (last accessed 11 March 2011).

473 *Ibid.*, recital 6 of which notes 'the important contribution made by industry and civil society to the development of the Kimberley Process Certification Scheme'. Information on the Kimberley Process is available at www.kimberleyprocess.com/home/index_en.html (last accessed 11 March 2011).

474 *Ibid.*

475 SC Res. 1173 (1998) instituted an embargo on the importation of diamonds from Angola, which were not certified by the Government of Unity and National Reconciliation (para. 12 (b)): see also SC Res 1176 (1998); SC Res 1306 (2000), embargo on imports of rough diamonds from Sierra Leone which are not certified by Sierra Leone's certification of origin regime (paras. 1, 5).

476 GA Res 55/56 (2000); see also GA. Res 56/263 (2002).

477 See, e.g., GA Res 57/302 (2002) and SC Res 1459 (2003).

478 See also the classification by Ruggie, 'Business and Human Rights', 819, 839.

that only rough diamonds which are accompanied by a so-called Kimber-ley Process Certificate[479] are imported and exported;[480] and participants *should* neither import rough diamonds from non-participants nor export rough diamonds to non-participants.[481]

For its effectiveness[482] the KPCS depends on implementation of the substantive non-binding requirements through binding domestic legisla-tion and enforcement of this legislation.[483] Since the obligations set out in the KPCS are non-binding, participants who do not comply do not violate international law, and thus do not incur any state responsibility under general international law. However, non-compliance is sanctioned by exclusion from the market. States who do not implement the minimum requirements set out in the KPCS can be considered as non-participants, with the consequence that exports from and imports to them should be prohibited by participants. Whether the minimum requirements are met is assessed by the Participation Committee.[484] Currently the KPCS has forty-seven participants who meet the minimum requirements – the EC and its member states counting as one – representing the vast majority of trade in rough diamonds.[485]

Already during the drafting stage participants in the Kimberley Pro-cess were aware of potential conflicts between the prohibition of trade with non-participants and WTO norms, in particular the prohibition of quantitative restrictions (Art. XI:1 GATT), the obligation to admin-ister quantitative restrictions non-discriminatorily (Art. XIII:1 GATT), and the obligation to grant most-favoured-nation treatment (Art. I:1

---

479 The KPCS sets out certain requirements for the process of issuing certificates. Most importantly, participants should 'establish a system of internal controls designed to elim-inate the presence of conflict diamonds from shipments of rough diamonds imported into and exported from its territory' (Section IV(a)). The certificate will thus ensure that only diamonds which come from areas which are controlled by the legitimate government of a country enter the market.
480 Section III(a) and (b).   481 Section III(c).
482 For criticism of the effectiveness of the KP see Smillie, *Blood on the Stone*, 177 *et seq.*
483 The EC has implemented the KPCS by Council Reg. 2368/2002, OJ (2002) L358/28, the US by the Clean Diamond Trade Act (Public Law 108-19 (25 April 2003)).
484 See Terms of Reference of the Participation Committee, Administrative Decision on Participation Committee of 29 October 2004. available at www.kimberleyprocess.com/structure/working_group_en.html (last accessed 11 March 2011). Para. 4.3 of the Terms of Reference reads: '[i]f the Committee concludes that the Participant no longer meets the said requirements it will inform the Chair in writing of the reasons for such a conclusion and may recommend any further action that the Committee believes is appropriate'.
485 For a list of KPCS Participants who meet the minimum requirements, see www.kimberleyprocess.com/structure/participants_world_map_en.html (last accessed 11 March 2011).

GATT).[486] While some WTO members, in particular Switzerland and the EC, were of the view that the trade bans vis-à-vis non-participants were justified under WTO law,[487] some WTO members did not want to proceed with the implementation of the KPCS unless the potential violation by these measures of GATT norms was addressed and justified by a waiver decision.[488]

Consequently, a waiver was requested on 11 November 2002 by three WTO members[489] and, after formal and informal discussions and consultations[490] it was granted by the General Council on 15 May 2003.[491] The waiver suspends Articles I:1, XI:1, and XIII:1 of GATT retroactively as of 1 January 2003 (the date the KPCS was launched) and until 31 December 2006. The waiver decision was extended until 31 December 2012 by a second decision of 15 December 2006.[492] The mentioned obligations are waived for all members which are listed in the annex to the waiver decision and for members which notify the Council for Trade in Goods of their desire to be covered by the waiver.[493] They are waived with respect to measures taken by these members which are 'necessary to prohibit the export of rough diamonds to [and import from] non-Participants in the

---

486 See Chairman of the Kimberley Process, Non-Paper, Kimberley Process Workshop on WTO Conformity, 15–17 February 2002 (revised version 14 March 2002), available at www.kimberleyprocess.com/download/getfile/42 (last accessed 11 March 2011). With respect to the prohibition on trade in uncertified diamonds between participants, the predominant view seemingly was that this prohibition was in conformity with WTO law.

487 It also seems to be the predominant view in the literature that the trade bans are justified under the general exceptions in Art. XX GATT or the security exception in Art. XXI GATT. See e.g. Price, 'Kimberley Process', 1, 48 et seq.; Pauwelyn, 'WTO Compassion or Superiority Complex?', 1177, 1189 et seq.; Nadakavukaren Schefer, 'Stopping Trade in Conflict Diamonds', 391, 418 et seq.; more critical as to the justification of the trade restrictions under GATT exceptions is Gray, 'Conflict Diamonds and the WTO', 451.

488 See Price, 'Kimberley Process', 1, 5.

489 Communication from Canada, Japan, and Sierra Leone, Kimberley Certification Scheme for Rough Diamonds – Request for a WTO Waiver, 11 November 2002, G/C/W/431 (12 November 2002).

490 See Council for Trade in Goods, Minutes of the Meetings on 22 November 2002, G/C/M/66 (4 December 2002) (suggestion by the chairman that Canada carry out consultations and that the Council for Trade in Goods revert to the issue at a later time (para 6.16)) and on 23 January 2003 and 26 February 2003, G/C/M/68 (6 March 2003) (these minutes refer to consultations on 16 January 2003 with thirty delegations (para. 1.2) and an open-ended informal meeting on 18 February 2003 (para. 1.4)).

491 General Council, Decision of 15 May 2003, WT/L/518 (27 May 2003). By that time Australia, Brazil, Israel, the Philippines, Thailand, the United Arab Emirates and the US had joined the waiver request: see G/C/W/431/Corr. 1 and Corr. 2.

492 General Council, Waiver Concerning Kimberley Process Certification Scheme for Rough Diamonds, Decision of 15 December 2006, WT/L/676 (19 December 2006).

493 WT/L/518, paras. 1, 3; WT/L/676, paras. 1, 3.

Kimberley Process Certification Scheme consistent with the Kimberley scheme'.[494] The waiver does not cover measures restricting trade in rough diamonds with participants since these were held to be consistent with WTO law. To accommodate those members who were of the view that the trade bans vis-à-vis non-participants were also consistent with WTO law, and a waiver decision therefore unnecessary, the decision notes in the preamble that the waiver is granted for legal certainty and does not prejudge the consistency with WTO law of domestic measures which are consistent with the KPCS.[495]

The Kimberley Waiver immunizes trade measures that are adopted to implement the KPCS from claims of illegality under WTO law by suspending GATT norms. It thus coordinates WTO law and KPCS norms and resolves potential conflict in favour of the KPCS. It does not take a stance on the compatibility of KPCS implementing measures with WTO law, and in particular their justification under the general exceptions of the GATT. Since the waiver suspends the application of certain norms with respect to concretely defined measures, it constitutes a real exception to WTO law for these measures.[496]

So far the Kimberley Waiver has been the only waiver decision that suspends an obligation with respect to trade measures foreseen in another international legal regime. However, the extensive debate among academics and within the WTO on how to ensure the compatibility of multilateral environmental agreements with GATT 1994 has frequently referred to the waiver power as one possible coordination device.[497]

---

494 WT/L/518, para. 1 on exports, para. 2 on imports.
495 WT/L/518, preamble, recital 4; WT/L/676, preamble, recital 5.
496 In order to safeguard WTO members' interests the waiver provides for consultations between members benefiting from the waiver and a member which considers that a measure covered by the waiver unduly impairs benefits accruing to it under the GATT. If such consultations do not lead to a satisfactory solution such member may bring the matter before the General Council which shall examine it and make recommendations (WT/L/518, para. 6). Finally, the waiver makes it clear that recourse to consultation and dispute settlement by affected members pursuant to Arts. XXII and XXIII GATT shall not be precluded (para. 7).
497 See Caldwell, 'International Environmental Agreements and the GATT', 173; for further references to academic literature on this point, see Böckenförde, *Grüne Gentechnik und Welthandel*, fn. 1242; Note by the Secretariat, Approaches to the Relationship Between the Provisions of the Multilateral Trading System and Trade Measures Pursuant to Multilateral Environmental Agreements, WT/CTE/W/4 (10 March 1995); Note by the Secretariat, Multilateral Environmental Agreements (MEAs) and WTO Rules; Proposals made in the Committee on Trade and Environment (CTE) from 1995–2002, TN/TE/S/1 (23 May 2002).

4 Conclusion

Collective waivers so far have addressed various flexibility needs of a systemic and not merely an incidental nature. They have taken account of implementation difficulties by deferring the obligation to comply. Collective waivers have further codified the results of political contestation within the organization as to its proper objectives as well as the legal disciplines required to achieve these objectives. Finally, collective waivers have coordinated the WTO with other international legal regimes, the World Customs Organization's Harmonized System Convention and the Kimberley Process Certification Scheme. In the first case, the collective Harmonized System waivers are an important element in the division of labour between both institutions towards the common end of trade facilitation. In the latter case, coordination takes the form of deference by the WTO to the jurisdiction of the other regime, the KPCS, with respect to trade measures to combat trade in conflict diamonds and thus to protect human security.

III One waiver power – multiple flexibility instruments: a typology of waiver decisions

The waiver practice abundantly demonstrates that it would be mistaken to qualify the waiver power merely as a safeguard clause that allows for deviation from the legal rules in narrowly defined circumstances. Instead, one can broadly distinguish between three types of waiver decisions which may be further subdivided according to their varying functions. These distinctions are important in that they inform the doctrinal analysis in the next chapter. They are, inter alia, relevant for determining the appropriate method of interpretation or the scope of review. The distinctions are furthermore relevant for questions of legal policy, such as which terms and conditions should be included in a waiver or whether a waiver should exclude the option of non-violation complaints or not.

The three waiver types are as follows: firstly, individual exceptions; secondly, general exceptions; and thirdly, rule-making instruments. Waivers as individual exceptions may be subdivided into waivers that address capacity problems of the beneficiary and waivers that accommodate specific policy choices of the beneficiary. A particular group, within the latter category of individual exceptions that accommodate policy choices, is constituted by waivers that are adopted to legalize developed country members' special preference arrangements. These are the only individual exceptions regularly adopted to allow developed country members to pursue (foreign) policy objectives. By contrast, individual exceptions granted to developing country members, even if accommodating a policy choice, are usually justified on the basis of an exceptional situation which would make compliance unduly burdensome.

Secondly, collective waivers, granted either for the benefit of all members or abstractly defined groups of members, that suspend obligations in their entirety or that suspend obligations to allow for compliance with the obligations of another international legal regime, can be understood as general exceptions. While the general suspensions address capacity problems, the suspensions to allow for compliance with another legal regime perform two functions. On the one hand, such waivers (as the collective HS waivers) may be adopted to enhance effective cooperation with another international legal regime; on the other hand, they may be adopted to address potential norm conflict in case of conflicting objectives by limiting the WTO's jurisdiction in favour of the other regime.

Finally, waivers as rule-making instruments abstractly modify existing legal rules, by making the suspension dependent on abstractly defined terms being met. They can thus be interpreted as establishing new rules. While waivers as general exceptions either suspend the application of a norm entirely or refer for the extent of the suspension to another legal regime, waivers as rule-making instruments establish abstract legal requirements whose interpretation falls within the WTO's jurisdiction.

C. UNADOPTED AND UNREQUESTED WAIVER DECISIONS

An overview of the waiver practice would be lacking if no account were taken of waivers requested, but not granted, as well as situations in which members abstained from requesting a waiver even though maintaining illegal measures. Therefore, before turning to an analysis of the law on waivers under GATT 1947 and in the WTO, I shall briefly address this non-existent waiver practice.

As was seen in this chapter and will be discussed in more detail in Chapter 5, there are hardly any substantive limitations on the waiver power. In particular, the requirement that waivers need to be justified by the existence of exceptional circumstances has not proved a substantive restriction on the waiver power.[498] Nonetheless, waivers have been granted for a relatively limited number of situations, even more limited in the

---

498 Chapter 5 B.III.1.

WTO than under the GATT. The narrower scope of the waiver practice in the WTO as compared to the GATT can be explained by the practice of decision-making by consensus which makes it appear unlikely that the General Council will adopt waivers to legalize protectionist measures comparable in extent to those justified by the 1955 Agricultural Waiver.

Two considerations seem to play a decisive role for the question whether waivers are granted or not: on the one hand, the impact of the measure to be legalized by a waiver on the commercial interests of other members; on the other hand, the question whether a waiver creates a precedent that might lead to an erosion of a fundamental rule or principle. Once a certain practice is established according to which waivers are routinely granted, members might not veto a waiver even though it negatively affects them, if they hope to (or already do) benefit from such a waiver themselves.

The only two GATT working party reports on waiver requests which eventually did not lead to the adoption of a waiver suggest that opposition was based on both: commercial interest as well as the fear that the fundamental most-favoured-nation principle would be weakened.[499] In the case of the EEC's request in 1969 for a waiver of Art. I:1 GATT, to allow it to reduce customs duties on certain citrus fruit originating in Israel and Spain,[500] it was clearly the negative trade effects on third party suppliers which motivated the strict opposition to this waiver, in particular by the United States. This opposition eventually led the EEC to withdraw the request.[501] A Greek request in 1970 for a waiver of Art. I:1 GATT to accord certain trade preference to the Soviet Union likewise was opposed by the United States. While the working party members acknowledged that Greece was in an unfavourable balance-of-payments situation – a situation which frequently prompted the granting of waivers of Art. II:1 GATT to allow the imposition of tariff surcharges[502] – they held the view that such a situation should not justify the adoption of discriminatory trade preferences.[503] Thus, in this case opposition to the

---

499 Report of the Working Party on Citrus Fruit, L/3281 (5 December 1969) (the working party considered it, due to the divergences in opinion, pointless to draft a waiver decision to be submitted to the CONTRACTING PARTIES); Report of the Working Party on Greek Tariff Quotas, L/3447 (14 October 1970) (the report stated that a large majority did not recommend that a waiver be granted (para. 16)).

500 For the request, see Annex III to the Working Party Report in L/3281.

501 GATT Council, Minutes of the Meeting on 16 December 1969, C/M/59, 4 (6 January 1970). On the US opposition to EEC preferences for citrus fruit, see Hudec, *GATT Legal System and World Trade Diplomacy*, 2nd edn, 1990, 253 *et seq.*

502 On this waiver practice, see B.I.2.2(a) above.

503 Report of the Working Party on Greek Tariff Quotas, L/3447 (14 October 1970), paras. 6 and 11; R. E. Hudec, *GATT Legal System and World Trade Diplomacy*, 255.

waiver request was additionally motivated by the will to limit the granting of tariff preferences as a matter of principle.

Over time the most-favoured-nation principle eroded more and more, in particular as concerns trade preferences granted to products from developing countries. While in 1984 the working party on the United States' request for a waiver for preferences to be granted on the basis of the Caribbean Basin Economic Recovery Act could not agree to recommend the adoption of a waiver,[504] the attitude towards such waivers changed once the CBERA Waiver had set a precedent, followed by the waivers for preferences under the United States' Andean Trade Preferences Act, the Canadian CARIBCAN initiative, the Fourth Lomé Convention, the Cotonou Agreement and most recently the United States' African Growth and Opportunities Act. Considerations of principle no longer have much weight in the examination of requests for such waivers. Instead commercial interest and bargaining power are decisive for the success of a waiver request.[505]

While very few waiver requests that were formally submitted and examined did not result in the adoption of a waiver decision,[506] there are many instances of non-compliance in which no legalizing waiver is sought at all. In particular, in cases where illegality was determined in dispute settlement proceedings, but the respondent member nonetheless has a strong preference to maintain the illegal measure, it may be asked why no attempt is being made by the respondent to obtain a waiver in order to legalize the measure. Cases in point are the United States' maintenance of the zeroing method in antidumping proceedings which was found by the Appellate Body to violate provisions of the Antidumping Agreement,[507] the US ban on Internet gambling in violation of the GATS,[508] or the

---

504 Report of the Working Party on United States Caribbean Basin Economic Recovery Act (CBERA), L/5708 (26 October 1984). The working party did, however, prepare a draft waiver which was put to a vote by the CONTRACTING PARTIES and was accepted. On this waiver, see B.II.3.3(b).

505 See also the discussion in Chapter 7 A.II.

506 Under the GATT 1947 these were the requests by the EC and Greek waiver requests discussed above; in the WTO the EC had submitted requests for its GSP + arrangement as well as an extension of the Bananas Waiver neither of which led to the adoption of waiver decisions.

507 Appellate Body Report, *US – Zeroing (EC)*, WT/DS294/AB/R, adopted 9 May 2006; Appellate Body Report, *US – Zeroing (Japan)*, WT/DS322/AB/R, adopted 23 January 2007; Appellate Body Report, *US – Continued Zeroing*, WT/DS350/AB/R, adopted 19 February 2009.

508 Appellate Body Report, *US – Gambling*, WT/DS285/AB/R, adopted 20 April 2005.

EC ban on the sale of hormone-treated beef in violation of the SPS Agreement.[509]

In the first case the US defend the position that the zeroing method should be admissible and argues for a clarification of the Antidumping Agreement to this effect. This position is opposed by most other WTO members.[510] It is therefore highly unlikely that consensus on a waiver decision could be achieved. Moreover, a temporary waiver would not remedy the situation due to the general disagreement of the US with the Appellate Body's interpretation of the antidumping rules which is not limited to specific instances of the application of these rules. A waiver request might be interpreted as an acknowledgement that zeroing is illegal. The US maintains, however, that even under the existing rules zeroing should be permissible.[511]

In the *Gambling* dispute the US aimed to legalize the maintenance of its Internet gambling ban by withdrawing its market access commitment for Internet gambling services according to Art. XXI GATS.[512] In the given situation this strategy provided for several advantages over a waiver request. Most importantly, the decision to withdraw a market access commitment can be made unilaterally. Had the US requested a waiver, members might have been reluctant – again as a matter of principle – to consent to a waiver for a measure that discriminates between foreign and domestic services providers as does the United States' gambling legislation.[513] It is unlikely that a consensus would form to legalize discrimination for which the US did not provide any justification in terms of generally acknowledged public interests and thus to potentially set a precedent for future waiver requests.

The situation seems different with respect to the EC's ban on hormone-treated beef. The EC still attempts to bring its legislation into conformity with the SPS Agreement while upholding its ban on hormone-treated

---

509 Appellate Body Report, *EC – Hormones*, WT/DS26/AB/R, WT/DS48/AB/R, adopted 13 February 1998.
510 For the different positions in the ongoing rules negotiations of the Doha Round, see Negotiating Group on Rules, New Draft Consolidated Chair Texts of the AD and SCM Agreements, TN/RL/W/236 (19 December 2008), para. 2.4.4 (noting that delegations remain profoundly divided on the issue of zeroing).
511 This interpretation, in deviation from Appellate Body jurisprudence, was supported by the Panel Report in *US – Zeroing (Japan)*, WT/DS322/R (20 September 2006).
512 See below Chapter 6 A.II.
513 The Appellate Body had not found that the legislation unjustifiably discriminated against foreign service suppliers, but it did find that the US had not demonstrated that it complied with the chapeau of Art. XIV GATS), Appellate Body Report, *US – Gambling*, WT/DS285/AB/R, adopted 20 April 2005, para. 371.

beef.[514] In this constellation it seems least unlikely that legality of the ban might be put beyond dispute by the granting of a waiver. It differs from the *Gambling* case, firstly, in that there is strong and broad support by the European public for the ban on hormone-treated beef. Secondly, the ban is administered in a non-discriminatory way as towards domestic and foreign producers. And thirdly, the case does not evidence a principled disregard on behalf of the EC for the rules of the SPS Agreement as interpreted by the dispute settlement organs. Rather, in this specific instance a strong consumer preference is irreconcilable with the rational scientific approach of the SPS Agreement with which the EC agrees in principle.[515] Therefore a consensus might develop that the hormones ban be legalized through a waiver. This could be done while demanding that the EC affords some compensation, for example in the form of additional market access concessions to those members whose exports are negatively affected by the ban. To date, however, no such waiver has been requested. Instead, the *Hormones* dispute was settled preliminarily between the EU and the United States by a memorandum of understanding, according to which the EU agreed to a duty-free import quota for hormone-free beef and the US agreed to cease imposing trade sanctions on products from the EU.[516] A waiver would have the advantage over such a bilateral settlement in that it provides a multilateral solution that can take account of the interests of all affected members and ensures conformity with the WTO agreements.

To conclude: it is difficult to make any general statements as to what motivates governments to request waivers or not to do so and similarly to try to explain why states join a consensus to adopt a waiver decision or refuse to do so. Nonetheless, it seems safe to say the following. Waiver requests are less likely to be successful, firstly, if the measure for which a waiver is sought strongly impacts commercial interests of other members and, secondly, where the measure generally calls into doubt a legal rule or principle for which there exists broad support by the membership.

---

514 The dispute between the EC on the one hand and Canada and the US on the other is ongoing. In its last report the Appellate Body recommended that the DSB request all the parties 'to initiate Article 21.5 proceedings without delay in order to resolve their disagreement as to whether the European Communities has removed the measure found to be inconsistent in *EC – Hormones* and whether the application of the suspension of concessions by [the United States and Canada] remains legally valid', Appellate Body Reports, *EC – Hormones*, WT/DS320/AB/R,WT/DS321/AB/R, adopted 14 November 2008.

515 See discussion in Chapter 6 A.III.4.2.

516 Joint Communication from the European Communities and the United States, *EC – Hormones*, dated 25 September 2009, WT/DS26/28 (30 September 2009).

5

The law of waivers

This chapter analyses the waiver practice in doctrinal terms. It presents the legal rules with respect to waivers conceptualized as acts of secondary law. The WTO is usually referred to as the prime example for a highly legalized international regime. This is due in particular to the detailed content of the substantive legal rules as well as the compulsory dispute settlement system. As regards, however, the procedural rules that govern the activities of the WTO's organs, the WTO, like most other international organizations, evidences a rather low degree of legalization in that there is only little written law on procedure. This makes it all the more important to take a close look at the institutional practice to identify the complete body of norms that legally frame the exercise of the waiver power.

A. WAIVER DECISIONS AS SECONDARY LAW

I Qualification as secondary legal acts

With the entry into force of the WTO Agreement, the WTO – an organization with legal personality (Art. VIII:1 WTO Agreement) – was established and WTO members attributed to it the power to take legally binding waiver decisions.[1] This power is to be exercised by the Ministerial Conference and the General Council acting on its behalf.[2] The waiver power is

---

1 On the legal concept of conferral of decision-making powers to international organizations, see Sarooshi, *International Organizations and their Exercise of Sovereign Powers*. The WTO Agreement does not use the term power or competence, but instead speaks of functions and authority.
2 Art. IX:3 specifies that the Ministerial Conference is the organ which is competent to adopt waiver decisions. When the WTO agreements do not indicate which organ is to exercise a power that is attributed to the organization Art. IV:1 cl. 1 WTO Agreement specifies that such a power of the WTO is to be carried out by the Ministerial Conference. Art. IV:2 cl. 2 foresees that during the intervals between Ministerials, the General Council exercises the powers that the law entrusts to the Ministerial Conference.

defined by the requirements laid down in Art. IX:3 and 4 WTO Agreement and in the Understanding in Respect of Waivers of Obligations under the General Agreement on Tariffs and Trade 1994. Further procedural rules have been laid down in decisions adopted under the GATT and in the WTO.[3]

Since waiver decisions are adopted by organs of the organization on the basis of a competence included in the constitutive document they can be qualified as secondary law of the WTO.[4] Under the GATT 1947 waiver decisions could also be qualified as secondary legal acts even though the GATT 1947 was not formally an international organization. This qualification was justified since the contracting parties acting jointly ('the CONTRACTING PARTIES') could be considered the organ of a de facto organization and also acted on the basis of a competence (Art. XXV:5 GATT) which had been attributed to it by the contracting parties.[5]

The term secondary law, which is commonly used with respect to legal acts adopted by the organs of the European Union, has not yet been firmly established with respect to legal instruments adopted by organs of international organizations.[6] The concept of secondary law implies a hierarchy of norms with treaty law as primary law ranking above secondary law. Secondary law has to conform to treaty law; if it does not, it is illegal. Furthermore secondary law may only be adopted if the organization has a competence to do so.[7]

---

3 These will be discussed in detail in the following sections of this chapter.
4 For a characterization of the legal decisions of the organs of the WTO as secondary law see Kuijper, 'Some Institutional Issues Presently before the WTO', 81, 109.
5 For the qualification of the GATT 1947 as an international organization and its legal acts as secondary law, see Benedek, *Die Rechtsordnung des GATT aus völkerrechtlicher Sicht*. The existence of an international organization is not generally seen to be a prerequisite for the creation of secondary law. For example COP/MOP decisions on the basis of the Kyoto and the Montreal Protocol may be characterized as secondary law even though neither the Vienna Convention for the Protection of the Ozone Layer nor the United Nations Framework Convention on Climate Change establish international organizations. On the legal instruments adopted by Conferences of the Parties under Multilateral Environmental Agreements that can be qualified as acts of secondary law, see Brunnée, 'COPing with Consent', 1.
6 Neither the important work on international institutional law by Schermers and Blokker (*International Institutional Law*, 4th edn 2003) nor the extensive study on law-making by international organizations by Alvarez (*International Organizations as Law-Makers*, 2005) include the term 'secondary law' in the index. By contrast the *Max Planck Encyclopedia of International Law* includes a separate entry on the topic, see Benzing, 'International Organizations or Institutions, Secondary Law' (March 2007).
7 On the doctrine of competences in the European Union, see Bogdandy and Bast, 'Federal Order of Competences', 275.

International institutional law doctrine is still at a very rudimentary stage. It generally states that international organizations may only adopt binding legal acts on the basis of a power – implied or explicitly attributed to them. It further holds that legal acts that do not remain within the confines of such powers are ultra vires and consequently invalid: a legal act which does not originate from an institutional power cannot come into existence.[8] While doctrine is clear in stating that legal acts of an organization need to be based on a competence and conform to treaty law, it does not clearly delimit when a legal act counts as an act of the organization and when it is attributable to the member states. Acts that are adopted by an organ of an international institution, either unanimously or by consensus, are sometimes qualified as international agreements.[9] Such a qualification has the consequence that the legal principles that limit the law-making powers of international organizations, in particular the principle of attribution of powers and the ultra vires doctrine, do not apply.

With respect to the WTO, as well, it is sometimes argued that decisions taken by the WTO plenary organs can be qualified as international agreements.[10] The ambivalence of the General Council and the Ministerial Conference which are organs of the WTO, but at the same time evidence a self-understanding as intergovernmental meetings of state representatives, becomes apparent in the formulation of waiver requests and waiver

---

8 'Legality of the Use by a State of Nuclear Weapons in Armed Conflicts', Advisory Opinion of 8 July 1996, ICJ-Reports 1996, 80–1. On the wide interpretation of the attribution of powers doctrine which renders meaningless the ultra vires doctrine, see Bernstorff, 'Procedures of Decision-Making and the Role of Law in International Organizations', 777, 784 et seq.; generally on the doctrine of law-making by international institutions, see Klabbers, *Introduction to International Institutional Law*, Chapters 10 and 11.

9 Cf. Klein, 'International Organizations or Institutions, Decision-Making' (distinguishing between two forms of law-making in international organizations: firstly treaty-making in the forum of an international organization and, secondly, the adoption of unilateral acts by the international organization which reflect its will and autonomy from its members); Simma, Brunner and Kaul, 'Article 27', 476, paras. 56–60.

10 Mavroidis, 'Judicial Supremacy, Judicial Restraint', 583, 600 (stating that the political organs are not truly international organs exercising conferred powers, but intergovernmental in character). On the distinction between treaty changes by mini diplomatic conferences as opposed to decisions of an organ of the organization in the context of the WTO, see Kuijper, 'Some Institutional Issues Presently before the WTO', 81, 93 et seq.; generally on the ambivalence with respect to the qualification of WTO decisions as secondary law, *sui generis* decisions or treaty law, see Kuijper, 'WTO Institutional Aspects', 79, 95; Charnovitz, 'Legal Status of the Doha Declarations', 207 (leaving the question as to the qualification of WTO Ministerial Declarations open, proposing that they could be qualified as subsequent agreements within the meaning of Art. 31:3(a) VCLT (at 211)).

decisions. Thus waiver requests are frequently directed by the requesting member to the WTO 'members' and not the Ministerial Conference or General Council; and some waiver decisions include the introductory phrase 'Members decide . . .'. Recent waiver decisions, however, refer to the General Council or the Ministerial Conference as the author of the decision.

The state of institutional law doctrine, which does not establish clearly when a legal act constitutes an act of secondary law and when it may be interpreted as an international agreement that binds states even if it cannot be based on a competence in the constituent treaty is not satisfactory. It is particularly problematic in light of the activities of international institutions which increasingly implicate societal interests. In such a setting a clear doctrine of secondary law constitutes an important safeguard. On a general level it ensures legality and legal clarity.[11] More importantly, a doctrine of secondary law would serve to safeguard individual freedom and domestic democratic government.

Such doctrine should establish the presumption that if state representatives meet as an organ of an international organization and adopt legal instruments these instruments qualify as secondary law and as such have to conform to the constituent treaty. This still leaves the possibility that ministers or heads of states may act outside the confines of treaty law. If they intend to do so, they should, however, clarify that they are acting in an intergovernmental capacity and not as an organ of the international institution.[12]

For the WTO this would mean that where one of the organs acts, such action may not be conceptualized as an international agreement. This principle should also hold true for the Ministerial Conference which may be seen as having a double function, on the one hand acting as an organ of the organization and, on the other hand, representing the conference of state parties acting collectively. If the Ministerial Conference purports to act on the basis of a legal competence laid down in the WTO Agreements, it acts as an organ and thus must remain within the confines of this competence.

Consequently, waiver decisions whether adopted by the General Council or the Ministerial Conference should be qualified as acts of secondary

11 Kumm, 'Legitimacy of International Law', 907 (conceptualizing the principle of legality as an important factor for the legitimacy of international law).
12 On the double role of states in international organizations as sovereigns and constituent members of the organization, see Blokker, 'International Organizations and their Members', 139.

law. The legal status of a waiver decision was at issue in the second compliance proceeding in *EC – Bananas III*. In this case the panel found that the Bananas Waiver, which was adopted during the Doha Round by the Ministerial Conference to legalize the preferential tariff quota of the EC for bananas from ACP countries,[13] constituted a subsequent agreement by the WTO members to extend the duration of the tariff quota concession.[14] On appeal, the Appellate Body concentrated on the substantive scope of the waiver decision and did not address the question whether the waiver qualified as an act of the organization or an international agreement between its members. However, it did stress – in order to distinguish a waiver decision from an amendment according to Art. X WTO Agreement – that a waiver is a 'decision taken by the Ministerial Conference, which [does] not require formal acceptance by the Membership as foreseen under Art. X:7' to take effect.[15] This statement supports the view that waivers are decisions of the organization and not agreements among its members.

The question as to the qualification of waiver decisions as secondary law has to be distinguished from the evaluation of the material content of the respective legal act. Thus, it can be argued that the plenary composition of the law-making organ, the consensus practice and the domination of national interests do not allow qualifying certain legal acts as the expression of a collective will of the organization that reflects the organization's autonomy from its members.[16] While not decisive for the question whether waiver decisions can be formally qualified as secondary law, the dominant role of members in the decision-making process and the limited degree of autonomy of the international organization and its organs may nonetheless be relevant, in particular concerning questions of state responsibility. Thus, even though formally an act of secondary law, a measure may give rise to the responsibility of a state whose representative consented to the measure in the organ of an international institution.[17]

---

13 On this waiver decision, see Chapter 4 B.I.3.3(b).
14 Panel Report, *EC – Bananas III*, Second Recourse to Art. 21.5 of the DSU by Ecuador, WT/DS27/RW2/ECU (7 April 2008), para. 7.446 and para. 7.492.
15 Appellate Body Report, *EC – Bananas III (Article 21.5 – ECU II, US)*, WT/DS27/AB/RW2/ECU, adopted 11 December 2008, and WT/DS27/AB/RW/USA, adopted 22 December 2008, para. 394.
16 Blokker, 'International Organizations or Institutions, Decision-Making Bodies' (noting that only very few international organizations have supranational decision-making bodies while in most international organizations members dominate decision-making).
17 Cf. D'Aspremont, 'Abuse of the Legal Personality of International Organizations', 91 (arguing that member states exerting an excessive control over the decision-making

One further note should be added with respect to a doctrine of secondary law of international institutions. In light of the various law-making activities by international organizations[18] it would be desirable to distinguish between different types of legal acts.[19] The distinction between different legal instruments would not only serve to give a better understanding of the law-making activities of international institutions, it could also be the basis for differentiated rules on interpretation, judicial review and further development of procedural law to ensure accountability and legitimacy of law-making processes in international institutions.[20] A refinement of the legal regimes for the adoption of acts of secondary law would also allow a departure from the all or nothing ultra vires doctrine.[21] Combined with judicial review they would permit the distinction between illegal, but valid acts on the one hand and illegal and invalid acts on the other – a distinction which is known from EU law as well as domestic administrative law.

As of now doctrine does not clearly distinguish between different legal acts. Instead, scholarship on law-making by international institutions generally employs very wide categories. For example, it differentiates between binding legal acts and non-binding 'soft' law or between legislative acts which lay down abstract rules of general application and decisions which apply to a concrete situation.[22] With respect to WTO law, scholarship often is even less differentiated, a common view being that hardly any

process of an organization must be held responsible for violations of international law committed by the organization).

18 For a recent study on the wide-ranging law-making activities of international organizations see Alvarez, *International Organizations as Law-Makers*.

19 On the juridical method of systematization and conceptualization in public law which established the functional autonomy of the legal science of public law, see Bogdandy, 'Wissenschaft vom Verfassungsrecht', 807, paras. 20 *et seq.*

20 Accountablity and legitimacy are among the main concerns of the Global Administrative Law Project. For an introduction to this project, see Kingsbury, Krisch and Stewart, 'Emergence of Global Administrative Law', 15. For an approach that identifies and differentiates between different legal forms of action in European Union Law, see Bast, *Grundbegriffe der Handlungsformen der EU*; see also Bogdandy, 'Lawmaking by International Organizations', 171; Goldmann, 'Inside Relative Normativity', 661 and the comment on this text by Klabbers, 'Goldmann Variations', 713.

21 For the proposal of such a legal regime for national policy assessments by international organizations see Bogdandy and Goldmann, 'Exercise of International Public Authority Through National Policy Assessment', 241.

22 Klabbers, *Introduction to International Institutional Law*, 181 *et seq.*; Aston, *Sekundärgesetzgebung internationaler Organisationen*.

law-making takes place in the WTO.[23] That this view is incorrect, was demonstrated in Chapter 4 where it was shown that the competence to adopt waiver decisions is used extensively and gives rise to different types of legal decisions, individual exceptions and general exceptions, as well as rule-making instruments.

II Legal effects of waiver decisions

A waiver decision changes the pre-existing legal situation by suspending a legal obligation and thus freeing the beneficiary from the duty to comply with this obligation. It therefore has to be characterized as a legally binding decision.[24] Waiver decisions not only have legal effects for the members whose obligations are suspended, but for the membership as a whole in that no member can successfully claim that the waived obligation is being violated. Due to its effects *erga omnes partes* a waiver decision is not addressed to the individual member whose obligation is being waived. Therefore, this study refers to the member whose obligation is suspended as beneficiary and not as addressee of the waiver decision.[25] The term beneficiary refers to the legal benefit that the member whose obligation has been waived obtains because it is not required by law to comply with the waived obligation. The term thus does not refer to commercial benefits. Commercial benefits sometimes accrue to beneficiaries of waiver decisions; often, however, they also accrue to other members or non-members, which are not beneficiaries in the legal sense of the term. Examples are tariff preference waivers which commercially benefit the preference-receiving countries and not necessarily the beneficiary of the waiver who grants the preferences.[26]

1 Legal effects for the beneficiary of the waiver decision

A waiver decision has the effect that measures falling within the scope of the waiver decision do not violate the waived obligation. It may also be said that a waiver decision provides a justification for an otherwise

---

23 Exceptions are the studies by John H. Jackson and Wolfgang Benedek on the GATT 1947 which deal in detail with different types of legal instruments: Jackson, *World Trade and the Law of GATT*; Benedek, *Die Rechtsordnung des GATT aus völkerrechtlicher Sicht.*

24 Schermers and Blokker, *International Institutional Law*, § 811.

25 Cf. Kimberley Waiver, which requires 'Members *benefiting from this waiver*...' to notify certain measures, WT/L/518 (27 May 2003), para. 4 (emphasis added).

26 On these waivers see Chapter 4 B.I.3.

(potentially)[27] unlawful measure. This interpretation was called into question by the EEC in the *Sugar* dispute. The EEC argued that a waiver merely constituted an exemption from the obligation to bring a measure which is inconsistent with the law into conformity with the law. The measure itself, however, was still illegal and thus could be the object of a violation complaint.[28] To support this claim the EEC referred to a footnote in another panel report which states that the 'status of a measure (that is, whether or not it is consistent with GATT) is not to be affected by a waiver decision'.[29] The panel did not follow the EEC's argument. It stated that a measure which is in conformity with a waiver decision does not constitute a violation of the GATT.[30] With respect to the cited footnote it held that this could also be interpreted to suggest that a waiver decision did not constitute a ruling that the measure for which the waiver suspended an obligation was unlawful.[31]

2 Legal effects for the organization and members who are not beneficiaries of the waiver decision

The conceptualization of the right/obligation relationships to which legal rules give rise determines the legal effects of waiver decisions for members, other than the beneficiary of a waiver decision, as well as for the organization as a whole. If an obligation is conceptualized as giving rise to a substantive legal right of another member, a waiver of this obligation at the same time entails a waiver of the corresponding right.[32] If, however, an obligation does not give rise to substantive rights of individual members, a waiver does not affect such rights. Nonetheless, a waiver may affect procedural rights to claim that the waived obligation has been violated.

When addressing these questions it is useful to distinguish between two types of obligations: firstly, obligations of members in their internal

---

27 Sometimes waivers are granted for reasons of legal security for measures whose unlawfulness is not determined, see section B.III.2. below.
28 Panel Report, *US – Sugar Waiver*, adopted 7 November 1990, L/6631, BISD 37S/228, paras. 3.28, 5.17.
29 Panel Report, *Uruguayan Recourse to Article XXIII*, adopted 16 November 1962, L/1923, BISD 11S/95, 100, fn. 1.
30 Panel Report, *US – Sugar Waiver*, adopted 7 November 1990, L/6631, BISD 37S/228, para. 5.18.
31 *Ibid.*, para. 5.19.
32 Cf. Report of Working Party 4 on the European Coal and Steel Community, G/35 (7 November 52), para. 6 (noting the position that a waiver constituted a surrender of rights).

capacity as constituent elements of the organizations, such as, for example, the obligation to pay membership dues; and secondly, obligations of members in their external capacity that mandate a certain behaviour of members as subjects of international law.[33]

Internal obligations do not give rise to rights to performance of individual members, but merely to a right of the organization.[34] Consequently, it has been argued that each international organization has the implied power to waive obligations of members in their internal capacity, such as the obligation to pay membership contributions (Art. VII:4 WTO Agreement).[35] Waivers of such obligations do not affect the rights of other individual members.[36]

The situation is different when external obligations are waived. Such waivers usually affect the position of other members. The question may be posed, however, whether such waivers merely have the effect that other members may not successfully bring a violation complaint or whether they affect the substantive rights of other members. This depends on whether one conceptualizes WTO obligations as giving rise to individual rights to performance by other members. The alternative would be to conceptualize the obligations as giving rise to a collective right to compliance of the organization. Such a collective right may then be enforced by individual members. The latter conception would mean that a waiver decision does not entail a surrender of individual rights to performance.

Around the question whether WTO obligations give rise to bilateral right/obligation relationships among members, or whether they constitute collective obligations in the sense that performance is not owed to individual members, an intense – and mainly scholarly – debate has evolved. I shall not enter into a detailed analysis of this question, but merely want to sketch the different approaches and their implications for the characterization of waiver decisions.[37] The majority view among

---

33 For this distinction see Schermers and Blokker, *International Institutional Law*, § 155.
34 Joost Pauwelyn, with reference to the categorization of international obligations into bilateral, collective and integral obligations by Sir Gerald Fitzmaurice, qualifies such internal obligations as integral obligations: Pauwelyn, 'Nature of WTO Obligations'.
35 Schermers and Blokker, *International Institutional Law*, § 157.
36 To date no waiver of internal obligations has been adopted by WTO organs on the basis of Art. IX:3 WTO Agreement.
37 Other implications of the characterization of WTO obligations as bilateral or collective concern questions of interpretation, standing, responsibility for breach, the possibility of *inter se* modifications of WTO law and the relationship between WTO obligations and other obligations of international law.

international trade lawyers is that WTO norms which impose legal obligations on WTO members give rise to correlative and bilateral right/obligation relationships between members.[38] Mostly, proponents of this view refer to the nature of trade and an interpretation of the objectives of the WTO as primarily aiming at market access, to bolster the argument that WTO law is not collective but bilateral in nature.[39] On this account, which conceptualizes the substantive obligations as right/obligation relationships bundled together in multilateral treaties, a waiver of an obligation necessarily affects the rights of individual members. The exercise of the waiver power could accordingly be conceptualized as the exercise of a competence of the organization to waive the rights to performance of WTO members.[40]

If, on the other hand, obligations of WTO law are conceived not as bilateral but as collective[41] and thus not as giving rise to rights of individual

38 According to Roberto Ago correlativity is a general feature of international law which allows for no exceptions; each obligation of a state gives rise to a corresponding right of another state: Ago, 'Second Report on State Responsibility', 40; see also Willem Riphagen for whom legal relationships (corresponding rights and obligations) between states could be bilateral only, even though resulting from a norm applicable to all states: Riphagen, 'State Responsibility', 583. For a theory explaining why each promise results in a right of the promisee, even if the promisee has no interest in the object of the promise, see Raz, *Concept of a Legal System*. The concept of correlativity is not limited to norms arising from contracts or treaties. According to Wesley N. Hohfeld all law is correlative in that obligations are matched with rights, either individual rights or the right of the collective: Hohfeld, 'Fundamental Legal Conceptions as Applied in Judicial Reasoning', 710. This clarifies that the assumption that obligations do give rise to rights in the context of the conclusion of international treaties does not necessarily lead to the conclusion that multilateral treaty obligations need to be matched with correlative rights of states, but allows for the view that obligations only give rise to collective rights held by the other contracting states. For an in-depth discussion of the theory of correlativity with respect to international law, see Simma, *Das Reziprozitätselement im Zustandekommen völkerrechtlicher Verträge*, 51 *et seq.*

39 See e.g. Pauwelyn, 'Typology of Multilateral Treaty Obligations', 907; Hahn, *Die einseitige Aussetzung von GATT-Verpflichtungen als Repressalie*, 111 *et seq.*; for a critique of the general characterization of WTO law as reciprocal or bilateral, see Trachtman, 'Review of *Conflict of Norms in Public International Law*', 855, 860.

40 For the view that waivers under GATT are waivers of rights, see Bogdandy, 'Eine Ordnung für das GATT', 55, 60. Such a view corresponds to the use of the term waiver in general international law where it generally refers to a voluntary and express renunciation of rights or claims. On waivers as unilateral renunciations of rights or claims see e.g. Suy, *Les Actes juridiques unilatéraux en droit international public*.

41 See Hodu, 'Third Party Rights and the Concept of Legal Interest', 757, 768; Carmody, 'WTO Obligations as Collective', 419; Charnovitz, 'Appellate Body's GSP Decision', 239, 241 (raising the question whether WTO obligations should be understood as granting substantive rights to other members or as merely laying down obligations). For a

members, but rather a collective right to compliance, the waiver power and the effects of waivers have to be characterized differently. Following such a conceptualization, waivers can only be granted by the collective and not by individual members. While under the former conception members can still individually waive their rights to compliance, under the latter it has to be asked whether such individual waivers are precluded by the attribution of the waiver power to the WTO.[42] A good argument for the conceptualization of WTO obligations as collective is found in the Dispute Settlement Understanding which prescribes that 'all solutions to matters raised under the consultation and dispute settlement provisions shall be consistent with the agreements' (Art. 3.5 DSU). This shall also be the case for mutually acceptable solutions by which members may settle their bilateral disputes (Art. 3.6 DSU).[43] If obligations were truly bilateral, members could agree to modifications of the obligations *inter se* and thus agree on solutions which are not consistent with the agreements so long as no rights of other members are affected. In practice, members do, however, sometimes settle their disputes in ways which do not strictly conform to the agreements.[44]

B. SUBSTANTIVE REQUIREMENTS FOR THE EXERCISE OF THE WAIVER COMPETENCE

I The waiver competence

Art. IX:3 cl. 1 WTO Agreement constitutes the WTO's competence to adopt waiver decisions.
It reads:

> In exceptional circumstances, the Ministerial Conference may decide to waive an obligation imposed on a Member by this Agreement or any of the Multilateral Trade Agreements, provided that any such decision shall

characterization of the obligation under Art. 4:7 SCM by an arbitration panel as an *erga omnes* obligation, see *US – FSC (Article 22.6 – US)*, WT/DS108/ARB (30 August 2002), Rn. 6.10.

42 Mary Footer notes one instance in which an individual member 'waived' another member's WTO obligations. She refers to an agreement between the United States and the Philippines whereby the US granted a waiver of obligations under the Agreement on Trade Related Investment Measures: see Footer, *Institutional and Normative Analysis of the World Trade Organization*, 261.

43 Stoll, 'Article 3 DSU', 281, para. 64 (noting that Art. 3.6 DSU 'reflects some sort of a common interest').

44 See e.g. ICTSD, 'Truce Declared in Beef Hormones Dispute'.

be taken by three fourths of the Members unless otherwise provided for in this paragraph.

A footnote to this provision which modifies the voting requirement states:

> A decision to grant a waiver in respect of any obligation subject to a transition period or a period for staged implementation that the requesting Member has not performed by the end of the relevant period shall be taken only by consensus.

Art. XVI:3 WTO Agreement contains a conflict rule that determines the relationship between the GATT 1994 and the WTO Agreement. It provides that '[i]n the event of a conflict between a provision of [the WTO Agreement] and a provision of any of the Multilateral Trade Agreements, the provision of this Agreement shall prevail to the extent of the conflict'. Accordingly, Art. IX:3 WTO Agreement supersedes Art. XXV:5 GATT[45] as the competence norm for the adoption of waiver decisions and as the applicable legal rule on voting requirements.

Further legal requirements with respect to the adoption, renewal and review of waiver decisions are found in other treaty provisions and acts of secondary law. The Understanding in Respect of Waivers of Obligations under the General Agreement on Tariffs and Trade 1994 ('Understanding') which was negotiated during the Uruguay Round and forms part of the GATT 1994[46] is of particular relevance. It sets out, inter alia, requirements concerning requests for waivers of obligations under the GATT 1994.

Even though there is no legal continuity between the GATT 1947 and the WTO[47] and even though the law on waivers differs in the WTO from the law that governed waivers under the GATT 1947, GATT law and practice are still relevant today. The GATT 1947 as well as legally binding decisions of the CONTRACTING PARTIES are incorporated into the GATT 1994 through the so-called Introductory Note to the GATT 1994.[48] With the entry into force of the WTO Agreement the latter have become

---

45 Art. XXV:5 GATT reads in part: 'In exceptional circumstances not elsewhere provided for in this Agreement, the CONTRACTING PARTIES may waive an obligation imposed upon a contracting party by this Agreement; *Provided* that any such decision shall be approved by a two-thirds majority of the votes cast and that such majority shall comprise more than half of the contracting parties.'

46 See Introductory Note to the General Agreement on Tariffs and Trade 1994, Section 1 (c) (v).

47 See Article II:4 WTO Agreement. On the relationship between the GATT 1947 and the GATT 1994 see Bogdandy and Stelzer, 'Article II WTO Agreement', 20, 25 *et seq.*

48 On the Introductory Note and the question which decisions taken under the GATT 1947 are incorporated into the GATT 1994, see Feichtner, 'GATT 1994', 25.

a part of primary law. Moreover, GATT panel reports and working party reports on waiver requests, and, more generally, the GATT waiver practice are recognized as relevant *acquis* by Art. XVI:1 WTO Agreement and as such provide guidance to WTO organs.[49]

II Obligations that can be waived

Art. IX:3 WTO Agreement provides that the Ministerial Conference may decide to waive 'an obligation imposed on a Member by this Agreement or any of the Multilateral Trade Agreements'. It does not include a competence for waivers of obligations under the Plurilateral Trade Agreements.[50] Art. IX:5 WTO Agreement clarifies that such waiver decisions shall be governed by the provisions of the respective Plurilateral Trade Agreement.

The term 'Multilateral Trade Agreements' is defined in Art. II:2 WTO Agreement and refers to the agreements and associated legal documents included in Annexes 1, 2 and 3 to the WTO Agreement, namely the multilateral agreements on trade in goods (including the General Agreement on Tariffs and Trade (GATT)), the General Agreement on Trade in Services (GATS), the Agreement on Trade-Related Aspects of Intellectual Property (TRIPS Agreement) (Annex 1); the Dispute Settlement Understanding (DSU) (Annex 2) and the Trade Policy Review Mechanism (TPRM) (Annex 3). The schedules of concessions which are annexed to the GATT and the GATS form integral parts of these two agreements (Art. II:7 GATT, Art. XX:3 GATS).

With respect to the formulation 'obligation imposed . . . by this Agreement' the question arises whether the term 'this Agreement' merely refers to the preamble and the following Articles I–XVI of the WTO Agreement or whether it refers to the WTO Agreement as defined in Art. II:2 WTO

---

49 According to Art. XVI:1 WTO Agreement 'the WTO shall be guided by the decisions, procedures and customary practices followed by the CONTRACTING PARTIES to GATT 1947 and the bodies established in the framework of GATT 1947'. On Art. XVI:1 WTO Agreement, see Broek, 'Article XVI WTO Agreement', 170, 172 *et seq.*; on the legal relevance of GATT panel reports, Mavroidis, 'Remedies in the WTO Legal System', 763, 782.

50 The Plurilateral Trade Agreements are included in Annex 4 to the WTO Agreement. They are the Agreement on Trade in Civil Aircraft, the Agreement on Government Procurement, the International Dairy Agreement and the International Bovine Meat Agreement. The latter two agreements were terminated as of 1 January 2008: see WTO, Termination of the International Dairy Agreement, Decision pursuant to Article VIII:3, IDA/8 (30 September 1997); WTO, Termination of the International Bovine Meat Agreement, Decision pursuant to Article VI:3, IMA/8 (30 September 1997).

Agreement. According to Art. II:2 WTO Agreement the Annexes form an integral part of the WTO Agreement. Since Art. IX:3 WTO Agreement refers to this Agreement and the Multilateral Trade Agreements separately and, moreover, since Art. IX:5 WTO Agreement states that decisions, including waiver decisions, under a Plurilateral Trade Agreement shall be governed by the respective agreement, it is safe to conclude that the term 'this Agreement' in Art. IX:3 WTO Agreement only refers to the WTO Agreement without its annexes.

In the early years of the GATT 1947 the scope of the waiver power had been an issue of contention. It was questioned whether any obligation under the GATT, including obligations under Part I of the GATT, could be waived. This issue arose in particular in connection with the discussion of a waiver to legalize trade preferences under the European Coal and Steel Community (ECSC).[51] The report of the working party which considered the request for a waiver by the founding members of the ECSC stated:

> The Working Party is of the view that the text of paragraph 5(a) of Article XXV is general in character; it allows the CONTRACTING PARTIES to waive any obligations imposed upon the contracting parties by the Agreement in exceptional circumstances not provided for in the Agreement, and places no limitation on the exercise of that right.[52]

Cuba in particular was opposed to this position. It was of the opinion that obligations under Part I, which constituted fundamental obligations of the GATT, should not be waived on the basis of Art. XXV:5 GATT by a two-thirds majority while a decision for amendment of these provisions, according to Art. XXX GATT, required unanimity.[53]

---

51 There had been opposition to waivers of the most-favoured-nation obligation before, in particular by Cuba, see e.g. CONTRACTING PARTIES, Tenth Session, Summary Report of 17th Meeting on 25 November 1955 SR.10/17 (7 December 1955), 192 (statement by the Cuban representative); on the ECSC Waiver, see Chapter 4 B.I.1.3.

52 Working Party Report, The European Coal and Steel Community, adopted 10 November 1952, BISD 1S (1953), 85, para. 2.

53 While Cuba defended the position that such waiver decisions should only be adopted unanimously it stressed that it was not of the opinion that Art. XXV:5 GATT could not be applied to all obligations under the GATT. For Cuba's position on this matter, see Statement by the Representative of Cuba at the meeting of the CONTRACTING PARTIES on 30 November 1955, Waiver Granted by the CONTRACTING PARTIES. Voting Requirements under Article XXV:5(a), L/459 (2 December 1955); Statement by the Representative of Cuba at the plenary meeting of the CONTRACTING PARTIES on 1 November 1956, Votes Required for Granting Waivers, L/579 (7 November 1956). See also criticism by the Czech delegate of the waiver for the European Coal and Steel

The Executive Secretary[54] dealt with this question in a note that was to form the basis for discussions of this issue by the CONTRACTING PARTIES during their Tenth Session. Based on the wording of Art. XXV:5 and Art. XXX GATT, the legislative history, as well as the waiver practice, the Executive Secretary reached the conclusion that Art. XXV:5 GATT did indeed allow the CONTRACTING PARTIES to waive obligations under Part I of the GATT.[55] The note refers on the one hand to the clear wording of Art. XXV:5, which does not explicitly exclude any GATT obligations from its scope, but merely states that the CONTRACTING PARTIES may waive 'an obligation imposed upon a contracting party by this Agreement'. On the other hand it points to the wording of Art. XXX GATT which acknowledges the possibility of modifications other than through the amendment procedure by stating in paragraph 1: 'Except where provision for modification is made elsewhere in this Agreement, amendments to the provisions of Part I of this Agreement . . . shall become effective upon acceptance by all the contracting parties'.

The Executive Secretary's note also refers to the negotiations leading to the adoption of the Havana Charter. There it had been discussed whether the organization's waiver power should only extend to commercial obligations or to all obligations under the Charter. The United States had originally introduced a waiver provision only with respect to tariff and customs obligations.[56] At the London Conference the French delegate proposed the extension of the waiver power to all obligations under the charter. This proposal was debated and eventually accepted.[57] While

Community, CONTRACTING PARTIES, Summary Record of the Seventh Session at the Seventeenth Meeting on 10 November 1952, SR.7/17 (18 November 1952), 5, 6.

54 In the early years of the GATT the executive secretary of the Interim Commission for the International Trade Organization had also performed the function of Executive Secretary for the GATT, see Jackson, 'History of GATT', 1, para. 49. In 1965 the position of Executive Secretary was named Director-General, see Director-General, Change of Title from 'Executive Secretary', Decision of 23 March 1965, BISD 13S (1965), 19.

55 Executive Secretary, Article XXV:5(a). Applicability of Article XXV:5(a) to Obligations defined in Part I of the General Agreement, L/403 (7 September 1955).

56 Art. 55:2 of the United States' 'Suggested Charter for an International Trade Organization' (1946), UN Document E/PC/T/33, 22.

57 For a discussion of this proposal at the London Conference, see United Nations Economic and Social Council Preparatory Committee of the International Conference on Trade and Employment, Verbatim Report of the Ninth Meeting of Committee V held on 7 November 1946, E/PC/T/C.V/PV/9, 4 et seq.; see also United Nations Economic and Social Council Preparatory Committee of the International Conference on Trade and Employment, Ninth Meeting of Committee V held on 7 November 1946, Report of ad hoc sub-committee on Articles 52, 54, 55, 59, 60 and 62, E/PC/T/C.V/25 (11 November 1946), 1–4.

Art. XXV:5 GATT did not differ in substance from the provision on waivers in the Havana Charter,[58] the amendment provision in the GATT 1947 differed substantially from the amendment provision in Art. 100 Havana Charter. The latter had provided for amendments by a two-thirds majority of members. Art. XXX:1 GATT, by contrast, required unanimity for amendments of obligations under Part I of the GATT. In his note the Executive Secretary argued that the drafters of the GATT had been aware of the resulting tension between the voting requirements for waivers of obligations under Part I and for amendments of the same obligations and that they had resolved this tension by the inclusion into Art. XXX GATT of the exception for other modifications mentioned above. This exception was intended to avoid conflict with provisions on treaty modifications that required less than unanimity.[59]

Finally, the Executive Secretary pointed to the GATT practice at that time of granting waivers of obligations under Part I, in particular of the most-favoured-nation obligation in Art. I GATT. The Executive Secretary noted that several of these waivers had been granted over the dissenting votes of individual contracting parties and that none of them had been accepted by a unanimous vote.[60]

On the basis of the Executive Secretary's note, as well as a statement by Cuba, detailing its criticism of the practice of granting waivers of obligations under Part I by majority vote,[61] the Intersessional Committee[62] issued a report to the Eleventh Session of the CONTRACTING PARTIES. While it did not, as requested by Cuba, recommend different voting requirements for waivers of Part I obligations, it recommended 'that the CONTRACTING PARTIES . . . should affirm their intention to proceed with caution in considering requests for waivers of obligations in

---

58 Art. 77:3 Havana Charter.
59 Executive Secretary, Article XXV:5(a). Applicability of Article XXV:5(a) to Obligations defined in Part I of the General Agreement, L/403 (7 September 1955), paras. 6, 7. The document also notes, however, that during the discussions on Art. XXX no reference was made to the waiver provision, *ibid.* para. 7.
60 For a list of these waivers granted by September 1955, see *ibid.*, para. 9.
61 Statement by the Representative of Cuba at the meeting of the CONTRACTING PARTIES on 30 November 1955, Waiver Granted by the CONTRACTING PARTIES. Voting Requirements under Article XXV:5(a), L/459 (2 December 1955).
62 The Intersessional Committee was established during the 1954/1955 session of the CONTRACTING PARTIES to deal with matters arising during the sessions of the CONTRACTING PARTIES. In 1960 the CONTRACTING PARTIES established the GATT Council which replaced the Intersessional Committee (Decision of 4 June 1960, BISD 9S (1961), 7, 8).

Part I, or from other important obligations of the Agreement'.[63] This settled the issue whether Art. XXV:5 GATT authorized waivers of any obligation under the GATT by majority vote.

Years later, with regard to a waiver granted to the EC in connection with German reunification,[64] the question arose whether the CONTRACTING PARTIES could, on the basis of Art. XXV:5 GATT, waive obligations under one of the plurilateral agreements concluded during the Tokyo Round. The waiver granted in 1990 to the EC suspended Art. I:1 GATT to permit the EC to grant duty-free treatment to certain imports from Eastern European countries. The EC had requested this waiver in order to be able to honour the obligations of the former German Democratic Republic under international trading agreements with its Eastern European trading partners.[65] The EC not only granted preferential tariff treatment, but also derogated from certain product standards with respect to these products in violation of Art. 2.1 of the Agreement on Technical Barriers to Trade. The EC argued that the waiver granted under Art. XXV:5 GATT should be interpreted as justifying this violation as well, since the TBT Agreement did not itself contain a waiver provision and constituted a further development of Art. I:1 GATT.[66] While this issue was not formally resolved, delegates of the United States and New Zealand rejected this interpretation in a working party on the transitional measures for which the waiver had been granted. They argued that the EC had to follow the procedures provided for in the TBT Agreement.[67]

---

63 Report by the Intersessional Committee, Votes Required for Granting Waivers, L/532 (21 September 1956). The report further recommended measures to safeguard the interests of contracting parties, such as prior notice of waiver requests, full consultation, reporting and review. On 1 November 1956 the CONTRACTING PARTIES, in response to the recommendations by the Intersessional Committee, adopted the decision, Article XXV – Guiding Principles to be Followed by the Contracting Parties in Considering Applications for Waivers from Part I or other Obligations of the Agreement (L/532), BISD 5S (1957), 25.

64 CONTRACTING PARTIES, European Communities – Transitional Measures to Take Account of the External Economic Impact of German Unification, Decision of 13 December 1990, L/6792 (14 December 1990).

65 Communication from the European Communities, European Communities – Transitional Measures to Take Account of the External Economic Impact of German Unification, Request for a Waiver under Art. XXV:5, L/6759 (31 October 1990), para. 4.

66 Working Party Report, German Unification – Transitional Measures Adopted by the European Communities, L/7119 (18 December 1992), para. 15. The report was adopted by the GATT Council at its meeting on 9–10 February 1993, C/M/261 (12 March 1993), para. 14.

67 *Ibid.*

In the WTO waiver decisions have been adopted that waive obligations under the GATT, the Customs Valuation Agreement, the Agreement on Trade-Related Investment Measures, the Agreement on Agriculture, the GATS and the TRIPS Agreement. No waiver to date has been granted of an obligation of the WTO Agreement. So far there never has been any discussion as to whether a particular obligation could be waived according to Art. IX:3 WTO Agreement or not. Several waiver decisions, however, lack precision as to the obligation which they are waiving. Thus, for example, the waiver granted to Albania of its obligation to comply with certain tariff reduction commitments states that 'the commitments to make effective the interim bound rates in Schedule CXLVI... are waived'.[68] Correctly speaking, however, the decision waives the obligation in Art. II GATT which obliges members to 'accord to the commerce of the other contracting parties treatment no less favourable than that provided for in the... Schedule' annexed to the GATT. Other examples for such imprecision are the waiver decisions that waive the prohibition on determining customs value on the basis of minimum customs values in Art. 7:2 (f) of the Customs Valuation Agreement. Without referring to a provision of the CVA, these decisions typically only state that the requesting WTO member 'may use the officially established minimum values'[69] subject to certain terms and conditions.

One waiver granted to Mongolia in 2007 waives Mongolia's commitment to phase out and eliminate its export duty on raw cashmere as contained in paragraph 2 of the Protocol for the Accession of Mongolia to the WTO Agreement.[70] Protocols of accession become integral parts of the WTO Agreement.[71] Specific commitments of the acceding member relating to trade in goods and trade in services are contained in schedules annexed to the protocol. These become the Schedule of Concessions and Commitments annexed to the GATT 1994 and the Schedule of Specific Commitments annexed to the GATS relating to the acceding member.[72] As such they are integral parts of the GATT (Art. II:7 GATT) and the GATS (Art. XX:3 GATS). A waiver decision which intends to free a member from an accession commitment contained in such a schedule would

---

68 WT/L/610, para. 1; on this waiver, see Chapter 4 B.I.2.1(b).
69 See e.g. WT/L354, para. 1; on the waivers of obligations under the Customs Valuation Agreement, see Chapter 4 B.I.1.1.
70 WT/L/695, para. 1; on this waiver see Chapter 4 B.I.2.1(b).
71 For the protocol of accession of Mongolia this is stated in Part I, para. 2 of the Protocol, WT/ACC/MNG/11 (25 July 1996).
72 See e.g. WT/ACC/MNG/11, Part 2, para. 5.

have to waive the obligation contained in the respective multilateral trade agreement to comply with the specific commitment as laid down in the members' schedule. Accession protocols, however, also comprise commitments which are not part of the acceding member's schedules, such as Mongolia's commitment to phase out export duties on cashmere which is found in the working party report[73] and by reference is included in the accession protocol.[74] Strictly speaking, these commitments are not an integral part of the Multilateral Trade Agreements, nor of the WTO Agreement narrowly defined, but instead form part of the Marrakesh Agreement, understood as the WTO Agreement including its annexes. Nonetheless, the waiver decision which suspends Mongolia's accession commitment is based on Art. IX:3 WTO Agreement and this has not been challenged by any WTO member.

III Substantive requirements

It appears from the relevant legal provisions that the existence of exceptional circumstances is a substantive requirement for the exercise of the waiver power. At first sight it seems to be the only substantive requirement, albeit one which has to be taken seriously. Not only does Art. IX:3 WTO Agreement state that '*[i]n exceptional circumstances* the Ministerial Conference may decide to waive an obligation'.[75] In addition, waiver requests have to state the exceptional circumstances that justify a waiver (Understanding, para. 1),[76] and so do the waiver decisions (Art. IX:4 cl.1 WTO Agreement). Finally, during the annual review of waivers, the Ministerial Conference 'shall examine whether the exceptional circumstances justifying the waiver still exist' (Art. IX:4 cl. 3 WTO Agreement).

The wording of Art. XXV:5 GATT (which was the general waiver power under the GATT 1947) suggests a further substantive requirement for the exercise of the waiver competence. According to Art. XXV:5 GATT waivers may be granted '[i]n exceptional circumstances *not elsewhere provided for in this Agreement*'.[77] This wording supports an interpretation according to which the waiver power shall only be used to justify non-compliance which is not justified under any other treaty provision. The question whether the waiver power shall only be used to justify measures

---

73 WT/ACC/MNG/9 (27 June 1996), para. 24.   74 WT/Acc/Mng/11, para. 2.
75 Emphasis added.
76 On the requirements that waiver requests have to meet, see below section C.I.
77 Emphasis added.

that would otherwise be illegal has been raised several times in practice. It is of particular relevance, for if this question was answered in the affirmative then the adoption of a waiver decision could be interpreted as a determination of illegality with respect to the measure for which the waiver is being granted.

Finally, this section will deal with two further claims – made in particular by contracting parties under the GATT 1947 – in connection with the exercise of the waiver power. These are: firstly, the claim that waiver decisions should not lead to trade diversion and, secondly, that waiver decisions should not contradict the objectives of the GATT/the WTO.

1 The 'exceptional circumstances' requirement

The term 'exceptional circumstances' has never been authoritatively defined, either under the GATT 1947 or in the WTO. Art. XXV:5 GATT expressly authorizes the organization to 'define certain categories of exceptional circumstance to which other voting requirements shall apply for the waiver of obligations' (Art. XXV:5 (i) GATT) and to 'prescribe such criteria as may be necessary for the application of this paragraph' (Art. XXV:5 (ii) GATT). These competences were, however, never used. Under the GATT 1947 the question whether a certain situation gave rise to exceptional circumstances was frequently raised. In the WTO, by contrast, the existence of exceptional circumstances is hardly ever the subject of an open debate.[78]

While interpretation suggests that the waiver power should be used restrictively as an escape clause to address individual situations in which compliance would temporarily result in undue hardship, the waiver practice contradicts such a reading. However, even though the exceptional circumstances requirement did not place a substantive restriction on the waiver power, I shall argue that it is not without meaning and that it might perform an even more important role in the future. For one, the exceptional circumstances language provides members with a legal argument to support their opposition to a waiver decision. More importantly,

---

78 The only publicly accessible minutes in which the term appears are those which document discussions in the Council on Trade in Goods on the EC's request for a waiver of Art. I:1 GATT for trade preferences under the Cotonou Agreement and the request for a waiver of Art. XIII GATT for the EC's banana import regime. On these waivers, see Chapter 4 B.I.3.3(b).

however, the proceduralization of this requirement may enhance transparency, facilitate control of the waiver process and waivers, and prevent arbitrariness in the examination of waiver requests.

1.1 Textual, systematic and historical interpretation

The legal texts, as well as the systematic position of the waiver power and the *travaux préparatoires* suggest that the waiver is an instrument which justifies non-compliance by individual members with particular obligations in temporary situations where compliance would result in undue hardship.

The term 'exceptional circumstances' can be interpreted to refer to a situation which deviates from the normal state of affairs. 'Exceptional' entails the expectation of a return to the state of normality when the exceptional circumstances subside. Neither Art. IX:3 WTO Agreement nor Art. XXV:5 GATT clarify, however, whether the exceptional circumstances shall exist in the territory of the member requesting the waiver or whether such member may also react to exceptional circumstances outside its territory. This ambiguity can be resolved by reference to the *travaux préparatoires* which suggest that the drafters had in mind circumstances within the jurisdiction of the requesting member which differ from the usual circumstances.[79]

The wording of Art. IX:3 WTO Agreement, which states that 'the Ministerial Conference may decide to waive an obligation of *a* Member', and of the Understanding, which requires that a waiver request 'shall describe *the measures* which *the Member* seeks to pursue' (para. 1), further suggest that individual members will be requesting waivers and not that waivers will be adopted for the benefit of whole groups of members or even all members.[80] The reference to specific measures in the Understanding implies that the waiver power is not intended to be used to suspend obligations in their entirety, but only with respect to specific measures which are necessitated by the exceptional circumstances.

A narrow scope of the waiver power is also supported by a systematic interpretation. When seen in the context of the competence of the Ministerial Conference and General Council to adopt authoritative interpretations (Art. IX:2 WTO Agreement) as well as the competence to propose amendments (Art. X:1 WTO Agreement), the argument can be made that each of these powers intends to address a different situation. While an authoritative interpretation and an amendment are instruments

---

79 E/PC/T/C.V/PV/9, 8, 9.   80 Emphasis added.

to clarify or modify the legal rules in an abstract way and for the whole membership, the waiver power – it could be argued – will be used to address individual cases and concrete situations.

The *travaux préparatoires* suggest the intention of the drafters[81] to limit the exercise of the waiver power to particular members and specific situations of a temporary nature. During the London Preparatory Conference for an International Trade Organization, the delegate from the United States, Edward H. Kellogg, stated that the proposed waiver power was meant to 'cover cases which were exceptional and caused particular hardship to any particular member'.[82] The French delegate at the same meeting stated that the waiver power should allow the suspension of obligations if they 'would impose some economic hardship on some countries, those hardships . . . being of a temporary character'.[83] From the *travaux préparatoires* it appears that this interpretation was undisputed.

1.2 Case law

To date only a few panel and Appellate Body reports have addressed the waiver power. The first of these dispute settlement reports had to deal with the question that arose in the *Sugar Waiver* dispute between the EEC and the United States whether certain US trade restrictions were justified under the 1955 Agricultural Waiver.[84] The Agricultural Waiver was one of the few GATT waiver decisions which was not limited in duration and which enabled the United States to impose wide-ranging restrictions on agricultural products to protect its domestic agricultural industry.[85] Nonetheless, the panel stressed that waivers were only granted in exceptional circumstances, a fact from which it deduced the duty to interpret waiver decisions narrowly.[86] It refrained, however, from engaging in a review whether the requirement of 'exceptional circumstances' had been met in case of the Agricultural Waiver.[87]

---

81 According to Art. 32 VCLT the negotiating history of treaties constitutes a supplementary means of interpretation. On the relevance of negotiating history in interpretation of international law in general as well as by the Appellate Body, see Van Damme, *Treaty Interpretation by the WTO Appellate Body*, 44 *et seq.*, 306 *et seq.*

82 E/PC/T/C.V/PV/9, 8, see also E/PC/T/C.V/25, 3.   83 E/PC/T/C.V/PV/9, 9.

84 Panel Report, *US – Sugar Waiver*, adopted 7 November 1990, L/6631, BISD 37S/228.

85 On this waiver decision, see Chapter 4 B.I.2.2(a).

86 Panel Report, *US – Sugar Waiver*, adopted 7 November 1990, L/6631, BISD 37S/228, para. 5.9.

87 For a discussion of the judicial review of waiver decisions, see section F.II. below.

Later reports, all prompted by the *Bananas III* dispute, reiterated the exceptional nature of waivers.[88] They moved from the claim that waiver decisions had to be interpreted narrowly to the statement that they had to be interpreted 'with great care'.[89] The Appellate Body report in the second compliance proceeding in *Bananas III* made a further statement based on the exceptional circumstances requirement as well as the systematic position of the waiver as one of three methods to interpret or modify WTO law.[90] Apart from stressing the exceptional nature of waivers and the need to interpret them with great care, the Appellate Body in this report emphasized that the purpose of a waiver was 'not to modify existing provisions in the agreements, let alone create new law or add to or amend the obligations under a covered agreement or Schedule'.[91] This last statement, as well as the interpretation put forward in the preceding section, have been contradicted by the waiver practice.

1.3 Waiver practice

The narrow interpretation of the waiver power that was proposed at the London Conference was from time to time invoked under the GATT 1947 by individual contracting parties that opposed particular waiver decisions.[92] Furthermore, the general modification of norms by way of the adoption of waiver decisions was criticized by the proponents of such norm change who desired an instrument which would be less evocative of

---

88 Panel Report, *EC – Bananas III*, WT/DS27/R/ECU (22 May 1997), para. 7.105; Appellate Body Report, *EC – Bananas III*, WT/DS27/AB/R, adopted 25 September 1997, para. 185; Panel Report, *EC – Bananas III (Article 21.5 – US)*, WT/DS27/RW/USA (19 May 2008), 7.569; Appellate Body Report, *EC – Bananas III (Article 21.5 – US)*, WT/DS27/AB/RW/USA, adopted 22 December 2008, paras. 378 *et seq.*

89 Appellate Body Report, *EC – Bananas III*, WT/DS27/AB/R, adopted 25 September 1997, para. 185; Appellate Body Report, *EC – Bananas III (Article 21.5 – ECU II, US)*, WT/DS27/AB/RW2/ECU, adopted 11 December 2008, WT/DS27/AB/RW/USA, adopted 22 December 2008, para. 382.

90 The other two methods being the adoption of an authoritative interpretation or an amendment decision.

91 Appellate Body Report, *EC – Bananas III (Article 21.5 – ECU II, US)*, WT/DS27/AB/RW2/ECU, adopted 11 December 2008, WT/DS27/AB/RW/USA, adopted 22 December 2008, para. 382.

92 Czechoslovakia, for example, vehemently criticized the ECSC Waiver. It argued that Art. XXV:5 GATT was meant to cover situations different to the integration project of the ECSC. According to the Czech view – referring to the *travaux préparatoires* – the waiver power was meant to address economic difficulties with compliance of a temporary character arising from situations such as floods or droughts. Working Party 4 on the European Coal and Steel Community, Statement by the Czechoslovak Delegation at the Tenth Meeting of the Seventh Session, W.7/47 (29 October 1952), 4.

the idea of 'exceptionality' than a waiver.[93] Apart from the dispute settlement bodies, other organs also referred to the exceptional circumstances requirement as limiting the scope of the waiver power. The Executive Secretary in 1955 stated in his legal opinion on the scope of Art. XXV:5 GATT:

> The words 'in exceptional circumstances not elsewhere provided for in this Agreement' are clearly designed to limit the use of the waiver provision to individual problems to which the Agreement as written does not provide an adequate solution and where an amendment would result in a modification both broader in its application and more permanent than is required.[94]

The waiver practice reveals, however, that the exceptional circumstances requirement has not led to a substantive restriction of the waiver power.[95] Waivers under the GATT 1947 and in the WTO have not merely addressed individual cases and have not been restricted to situations of economic hardship or those of a temporary nature.

A few waiver decisions did indeed address exceptional situations such as those envisaged by the drafters of the Havana Charter's waiver power, namely situations particular to individual members and temporarily imposing economic hardship. They were prompted by financial crises or natural disaster.[96] Many other individual waivers adopted in the WTO, however, are not justified by similar situations. Many of the capacity problems which are addressed by individual waivers are due to structural deficits which are shared by many developing countries and cannot be

---

93 See Gros Espiell, 'GATT: Accommodating Generalized Preferences', 341 (criticizing the choice to legalize the Generalized System of Preferences through adoption of a waiver decision).

94 Executive Secretary, Article XXV:5(a). Applicability of Article XXV:5(a) to Obligations defined in Part I of the General Agreement, L/403 (7 September 1955). This statement was cited again in a Secretariat note of 1993 to the Group on Environmental Measures and International Trade on the waiver power, TRE/W/18 (1 October 1993), para. 3.

95 This was already noted by John H. Jackson with respect to the waiver practice under the GATT 1947: see Jackson, *World Trade and the Law of GATT*, 544. For a critique of this practice in the WTO, see Marinberg, 'GATT/WTO Waivers', 129.

96 For example, Albania's request for a waiver from its commitments under the GATS to liberalize its telecommunications sector was justified by reference to Albania's economic situation after the war in Kosovo as well as the 9/11 terrorist attacks: see S/L/148 (21 November 2003). El Salvador justified the need for a waiver of obligations of the Customs Valuation Agreement with the unforeseen delay in the passage of domestic legislation which was caused by two major earthquakes in January and February 2001: see WT/L/453 (17 May 2002), preamble. An example for a GATT waiver that addressed such circumstances is the waiver allowing Pakistan to maintain a temporary Flood Relief Surcharge in violation of Art. II:1 GATT: see CONTRACTING PARTIES, Pakistan – Flood Relief Surcharge, Decision of 28 January 1974, L/4003, BISD 21S (1975), 27.

described as temporary even though the general aim is repeatedly formulated that these problems should be overcome at some time in the future. Even farther removed from the situations that were anticipated when the waiver power was included in the General Agreement are the requests for waivers to legalize special preferences. The drafters of the waiver power clearly envisaged that the situation which justifies a waiver decision is faced by the requesting member who seeks a suspension of its obligations. However, waivers to legalize special preferences usually do not refer to exceptional circumstances in the preference-granting member but to the situation in the developing countries that are to benefit from the preferences.[97] Moreover, in these cases compliance would not impose a particular economic burden on the preference-granting member.

Finally, collective waivers are adopted which relieve all members or groups of members from the burdens of compliance. Some of them address structural deficits which render compliance difficult for all countries or whole groups of countries. Others generally modify legal rules to take account of a changed consensus with respect to the objectives of the law or coordinate WTO law with other legal regimes. None of these collective waiver decisions conform to the narrow interpretation. Due to this long-standing practice, in which all members have joined over time, it can be said that to date no substantive meaning can be ascribed to the term 'exceptional circumstances' in the waiver competence.[98]

The effect of the waiver practice under the GATT 1947 on the 'exceptional circumstances' requirement is somewhat reflected in the wording of the Understanding in Respect of Waivers of Obligations under the GATT. The Understanding requires that waiver requests describe not only the measure for which the waiver is sought, but also 'the specific policy objectives which the Member seeks to pursue and the reasons which prevent the Member from achieving its policy objectives by measures consistent with its obligations under the GATT' (section 1). The Understanding does

---

97 See Chapter 4 B.I.3.3. In the working party on the United States' request for a waiver for preferences granted under the Caribbean Basin Economic Recovery Act the United States argued that exceptional circumstances consisted, on the one hand, in the need for economic recovery in the preference-receiving countries and, on the other hand, in the legal situation that the preferences were not covered by the Enabling Clause, but were consistent with its objectives. Some members of the working party were of the view that no exceptional circumstances existed which would justify the granting of the waiver. Consequently the working party did not recommend the adoption of a waiver to the CONTRACTING PARTIES (BISD 31S/189).

98 On the role of subsequent practice in interpretation by the Appellate Body, see Van Damme, *Treaty Interpretation by the WTO Appellate Body*, 338 *et seq.*

not mention the term 'exceptional circumstances', but instead acknowledges that waivers are requested in the pursuit of certain policy objectives and not merely out of necessity in situations in which compliance is impossible.

1.4 The rhetorical and procedural function of the 'exceptional circumstances' requirement in the waiver process

Even though the exceptional circumstances requirement does not place a substantive limitation on the waiver power, it is not without meaning. Waiver requests have to be reasoned; waiver decisions have to state the 'exceptional circumstances justifying the decision' (Art. IX:4 WTO Agreement) and in each annual review it shall be examined 'whether the exceptional circumstances justifying the waiver still exist'.

This emphasis on the need for a justification of waivers on the basis of the existence of exceptional circumstances provides members who wish to veto a waiver decision with a legal argument to oppose the adoption of a waiver. The only other valid legal arguments that can be made during the waiver process are arguments referring to the correct procedure. Within the WTO the only time when the existence of exceptional circumstances was openly disputed was in response to the highly contentious waiver request submitted by the EC for an extension of the waiver of Art. XIII GATT for the EC's banana import regime. Latin American banana exporting countries who were opposed to an extension argued, inter alia, that the exceptional circumstances which had existed when the waiver was first granted (due to the understandings reached between the EC and the United States and between the EC and Ecuador on a preliminary settlement of the *Bananas* dispute) now had ceased to exist.[99] In all the other formal discussions on waivers the term 'exceptional circumstances' either does not appear at all or it is simply stated (mostly by the requesting member) that exceptional circumstances exist.

While the requirement of exceptional circumstances may be used rhetorically to support or oppose a waiver request and thus is not meaningless, a normative argument can be made in favour of the proceduralization of the exceptional circumstances requirement. Such a proceduralization is already foreseen by the legal provisions. Thus, members have to substantiate their waiver requests with reasons why a waiver is necessary, and the waiver decision has to document the reasons which justify the decision in view of the organization. These reasons then serve

99 Council for Trade in Goods, Minutes of the Meeting on 10 March 2006, G/C/M/83, paras. 5.8., 5.9., 5.12 (May 2006) (statements by the representatives of Honduras and Panama).

as a reference in the annual review to determine whether the need for a waiver persists. This proceduralization has the potential to make the waiver process more transparent and to facilitate scrutiny and review[100] while at the same time not limiting the range of situations which may be deemed by the membership to necessitate a waiver decision. It could also be envisaged that it be assessed on the basis of the justification set out in the waiver request and in the waiver decision whether the measures legalized by the waiver have proven effective to remedy the situation or attain the policy objectives which gave rise to the request.[101] Furthermore, the reasons given in support of waiver decisions will have the effect of guiding future examinations of waiver requests. They establish a further justificatory burden in cases in which members intend to treat similar situations differently. The reason-giving requirement may thus serve to contain arbitrariness of the waiver practice.[102]

2 No other legal justification

Apart from the existence of exceptional circumstances, the waiver competence could be interpreted to be limited to situations in which no other justification applies. Again the *travaux préparatoires* are quite clear on this point as is the wording of Art. XXV:5 GATT. At the London Conference the US representative when elaborating on the waiver clause clarified that it was to apply to cases not only exceptional in nature but also 'not covered by specific escape clauses provided elsewhere in the Charter'.[103] This language reappears in Art. XXV:5 GATT which allowed the adoption of waiver decisions 'in exceptional circumstances *not elsewhere provided for* in this Agreement'. Similar language is not included in Art. IX:3 WTO Agreement which merely states that 'in exceptional circumstances, the Ministerial Conference may decide to waive an obligation'. An argument that the restriction foreseen in the GATT nonetheless applies also in the WTO[104] is supported by the wording of the Understanding which states that a waiver request 'shall describe . . . the reasons which prevent the

---

100 On the judicial and political review of waivers, see below sections F.I. and F.II.
101 It has to be observed, however, that so far the annual reviews of waivers in the WTO have been mere formalities and no assessment of the persistence of the circumstances justifying the waiver has taken place.
102 For further discussion of the reason-giving requirement, see Chapter 7 B.V.
103 E/PC/T/C.V/PV/9, 8, see also E/PC/T/C.V/25, 3.
104 Marinberg, 'GATT/WTO Waivers', 129, 325; Wolfrum, 'Article IX WTO Agreement', 110, 117.

Member from achieving its policy objectives by measures consistent with its obligations under GATT 1994' (para. 1).

A requirement that no other justification may apply before use is made of the waiver competence could be interpreted in two ways. Firstly, it could be understood simply to mean that a waiver shall only be granted for measures which without the waiver would be in violation of WTO law. Secondly, and more far-reaching, it could be argued that a waiver should only be granted in situations which do not fall within the scope of one of the legal exceptions.[105] According to the latter view one might come to the conclusion that a waiver may not be granted even if the measure for which the waiver is sought is not justified, as long as the situation is addressed by another exception. To give an example: with respect to the requests for a suspension of Art. II:1 GATT to allow the imposition of tariff surcharges to address balance-of-payments problems it could have been argued that this situation, balance-of-payments problems, is addressed by Art. XII and Art. XVIII GATT. Consequently, it could have been concluded that balance-of-payments problems are not circumstances not elsewhere provided for in the GATT and that therefore no waiver could be granted.

This example already shows that the latter interpretation was not adopted by the GATT CONTRACTING PARTIES who on several occasions did waive Art. II:1 GATT to allow developing contracting parties to impose tariff surcharges in order to address balance-of-payments difficulties.[106] Similarly, trade preferences under regional-type arrangements which did not meet the requirements of the pertinent exception in Art. XXIV GATT were consistently justified by waivers.[107]

The first interpretation – that waivers may only be granted for measures otherwise illegal – is also not reflected in any consistent waiver practice. It is true that most waivers are requested because the requesting member believes that the measure for which it requests the waiver violates the law[108] or because the measure was found in dispute settlement proceedings to violate the law.[109] Sometimes working party reports or waiver decisions even explicitly state that the measure in question is not justified

---

105 Jackson, *World Trade and the Law of GATT*, 586, fn. 13.   106 *Ibid.*   107 *Ibid.*
108 Examples are the requests by the UK for the Margins of Preferences Waiver (Chapter 4 B.I.2.2(a)(iii)) or by the US for the Agricultural Waiver (Chapter 4 B.I.2.2(a)(i)).
109 The trade preferences granted by the EC under the Lomé Convention were found to violate the law by GATT panels, which recommended that the EC request a waiver, see Chapter 4 B.I.3.3(a).

under any other legal provision.[110] However, under the GATT 1947, as well as in the WTO, waiver decisions did not always reflect an agreement by the membership that the measure in question was not justified under any other GATT or WTO provision. There have been several instances in which requesting members explicitly defended the view that the measures in question were not illegal and that the waiver was merely requested for reasons of legal certainty. Waivers were requested in these cases to achieve legal certainty in light of contestations of the legality of the requested measures by other GATT contracting parties or WTO members.[111] The waiver decisions adopted in these cases often incorporate the view of the requesting party that the waiver is granted for reasons of legal certainty and does not include a verdict on the inconsistency of the measure with the waived obligation. Examples from GATT practice are a waiver granted to Germany for certain quantitative restrictions on agricultural products[112] or the waivers granted to the EEC for tariff preferences under the Lomé IV Convention.[113] In the WTO the EC supported its request for an extension of the Bananas Waiver[114] with the need for legal certainty and at the same time emphasized its view that a waiver was not required.[115] The

---

110 The GATT waiver decisions allowing the imposition of tariff surcharges regularly noted that tariff surcharges were not provided for in Art. XII GATT and were inconsistent with Art. II GATT, see e.g. BISD 8S (1960), 29, 30 recital 6, 10S (1962), 51, recital 4. The working party reports on several waiver requests for trade preferences stated that there was no other provision in the GATT that could justify the granting of such preferences, see e.g. Report of Working Party No. 3 on the Request of the United States for a Waiver in Respect of Preferential Treatment for the Trust Territory of the Pacific, GATT/CP.2/36 (7 September 1948), 1, para. 1.

111 See e.g. CONTRACTING PARTIES, German Import Restrictions, Decision of 30 May 1959, BISD 8S (1960), 31 (reserving Germany's position that the quantitative restrictions for which the waiver was granted were legal); General Council, Waiver Concerning Kimberley Process Certification Scheme for Rough Diamonds, Decision of 15 May 2003, WT/L/518 (27 May 2003); General Council, Decision of 15 December 2006, WT/L/676 (19 December 2006) (extension decision).

112 The waiver decision includes Germany's contention that the import restrictions were covered by the existing legislation clause in the protocol by which Germany acceded to the GATT, BISD 8S (1960) 31, para. 2.

113 L/7604, preamble, 5th recital: 'Noting that the Parties to the [Lomé] Convention have made a request for a waiver under Article XXV:5 without prejudice to their position that the Convention is entirely compatible with their obligations under Article XXIV in light of Part IV'.

114 On this waiver, see Chapter 4 B.I.3.3(b).

115 Council for Trade in Goods, Minutes of the Meeting on 9 May 2006, G/C/M/84 (29 June 2006), para. 6.3 (statement by the delegate of the EC: 'Finally, his delegation wished to note again that its request for a waiver should not be interpreted as a recognition that the ACP TRQ [tariff rate quota] was inconsistent with Article XIII. The objective of the

Kimberley Waiver expressly leaves open the question whether the trade bans for which the waiver is granted are GATT-consistent or not. It states that the waiver decision 'does not prejudge the consistency of domestic measures taken consistent with the Kimberley Process Certification Scheme with provisions of the WTO Agreement including any relevant WTO exceptions, and that the Waiver is granted for reasons of legal certainty'.[116] This language was included on the insistence of WTO members who are of the view that the trade bans are justified under the GATT general exceptions. Both the 2003 TRIPS Waiver and the 1999 Preferences Waiver include clauses stating that they do not prejudice the rights of members under the TRIPS Agreement and the Enabling Clause respectively.[117]

It thus appears from the waiver practice that the political organs do not consider it a mandatory requirement for the exercise of the waiver power that measures for which waivers are granted are inconsistent with the law. There are good reasons too why the waiver power should not be limited by a requirement that no other justification applies. Members would be very reluctant to request waivers in cases where illegality is neither beyond doubt nor already established in dispute settlement. If a waiver decision entailed a determination of illegality this could be interpreted to mean that non-violation complaints would be successful without the need of the complaining member to prove nullification or impairment of benefits.[118] Furthermore, a waiver could be used more easily by other members as a bargaining chip vis-à-vis the beneficiary of the waiver.[119]

Even though waiver decisions do not necessarily entail a determination by the political organs of the illegality of the measure for which the waiver is requested it has nonetheless been argued that waiver decisions might

request was not to fulfil a legal requirement but rather to provide legal certainty for ACP, but also MFN, operators.').

116 WT/L/518 (27 May 2003), preamble, recital 4; WT/L/676 (19 December 2006) (extension decision), preamble, recital 5.
117 General Council, Implementation of Paragraph 6 of the Doha Declaration on the TRIPS Agreement and Public Health, Decision of 30 August 2003, WT/L/540 (2 September 2003), para. 9, General Council, Preferential Tariff Treatment for Least-Developed Countries, Decision of 15 June 1999, WT/L/304 (17 June 1999), para. 6.
118 On non-violation complaints with respect to measures justified by waivers, see below section F.II.3.2.
119 Jackson, Law of World Trade, 714 (suggesting that the practice of granting individual waiver decisions of Art. II GATT for the imposition of tariff surcharges to address balance-of-payments difficulties instead of generally modifying the law was motivated by the interest of industrialized states to use the waiver decisions as bargaining chips with developing countries).

give rise to a presumption of illegality.[120] This alleged stigma was one of the reasons why developing contracting parties resisted a reference to Art. XXV:5 GATT in the 1971 decision which suspended Art. I:1 GATT to allow developed contracting parties to implement the General System of Preferences.[121] These developing countries were of the view that preferences under the GSP were justified under Part IV of the GATT and feared that a waiver decision might support the view that without a waiver they would be illegal. In light of the existing waiver practice this negative connotation of waivers, however, should not be overestimated.

3 No substantial trade diversion

Under the GATT 1947 many working party reports and discussions on waiver requests focused on the question whether the measures for which waivers were requested would result in substantial trade diversion or substantial injury to the trade of third parties.

Some waiver decisions conditioned justification for a measure on the requirement that it did not have any negative effects on the trade with third countries.[122] However, there exists no general requirement that the waiver power may only be used to justify measures that do not negatively affect trade. In fact, most of the tariff preferences justified by waiver decisions result in some trade diversion. The economic rationale for tariff preferences is that they increase exports from the preference-receiving country, on the one hand because these exports replace domestic production in the preference-granting country and, on the other hand, because they replace imports to the preference-granting country from third countries.[123] Tariff preferences are thus in part justified on the basis of their trade diverting effects.[124] While no legal requirement can be discerned that relates to the

---

120 Pauwelyn, 'WTO Compassion or Superiority Complex?', 1177, 1198 *et seq.*

121 See Chapter 4 B.II.2.1(a).

122 CONTRACTING PARTIES, Waiver Granted to the United Kingdom in Connection With Items Not Bound in Schedule XIX and Traditionally Admitted Free of Duty from Countries of the Commonwealth, Decision of 24 October 1953, BISD 2S (1954), 20 (on this waiver, see Chapter 4 B.I.2.2(a)); CONTRACTING PARTIES, United States Imports of Automotive Products, Decision of 20 December 1965, L/2528 (28 December 1965) (on this waiver, see Chapter 4 B.I.2.2(b)).

123 See Report of the then Secretary-General of UNCTAD Raúl Prebisch to the first United Nations Conference on Trade and Development: Prebisch, 'Towards a New Trade Policy for Development', 5, at 21.

124 On the statements in waiver decisions' preambles as to the trade effects of the legalized measures, see below D.III.1.

trade effects of measures legalized by a waiver, these effects obviously are important factors in the consideration of waiver requests.[125]

4 Consistency with the organization's objectives

An argument frequently voiced in support of a waiver request is that the measure for which the waiver is requested – while inconsistent with specific provisions – is nonetheless consistent with the organization's objectives or even promotes such objectives.

Consistency of a waiver decision with the functions and objectives of the organization can even be seen as required by the law. According to the doctrine of delegated powers, an international institution may only act within its functional limits. If it does not remain within these limits it acts ultra vires and cannot produce legal effects.[126] In this doctrine lies an explanation for the statement of the working party which examined the ECSC Waiver request:

> [I]t would be appropriate for the CONTRACTING PARTIES, before granting a waiver under paragraph 5(a) of Article XXV, to consider whether the objectives of the European Coal and Steel Community were consistent with those of the General Agreement.[127]

Since it is the objective of the waiver power to relieve members from the duty to comply it is, however, difficult to envisage a situation which justifies the argument that a waiver violates the objectives of the organization. This might be the case if a waiver generally modifies legal rules to promote an objective which cannot be located in the agreements. So far, the aims of rule-making waivers could be construed as falling within the organization's objectives. Thus, of the WTO rule-making waivers the 1999 Preferences Waiver aims at the economic development of least-developed countries and the 2003 TRIPS Waiver intends to promote the conduciveness of patent protection to social welfare, an objective recognized by Art. 7 of the TRIPS Agreement.

Mostly, however, arguments as to the consistency of a waiver with the organization's objectives are made not to defend a waiver's legality, but rather in an attempt to present waivers not only as a matter of individual preference, but as generally desirable or a matter of equity. An example is the justification put forward by the United Kingdom for the requested

---

125 See below discussion in Chapter 7 A.II.   126 See *supra* section A.I.
127 BISD 1S (1953), 85, 86, para. 3.

waiver of Art. I:4 GATT to enable it to legally raise tariffs on products for which its tariffs were unbound without having to adopt legislation imposing tariffs on the same products from Commonwealth countries that benefited from historical preferences. The UK argued that the waiver was a mere technicality since the tariff increases would not result in trade diversion, i.e. imports from third countries which were to be subjected to higher customs duties would not be replaced by imports from Commonwealth countries.[128] Similarly, in support of waivers for special preference schemes it is sometimes said that special preferences – even though in violation of Art. I GATT and the Enabling Clause – are in fact promoting the objective of increased export earnings to promote economic development and thus further an aim of the organization. Accordingly, waivers justifying tariff preferences for developing country products in their preambles frequently refer to objectives of the GATT.[129]

It is indeed not seldom the case that a rule in certain instances appears over-inclusive by prohibiting certain measures which do not compromise its objective, or under-inclusive by not allowing measures which would further its objectives.[130] The former was arguably the case with the UK tariffs, the latter with respect to the GATT rules on balance of payments restrictions. Thus it could be argued in the first case that the UK tariffs should not be prohibited since in fact they did not create new preferences, and in the second case that tariff surcharges should be allowed since they more efficiently addressed balance-of-payments difficulties than quantitative restrictions.[131]

How convincing such arguments are depends on whether there is a consensus among the membership as to the objectives of the legal rules. If consensus exists, arguments that a waiver would be conducive to the realization of certain objectives may be of great weight in the waiver process. A waiver in such a situation can ensure the consistency of the legal rules with the desired objectives without endangering the validity of the law. By contrast the concept of validity cannot be maintained if rules

---

128 On this waiver, see Chapter 4 B.I.2.2(a).

129 Such waiver decisions often state that the 'preferential treatment . . . is intended to promote economic expansion . . . in a manner consistent with the objectives of the GATT 1994 and not to create barriers for the trade of other Members': Switzerland – Preferences for Albania and Bosnia–Herzegovina, Decision of 18 July 2001, WT/L/406 (26 July 2001), preamble 7th recital.

130 In Chapter 6 I shall come back to this issue and argue that the over-inclusiveness of rules provides a justification for a waiver power of international institutions.

131 On the tariff surcharges waivers granted under the GATT 1947, see Chapter 4 B.I.2.2(a).

simply cease to be binding if compliance does not promote the desired objectives.[132]

C. THE WAIVER PROCEDURE AND PROCESS

The previous section yielded the conclusion that neither the 'exceptional circumstances' nor the 'not elsewhere provided for' language limit the exercise of the waiver power to certain situations or measures. The difficulty and also undesirability of restricting the waiver power through the imposition of substantive limitations is recognized by WTO law. The new rules negotiated during the Uruguay Round did not impose any further substantive requirements, but instead, in addition to changing the majority necessary for the adoption of a waiver decision and requiring that waivers be limited in time, introduced further procedural requirements. This can be seen as an acknowledgement that the waiver process should be a political process merely to be framed by procedural law in order to ensure transparency and accountability. The new rules potentially increase transparency and may facilitate the multilateral control of action justified by waiver decisions. However, despite these rules, the waiver process in the WTO frequently appears less transparent and control less thorough than under the GATT 1947.

This section will take a closer look not only at the procedural rules and their implementaion in practice, but also at the waiver process. The distinction made between procedure and process is the following: Procedure refers to the formal requirements set out in treaty law and secondary law that have to be met so that a waiver decision is legally adopted. By contrast, the term process is wider and refers to the practice by which the content of the decision is established such as the holding of formal and informal consultations and meetings.[133] Such institutional practice over time can lead to the establishment of further binding procedural rules.[134]

WTO law broadly provides for the following procedure for the granting of waivers: the member who wishes to benefit from a waiver submits a waiver request either to the Ministerial Conference or to one of the competent councils – the Council for Trade in Goods, the Council for Trade

---

132 See the discussion in Chapter 3 B.I.2. of the efficient breach doctrine which makes bindingness dependent on whether compliance is efficient.
133 For this distinction, see Bogdandy, *Gubernative Rechtsetzung*.
134 See Benedek, *Die Rechtsordnung des GATT aus völkerrechtlicher Sicht*, 126 *et seq.* (on custom as a source of GATT law).

in Services or the Council for TRIPS. This request will then be examined within a time frame of ninety days (Art. IX:3 WTO Agreement). Before the waiver request is examined by the competent organ adequate notice as well as the possibility for consultations must be given to the other members. A decision to suspend an obligation will be taken by the Ministerial Conference (Art. IX:3 WTO Agreement) or the General Council acting on its behalf (Art. IV:2 WTO Agreement). A waiver decision needs to be approved either by consensus, or – if consensus cannot be reached – by three-fourths of the members (Art. IX:1, 3 WTO Agreement).[135]

I The waiver request

The Understanding in Respect of Waivers of Obligations under the GATT 1994 sets out the requirement that members seeking a waiver submit a reasoned request. Para. 1 of the Understanding reads:

> A request for a waiver or for an extension of an existing waiver shall describe the measures which the Member proposes to take, the specific policy objectives which the Member seeks to pursue and the reasons which prevent the Member from achieving its policy objectives by measures consistent with its obligations under GATT 1994.

Art. IX:3 subparagraphs (a) and (b) WTO Agreement also deal with the waiver request and require that requests for waivers of obligations of the WTO Agreement be submitted to the Ministerial Conference and that requests for waivers of the Multilateral Trade Agreements in Annexes 1A, 1B and 1C initially be submitted to the Council for Trade in Goods, the Council for Trade in Services or the TRIPS Council, respectively, for consideration. Arguably, the provisions of the WTO Agreement merely determine the competent WTO organs to consider waiver requests, but do not give rise to a requirement for the formal submission of a waiver request as does the Understanding. This interpretation is supported by the fact that Art. IX:3 WTO Agreement does not deal with requests for waivers of obligations of the Multilateral Trade Agreements in Annex 2 (Dispute Settlement Understanding) and Annex 3 (Trade Policy Review Mechanism) which also fall within the scope of the waiver power.

---

135 Unless the request concerns an obligation subject to a transition period or a period for staged implementation which the requesting member has not performed (footnote 4 to Art. IX:3 WTO Agreement).

However, even though the written treaty law contains a requirement to submit a reasoned request only with respect to waivers of GATT obligations, in practice requests are submitted whenever individual members seek a waiver of one of their obligations under the WTO Agreements. A request is a precondition for the initiation of discussions in the competent organs. It provides the basis for an examination of the measure for which the waiver is requested, its effects as well as the circumstances put forward for its justification.

By requiring that a waiver request specify the policy objectives which the requesting member pursues as well as the reasons why these objectives cannot be achieved in a GATT-consistent manner, the Understanding acknowledges the indeterminacy of the 'exceptional circumstances' requirement. Exceptional circumstances exist if the relevant WTO organs so decide. In order for this decision to be an informed decision the request needs to provide the relevant information. The requirement of a reasoned request can thus be seen as a proceduralization of the exceptional circumstances requirement. It enhances transparency and enables other members to assess the situation that gives rise to the need for a waiver as well as the economic impact that the measure in question will have.

In practice, waiver requests have not been submitted exclusively by the member seeking a suspension of its legal obligation. Thus, the waivers for trade preferences under the Lomé IV Convention and the Cotonou Agreement were not only requested by the EC, but also by the ACP states parties to these conventions.[136]

When members request a waiver for a certain policy measure, this measure is described in the request. Thus, for example, requests for waivers of the obligations under the TRIMs Agreement refer to the trade-related investment measure that shall be maintained,[137] waivers to allow the use of officially established minimum values to determine customs value specify the products to which they will be applied,[138] and waivers for trade preferences refer to the domestic legislation or international agreement which

---

136 ACP Countries–European Communities. Fourth Lomé Convention, Request for a Waiver from the Parties to the Fourth Lomé Convention, dated 10 October 1994, L/7539 (10 October 1994); New ACP–EC Partnership Agreement, Request for a WTO Waiver, communication from the EC and from Tanzania and Jamaica on behalf of the ACP countries dated 29 February 2000, G/C/W/187 (2 March 2000).

137 See e.g. G/C/W/340 (6 November 2001).

138 See e.g. G/VAL/W/55 (22 December 1999).

is the legal basis for the preferences. Sometimes, the text of the relevant domestic or international legal instrument is included in the request.[139]

As demanded by the Understanding, requests specify the policy objectives which the requesting members seek to pursue. These range from domestic reform in order to gradually implement WTO norms[140] and internal non-economic policies[141] to the pursuit of the economic development of third states[142] and other non-economic foreign policy objectives such as the pursuit of human security or peace.[143] Furthermore, the requests frequently set out how the envisaged measure will contribute to the achievement of the pursued policy objective.

When it comes to the requirement that a member describes the reasons which prevent it from achieving its policy objectives by measures consistent with its legal obligations, requests that seek a postponement of compliance due to certain impediments to compliance usually set out these difficulties. However, requests for waivers for trade preferences are often not very specific on this point. Sometimes they mention that special preferences beyond those granted under GSP are needed to support the preference-receiving state, sometimes they additionally refer to reasons why the conclusion of a free trade agreement consistent with Art. XXIV GATT is not (yet) feasible.[144] There is, however, usually no principled discussion as to why the pursued objectives cannot be achieved within either the framework of the Generalized System of Preferences or a regional trade agreement that meets the requirements of Art. XXIV GATT. Instead, such requests regularly include statements as to the

---

139 See, e.g. G/C/W/510/Add.1 (17 March 2005).
140 This is the case for waivers of obligations of the Customs Valuation Agreement which are discussed in Chapter 4 B.I.1.1. or waivers for trade-related investment measures discussed in Chapter 4 B.I.2.1(a).
141 The request by the US for preferences under the Andean Trade Preferences Act (Chapter 4 B.I.3.3(b)) and the request by Mongolia for a waiver of its commitment to abolish export duties on raw cashmere (Chapter 4 B.I.2.1(b)) indicated domestic policy objectives, namely the fight against drug consumption in the first case and the protection of the environment in the second.
142 This is the common justification for special preferences waivers, discussed in Chapter 4 B.I.3.3.
143 The US ATPA preferences not only aim to contain drug consumption within the US, but also to put an end to drug production and trafficking in the Andean states (Chapter 4 B.I.3.3(b)); the Kimberley Waiver is justified by the aim to stop trade in so-called blood diamonds and thus to protect human security, in particular in African countries (Chapter 4 B.II.3.2).
144 See e.g. L/5573 (US request for a waiver of Art. I GATT for CBERA preferences); L/5948 (Canadian request for a waiver of Art. I GATT for CARIBCAN preferences).

anticipated trade effects as well as the consistency of the preferences with the organization's objectives.[145] Waiver requests frequently include a draft waiver decision. Often the requests are amended to include further information that was demanded by other members, frequently relating to the measure for which the waiver is requested.[146]

In the WTO it has been a point of criticism that waiver requests are sometimes submitted at a time when the measure for which the waiver is requested is already in force.[147] Despite demands that submissions be made early enough to allow for an examination before the entry into force of the measure in question, the practice of submitting waiver requests after the fact has persisted.[148] In some instances this may be explained by the fact that the full extent of a measure will only be known once it has been adopted domestically. At that time it often, however, also takes effect.

A number of collective waiver decisions were not adopted on the basis of a waiver request, but instead on the basis of a mandate by the Ministerial Conference. The TRIPS Waiver, as well as the waiver that suspends Art. 70.9 TRIPS Agreement for pharmaceutical products, implement provisions of the Doha Declaration on the TRIPS Agreement and Public Health.[149] The 1999 Waiver suspending Art. I:1 GATT to allow developing country members to afford preferential tariff treatment to products from least-developed countries is based on the Comprehensive and Integrated WTO Plan of Action for the Least-Developed Countries which the Ministerial Conference adopted in Singapore in 1996.[150] This Integrated WTO Plan of Action calls on members to 'explore the

---

145 See e.g. G/C/W/257 (28 March 2001).

146 See e.g. Council for Trade in Goods, Request for a WTO Waiver – New ACP–EC Partnership Agreement, G/C/W/187 (2 March 2000) and the various addenda and revisions to this request in G/C/W/187 Add. 1, Add. 2, Add. 2 Rev. 1, Add. 2 Rev. 2, Add. 2, Add. 3.

147 See Council for Trade in Goods, Minutes of the Meeting on 5 April and 18 May 2000, G/C/M/43 (13 June 2000), para. 5.5 (criticism by the representative of Canada), para. 5.6. (statement by the chairman of the General Council 'that it was important to take note of ... the request that submissions were provided in a timely enough way to allow the Goods Council to consider waivers in a meaningful fashion').

148 Extreme examples are the US requests for waivers in relation to preferences under the amended Caribbean Basin Economic Recovery Act and the African Growth and Opportunity Act. These preferences had been granted for years without a legalizing waiver before the US submitted waiver requests in 2005, see Chapter 4 B.I.3.3(b).

149 See Chapter 4 B.II.1.2. and B.II.2.2.

150 Comprehensive and Integrated WTO Plan of Action for the Least-Developed Countries, adopted 13 December 1996, WT/MIN(96)/14 (7 January 1996). The Ministerial Conference had already called for the adoption of positive measures to facilitate the expansion of trading opportunities in favour of least-developed countries in the 1994 Decision

possibilities of granting preferential duty-free access for the exports of least-developed countries' and further states that exceptions should be provided for such preferences.[151] While mandates by the highest political organ, the Ministerial Conference, may be seen as an important legal prerequisite to legitimate autonomous law-making by organs of international institutions,[152] they are of limited relevance within the WTO where all waiver decisions are adopted by the Ministerial Conference or the General Council acting on the basis of consensus. This would change if members returned to voting on waivers. Then a mandate adopted by consensus would be an additional legitim-ating factor for subsequent waivers adopted by a majority decision to implement such a mandate.

Another group of collective waivers, namely the collective Harmonized System waivers, have also not been adopted on the basis of individual requests. In contrast to the high level mandates for the legislative waiver decisions, these waivers were adopted on the initiative of the Committee on Market Access. That in these instances the waiver process was initiated at the level of technical experts is explained by the rather technical and non-contentious nature of the process of adapting schedules to changes in the Harmonized System.[153]

II Examination of waiver requests

Between the submission of the waiver request and the adoption of a waiver decision by the General Council (or in exceptional cases the Ministerial Conference) there is a period of examination of the proposed waiver. This examination is conducted in formal and informal meetings as well as bilateral consultations. When comparing the practice under the GATT 1947 with that in the WTO, it appears – somewhat counterintuitively – that this period of examination was more regulated and transparent under the GATT than it is in the WTO. Most importantly, waiver requests under the GATT 1947 were habitually examined by working parties set up with

---

on Measures in Favour of Least-Developed Countries, LT/UR/D-1/3 (15 April 1994), para. 3.
151 *Ibid.*, para. 11.
152 On the need for mandates to ensure the legitimacy of the exercise of public authority by international institutions, see Bogdandy and Goldmann, 'Exercise of International Public Authority Through National Policy Assessment', 241, 289 *et seq.*
153 See Chapter 4 B.II.3.1. and Chapter 7 A.II.2.

the mandate of examining the waiver request. This practice was abandoned in the WTO. The main part of the examination is now conducted in informal meetings and consultations, a practice which leads to a loss of transparency. Moreover, it reduces even further the opportunities for a principled discussion on the merits of a waiver which takes into account interests beyond the immediate commercial interests of individual members.

1 The organs involved

Art. IX:3 WTO Agreement authorizes the Ministerial Conference to adopt waiver decisions. In practice most waiver decisions are adopted by the General Council which conducts the functions of the Ministerial Conference between its meetings (Art. IV:2 WTO Agreement).[154] Under the GATT 1947 waiver decisions were exclusively adopted by the CONTRACTING PARTIES. Even when most decision-making competences were delegated to the Council, the CONTRACTING PARTIES retained the exclusive competence to grant waivers.[155]

The Ministerial Conference and the General Council are both plenary organs composed of representatives of all members (Art. IV:1, 2 WTO Agreement).[156] While a plenary organ such as the Ministerial Conference is a general feature of international organizations, it is a special characteristic of the WTO that the General Council, as the organ which conducts the 'everyday business' of the organization, also consists of

---

154 The Ministerial Conference generally only meets once every two years for one week. The Bananas Waiver and the Cotonou Waiver for preferences granted by the EU to ACP states are to date the only WTO waivers which were adopted by the Ministerial Conference, see Chapter 4 B.I.3.3(b).

155 The decision of the CONTRACTING PARTIES on the establishment of the Council of 4 June 1960 stated that the power to take waivers could not be delegated to the Council, BISD 9S (1961), 8; frequently the CONTRACTING PARTIES adopted waiver decisions by ballot. For the voting procedures with respect to waiver decisions, see below section C.III.

156 Under the GATT 1947 membership in the Council was open to 'representatives of all contracting parties willing to accept the responsibilities of membership'. Contracting parties with an interest in a matter could be co-opted as full members, BISD 9S (1961), 8. On the GATT Council and its competences, see Jackson, *World Trade and the Law of GATT*, 154 *et seq.* When the GSP Waiver was discussed in the GATT Council all contracting parties which were not members of the Council were co-opted as full members, C/M/69 (28 May 1971).

representatives of all members.[157] Due to this composition of the decision-making organs all members have a voice in the decision-making procedure under Art. IX:3 WTO Agreement. The Ministerial Conference is generally composed of members' ministers responsible for foreign trade. It is usually members' ambassadors and heads of delegations in Geneva who convene in the General Council.[158]

Not only may all members participate in the decision-making, but the process leading to the adoption of a waiver decision is also formally accessible to all interested members. Membership in the specialized councils and committees, such as the Committee on Market Access (which deals with HS waivers) or the Customs Valuation Committee (which deals with waivers from obligations of the Customs Valuation Agreement) as well as working parties that examine waiver requests, is open to representatives of all members.[159] In practice, however, members and in particular developing country members are not able to attend all meetings of the specialized councils and committees due to capacity restraints.[160] Frequently, it is even difficult for developing country members to send delegates to all meetings of the higher organs. Thus, when Cape Verde's request for a waiver of its tariff reduction commitments was discussed in the Council for Trade in Goods no delegate from Cape Verde could attend the meeting due to 'conflicting commitments'.[161]

Apart from the political organs, chairpersons and Secretariat also play a – sometimes considerable – part in the waiver process. Their informal role in the waiver process will be discussed below (II.3).

---

157 Most international organizations have a non-plenary organ such as the Executive Board of Directors of the IMF and the World Bank. The reason why the WTO does not has been explained by reference to the wariness of the US Congress. US negotiators feared that more far-reaching institutional changes would have resulted in the need to submit the agreement to the Congress for approval, who might not have accepted it. With the limited institutional changes the WTO Agreement could be adopted as an executive-congressional agreement under the fast-track authority that had been granted by the Congress to the US Trade Representative: see Kuijper, 'WTO Institutional Aspects', 79, 83 *et seq*. On the problems caused by the absence of a non-plenary body for efficient decision-making and de facto techniques such as so-called Green Room negotiations, *ibid.*, 112 *et seq.*

158 Footer, *Institutional and Normative Analysis of the World Trade Organization*, 43, 48.

159 Art. IV para. 5 cl. 7 WTO Agreement.

160 Footer, *Institutional and Normative Analysis of the World Trade Organization*, 54.

161 Council for Trade in Goods, Minutes of the Meeting on 12 May 2009, G/C/M/97 (22 June 2009); on this waiver see Chapter 4 B.I.2.1(b).

2 The examination process

The waiver process starts when a member submits a request for a waiver either to the General Council, a specialized council or the committee which is competent for the matter in question. Even though the submission of requests to a committee is not foreseen in Art. IX:3 WTO Agreement, in practice requests which concern a matter that falls within the mandate of a particular committee are submitted to this committee. Thus, the requests for Harmonized System waivers are submitted to the Committee on Market Access, requests for waivers from the Customs Valuation Agreement to the Customs Valuation Committee. The 'Guiding Principles to be Followed by the Contracting Parties in Considering Applications for Waivers from Part I [GATT] or other Important Obligations of the Agreement' (Guiding Principles) which were adopted by the CONTRACTING PARTIES for the consideration of waivers provide that '[a]pplications for waivers from Part I or other important obligations of the General Agreement should be considered only if submitted with at least thirty days' notice'. The guidelines further recognize that in cases of urgency this requirement may be relaxed.[162] After submission of the request and before its consideration by the competent body, the requesting member should give full consideration to representations made by other members and engage in full consultations with them.[163] After members have had time to study the request, it is considered in the meeting of the competent body. The agendas which are distributed to all delegations prior to the formal meetings of WTO organs ensure that delegates know before a meeting whether a waiver request will be discussed.

In the WTO the competent committees or councils usually discuss waiver requests and draft waiver decisions in formal and informal meetings. Formal meetings are usually held in private.[164] When waiver requests are particularly contentious the waiver process may include a question

---

162 CONTRACTING PARTIES, Article XXV – Guiding Principles to be Followed by the Contracting Parties in Considering Applications for Waivers from Part I or other Important Obligations of the Agreement, Decision of 1 November 1956, (L/532), BISD 5S/25, para. (a). The Guiding Principles form part of the GATT 1994 according to Introductory Note to the General Agreement on Tariffs and Trade 1994, Section 1 (b) (iv).

163 *Ibid.*, para. (b).

164 See Rule 32 of the Rules of Procedure for Sessions of the Ministerial Conference and Meetings of the General Council, adopted by the General Council on 31 January 1995, WT/L/28 (7 February 1995). According to this rule it can be decided that a meeting shall be public.

and answer process. Interested members submit questions to the requesting member who addresses them. Questions and answers are published on the WTO website.[165] The minutes of the formal meetings are also posted on the website.[166]

The only publicly accessible formal information on the informal meetings consists of the short summaries given by the chairpersons in formal meetings which are included in the minutes. Since most discussions on waiver requests do take place in informal meetings and bilateral consultations, the waiver process in the WTO is characterized by a relatively great lack of transparency. It lacks transparency not only for outsiders, but also for members who do not have the capacity to participate in all informal meetings.

When the body in which the request is being discussed reaches a consensus on a draft waiver decision, this decision is submitted to the organ which is next in the institutional hierarchy and – if this organ is not the General Council – from there to the General Council for adoption. Usually, the higher organs do not consider the waiver request anew, but follow the recommendation of the lower organ to submit the waiver decision to the General Council for adoption or – when the draft decision is submitted directly to the General Council – to adopt the waiver decision. To illustrate this process by way of example: requests for individual Harmonized System waivers are submitted to the Committee on Market Access which was established with the mandate 'to ensure that GATT Schedules are kept up-to-date, and that modifications, including those resulting from changes in tariff nomenclature, are reflected'.[167] In the committee the requests are discussed in formal and informal meetings and after approval in a formal meeting are referred to the Council for Trade in Goods together with a draft decision. The Council for Trade in Goods approves a request usually on the basis of the committee's approval and without further discussion transmits it to the General Council for adoption. The General Council then adopts the decision on

---

165 A question and answer process was conducted for example with respect to the EC request for the Bananas Waiver and the United States' 2005 requests for waivers for preferences granted under CBERA, ATPA and AGOA.

166 They are available under http://docsonline.wto.org/gen_home.asp?language=1&_=1 (last accessed 12 March 2011).

167 General Council, WTO Committee on Market Access, Decision adopted on 31 January 1995, WT/L/47 (17 February 1995), para. C. The Committee on Market Access is a subsidiary organ of the Council for Trade in Goods which is established by the WTO Agreement and operates under the general guidance of the General Council (Art. IV para. 5 WTO Agreement).

the basis of the respective recommendation by the Council for Trade in Goods.

Art. IX:3 WTO Agreement provides that the consideration of a waiver request by WTO bodies shall not exceed ninety days. In case the request concerns an obligation of one of the Multilateral Trade Agreements, the organ considering the request shall at the end of this time period submit a report to the Ministerial Conference (Art. IX:3(b) cl. 2 WTO Agreement).[168] In practice this time limit is not observed strictly. However, the rule is followed in so far as chairpersons of the organ considering the request inform the General Council of the state of discussions in case the organ cannot agree on a request for several months. When in the past the competent organ in such a case could not agree on a report, chairpersons submitted reports in their personal capacity.[169] These reports are usually not very detailed, but merely state the main points of contention without detailing individual positions or reasons for the opposition to a waiver request.[170]

When the EC's request for a waiver of Art. XIII GATT for its preferential tariff quotas for imports of bananas from ACP states was discussed in the Council for Trade in Goods, other members with significant commercial interests in the EC market for bananas claimed that the EC's request insufficiently described the banana import regime for which the waiver was requested as well as the policy objectives which necessitated the waiver. These members claimed that the ninety-day period for the consideration of a waiver request could not begin unless the request was amended.[171] It was eventually agreed that the chairperson of the Council for Trade in Goods would submit a report to the General Council in his personal

---

168 A similar rule is found in the rules of procedure of WTO bodies. According to this rule matters on which no consensus can be reached have to be referred to the higher body which is next in the institutional hierarchy for consideration, see e.g. Rules of Procedure of the Council for Trade in Goods, WT/L/79 (7 August 1995), Rule 33.

169 See e.g. Council for Trade in Goods, Minutes of the Meeting on 12 July 2006, G/C/M/85 (14 September 2006), para. 4.4 (statement of the chairman with respect to his obligation to report to the General Council on the ongoing discussions with respect to the EC's request for an extension of the Bananas Waiver).

170 Council for Trade in Goods, Minutes of the Meeting on 20 November 2006, G/C/M/86 (3 January 2007, para. 6.2 (text of the factual report that the chairman of the Council for Trade in Goods intended to make to the General Council on the state of considerations of the EC's request for an extension of the Bananas Waiver)).

171 See e.g. Council for Trade in Goods, Minutes of the Meeting of 5 April and 18 May 2000, 13 June 2000, G/C/M/43 (13 June 2000), 7 *et seq.*

capacity to update the General Council on the status of discussions on the request in the Council for Trade in Goods.[172]

The time frame for the consideration of waiver requests which is set out in Art. IX:3 WTO Agreement helps to ensure that the discussion of a request is not unduly delayed.[173] Through the requirement to report to the General Council if no decision can be reached contentious requests gain visibility and are taken from the lower bodies of trade experts to the more politicized level of the General Council.[174]

The examination process of waiver requests under the GATT 1947 differed from that in the WTO in one important respect. Under the GATT 1947 it was common practice that upon the submission of a waiver request a working party was established to examine the request. Participation in the working party was open to all interested contracting parties and it was headed by a chairperson.[175] Usually the working party, after a question and answer process, consideration of the request and – if the working party supported the adoption of a waiver – the drafting of a waiver decision, issued a report which was drafted by the Secretariat. This working

172 Council for Trade in Goods, Minutes of the Meeting on 7 July and 16 October 2000, G/C/M/44 (30 October 2000), 22 (statement by the chairman that he would make a factual report to the General Council on his own responsibility).

173 Consideration of the EC's request for a waiver for trade preferences granted under the Cotonou Agreement was, however, substantially delayed, since members opposing the waiver argued that the request did not meet the procedural requirements, see *ibid.*, 18.

174 Pieter Jan Kuijper is more critical and of the view that moving up draft decisions to higher levels only makes sense if some change can be expected from the move because either composition or decision-making modus changes: Kuijper, 'WTO Institutional Aspects', 79, 112.

175 The working party that examined the US request for a waiver of Art. I GATT with respect to CBERA preferences was also open to CBERA eligible beneficiary countries who were not GATT contracting parties (L/5708, para. 2). Generally excepted from this practice of examining waiver requests in working parties were requests concerning the adaptation of GATT schedules to the Harmonized System and Harmonized System changes. Since these waiver decisions were routinely and frequently granted they were considered by the GATT Committee on Tariff Concessions and not by specially established working parties. In a few other instances working parties were not established due to a lack of time. When the EC requested a waiver for trade preferences to be granted to trading partners of the former German Democratic Republic after German unification it opposed the establishment of a working party to consider the waiver request for time reasons. The US was opposed and asked other contracting parties to support its request for the establishment of a working party as a precondition to any decision on a waiver (C/M/246, 6). When the EC nonetheless requested a vote on the waiver decision, the United States voted against. After the adoption of the waiver decision a working party was established to examine the preferences legalized by the waiver decision.

party report listed all relevant documents, including the request and relevant domestic legislation. It summarized the position of the requesting contracting party as well as the opinions formed in the working party, giving a detailed picture of diverging views on factual, policy, as well as legal questions. Annexes to the working party report included relevant documents and – depending on its conclusions – the draft decision. When the working party came to the conclusion that a waiver should be adopted it recommended the adoption to the CONTRACTING PARTIES.[176]

The working party reports were formally adopted by the CONTRACTING PARTIES and like waiver decisions they were published in the Basic Instruments and Selected Documents Supplements. These working party reports constitute an important documentation not only of the situation and objectives justifying the waiver request and of the views of GATT contracting parties with respect to the specific waiver in question, but also, more generally, of the interpretation of the legal requirements of the waiver competence and general waiver practice. In the WTO to date a working party has been established only once, namely to consider the request by the EC and ACP states for a waiver for preferences granted under the Cotonou Agreement.[177] In contrast to GATT working parties no report was drafted.

The practice of establishing working parties for the examination of waiver requests can be seen as an attempt to guarantee that the legitimate interests of the contracting parties are adequately safeguarded. In the WTO, due to the consensus practice, individual members can veto a waiver decision which they think impedes their interests. However, even though the establishment of special working parties in the WTO due to the consensus practice might not be necessary to safeguard the legitimate interests of all members, the lack of a formalized and in-depth multilateral examination of waiver requests has serious disadvantages. Apart from the lack of transparency which results from the practice of considering waiver requests mainly in informal meetings, the bilateralization through

---

176 In a few instances working parties did not recommend the adoption of a waiver. In two cases the requesting member withdrew the request (the EC its request for a waiver to legalize preferences for citrus fruit and Greece its request to legalize preferences for steel from the Soviet Union, see Chapter 4 C). In the other two instances the US proceeded to put its requests (for the Automotive and CBERA Waivers, Chapter 4 B.I.2.2(b) and B.I.3.3(b)) to a vote by the CONTRACTING PARTIES who adopted waiver decisions.

177 Council for Trade in Goods, Minutes of the Meeting on 5 October 2001, G/C/M/53 (14 November 2001), para. 3.1.

consultations between the requesting and interested members prevents a principled examination in which not only individual interests are taken into account, but in which the proposed measure can be assessed against the purported policy objectives as well as its effects on the objectives of the organization or other public interests.

3 Representation of the collective interest – the role of Secretariat and chairpersons

As was argued in the previous section the current process of considering waiver requests predominantly in informal meetings and bilateral consultations is not conducive to a rigorous assessment of the overall effects of waivers. Rather it ensures that each member has the opportunity to safeguard its own interests as defined by the domestic actor entrusted to formulate a response to the waiver request. This raises the question whether the institution's bureaucracy assumes the role of representing collective interests during the waiver process.

A distinct will represented by one organ is considered by some scholars to be an essential characteristic of an international organization.[178] Given the WTO's self-depiction as a member-driven organization,[179] which finds its main expression in the plenary composition of its political organs as well as the consensus practice, it can be questioned whether the WTO represents a collective interest or a distinct will, beyond the legal norms. Pieter Jan Kuijper provocatively expresses these doubts:

> One wonders at times whether 'Member-driven organization' is still even a tautology [since all organizations are driven by their members] and has not rather become a contradiction in terms, i.e. that the WTO has become so much Member-driven that no organization remains with its own will, independent of that of the Member States.[180]

It is a common feature of international organizations that the institutionalization of the formulation, implementation and enforcement of collective interests does not reach the same extent as in the European Union where the 'community interest' is an established legal concept and where

---

178 See Schermers and Blokker, *International Institutional Law*, §44. On this concept and the problems associated with it, see Klabbers, *Introduction to International Institutional Law*, 12.

179 See e.g. WTO, *Understanding the WTO*, 101, www.wto.org/english/thewto_e/whatis_e/tif_e/tif_e.htm (last accessed 11 March 2011).

180 Kuijper, 'Sutherland Report and the WTO's Institutional Law', 191, 197, 198.

the Commission has been entrusted to safeguard this community interest and, inter alia, to represent it in the law-making procedure.[181] Nonetheless, the bureaucracies of other international institutions have, compared with the WTO Director-General and WTO Secretariat, more formal competences and, moreover, play an important informal role in shaping the organizations' activities, including law-making.[182] The Secretary-General of the United Nations, for example, has the competence, according to Art. 99 UN Charter to 'bring to the attention of the Security Council any matter which in his opinion may threaten the maintenance of international peace and security'. The Secretary-General has been identified to articulate a genuine international collective interest which is more than the sum of the interests of the member states.[183] International secretariats (mostly informally) also play an important role in law-making, for example by drafting legal documents. Thus, international secretariats of environmental agreements routinely engage in extensive preparations of decision-making by conferences and meetings of the parties.[184]

In comparison, the part which the WTO Director-General and Secretariat play in the organization's internal policy and law-making processes seems to be more limited.[185] This is only partly due to the WTO's limited staff and budget[186] and owes more to the notion of the WTO as

---

181 See Art. 17 of the Treaty on European Union. On the concept of community interest in the European Community, see Calliess, 'Gemeinwohl in der EU', 174. Armin von Bogdandy notes the lack of a similar concept in the WTO: Bogdandy, 'Preamble WTO Agreement', 1, 9.

182 According to José Alvarez the 'power of secretariat members to become active in treaty-making . . . has been generally assumed as part of a secretariat's "implied powers"': Alvarez, International Organizations as Law-Makers, 284.

183 Uerpmann, Das öffentliche Interesse, 35.

184 Röben, 'Institutional Developments under Modern International Environmental Agreements', 363, 423 et seq.

185 But see Hoekman and Kostecki, Political Economy of the World Trading System, 54 (stating that the Director-General is seen as 'the guardian of the collective interest of Member States'); for claims to strengthen the role of the Secretariat and the Director General, see e.g. Petersmann, 'From "Member-Driven Governance" to Constitutionally Limited "Multi-Level Trade Governance" in the WTO', 86, 109 (arguing that 'WTO Members should empower the Director-General to defend the collective WTO interests more strongly'); Sutherland et al., Future of the WTO, 73 et seq.

186 In 2009 the Secretariat had 629 regular staff and a consolidated budget of CHF 189,257,600 (≈ EUR125 million). This information can be found on the WTO's website at www.wto.org. By contrast the OECD with thirty members has a staff of 2500 and a budget of 303 million EUR (www.oecd.org).

a member-driven organization.[187] The activities of the Secretariat are, however, not negligible. While it might not play a substantial part in law and policy-making processes[188] it engages in a host of external activities, including the dissemination of information on the organization, as for example through the WTO website, joint studies with other international institutions,[189] and education or capacity-building projects in developing countries, for example through the organization of workshops for trade officials.[190] It further draws up reports for the trade policy review of members (section C (v) (b) Trade Policy Review Mechanism) and influences panel proceedings not only through its key role in the selection of panellists, but by giving legal advice on substantive matters.[191]

In the waiver process the Secretariat provides information (mainly on past waiver practice),[192] gives advice on legal questions[193] and assists in

---

187 Kuijper, 'Sutherland Report and the WTO's Institutional Law', 191, 197–9. Again it was due to the resistance by the United States who wished to maintain the character of the agreement as an executive-congressional agreement that the Secretariat was given such limited powers: Kuijper, 'WTO Institutional Aspects', 79, 83 *et seq.*

188 However, here also the impact of the Secretariat is not as negligible as it might seem to be at first sight. On multilateral negotiations, see Yi-Chong and Weller, *Governance of World Trade* (coming to the conclusion that the Secretariat's influence is substantial); R. Howse, 'For a Citizen's Task Force on the Future of the World Trade Organization', 877 (noting that the Director-General and senior WTO officials controlled information, access, and declaration drafting during the Cancun Ministerial).

189 See for example the recent joint study by the WTO and UNEP, *Trade and Climate Change*, www.wto.org/english/res_e/publications_e/trade_climate_change_e.htm (last accessed 11 March 2011).

190 The WTO regularly reports on these activities on its news page at www.wto.org/english/news_e/news_e.htm (last accessed 11 March 2011).

191 Weiler, 'Rule of Lawyers and the Ethos of Diplomats', 191, 205 *et seq.* (criticizing the Secretariat's hidden impact on dispute settlement reports); Howse, 'For a Citizen's Task Force on the Future of the World Trade Organization', 877, 882.

192 See e.g. Note by the WTO Secretariat, Paragraph 6 of the Doha Declaration on the TRIPS Agreement and Public Health: Information on Waivers, IP/C/W/387; Note by the GATT Secretariat on the Waiver Power to the Group on Environmental Measures and International Trade, TRE/W/18 (1 October 1993).

193 Working Party Report on the United States' Waiver Request for Preferences under the Caribbean Basin Economic Recovery Act, BISD 31S/189 (referring to the Secretariat's understanding of footnote 2 of paragraph 2 of the Enabling Clause which it provided at the request of the working party); Hector Gros Espiell refers to an (unpublished) note by the GATT Secretariat on the different legal options to ensure compatibility of the Generalized System of Preferences with the GATT: Gros Espiell, 'GATT: Accommodating Generalized Preferences', 341, 349; Statement by the Deputy Director-General in the Committee on Trade and Development, Note on the Meeting of 2 March 1999, WT/COMTD/M/24 (27 April 1999), para. 32 (on the question whether the Enabling

the drafting of waiver decisions.[194] The most important function of the Secretariat seems to be that of an institutional memory of the organization that can provide information on legal questions as well as on former practice.[195] Its influence varies, depending on the subject matter, and is considerably greater in processes which can be characterized as aiming at effective administration, such as the adaptation of GATT schedules to changes in the Harmonized System, than in areas where diverging member interests collide.[196]

While it is difficult to speak of collective interests in the WTO due to the diversity of views as to the objectives of the organization,[197] the waiver process might be made more transparent and better informed by attributing an even greater part to the Secretariat. Thus, the Secretariat could assist a more rigid assessment of the effects of waivers, or rather the measures which are legalized by waiver decisions, on international trade as well as their effectiveness with respect to the alleged policy objectives such as economic development. It could do so by providing expertise and analysis of these questions so as to inform and structure a multilateral examination of waiver requests. In such an informed multilateral examination the potential effects of measures to be justified by a waiver might become more apparent, not only to members' representatives, but – depending on the publicness of information – also to other actors such as other international institutions, NGOs or even the public in the requesting member.[198] While expertise and analysis would not legally determine the outcome of a waiver process they would increase the justificatory burden of the requesting member and thus might lead to a more reasoned decision. If the influence of the Secretariat in the waiver

Clause justifies tariff preferences granted by developing countries to least-developed countries or whether a waiver is needed).

194 The first collective Harmonized System waiver concerning the transposition of HS2007 changes was, for example, drafted together with the HS2007 procedures by the Secretariat's Market Access Division with the help of the Legal Affairs Division. The draft waiver is contained in G/MA/W/82 (21 September 2006).

195 Weiler, 'Rule of Lawyers and the Ethos of Diplomats', 191, 205 (noting the role of the Secretariat as the repository of institutional memory).

196 See Chapter 7 A.II.

197 There were stronger expressions of collective interests within the early GATT 1947 than in the WTO, see Hudec, 'GATT or GABB?', 1299, 1339; Weiler, 'Rule of Lawyers and the Ethos of Diplomats', 191, 194 *et seq.*

198 Dam, '*GATT: Law and International Economic Organization*', 50, 51 (noting that 'effective analytical work at the international organization level would have an indirect influence both in improving the quality of political discussion within the individual contracting parties and in furthering the goal of economic efficiency with the GATT').

process were to be increased its accountability should, however, also be ensured, meaning that the Secretariat should become more representative of the membership and the selection process for Secretariat officers more transparent.[199]

The chairpersons of the councils and committees that consider waiver requests have also played an important part in waiver processes. Even though chairpersons are representatives of WTO members, as chairpersons they also represent the organ whose meetings they chair. Their personal leadership is often decisive for finding a compromise and thus the successful conclusion of discussions or implementation of procedures.[200] For example, chairman Motta and his successor as chairmen of the TRIPS Council significantly contributed to achieving consensus on the TRIPS Waiver by providing decision drafts and formulating statements to accompany the waiver decision.[201] The chairpersons of the Committee on Market Access played an important role in maintaining legality by regularly reminding members to request extensions of their HS waivers in case they had not yet completed the adjustment of their schedules to HS changes. Through their personal engagement with individual members they substantially contributed to an acceleration of the adaptation exercise.[202]

4 Institutional linkages and participation of NGOs

Other international institutions generally do not play any significant part in the waiver process. Under the GATT this was slightly different with respect to waivers that allowed developing countries with balance of payments difficulties to impose tariff surcharges.[203] In these waiver processes the Committee on Balance-of-Payments Restrictions consulted with the IMF in accordance with Art. XV GATT[204] and a representative of the IMF was invited to make a statement on the balance-of-payments situation of

---

199 Howse, 'For a Citizen's Task Force on the Future of the World Trade Organization', 877, 882; see also the recent proposal by China which was joined by India seeking better representation in the WTO Secretariat, *Economic Times*, 'At Odds Elsewhere: India, China on Same WTO Team', 23 November 2009.

200 Odell, 'Chairing a WTO Negotiation', 425 (on the different techniques used by chairpersons to build consensus and mediate deadlock); Ruse-Khan, 'Role of Chairman's Statements in the WTO', 475.

201 See Abbott, 'WTO Medicines Decision', 317, 326 *et seq.*

202 Feichtner, 'Administration of the Vocabulary of International Trade', 1481, 1501, 1503.

203 On these waiver decisions, see Chapter 4 B.I.2.2(a).

204 Art. XV:2 cl. 1 GATT reads: 'In all cases in which the CONTRACTING PARTIES are called upon to consider or deal with problems concerning monetary reserves, balances

the respective contracting party and the appropriateness of the measures adopted.[205]

Within the WTO several international institutions have the status of observers and as such may participate in formal meetings.[206] The IMF and the World Bank have observer status in WTO bodies on the basis of their respective agreements with the WTO.[207] Other international organizations are admitted according to the Guidelines on Observer Status which are relatively restrictive.[208] They provide that requests for observer status shall be considered 'from organizations which have competence and a direct interest in trade policy matters',[209] thus prima facie excluding certain institutions, such as secretariats of Multilateral Environmental Agreements. International institutions that wish to be admitted as observers have to submit requests to each body whose meetings they would like to attend as observers. These requests are considered by the respective body on a case-by-case basis. The rights that go along with observer status are limited. International organizations that are granted observer status may be invited to speak at meetings. The right to speak does not include, however, the right to circulate papers or make proposals, unless the organization is specifically invited to do so.[210]

The World Customs Organization has observer status in the Committee on Market Access. During discussions on the implementation of Harmonized System changes in members' schedules of tariff concessions, representatives of the World Customs Organization are invited to take the floor to explain the process of amending the Harmonized System or to explain the changes which were made.[211] These representatives do not,

---

of payments or foreign exchange arrangements, they shall consult fully with the International Monetary Fund.'

205 See, for example, Report of the Committee on Balance of Payments Restrictions on the Consultations under Art. XVIII:12(B) with Chile, L/2392 (13 March 1965).

206 The relevant treaty provision is Art. V:1 WTO Agreement according to which '[t]he General Council may make appropriate arrangements for effective cooperation with other intergovernmental organizations that have responsibilities related to those of the WTO.' A list of international organizations which currently have observer status within the WTO can be found on the WTO's website at www.wto.org/english/thewto_e/igo_obs_e.htm.

207 WTO Agreements with the Fund and the Bank, Approved by the General Council at its Meeting on the 7, 8 and 13 November 1996, WT/L/195 (18 November 1996).

208 The Guidelines on Observer Status for International Intergovernmental Organizations in the WTO are included in Annex 3 to the Rules of Procedure for Sessions of the Ministerial Conference and Meetings of the General Council, WT/L/161 (15 July 1996).

209 Ibid., para. 2.   210 Ibid., para. 8.

211 See e.g. G/MA/M/39 (13 May 2005), paras. 4.9–4.19.

however, express an opinion as to how these changes should be implemented in GATT schedules. By contrast, the World Health Organization, which has ad hoc observer status in the TRIPS Council, introduced a very specific proposal regarding the most suitable mechanism to implement paragraph 6 of the Doha Declaration on the TRIPS Agreement and Public Health.[212]

Through stronger institutional linkages and involvement of other international institutions the waiver process would be improved. Other perspectives could be introduced on the desirability of a waiver, including an assessment of the impacts of measures to be justified by a waiver on matters that fall within the expertise of other international institutions. If, for example, waivers are requested to legalize special preference arrangements, the World Bank or UNCTAD could give an opinion from the perspective of development economics on the suitability of these preferences to promote development in the preference-receiving countries and the potential negative impacts such preferences might have on third countries.

The participation of non-governmental institutions in the waiver process is even more limited than that of other international institutions. According to Art V:2 WTO Agreement the 'General Council may make appropriate arrangements for consultations and cooperation with non-governmental organizations concerned with matters related to those of the WTO'. In 1996 the General Council adopted guidelines according to which interaction between the WTO and NGOs shall take place mainly through information exchange and in discussion forums, for example in the form of symposia.[213] The guidelines also state that 'there is currently a broadly held view that it would not be possible for NGOs to be directly involved in the work of the WTO or its meetings'.[214]

---

212 See statement of the representative of the WHO in the meeting of the TRIPS Council held on 17–19 September 2002, which endorsed the provision of a limited exception under Art. 30 TRIPS Agreement as the solution most consistent with a basic public health principle, IP/C/M/37 (11 October 2002), para. 5.

213 General Council, Guidelines for Arrangements on Relations with Non-Governmental Organizations, Decision adopted by the General Council on 18 July 1996, WT/L/162 (23 July 1996), paras. IV, V. On the different forms of NGO involvement in the WTO, see Ripinsky and Bossche, *NGO Involvement in International Organizations. A Legal Analysis*, 192 *et seq.*

214 General Council, Guidelines for Arrangements on Relations with Non-Governmental Organizations, Decision adopted by the General Council on 18 July 1996, WT/L/162 (23 July 1996), para. VI.

Unless members include NGO representatives in their delegations, they may not participate in meetings of the organs examining waiver requests. Nonetheless, NGOs may participate indirectly, by publishing information on the issues discussed and by critically evaluating positions taken in the formal meetings (in so far as their minutes are accessible in time). NGOs, thus, substantially – if indirectly – participated in the process which led to the adoption of the TRIPS Waiver.[215]

Such participation may make the process more informed, representative and transparent. It further may have the important effect of connecting the international process to national public opinion which may then influence and control government representatives.[216]

III Decision-making

Under the GATT 1947 decisions on waivers were taken by vote while most other decisions were adopted by consensus.[217] Art. IX WTO Agreement codifies this general practice. According to Art. IX:1 WTO Agreement the WTO shall continue the GATT practice of consensus decision-making. Art. IX:3 WTO Agreement provides for voting on waivers when no consensus is reached during the ninety-day period. Waiver decisions shall be taken by three-fourths of the members. According to footnote 4 to Art. IX:3 WTO Agreement, consensus is, however, always required for a decision to waive obligations subject to a transition period or a period for staged implementation. This footnote was inserted since some developed countries were concerned that developing countries – who could achieve a three-fourths vote – might extend such periods against the opposition of developed country members. After the first few waiver decisions in the WTO had been adopted by vote, waiver decisions have since been adopted exclusively by consensus.[218]

---

215 Sell, 'Quest for Global Governance in Intellectual Property and Public Health', 363; Chapter 7 A.II.3. below.
216 On the latter point, Bernstorff, 'Zivilgesellschaftliche Partizipation in internationalen Organisationen', 277. See also Chapter 7 A.I. below.
217 An exception to voting on waivers in the GATT was the adoption by consensus of the 1971 decision on trade preferences among developing countries, SR.27/12 (22 December 1971), 165, 166; see Chapter 4 B.II.2.1(a).
218 See section C.III.2 below.

1 Decision-making by the GATT CONTRACTING PARTIES

Under the GATT 1947 a waiver could be adopted by a two-thirds majority of votes cast that had to comprise more than half of the contracting parties (Art. XXV:5 GATT).[219] Only the CONTRACTING PARTIES, and not the GATT Council, were allowed to adopt waiver decisions.[220] Between the sessions of the CONTRACTING PARTIES voting therefore usually took place by postal ballot.[221] When a waiver decision was adopted at a session of the CONTRACTING PARTIES it was also usually adopted by ballot in order to ensure an accurate count of the votes cast.[222]

In one instance the United States had originally requested a vote on a waiver – for trade preferences under the Caribbean Basin Economic Recovery Act[223] – at a session of the CONTRACTING PARTIES. It then requested to postpone the decision until it could be taken according to intersessional procedures.[224] The United States pursued this tactic due to the strong opposition to this waiver. A vote by postal ballot ensured that all contracting parties could cast a vote and not only those contracting parties that were present at the meeting of the CONTRACTING PARTIES thus increasing the likelihood that the required majority be reached.

Even though waiver decisions were taken by vote, great efforts were made to reach agreement on waiver requests and draft waiver decisions.

219 According to GATT practice abstentions did not count as votes cast: WTO, *Analytical Index of the GATT*, Vol. II, 1097.

220 The decision of the CONTRACTING PARTIES on the establishment of the Council of 4 June 1960 stated that the power to take waivers could not be delegated to the Council, BISD 9S (1961), 8.

221 Customarily voting cards were handed out to representatives at the Council meeting in which the working party report was adopted and contracting parties were given thirty days to cast their vote. The decision was adopted when the necessary two-thirds majority of all contracting parties was attained, but no later than thirty days following the meeting of the GATT Council. On this practice, see Statement by the Chairman of the Council, GATT Council, Minutes of the Meeting on 12–13 May 1993, C/M/263 (9 June 1993), 23. Generally on decision-making by the CONTRACTING PARTIES, see WTO, *Analytical Index of the GATT*, Vol. II, 1097 *et seq.*

222 Executive Secretary, Note on Voting Procedures, L/1477 (16 May 1961). An exception to this procedure is the adoption of the waiver requested by the EC in connection with German Unification. Due to time pressure the EC requested a vote by roll call. After some discussion on the admissibility of such a procedure the chairman decided that a roll call vote would be taken: SR.46/1 (1 February 1991), 21.

223 See Chapter 4 B.I.3.3(b).

224 SR.40/2 (9 January 1995), 12. The waiver was subsequently adopted by postal ballot with fifty-two votes in favour, two against and two abstentions, CONTRACTING PARTIES, Caribbean Basin Economic Recovery Act, Decision of 15 February 1985, L/5779 (20 February 1985), fn. 1.

Consequently, waiver decisions were usually adopted with no or very few negative votes. For some significant waivers it was politically very important to achieve wide support. Thus it was argued with respect to the 1971 GSP Waiver that massive approval was needed in order to demonstrate the political will behind the GSP initiative to individual contracting parties which had been hesitant to agree to the GSP.[225]

In the early years of the GATT there was some criticism, most vehemently by Cuba, of the practice of adopting waiver decisions by majority vote. Cuba argued that in particular waivers of GATT obligations under Part I should not be taken by majority vote since these were fundamental provisions. Waivers of such obligations taken by majority vote could circumvent the amendment procedure in Art. XXX GATT which demanded a unanimous decision.[226] The CONTRACTING PARTIES addressed these objections by adopting Guiding Principles to be followed when adopting waivers of obligations under Part I or other important obligations. The Guiding Principles do not address voting requirements, but call upon the CONTRACTING PARTIES to proceed with caution in considering requests for waivers from obligations under Part I of the GATT. [227]

2 Decision-making in the WTO

In the WTO votes were only taken at an early General Council meeting on 31 July 1995. They concerned the first accession to the WTO,

225 See e.g. C/M/69 (28 May 1971), 16 (statement by Norway). The decision was adopted with forty-eight votes in favour and none against, CONTRACTING PARTIES, Generalized System of Preferences, Decision of 25 June 1971, L/3545 (28 June 1971), fn. 1.

226 See *supra* section B.II. In order to avoid a circumvention of the amendment procedure Cuba suggested that the CONTRACTING PARTIES should establish criteria to distinguish mere suspensions of obligations from suspensions which in fact resulted in a modification of obligations. Cuba held the view that in particular waivers of Art. I:1 GATT to allow for systems of trade preferences beyond those permitted in Art. I:2 GATT constituted such modifications since the preferential systems were not of a transitory nature. Suspensions which were to be qualified as modifications would have to comply with the procedure for amendment laid down in Art. XXX GATT. But also other suspensions of obligations under Part I should, according to Cuba, be subject to stricter voting requirements. Therefore Cuba urged the CONTRACTING PARTIES to make use of Art. XXV:5(i) GATT which explicitly authorized the CONTRACTING PARTIES to prescribe by a two-thirds majority different voting requirements for certain cases.

227 The Intersessional Committee had considered it to be 'difficult and unwise to lay down special criteria for voting in respect of waivers affecting these obligations [contained in Part I GATT], particularly as similar caution would also be appropriate in dealing with waivers of other fundamental obligations such as those embodied in Articles XI and XIII': L/532 (21 September 1956), 1; see section B.II. *supra.*

by Ecuador, and the first eight waiver decisions.[228] After discussions and consultations on the question whether the General Council should seek to adopt accession and waiver decisions by consensus or whether it should proceed automatically to a vote on such decisions, the General Council on 15 November 1995 agreed on a statement of its chairman on decision-making procedures with respect to accessions and waivers.[229] According to these procedures the General Council shall seek consensus in accordance with Art. IX:1 WTO Agreement. When consensus cannot be achieved the issue shall be decided by voting except as otherwise provided for.[230]

Since then, waiver decisions have been adopted exclusively by consensus and there is currently no indication that members intend to return to the practice of voting on waivers. During the discussions on the waiver request by the EC related to trade preferences granted under the Cotonou Agreement some members referred to the possibility of voting. These statements were, however, met with resistance and were not pursued any further.[231] If the political will existed, the General Council could agree (by consensus) on certain categories of waiver decisions to be adopted by voting.

Even though the adoption of waiver decisions is sometimes significantly protracted due to the opposition of individual members,[232] the practice of the General Council to regularly adopt waiver decisions by consensus falsifies the general claim which is sometimes made, namely that the consensus practice is a barrier to virtually all decision-making by the political organs in the WTO.

The term consensus is clarified in footnote 1 to Art. IX:1 WTO Agreement which reads:

---

228 General Council, Minutes of Meeting on 31 July 1995, WT/GC/M/6 (20 September 1995); the draft decision on accession and the draft waiver decisions were submitted to a vote by postal ballot: Ehlermann and Ehring, 'Decision-Making in the World Trade Organization', 51, 64.

229 General Council, Minutes of the Meeting of 15 November 1995, WT/GC/M/8 (13 December 1995).

230 Decision-Making Procedures under Articles IX and XII of the WTO Agreement, Statement by the Chairman, as agreed by the General Council on 15 November 1995, WT/L/93 (4 November 1995). The statement also specifies that a member may request a vote at the time the decision is taken.

231 Council for Trade in Goods, Minutes of the Meeting on 5 April and 18 May 2000, G/C/M/43 (13 June 2000), paras. 6.11, 6.22, 6.33.

232 The United States, for example, was mainly responsible for the delay in the adoption of the TRIPS Waiver, see Sell, 'Quest for Global Governance', 363, 393.

> The body concerned shall be deemed to have decided by consensus on
> a matter submitted for its consideration, if no Member, present at the
> meeting when the decision is taken, formally objects to the proposed
> decision.[233]

On the one hand, consensus decision-making constitutes a facilitation as
compared to voting since it is not required for the adoption of a consensus
decision that three-fourths of the members actually participate in the
decision-making.[234] Given the large membership of the WTO and the
limited capacity of many developing country members to participate in
the work of the various WTO organs this is indeed significant.[235] On
the other hand, the consensus procedure affords each WTO member
formally the opportunity to veto a waiver decision. In order to ensure
that waiver decisions are not adopted over the objection of individual
members, the General Council agreed that members having problems
with a certain waiver request should be present at the respective meeting
or otherwise their absence would be assumed to imply that the member
has no comments or objections concerning the proposed decision.[236] The
meeting agendas which are distributed to all delegations prior to meetings
of WTO organs ensure that members know when waiver requests are to
be discussed in an upcoming meeting.[237]

233 On decision-making by consensus in the WTO, see Footer, 'Role of Consensus in
   GATT/WTO Decision-Making', 653; Steinberg, 'In the Shadow of Law or Power?',
   339.
234 Williams, *Handbook on Accession to the WTO*, 13 (noting that the absence of smaller
   delegations from the General Council meetings made it difficult to secure the necessary three-quarters majority); Bronckers, 'Better Rules for a New Millennium', 547, 552
   (noting that in many instances consensus is relatively easily achieved). Due to the differences between consensus decision-making and majority voting, Kuijper has expressed
   the view that the WTO practice constitutes an instance of a reinterpretation or de facto
   amendment of the relevant WTO provisions: Kuijper, 'WTO Institutional Aspects', 79,
   96.
235 John Jackson suggests that the consensus procedure gives rise to a sort of weighted voting
   since the larger powers will always be present if important decisions are taken, contrary
   to countries that find it politically or financially difficult to be adequately represented:
   World Trading System, 65, 68.
236 Decision-Making Procedures under Articles IX and XII of the WTO Agreement, Statement by the Chairman, as agreed by the General Council on 15 November 1995, WT/L/93
   (24 November 1995).
237 According to Rule 3 of the Rules of Procedure for Sessions of the Ministerial Conference
   '[t]he provisional agenda for each regular session shall be drawn up by the Secretariat
   in consultation with the Chairperson and shall be communicated to Members at least
   five weeks before the opening of the session'; The Rules of Procedure for Meetings
   of the General Council provide that an agenda shall be communicated to members

D. FORM AND CONTENT OF WAIVER DECISIONS

According to Art. IX:4 WTO Agreement a waiver decision shall state the terms and conditions governing the waiver, as well as a termination date. While under the GATT these requirements were not part of treaty law, most waivers nonetheless were time-limited and frequently contained very detailed terms and conditions concerning their application or dispute settlement procedures. The terms and conditions of a waiver are particularly important. They may not only instruct the political review of waivers, but moreover make them justiciable in the sense that a dispute settlement organ may find that a condition included in a waiver decision has not been met and therefore the waiver does not provide a justification of an otherwise illegal measure.[238]

I The form of waiver decisions

Art. IX:4 WTO Agreement sets out some requirements as to the form of a waiver decision: a waiver decision shall state the exceptional circumstances that justify the waiver, the terms and conditions that govern the application of the waiver and the date on which the waiver shall terminate.

Apart from these formalities which are specific to waiver decisions there is a lack of legal rules with respect to the form of secondary legal acts. There are no rules in the treaty or secondary law that require the written form of legal instruments, that legal instruments include an indication of their legal basis or that they are published. This lack of formal requirements with respect to secondary law-making is no peculiarity of the WTO, but a general characteristic of the law of international institutions. With the increase in secondary law-making activities, this feature of international institutions should change so as to ensure

---

together with the convening notice no later than ten calendar days prior to the date of the meeting (rules 2 and 3), WT/L/161 (25 July 1996). Sometimes, waiver decisions are adopted *ad referendum*, namely in cases when there seems to be a consensus, but one or more delegations still need authorization from their governments to formally join in the consensus. An *ad referendum* decision counts as adopted unless a member subsequent to the meeting and within an agreed time period notifies the Secretariat of its objections (see, for example, G/C/M/92, para. 4.10).

238 On judicial review of waivers, see section F.II. below.

transparency, legal certainty and legality.[239] European Union law, by contrast, includes rules on the form which legal instruments have to take.[240]

While there exists only little formal procedural WTO law, an institutional practice has developed with respect to waiver decisions. Accordingly, waiver decisions are regularly entitled 'Decision' and in the preamble they usually refer to their legal basis in Article IX WTO Agreement.[241] The designation as decision as well as reference to the legal basis are important since these features facilitate review of the legality of acts of secondary law. Frequently, waiver decisions also refer to Art. IV:2 WTO Agreement (which establishes the competence of the General Council to act on behalf of the Ministerial Conference), to the Guiding Principles which were adopted by the CONTRACTING PARTIES under the GATT 1947 for waivers of obligations in Part I and other important obligations,[242] as well as to the decision-making procedures adopted by the General Council on 15 November 1995.[243] Waivers of GATT obligations, moreover, refer to the Understanding. In comparison, decisions taken under the GATT 1947 often did not clearly state on which provision they were based. WTO Waiver decisions are published in the document series WT/L/*.[244] They are unrestricted and thus publicly available.[245] GATT 1947 waivers

---

239 On the need for further procedural law to ensure the legitimacy of law-making by international institutions, see Bernstorff, 'Procedures of Decision-Making and the Role of Law', 777. Generally on the principle of legality as one safeguard of the legitimacy of international law, see Kumm, 'Legitimacy of International Law', 907.

240 See in particular Art. 253 Treaty on European Union.

241 While this practice has been established with respect to waiver decisions, other decisions taken in the WTO still sometimes do not refer to any legal basis, see e.g. Doha Work Programme, Decision Adopted by the General Council on 1 August 2004, WT/L/579 (2 August 2004).

242 CONTRACTING PARTIES, Article XXV – Guiding Principles to be Followed by the Contracting Parties in Considering Applications for Waivers from Part I or other Obligations of the Agreement (L/532), BISD 5S (1957), 25.

243 Decision-Making Procedures under Articles IX and XII of the WTO Agreement, Statement by the Chairman, as agreed by the General Council on 15 November 1995, WT/L/93 (24 November 1995).

244 The Cotonou and the Bananas Waiver that were adopted at the Ministerial Conference were initially circulated as documents WT/MIN(01)/15 and WT/MIN(01)/16.

245 General Council, Procedures for the Circulation and Derestriction of WTO Documents, Decision of 14 May 2002, WT/L/452 (16 May 2002), para. 1; for waiver decisions taken before 14 May 2002, General Council, Procedures for the Circulation and Derestriction of WTO Documents, Decision of 18 July 1996, WT/L/160/Rev. 1 (26 July 1996), para. 1.

were published in the 'Basic Instruments and Selected Documents Supplements'.[246]

Waiver decisions are structured similarly to other legal decisions by international organizations, such as for example Security Council Resolutions. They have a preamble and an operative part. It is in the preamble that waiver decisions refer to the waiver competence, the decision-making procedures and – as the case may be – the Understanding and Guiding Principles. In the preamble they further set out – as required by Art. IX:4 WTO Agreement and the Understanding – the reasons why the waiver is granted, as well as the policy objectives pursued. In the preamble reference is frequently (but not always) made to the official document containing the waiver request.

The operative part of the decision states which obligation is being suspended and to what extent. As required by Art. IX:4 WTO Agreement it states the terms and conditions governing the application of the waiver as well as the date on which the waiver decision terminates. Decisions that extend a waiver sometimes differ from waiver decisions granted for the first time in that they refer for reasons, policy objectives and suspension to the original waiver decision.[247]

II The duration of waivers

Under the GATT 1947 waivers did not have to be of limited duration.[248] While most waivers were only granted for a specified period of time, some waiver decisions, such as the 1955 Agricultural Waiver, did not include a time limit.[249] This changed with the entry into force of the WTO Agreement. Art. IX:4 WTO Agreement states that a decision 'granting a waiver shall state . . . the date on which the waiver shall terminate'. With respect to waivers granted under the GATT 1947 it was agreed during the Uruguay Round that unless a decision was taken to extend such waivers they would terminate at the latest two years from the date of entry into

---

246 Those decisions, however, which in effect waived legal obligations, but were not designated as waivers did not appear in the section 'Waivers' of the Basic Documents Supplement.

247 See e.g. EC/France – Trading Arrangements with Morocco, Extension of the Waiver, Decision of 17 July 2000, WT/L/361 (19 July 2000).

248 Comments by delegates at the London Preparatory Conference suggest, however, that the waivers were intended by the drafters to be temporary only, see E/PC/T/C.V/PV/9, 9.

249 On the Agricultural Waiver, see Chapter 4 B.I.2.2(a).

force of the WTO Agreement, i.e. by the end of 1996 (Understanding, para. 2).

The duration of waivers varies from a few months up to ten years and frequently waiver decisions are extended once their term has expired.[250] All collective waiver decisions – apart from Harmonized System waivers which have been adopted for shorter periods as well – have been granted for multi-year periods.[251] Similarly, waivers that allow developed country members to extend tariff preferences to developing country members have been granted for several years in order to provide legal security for traders and investors.

A few waiver decisions adopted in the WTO do not include a specific termination date. The TRIPS Waiver of 30 August 2003 is one of them. It states in paragraph 11 that it 'shall terminate for each Member on the date on which an amendment to the TRIPS Agreement replacing its provisions takes effect for that Member'.[252] This formulation was to address fears of developing countries that if the waiver needed to be extended discussions on the merit of the decision might be reopened. Another waiver which was granted for France's preferential trading arrangements with Morocco did not specify a termination date either. Instead it suspended Art. I:1 GATT 'until the entry into force of the Euro-Mediterranean Agreement establishing an association between the European Communities and their Member States and the Kingdom of Morocco'.[253]

Waivers take effect with adoption of the decision, unless they state a different date for the suspension to take effect. One of the collective Harmonized System waivers specifies that the suspension shall take effect for each member from the date of domestic implementation of the Harmonized System changes.[254] Other waivers indicate as the date from which the obligation in question is suspended a date prior to the date of the adoption of the waiver decision.[255] These waivers retroactively legalize the measure for which the waiver is granted.

---

250 An extension is, however, subject to the same requirements as a request for a first waiver decision, meaning that a request has to be submitted which is subject to examination by the competent organ.

251 On these waiver decisions, see Chapter 4 B.II.

252 WT/L/540 (2 September 2003), para. 11.

253 EC/France – Trading Arrangements with Morocco, Extension of the Waiver, Decision of 17 July 2000, WT/L/361 (19 July 2000).

254 WT/L/469 (17 May 2002).   255 See e.g. WT/L/768 (31 July 2009).

III The terms and conditions governing the application of waivers

A waiver decision shall not only state the exceptional circumstances justifying the decision and the termination date of the waiver, but also the terms and conditions governing the application of the waiver (Art. IX:4 cl. 1 WTO Agreement). Legally binding terms and conditions have to be distinguished from non-binding statements which are often contained in the preambles to waiver decisions or in chairpersons' statements accompanying waiver decisions.

1 Preambles and chairperson statements

The preamble of a waiver decision frequently states the (exceptional) circumstances which are considered to justify a waiver.[256] The preamble not only sets out the factual and legal situation which prompted the request for a waiver. Moreover, it frequently includes 'assurances' by the requesting member; for example, the assurance to enter into consultations with other members or 'considerations' as to the anticipated trade effects of the measures for which the waiver is being granted.

Like the preambles of other legal documents, the preambles of waiver decisions are not legally binding.[257] Their recitals start with terms such as 'noting' or 'considering' which – in contrast to the term 'decides' which opens the operative part of waiver decisions – clarify that the recitals do not give rise to binding commitments. This was confirmed by the GATT panel in the *Sugar* dispute. The EEC had claimed that the United States had violated its assurances in consideration of which the CONTRACTING PARTIES had granted the Agricultural Waiver, as was recorded in the preamble.[258] The panel found that these assurances (to remove the trade restrictions justified by the waiver as soon as they were no longer required) were not legal requisites which the United States had to meet for its measures to be legalized by the waiver. Whilst they formed part of the grounds for the waiver decision they had to be distinguished from the binding conditions listed in the operative part.[259]

---

256 An exception is the waiver granted to Hungary to allow it to maintain export subsidies on certain agricultural products which merely refers to Hungary's waiver request, WT/L/238 (29 October 1997).

257 Mbengue, 'Preamble'.

258 Panel Report, *US – Sugar Waiver*, BISD 37S/228, adopted 7 November 1990, para. 3.12.

259 *Ibid.*, para. 5.15.

In the second compliance proceeding under Art. 21.5 DSU in the *Bananas III* dispute the panel and subsequently the Appellate Body had to address the question whether the Cotonou Waiver suspending Art. I:1 GATT included a binding tariff commitment by the EC. This waiver states in its preamble: '*Noting* that the tariff applied to bananas imported in the "A" and "B" quotas shall not exceed 75€/tonne until the entry into force of the new EC tariff-only regime.'[260] The panel interpreted this recital to constitute a binding international agreement between the WTO members which obliged the EC not to exceed the stated tariff.[261] The Appellate Body reversed this finding and concluded that this preambular statement was merely a reference to a tariff rate quota in the European Communities' schedule. It supported this conclusion with, inter alia, a finding that it was not a function of waiver decisions to modify existing obligations.[262] The Appellate Body further pointed to the placing of the statement on the tariff binding in the preamble and not in the waiver's operative part.[263]

Even though preambular statements do not give rise to binding obligations they may be of importance for the interpretation of the operative part of waivers. In particular, they can serve as an aid to determine the object and purpose of a waiver decision.[264] Furthermore, they are of political relevance. When waivers are reviewed by the General Council the fact that a beneficiary of a waiver has not complied with assurances noted in the preamble or that the measures taken do not conform to considerations stated in the preamble may support a decision of the General Council that a waiver should be terminated.[265] Similarly, they may provide arguments why a waiver should not be extended once it expires. As interpretative aids as well as a documentation of the grounds on which a waiver is granted the preambles to waiver decisions are of even more

---

260 WT/L/436 (7 December 2001), preamble, recital 9.
261 Panel Report, *EC – Bananas III (Article 21.5 – ECU II)*, WT/DS27/RW2/ECU (7 April 2008), para. 7.446.
262 Appellate Body Report, *EC – Bananas III (Article 21.5 – ECU II, US)*, WT/DS27/AB/RW2/ECU, adopted 11 December 2008, and WT/DS27/AB/RW/USA, adopted 22 December 2008, para. 381 *et seq.*
263 *Ibid.* para. 400.
264 In *EC – Tariff Preferences*, for example, the Appellate Body referred to the 1971 waiver decision's preamble for guidance in determinig the object and purpose of the Enabling Clause, WT/DS246/AB/R, adopted 20 April 2004, para. 92; Working Party Report on CARIBCAN, L/6090 (26 November 1986), para. 22 (statement by the representative of the Secretariat). According to Art. 31:2(a) VCLT the preamble of a treaty as part of the text constitutes context which is relevant for the determination of the ordinary meaning of the terms of a treaty.
265 On the political review of waivers, see section F.I. below.

relevance today than they were under the GATT 1947. Under the GATT 1947 working party reports served this function. With the cessation of the practice of mandating working groups with the examination of waiver requests, the waiver decision, apart from the request which evidences the views of the requesting member, remains the only instrument to document the reasons for granting a waiver as well as the understandings reached during the examination of the waiver request.[266]

Further relevant considerations in relation to legal acts, including waivers, are sometimes included in chairperson statements.[267] Chairpersons of WTO organs have no competence to adopt decisions which legally bind members in their external relations.[268] Formal statements of chairpersons may, however, like waiver preambles, provide important interpretative guidance.[269] Chairperson statements have been taken to constitute relevant context for interpretation in the sense of Art. 31:II(a) VCLT.[270]

In case of the TRIPS Waiver, the statement of the chairman of the General Council[271] that accompanied the decision served the function of appeasing fears that the decision might be misused for commercial purposes.[272] At first this statement was referenced in a footnote to the decision. This footnote was, however, deleted due to insistence by

---

266 The minutes of the meetings of the organ that examined the request are usually not very detailed in this respect, mostly because the greatest part of discussion on waiver requests takes place outside formal meetings.

267 Ruse-Khan, 'Role of Chairman's Statements in the WTO', 475.

268 The competences of chairpersons are set out in the rules of procedure for the respective organs. Chairpersons shall rule on points of order and, subject to the rules of procedure, have complete control of the proceedings: see rule 17 of the Rules of Procedure for Sessions of the Ministerial Conference and Meetings of the General Council, WT/L/161 (15 July 1996).

269 In *US – FSC* the Appellate Body referred to the chairman's statement to support its finding that a General Council decision did not constitute an authoritative interpretation, WT/DS108/AB/R, adopted 20 March 2000, para. 112.

270 Aust, *Modern Treaty Law and Practice*, 236 et seq.

271 Minutes of the General Council meeting, held on 30 August 2003, WT/GC//M/82 (13 November 2003), para. 29.

272 It says that members would ensure that the system should be used in good faith and not as an instrument to pursue industrial or commercial policy objectives. It encourages members to use best practices as developed by companies to prevent and discourage the diversion of medicines produced under compulsory licences to other markets than that of the importing member and to allow for expeditious review within the TRIPS Council of any complaints concerning the use of the new system (WT/GC/M/82 (13 November 2003), para. 29).

developing countries who were worried that legal obligations might be deduced from the statement if it was referenced in the waiver decision.[273]

2 Terms and conditions in the operative part of waiver decisions

The operative part of a waiver decision usually begins with a paragraph that states that 'subject to the terms and conditions set out hereunder' obligation X is waived with respect to measure Y until date Z.[274] Usually, waiver decisions include further provisions that relate to the measure authorized under the waiver or the situation that gives rise to the need for a waiver. These terms and conditions of waiver decisions can broadly be divided into: firstly, requirements that need to be met by the measure for which the waiver is granted; secondly, phase-out and implementation requirements; thirdly, notification, information and reporting require-ments; and lastly, provisions relating to compensation, consultation and dispute settlement.

2.1 Requirements relating to the measure which is legalized by the waiver

Unless a waiver decision suspends an obligation in its entirety, it speci-fies the extent of the suspension. This is mostly done by describing the measure that is legalized by the waiver. For example, waiver decisions that allow developing country members to use official minimum values for the determination of customs duties list the products for which minimum values may be used and specify that minimum values may not be applied to additional products.[275] Most elaborate with respect to the require-ments which members have to meet in order to benefit from the waiver is the TRIPS Waiver decision which specifies the situation in which com-pulsory licences for pharmaceutical products destined for export may be granted as well as requirements that the compulsory licence has to meet.[276]

Waivers that legalize tariff preferences under preferential trade arrange-ments usually include in their preambles a clause stating that the pref-erential treatment shall be designed to facilitate and promote trade and

273 Specifically on the legal status of the chairman's statement accompanying the TRIPS Waiver, see Hestermeyer, *Human Rights and the WTO*, 285 *et seq.*
274 See e.g. WT/L/436 (7 December 2001).
275 See e.g. WT/L/354 (8 May 2000), paras. 1, 2.   276 WT/L/540 (2 September 2003).

not raise new barriers to trade.[277] However, the most recent waiver decisions which legalize special tariff preferences provided for in US legislation, include this clause in their operative part. In the preamble they
furthermore state that the duty-free treatment is not expected to cause
significant trade diversion, thus implying that some trade diversion will
occur.[278]

2.2 Phase-out and implementation requirements

Waivers that address members' difficulties in complying with WTO obligations frequently include or require the submission of timetables for
the phasing out of the non-compliant measures and the gradual implementation of WTO obligations.[279] Harmonized System waivers call upon
the beneficiaries to enter, where necessary, promptly into negotiations
and consultations pursuant to Art. XXVIII GATT in order to renegotiate tariff bindings whose value has been affected by the transposition of
Harmonized System changes into the goods schedules. Such renegotiations are necessary in order to complete the transposition exercise and
ultimately to ensure compliance with Art. II GATT.

Phase-out and implementation requirements can be construed as part
of a 'compliance management' approach by the organization in cases in
which bilateral enforcement through formal dispute settlement proceedings would not be successful due to the capacity problems of the non-
compliant member.[280] The waiver is a recognition that the beneficiary is
not able to comply and consequently frees it from its duty to do so. At
the same time the decision is used to multilaterally control and supervise
incremental compliance by the beneficiary. This is done by including into
the waiver decision a phase-out plan as well as the obligation to report on
the steps taken towards compliance.

---

277 See e.g. WT/L/436 (7 December 2001), preamble, recital 5 (Cotonou Waiver).
278 General Council, United States – African Growth and Opportunity Act, Decision of 27
     May 2009, WT/L/754 (29 May 2009); General Council, United States – Caribbean Basin
     Economic Recovery Act, Renewal of Waiver, Decision of 27 May 2009, WT/L/753 (29
     May 2007); General Council, United States – Andean Trade Preference Act, Renewal of
     Waiver, Decision of 27 May 2009, WT/L/755 (29 May 2009); on these waiver decisions,
     see Chapter 4 B.I.3.3(b). See also WT/L/722 (15 May 2008), para. 2 (waiver granted to
     the EC for trade preferences to Moldova).
279 See e.g. WT/L/238 (29 October 1997) (Hungary agricultural subsidies); WT/L/439 (10
     January 2002) (CVA waiver granted to Haiti); WT/L/410 (7 August 2001) (TRIMS waiver
     granted to Thailand).
280 In general on the concept of compliance management, Chayes and Handler Chayes, *The
     New Sovereignty*, 22 *et seq.*

2.3 Notification, information and reporting requirements

Many waiver decisions demand that the beneficiary of the waiver informs the WTO and WTO members of the measures which it takes pursuant to the waiver or – when the waiver is granted for existing measures – any subsequent changes to these measures. The Kimberley Waiver, for example, provides that members benefiting from the waiver should notify their measures implementing the Kimberley Process Certification Scheme to the Council for Trade in Goods.[281] While the notification requirement in the Kimberley Waiver is not phrased in mandatory terms, the TRIPS Waiver obliges importing as well as exporting members under the TRIPS Waiver to make notifications to the TRIPS Council as to the need for imports of specific pharmaceutical products and the grant of a compulsory licence respectively.[282] Most of the waivers that justify preferential tariff treatment for certain products from selected developing countries require the preference-granting members to notify the General Council of the implementation of the preferences or any subsequent changes to the preferences, i.e. in particular a change with respect to the preference-receiving countries or a change in eligible products.[283]

Waivers that suspended the Customs Valuation Agreement's prohibition of the use of minimum values required beneficiaries to publish and make available information relevant for the determination of the official minimum values as well as any changes thereto sixty days before implementing such changes.[284] The collective Harmonized System waivers granted for the implementation of HS1996 and HS2002 changes require states to submit the documentation required by the WTO's HS procedures. These notifications and information allow members to determine whether their interests are being negatively affected by measures justified by a waiver. They further could assist the annual review of the waivers by the General Council.

The Guiding Principles state that waiver decisions 'should provide for an annual report'.[285] Thus, waivers of Art. I GATT for trade preferences

---

281 WT/L/518 (27 May 2003), para. 4.   282 WT/L/540 (2 September 2003), para. 2.

283 See e.g. WT/L/677 (19 December 2006) (the CARIBCAN Waiver requires notification to members and not as the other waiver decisions the General Council), WT/L/436 (7 December 2001) (Cotonou Waiver); WT/L/304 (17 June 1999) (notifications under the 1999 Preferences Waiver are handled by the Council for Trade in Goods who refers them for advice to the subcommittee on LDCs).

284 See e.g. WT/L/453 (17 May 2002).   285 L/532 (21 September 1956), section e.

require the beneficiaries to submit such reports on the implementation
of the preferential trade arrangements or the operation of the trade preferences. Some also require reports on the extent to which the trade preferences authorized by the waiver differ from the MFN tariffs and GSP
concessions.[286]

As already noted, waivers that suspend obligations of developing country members frequently require progress reports on implementation,
sometimes with respect to specific implementation plans. These often
have to be submitted more frequently than once a year.[287]

2.4 Compensation, consultation and dispute settlement

WTO members frequently fear that their economic interests may be
affected by the measures that are justified by a waiver decision. In particular non-compliance with Art. I GATT and Art. II GATT raise the
concern that trade may be diverted or the value of tariff concessions
impaired. Thus, under the GATT 1947 Sweden had claimed with respect
to the waiver request for the European Coal and Steel Community that
the beneficiaries of this waiver should compensate the other contracting
parties for their economic loss.[288] While some form of compensation is
sometimes negotiated bilaterally between requesting members and members that apprehend that their economic interests might be impaired,
waiver decisions in general do not contain provisions on compensation.
An exception are the Harmonized System waivers and the tariff surcharges
waivers adopted under the GATT 1947. The HS waivers provide that other
members will be free to suspend concessions in accordance with the provisions of Art. XXVIII:3 GATT.[289] The tariff surcharges waivers similarly
provided that if consultations were unsuccessful and the CONTRACT-
ING PARTIES determined that the surcharges caused serious damage
to the trade of a contracting party the latter could suspend concessions
negotiated with the beneficiary to an extent determined to be appropriate
by the CONTRACTING PARTIES.

While waiver decisions generally do not envisage compensation, many
do, however, provide for consultations between the requesting member

---

286 See e.g. WT/L/722 (15 May 2008), para. 5 (waiver granted to the EC for trade preferences
to Moldova).
287 See *supra* fn. 279.
288 Report of Working Party 4 on the European Coal and Steel Community, G/35
(7 November 52), para. 6.
289 See e.g. WT/L/744 (22 December 2008), para. (iii).

and any other member that considers that it might be negatively affected by the waiver. Kenneth Dam distinguished between what he called preaction and postaction consultation procedures.[290] An example for a preaction procedure is found in the UK Margins of Preferences Waiver which allowed the UK to raise tariffs on unbound items without at the same time imposing a tariff on products that benefited from historic preferences.[291] This waiver provided for a special consultation procedure which the UK had to follow to be allowed to take action under the waiver. The UK had to consult with contracting parties which had a substantial interest in trade in an item for which the UK intended to increase customs duties in order to determine whether there was a likelihood that the duties would result in substantial trade diversion. If no agreement was reached during such consultations, the UK could seek arbitration by the CONTRACTING PARTIES on the question of the likelihood of substantial diversion. Only if the CONTRACTING PARTIES determined that there was no likelihood of substantial diversion did the waiver take effect. In case the CONTRACTING PARTIES decided that evidence did not suffice for a determination the waiver was to apply conditionally until a determination could be made.[292] A consultation procedure such as this, to be complied with before the waiver took effect, constituted, however, the exception.

Waivers in the WTO so far have only provided for postaction consultations, i.e. consultations when the suspension is already in effect. Such provisions comply with the Guiding Principles which state that waiver decisions (that waive Article I GATT or other important obligations) 'should include procedures for future consultations on specific action taken under the waiver' (section (d)). In the WTO all waiver decisions granted for preferential trade arrangements as well as the Kimberley Waiver and the waiver granted to Cuba of its obligation under Art. XV:6 GATT include the following provision on consultations:

> [The beneficiary of the waiver] shall, upon request, promptly enter into consultations with any interested Member with respect to any difficulty or any matter that may arise as a result of the implementation of this waiver; where a Member considers that any benefit accruing to it under the GATT 1994 may be or is being impaired unduly as a result of such

---

290 Dam, *GATT: Law and International Economic Organization*, 45 *et seq.*, 53.
291 On this waiver, see Chapter 4 B.1.2.2(a).
292 BISD 2S (1954), 20, 21 *et seq.*; Dam, *GATT: Law and International Economic Organization*, 21, 22.

implementation, such consultation shall examine the possibility of action for a satisfactory adjustment of the matter.[293]

Some waiver decisions take account of the fact that not only a few individual members, but many or all members may have an interest in how the waiver is applied. These waiver decisions, which include the Kimberley Waiver, the Lomé Waiver, the Cotonou Waiver and the Bananas Waiver, provide that in case a member considers that consultations have proved unsatisfactory it may bring the matter before the General Council who will examine the matter promptly and make appropriate recommendations. The waiver decisions which include this provision are all waivers that are of interest to many WTO members – either because their trading interests may be negatively affected (Cotonou Waiver, Bananas Waiver) or because the waiver has many beneficiaries (Kimberley Waiver). This explains why these waivers envisage a multilateral solution to any disputed matters through a recommendation of the General Council.[294]

WTO waivers usually do not provide for the termination of a waiver decision as a possible consequence of consultations.[295] By contrast, the Automotive Waiver which was granted under the GATT 1947 foresaw that if a substantial injury to trade or an imminent threat of a substantial injury was determined either during consultations between the US and the affected contracting party or by the CONTRACTING PARTIES, the waiver would cease to apply to the respective product.[296] Similarly, the 1966 waiver that legalized tariff preferences by Australia to products from developing countries stated that Australia could not take action under the waiver if the CONTRACTING PARTIES determined, after unsuccessful consultations, that a certain preference resulted in a substantial threat of injury to trade.[297]

The Cotonou Waiver was special in that it included a specific arbitration procedure. An arbitrator upon request was to determine whether a

---

293 See e.g. General Council, United States – African Growth and Opportunity Act, Decision of 27 May 2009, WT/L/754 (29 May 2009), para. 4.

294 See e.g. WT/L/518 (27 May 2003), para. 6.

295 The Ministerial Conference or General Council, acting on its behalf, may, however, modify or terminate a waiver. This is clarified in Article IX:4 WTO Agreement. On the political review of waiver decisions, see section F.I. below.

296 CONTRACTING PARTIES, United States Imports of Automotive Products, Decision of 20 December 1965, L/2528 (28 December 1965); no comparable provision is included in the WTO extension decision, General Council, United States – Imports of Automotive Products, Decision adopted by the General Council at its meeting on 7, 8 and 13 November, WT/L/198 (18 November 1996).

297 BISD 14S (1966), 23, para. 4.

rebinding of the EC tariff on bananas resulted in maintaining total market access for MFN banana suppliers.[298] The waiver further provided that it would cease to apply to bananas in case a rebinding entered into force, even though an arbitrator had held that the rebinding did not maintain the required market access, the EC did not rectify this matter, and this was confirmed in a second arbitration proceeding. This procedure was used and when the new EC tariff entered into force – after two arbitration reports had found that the tariff rebinding did not maintain total market access for MFN bananas – the waiver ceased to apply.[299]

Finally, it should be noted that a number of waiver decisions do not include specific provisions on consultation or compensation even though they may affect the interests and benefits of other members. These are mainly waivers granted to developing countries that encounter difficulties in complying with their obligations under the WTO Agreements. The lack of such provisions acknowledges these difficulties which are frequently due to capacity problems. Were the beneficiaries in these cases asked to enter into consultations with the potential result of having to compensate other members the waiver might not achieve the aim of freeing them from the burden of compliance.

2.5 Consequences of non-compliance with terms and conditions

In the foregoing I broadly presented the terms and conditions frequently found in waiver decisions. They define the scope of waiver decisions, enable multilateral supervision and control, and protect members' interests. However, the legal consequences of non-compliance with these terms and conditions are not immediately apparent, either from Art. IX WTO Agreement or from the wording of most waiver decisions. The distinction in Art. IX:4 WTO Agreement between terms and conditions suggests that waiver decisions may include two types of requirements: if a requirement is qualified as a condition this might mean that the legal effect of the waiver is 'conditional' upon the requirement being met. If a requirement is qualified as a term, non-compliance might, by contrast, not result in the

---

298 This was a requirement in the Understandings between the EC and Ecuador and the EC and the United States. These Understandings provided that the EC would institute a tariff only system for bananas which would maintain total market access for MFN producers (see Chapter 4 B.I.3.3(b)).

299 Panel Report, *EC – Bananas III (Article 21.5 – ECU II)*, WT/DS27/RW2/ECU (7 April 2008), para. 7.200.

waiver failing to have its justificatory effect, but merely in the beneficiary not being in compliance with the terms of the waiver.

Requirements (described above under 1.1.) that determine the scope of the waiver, namely requirements that describe the measure to which the waiver applies or that describe the situation in which such a measure may be taken have to be interpreted as conditions, i.e. as requirements that need to be met for the waiver to have justificatory effect. They have to be complied with the same way as the requirements of the general exceptions in Art. XX GATT have to be met for Art. XX to justify measures that would otherwise be in violation of GATT obligations. To give an example: if a waiver decision provides that Art. I GATT shall be waived for non-discriminatory tariff preferences granted by developing country members to least-developed countries, this waiver does not have the effect of allowing a discriminatory preference arrangement.

More difficult is the question as to the consequence of non-compliance with information, reporting, notification or consultation requirements. With respect to these requirements one might hold the view that non-compliance – even though a violation of the decision – does not have the effect that the suspension ceases to apply. This interpretation in most cases, however, is not convincing. Sometimes such an interpretation is excluded by the clear wording of a waiver decision. The collective waiver granted for implementation of HS2002 changes, for example, states that members who have not submitted the documentation required by the HS procedures will not benefit from the waiver decision.[300] If documentation is not submitted, Art. II GATT is not suspended. Equally clearly phrased is the TRIPS Waiver that states in paragraph 2 that '[t]he obligations of an exporting Member under Article 31(f) of the TRIPS Agreement shall be waived ... in accordance with the terms set out below in this paragraph.'[301] Consequently, the terms that follow, regarding, inter alia, notifications to the Council for TRIPS, have to be regarded as requirements that have to be met for the waiver to take effect.

Another formulation which is commonly found in waiver decisions also supports the interpretation that all requirements included in these decisions are to be interpreted as real conditions. Waiver decisions frequently state that a certain obligation is waived 'subject to the terms and conditions' set out in the decision. This suggests that compliance with all requirements, including information, reporting, notification and

---

300 WT/L/469 (17 May 2002), Annex I, fn. 4.   301 WT/L/540 (2 September 2003).

consultation requirements, is indeed a condition for the waiver to have effect.

Finally, this interpretation finds support in the case law. The Appellate Body report in *EC – Tariff Preferences* suggests that all obligations in waiver decisions that are related to the measures for which the waiver is granted are to be interpreted as conditions that need to be met for the waiver to take effect. In this case the Appellate Body did not interpret a waiver, but the Enabling Clause which succeeded the 1971 GSP Waiver as the justification for contracting parties' Generalized System of Preferences legislation. Nonetheless, the Appellate Body's statements with regard to the Enabling Cause are relevant for the question at hand since the Enabling Clause – which, inter alia, codifies the GSP exception of the 1971 GSP Waiver[302] – contains several provisions which are also found in waiver decisions. The Appellate Body held in this case that the Enabling Clause 'excepts Members from complying with the obligation contained in Article I:1 [GATT] for the purpose of providing differential and more favourable treatment to developing countries, *provided that such treatment is in accordance with the conditions set out in the Enabling Clause*.'[303] According to the Appellate Body these conditions include the following: a provision, which is also found in many waivers on special preferences, that differential and favourable treatment 'shall be designed to facilitate and promote the trade of developing countries and not to raise barriers to or create undue difficulties for the trade of any other contracting parties' (para. 3(a) Enabling Clause). Furthermore, there is the requirement that preferential treatment shall not impede trade liberalization on a most-favoured-nation basis, and beneficiaries shall notify and inform the General Council with respect to any introduction, modification or withdrawal of preferential treatment and afford other members adequate opportunity for consultation (para. 4(b) Enabling Clause). Thus, the Appellate Body report suggests that the Enabling Clause only provides a justification for the preferential tariff treatment if not merely the requirements directly relating to the favourable treatment, but also the notification and consultation requirements are met.[304]

Similarly, the panel report in the *Sugar* dispute supports the view that all terms, conditions and procedures set out in a waiver decision have

---

302 On this waiver see Chapter 4 B.II.2.1(a).

303 Appellate Body Report, *EC – Tariff Preferences*, WT/DS246/AB/R, adopted 20 April 2004, para. 90.

304 Appellate Body Report, *EC – Tariff Preferences*, WT/DS246/AB/R, adopted 20 April 2004, paras. 90, 111, 112.

to be complied with for a waiver to justify measures that fall within its scope.[305] After the panel had found that the measure in question was one that fell within the scope of the waiver, it went on to examine whether the United States had met its reporting obligation under the waiver (and found that it had).[306] The fact that the panel examined compliance with the reporting obligation suggests that it considered compliance with this obligation to be a condition for the waiver to have effect.

It thus has to be concluded that in case of a legal dispute it is likely that the dispute settlement organs will hold that all provisions in the operative part of a waiver decision that determine the scope of the waiver, that set out requirements that measures have to meet, or that establish notification, information, reporting, or consultation requirements, give rise to conditions which have to be met for the waiver to take effect. This is the case unless the requirements are not phrased in mandatory terms. Indeed waiver decisions sometimes include language that the beneficiaries 'should' notify certain measures or 'will' submit annual reports.[307] Non-compliance with these terms will not result in an automatic termination of the suspension.

3 Creation of new obligations

One recent waiver decision, the 2003 TRIPS Waiver,[308] arguably not only contains terms and conditions in the sense of Article IX:4 WTO Agreement, but also creates new obligations for WTO members. The TRIPS Waiver, decision specifies requirements to be met by members that wish to import pharmaceuticals produced under a compulsory licence in other members, as well as requirements to be met by the member which grants the compulsory licence for production of pharmaceuticals to be exported. These requirements have to be met so that the suspensions of Art. 31(f) and Art. 31(h) TRIPS Agreement take effect. In fact these requirements constitute the new rule which replaces the suspended provisions. In addition, however, the decision imposes obligations on third members which neither issue a compulsory licence nor import pharmaceuticals produced under such a licence. Thus, paragraph 4 of the decision obliges developed country members to provide upon request technical and financial

---

305 Panel Report, *US – Sugar Waiver*, BISD 37S/228, adopted 7 November 1990, para. 5.9.
306 *Ibid.*, para. 5.13.
307 See WT/L/518 (27 May 2003) (Kimberley Waiver); WT/L/677 (19 December 2006) (CBERA Waiver).
308 WT/L/540 (2 September 2003). On the TRIPS Waiver see Chapter 4 B.II.2.2.

cooperation to developing country members to assist them in preventing re-exportation of the imported pharmaceutical products,.[309] Furthermore, the decision obliges all WTO members to 'ensure the availability of effective legal means to prevent the importation into, and sale in, their territories of products produced under the system set out in this Decision and diverted to their markets inconsistently with its provisions, using the means already required to be available under the TRIPS Agreement'.[310]

Since these provisions do not condition the waiver, but instead establish new obligations for WTO members other than the beneficiaries of the waiver they cannot be based on the waiver power in Art. IX:3 WTO Agreement. It can be argued that these obligations are merely specifications of general obligations included in the TRIPS Agreement, namely to provide technical cooperation to developing country members (Article 67 TRIPS Agreement) and to ensure the availability of enforcement procedures against acts of infringement of intellectual property rights covered by the TRIPS Agreement (Article 44 TRIPS Agreement). As such they could be based on the competence to adopt authoritative interpretations in Art. IX:2 WTO Agreement.[311] The fact that Art. IX :2 WTO Agreement is not referenced in the decision provides a further illustration of the lack of clear procedural rules on the enactment of secondary law in the WTO.

E. INTERPRETATION

Questions of interpretation are addressed throughout this doctrinal study of the waiver power. In this section, which deals specifically with interpretation, I firstly wish to question the generalized statement often made with respect to waivers, namely that they should be interpreted narrowly or restrictively. Secondly, I address the extent to which non-WTO law may need to be interpreted in order to determine the scope of a waiver decision.

I Narrow interpretation of waiver decisions?

The GATT panel report in *US – Sugar Waiver* stated:

---

309 *Ibid.*, para. 4 cl. 2.   310 *Ibid.*, para. 5 cl. 1.
311 Hestermeyer, 'Flexible Entscheidungsfindung in der WTO', 194.

The Panel took into account in its examination that waivers are granted according to Article XXV:5 only in 'exceptional circumstances', that they waive obligations under the basic rules of the General Agreement and that their terms and conditions consequently have to be interpreted narrowly.[312]

In *EC – Bananas III* the panel and Appellate Body referred to this statement. While the panel explicitly acknowledged that waiver decisions should be interpreted narrowly the Appellate Body in its report adopted a slightly different phrasing. The report states:

> Although the *WTO Agreement* does not provide any specific rules on the interpretation of waivers, Article IX of the WTO Agreement and the *Understanding in Respect of Waivers of Obligations under the General Agreement on Tariffs and Trade 1994*... stress the exceptional nature of waivers and subject waivers to strict disciplines. Thus, waivers should be interpreted with great care.[313]

Even though the Appellate Body does not explicitly state that waiver decisions should be interpreted narrowly it becomes clear that it regards waivers as exceptions, and consequently holds that they should be interpreted restrictively. In its report in the second compliance proceeding the Appellate Body elaborates on the function of waiver decisions and states:

> In our view, the function of a waiver is to relieve a Member, for a specified period of time, from a particular obligation provided for in the covered agreements, subject to the terms, conditions, justifying exceptional circumstances or policy objectives described in the waiver decision. Its purpose is not to modify existing provisions in the agreements, let alone create new law or add to or amend the obligations under a covered agreement or Schedule. Therefore, waivers are exceptional in nature, subject to strict disciplines and should be interpreted with great care.[314]

312 Panel Report, *US – Sugar Waiver*, BISD 37S/228, adopted 7 November 1990, para. 5.9. In the same case the United States, the defendant, defended the view that it was inappropriate to require that waivers be interpreted narrowly. Contrary to exceptions to GATT rules of which contracting parties could freely avail themselves, waiver requests were subject to rigorous examination and needed to be approved by a two-thirds majority (*ibid.*, para. 3.34).

313 Appellate Body Report, *EC – Bananas III*, WT/DS27/AB/R, adopted 25 September 1997, para. 185.

314 Appellate Body Report, *EC – Bananas III (Article 21.5 – ECU II, US)*, WT/DS27/AB/RW2/ECU, adopted 11 December 2008, and WT/DS27/AB/RW/USA, adopted 22 December 2008, para. 382 (emphasis added).

The Appellate Body proceeds from the assumption that waiver decisions are granted to individual members for limited periods of time until a certain exceptional situation is overcome or a policy objective achieved. It does not acknowledge the fact that the waiver power is used for more purposes than to provide a safety valve in case of individual difficulties with compliance.[315] In particular it does not take account of the practice of adopting collective waiver decisions that abstractly modify legal rules to adapt them to a (changed) consensus with regard to the proper balance of interests in WTO law, or of adopting waiver decisions that aim at the coordination of WTO law with other international legal regimes. As concerns individual waivers it ignores that these do not merely address situations of hardship caused by capacity problems or economic crisis, but are also adopted to allow members to freely pursue policy objectives in deviation from WTO rules. In regard to the multitude of purposes as well as differing legal effects of waiver decisions one single rule of interpretation is not appropriate.[316]

1 Interpretation of individual waiver decisions

With respect to waiver decisions as individual exceptions, which the Appellate Body apparently had in mind, a narrow interpretation at first sight seems plausible for the following reasons:[317] waiver decisions that suspend obligations for individual members grant these members a special benefit of non-compliance which may be seen to contradict the principle of equality before the law. Contrary to legal exceptions such as those in Art. XX GATT, which are available to each member who meets the legal requirements, waiver decisions only benefit the members designated in the decision. Furthermore, the organization's organs have always been very careful to stress that waiver decisions do not have precedential effect and are granted on a case-by-case basis, which means that even though each member may request a waiver there is no guarantee that a waiver

---

315 For a comprehensive overview of the WTO waiver practice, see Chapter 4.

316 With regard to domestic law it is recognized that different types of legal instruments require different methodologies of interpretation, see Barak, *Purposive Interpretation in Law*; for international law see Weiler, 'Interpretation of Treaties', 507, as well as the contributions to this EJIL symposium in the same issue.

317 On the narrow interpretation of safeguard clauses, see Huesa Vinaixa, 'Convention de Vienne de 1969, Article 57', 2015, 2031.

decision will be adopted – even in situations which are comparable to other situations for which waivers were adopted in the past.[318]

A general rule of restrictive interpretation cannot, however, change the need to take as a starting point for any interpretation the wording of the legal instrument that is being interpreted. The wording of waiver decisions is frequently not very restrictive. In particular, waiver decisions that allow for the granting of special tariff preferences to developing countries are often not specific in describing the tariff preferences they justify. For example, the waiver which legalizes trade preferences granted by the United States to its former trust territory of the Pacific Islands refers in its operative part to 'preferential treatment to eligible products' of the Pacific Island states named in the waiver. It neither includes a list of products nor does it refer to US legislation as the basis of such treatment.[319] Other waiver decisions, such as the CARIBCAN Waiver, do refer to such legislation, but by way of a dynamic reference thus allowing for the preferential treatment which is justified by the waiver to change over time.[320] More restrictively, the Cotonou Waiver merely justifies preferential treatment '*as required* by Article 36.3, Annex V and its Protocols of the ACP–EC Partnership Agreement'.[321] These different phrases clarify that the scope of a waiver primarily depends on the wording, resulting in a more or less restrictive scope. Absurdly, the panel in *EC – Bananas III* insisted on a narrow interpretation of waivers and then found that the Lomé Waiver not only suspended Art. I:1 GATT but also Art. XI GATT, even though Art. XI GATT was not mentioned anywhere in the waiver decision.[322] This finding was reversed by the Appellate Body who referred to the clear wording of the Lomé Waiver.[323]

When the wording – including the wording of relevant context such as the preamble – remains inconclusive, account should be taken of the intentions expressed by delegates in the organ which discussed and adopted the waiver decision. These are evidenced by official documents such as an accompanying chairperson's statement or working party reports. While treaties, especially public order treaties such as the WTO Agreements, should for good reasons be accorded a certain independence from the

---

318 The adoption of a waiver decision will, however, create a justificatory burden with respect to future requests in comparable situations.

319 WT/L/694 (1 August 2007).   320 WT/L/677 (19 December 2006), para. 1.

321 WT/L/436 (7 December 2001), para. 1.

322 Panel Report, *EC – Bananas III*, WT/DS27/R (22 May 1997), para. 7.110.

323 Appellate Body Report, *EC – Bananas III*, WT/DS27/AB/R, adopted 25 September 1997, para. 187.

parties that negotiated them, the same reasons are not convincing as regards the interpretation of individual waiver decisions. Public order treaties, like constitutions, bind not only their 'founders', but also states which accede and states which, even though they were among the original parties, over time change as to their constituencies and representatives. Furthermore, they apply over long periods of time during which the meanings attributed to legal concepts and principles may change.[324] All these factors justify a certain emancipation of the treaty from the intentions of the negotiators, even where these intentions are known. By contrast, waiver decisions are taken by an organ of the organization which maintains control over the decision. It can modify its terms and even terminate the waiver. The decision is only granted for a short period of time, usually a maximum of a few years for individual waivers. These circumstances justify it to accord more weight to expressions of intentions in the *travaux préparatoires* than is usually proposed as regards the interpretation of treaties.[325] More authoritative than statements of individual delegates, even if undisputed, are statements adopted on the basis of a consensus such as chairperson statements or statements included in a report of a working party that examined a waiver request. Under the GATT working party reports were adopted by the GATT Council or the CONTRACTING PARTIES and in some cases they included the explicit statement that the respective working party report should guide interpretation.[326] It may be concluded that only when recourse to the wording and the intentions as evidenced by the *travaux préparatoires* remain inconclusive is a narrow interpretation justified.

324 In *US – Shrimp* the Appellate Body adopted a dynamic interpretation which enabled it to subsume living resources under the term 'natural resources' in Art. XX (g) GATT, see Appellate Body Report, *US – Shrimp*, WT/DS58/AB/R, adopted 6 November 1998, paras. 128 *et seq.* (stating in para. 129 that the provision must be read 'in light of contemporary concerns'); see also Appellate Body Report, *China – Publications*, WT/DS363/AB/R, adopted 19 January 2010, paras. 396 *et seq.*

325 In *EC – Bananas* the Appellate Body referred to discussions in the CONTRACTING PARTIES on the wording of the waiver decision in order to determine the scope of the Lomé Waiver: see Appellate Body Report, *EC – Bananas III*, WT/DS27/AB/R, adopted 25 September 1997, para. 168.

326 Report of Working Party on United States Automotive Products Waiver Request, L/2509 (15 November 1965), para. 20 (clarifying the interpretation that should be given to the term 'substantive interest' in the waiver decision); CONTRACTING PARTIES, Summary Record of the Forty-Fifth Meeting at the Ninth Session, SR.9/45 (18 March 1955), 7 (agreeing that the working party report on a UK waiver 'should be regarded as a basic document for the interpretation of the waiver itself').

2 Interpretation of collective waiver decisions

The Appellate Body and panels that have pronounced so far on the inter-pretation of waivers did not take account of collective waiver decisions which either benefit (potentially) all members, such as the Kimberley or TRIPS Waivers, or groups of members, such as the 1999 Preferences Waiver. With respect to this waiver practice the general statement that waivers should be interpreted strictly or narrowly is not convincing. Fur-thermore, it is not reconcilable with the Appellate Body's own jurispru-dence with respect to the general exceptions in Art. XX GATT.

Waiver decisions such as the 1999 Preferences Waiver or the TRIPS Waiver that formulate abstract requirements to justify non-compliance, can be qualified as general exception rules comparable to those in Art. XX GATT. With respect to the general exception rules in Art. XX GATT the Appellate Body clarified in its case law – in deviation from former GATT jurisprudence – that they need not be interpreted narrowly. Panel reports under the GATT 1947 frequently and without much explanation stated a rule according to which exceptions were to be interpreted narrowly.[327] This interpretation rule can be explained with the relatively common perception that exceptions mitigate the effectiveness of the rules to which they form an exception and thus impede the attainment of the law's objectives. Under the GATT 1947 it was thus held that the exceptions in Article XX GATT – as exceptions to such fundamental rules as the most-favoured-nation and the national treatment obligations – impeded the attainment of the objectives of these rules and consequently the objectives of the GATT.[328]

Such a conclusion presupposes a conception of general exceptions as allowing the pursuit of policies in contradiction to the organization's objectives. By contrast, one may perceive of exception rules not as con-tradicting the organization's objectives, but as concretizing them. As a merely formal matter a rule and its exceptions can be reformulated by

---

327 Panel Report, *EEC – Restrictions on Imports of Apples*, adopted June 22, 1989, 36S/135, para. 5.13; Panel Report, *US – Countervailing Duties on Fresh, Chilled and Frozen Pork from Canada*, adopted 11 July 1991, BISD 38S/30, para. 4.4; Panel Report, *US – Measures Affecting Alcoholic and Malt Beverages*, adopted 19 June 1992, BISD 39S/206, para. 5.41; Panel Report, *Canada – Import Restrictions on Ice Cream and Yoghurt*, adopted 5 December 1989, BISD 36S/68, para. 59. ECJ case law consistently refers to the principle that the exceptions to the fundamental freedoms need not be interpreted narrowly, see Fennelly, 'Legal Interpretation at the European Court of Justice', 656, 673, 674.

328 Panel Report, *US – Tuna II* (unadopted), DS29/R (16 June 1994), para. 5.26.

integrating the exception into the rule.[329] The objective of this reformulated and integrated rule will be different to that of the rule looked at in
isolation from its exception.

This can be clarified when looking at the main obligations of the GATT
and the general exception of Art. XX GATT. Trade liberalization can be
seen as the aim of the obligation to respect tariff commitments (Art. II
GATT), the non-discrimination obligations (Art. I, III GATT), and the
prohibition on quantitative restrictions (Art. XI GATT). Art. XX GATT
justifies departures from all of these obligations in the pursuit of certain
values such as human and animal health, public morals or protection
of natural resources. Consequently, the application of the exceptions in
Art. XX GATT can be perceived as negatively affecting the main objective
of the GATT as derived from its main obligations (in Articles I, III and
XI GATT). This effect, it could be argued, and in fact was argued in the
cited GATT panel reports, justifies a narrow interpretation of Art. XX
GATT. If, however, one formulates the objectives of the GATT in light
of the general exceptions in Art. XX GATT, the objective would then be
'trade liberalization as far as it leaves members regulatory freedom in
matters of health, public morals and natural resources not exercised in a
protectionist manner'. This objective is not negatively affected if measures
are adopted which are inconsistent with one of the main obligations, but
justified under the general exception.

Such an integrated view of a treaty's objectives requires interpreters
not only to look at individual obligations to determine '*the* object and
purpose',[330] but rather to determine the objectives by viewing individual
obligations and their exceptions together. The Appellate Body has in
recent years explicitly abandoned the perception that exception norms
such as Art. XX GATT or the exception for GSP preferences in the Enabling
Clause impede the attainment of the organization's objectives and should
therefore be interpreted narrowly. In *EC – Hormones* the Appellate Body
acknowledged:

> [M]erely characterizing a treaty provision as an 'exception' does not itself
> justify a 'stricter' or 'narrower' interpretation than would be warranted

---

329 Raz, *Concept of a Legal System.*
330 Art. 31:1 VCLT states that a treaty shall be interpreted in light of 'its object and purpose'.
     Klabbers, 'On Rationalism in Politics', 405, 414, 415 (criticizing the Appellate Body
     for misreading this provision and arguing that the Appellate Body pursues a political
     strategy by presenting its interpretations as mandated by the rules on interpretation of
     the VCLT).

by examination of the ordinary meaning of the actual words, viewed in context and in the light of the treaty's objective.[331]

In *EC – Tariff Preferences* the Appellate Body further clarified that certain of the WTO's objectives may be pursued by members through the use of exceptions. It acknowledged that by adopting environmental measures that fall under the exception of Article XX (g) GATT, members may be seen to pursue the objective of 'sustainable development' recognized in the WTO Agreement's preamble.[332] The Appellate Body report in *EC – Tariff Preferences* is particularly relevant for the interpretation of waivers since the Enabling Clause which was interpreted in this case succeeded the 1971 GSP Waiver. In *EC – Tariff Preferences* the Appellate Body noted with respect to the 1971 GSP Waiver that it constituted a recognition that the most-favoured-nation principle failed to secure a fair share for developing countries in world trade and that different measures were necessary to pursue this objective of the GATT. In the view of the Appellate Body the 1971 GSP Waiver constituted an exception, albeit one the use of which was seen to further the organization's objectives.[333] The Appellate Body, thus, arguably took the view that objectives of the organization can be pursued not only through treaty exceptions, but also through exceptions stated in legal documents which are of limited duration such as waiver decisions.[334]

On the basis of this reasoning the 1999 Preferences Waiver can also be interpreted as a positive effort to ensure that developing countries secure a share in the growth in international trade as called for in the WTO Agreement's preamble.[335] That it has been adopted to further this objective becomes very clear from the waiver's preamble. It not only refers to the WTO objective of economic development, but also mentions several Ministerial Declarations and decisions that call upon members to improve the situation of developing countries in the world trading system.[336] Similarly, the 2003 TRIPS Waiver is an implementation of the 2001 Doha Declaration on the TRIPS Agreement and Public Health and as such intended to better realize the TRIPS Agreement's objective as stated

---

331 Appellate Body Report, *EC – Hormones*, WT/DS26/AB/R, WT/DS48/AB/R, adopted 13 February 1998, para. 104.

332 Appellate Body Report. *EC – Tariff Preferences*, WT/DS246/AB/R, adopted 20 April 2004, para. 94 (footnote deleted).

333 Cf. Jackson, *World Trade and the Law of GATT*, 31 (arguing that the CONTRACTING PARTIES used the waiver power to add new objectives to the GATT).

334 The 1971 GSP Waiver was granted for ten years, L/3545 (28 June 1971).

335 WT/L/304 (17 June 1999), preamble, 2nd recital.   336 See Chapter 4 B.II.2.1(b).

in Art. 7 TRIPS Agreement, namely to protect intellectual property rights 'in a manner conducive to social . . . welfare'.

To summarize: based on the Appellate Body's own case law it is not plausible to hold that waiver decisions of general application which were taken and justified on the basis of a consensus as to the proper balance of competing interests in the attainment of WTO objectives should be interpreted narrowly. Due to their purpose to give effect to such a consensus by modifying the legal rules, the status of these waiver decisions should not be relegated to that of exceptional measures detrimental to narrowly defined economic objectives. In the case of the TRIPS Waiver decision it becomes particularly clear that this would be a misinterpretation of its status, since this waiver is to be succeeded by an amendment with the same content. Instead of sticking to a rule of narrow interpretation, if wording and context remain inconclusive as to the meaning of a waiver decision, an openly teleological approach should be adopted. Such interpretation asks about the policy objectives which the decision aims to pursue and considers the effects of different interpretations in relation to such policy objectives.[337]

For similar reasons, waiver decisions which coordinate WTO law with another international legal regime also should not a priori be subjected to a rule of restrictive interpretation. The adoption of such a waiver is a decision to restrict the jurisdiction of the WTO in favour of another international regime, either to enable efficient division of labour (as in the case of the collective HS waiver decisions) or to defer to the greater expertise and representativeness of another international legal regime as concerns non-economic objectives (as in the case of the Kimberley Waiver).[338] These aims should guide interpretation within the limits of a waiver decision's text.

II References to non-WTO law to interpret waiver decisions

When interpreting waiver decisions the interpreter will frequently have to resort to non-WTO law in order to determine the scope of the waiver. Many waiver decisions justify measures 'consistent with',[339] 'authorized

---

337 Irwin and Weiler, 'Measures Affecting the Cross-Border Supply of Gambling and Betting Services', 71 (criticizing the 'textual fetish and policy phobia' of the Appellate Body); for an interpretative approach to WTO law guided by the policy objective of development, see Qureshi, *Interpreting WTO Agreements*, in particular 114 *et seq.*

338 On this function of collective waiver decisions, see Chapter 6 B.II.

339 E.g. WT/L/518 (27 May 2003) (Kimberley Waiver).

by',[340] or 'required by'[341] municipal or international legal instruments. To determine what these legal instruments permit, authorize or require, dispute settlement organs have to refer to the relevant provisions of these instruments.

In *EC – Bananas III* the Appellate Body made clear, confirming the Panel Report on this point, that when determining the scope of a waiver another international agreement may have to be interpreted by the dispute settlement organ to the extent its content bears on the meaning of the waiver.[342] The EC had argued that the panel had to accept the interpretation given to the Fourth Lomé Convention by its parties.[343] The panel did not agree and stated that through the reference to the Lomé Convention in the Lomé Waiver, the meaning of the Lomé Convention became a WTO issue and that therefore the panel had to interpret the provisions of the Lomé Convention in so far as this was necessary to interpret the waiver.[344]

The dispute settlement organs are, however, limited in their interpretative freedom with respect to international legal acts if an authoritative interpretation or consistent practice of interpretation exists.[345] Where a waiver refers to domestic law, the meaning of such law needs to be determined by reference to the domestic courts and executive authorities that apply this law.[346]

F. REVIEW OF WAIVER DECISIONS

I Political review

Waiver decisions are subject to review by the Ministerial Conference and the General Council acting on its behalf. These political organs can extend,

---

340 E.g. WT/L/677 (19 December 2006) (CBERA Waiver).

341 E.g. WT/L/186 (18 October 1996) (Lomé Waiver).

342 Appellate Body Report, *EC – Bananas III*, WT/DS27/AB/R, adopted 25 September 1997, para. 167; Panel Report, *EC – Bananas III (ECU)*, WT/DS27/R/ECU (22 May 1997), paras. 7.97, 7.98.

343 Panel Report, *EC – Bananas III (ECU)*, WT/DS27/R/ECU (22 May 1997), para. IV.67.

344 *Ibid.*, para. 7.98.

345 In *EC – Bananas III* the panel further pointed out that the parties to the Lomé Convention differed in their interpretations of the relevant provisions, *ibid.*

346 An example for such a waiver is the Agricultural Waiver. In the *Sugar* case the panel which had to interpret this waiver stated that the waiver authorized the United States to implement Section 22 'which is interpreted by the United States executive authorities and the United States courts'. Panel Report, *US – Sugar Waiver*, BISD 37S/228, adopted 7 November 1990, para. 5.9.

modify or terminate waiver decisions. Under the GATT 1947, while it was
from time to time asserted that the power to grant waivers also implied
the power to withdraw and modify waivers,[347] this power remained an
issue of contention.[348] The issue whether waivers may be modified or
terminated by the political organs is less pressing when waivers include
a termination date, as they have to in the WTO. Nonetheless, the WTO
Agreement explicitly confirms the competence for political review of
waiver decisions. Article IX:4, clauses 2 to 4 of the WTO Agreement states:

> Any waiver granted for a period of more than one year shall be reviewed by
> the Ministerial Conference not later than one year after it is granted, and
> thereafter annually until the waiver terminates. In each review the Min-
> isterial Conference shall examine whether the exceptional circumstances
> justifying the waiver still exist and whether the terms and conditions
> attached to the waiver have been met. The Ministerial Conference, on the
> basis of the annual review, may extend, modify or terminate the waiver.

Twice each year the General Council places the annual review of waiver
decisions on its agenda. So far the General Council has only once terminated a waiver decision on the occasion of such a review. This was in 2003
when the General Council agreed to terminate the waiver which it had
adopted in 2000 to allow Turkey to grant preferential tariff treatment to
products from Bosnia–Herzegovina.[349] Turkey had called for the termination of the waiver since it had concluded a free trade agreement with
Bosnia–Herzegovina and therefore no longer needed the waiver.[350]

Usually the annual review of waiver decisions in the WTO is conducted
as follows: the chairperson of the General Council points to the waiver
decisions under review and the annual reports which are required under

347 *Ibid.*, para. 5.16 (noting that the power of the CONTRACTING PARTIES to grant
     waivers under XXV:5 implies the power to withdraw or modify the waivers granted);
     GATT/CP.2/36 (7 September 1948), para. 6; G/59 (22 October 1953) (this working party
     report notes that waiver decisions except those for which a term of validity is prescribed,
     could be reviewed by the CONTRACTING PARTIES at any time). Klein, 'International
     Organizations or Institutions, Decision-Making', para. 12 (noting that as a general rule
     of institutional law an organ which adopted an act may decide to suspend or terminate
     it due to particular circumstances).

348 Jackson, Davey and Sykes, *Legal Problems of International Economic Relations*, 226.

349 General Council, Turkey – Preferential Treatment for Bosnia–Herzegovina, Decision
     of 8 December 2000, WT/L/381 (13 December 2000); for the termination see Gen-
     eral Council, Minutes of the Meeting on 15 and 16 December 2003, WT/GC/M/84
     (27 February 2004), para. 263.

350 *Ibid.*, para. 261 (statement by the representative of Turkey). The General Council inter-
     preted the conclusion of a free trade agreement to mean that exceptional circumstances
     no longer existed, *ibid.*, para. 262 (statement by the chairman).

some waivers and which are distributed to members before the meeting of the General Council. Rarely do delegates make statements. When they do, these are mostly expressions of gratitude for the adoption of a waiver.[351] Some have pointed to difficulties created for them by the measures justified under a waiver.[352] Never, however, has there been a substantive discussion concerning the situation which had prompted the waiver request, the implementation of a waiver decision or the effects of the measures justified under a waiver. In one General Council meeting the delegate from Tanzania speaking on behalf of least-developed country members pointed out that least-developed countries in many instances had difficulties in profiting from tariff preferences justified by the 1999 Preferences Waiver[353] due to stringent rules of origin and related burdensome administrative procedures.[354] This statement was noted by the General Council, but did not initiate a discussion on whether the waiver decision under review contributed to the policy objective of economic development even though this had been the justification for granting the waiver.[355]

Under the GATT the CONTRACTING PARTIES were not obliged to review waiver decisions annually. Many waiver decisions did, however, require the beneficiaries to submit annual reports.[356] In some instances these reports were examined by working parties specifically established

351 See, for example, General Council, Minutes of the Meeting on 31 July 2008, WT/GC/M/115 (10 October 2008), para. 71 (statement by the representative of Lesotho on behalf of the least-developed countries expressing gratitude for adopting the 1999 Preferences Waiver on tariff preferences from developing to least-developed countries and the waiver suspending Article 70.9 TRIPS Agreement with respect to pharmaceutical products).

352 See, for example, General Council, Minutes of the Meeting on 27 July and 1 August 2004, WT/GC/M/87 (4 October 2004), para. 60 (statement by the representative of Sri Lanka on the economic effects of the 1999 Preferences Waiver on developing countries which are not LDCs); General Council, Minutes of the Meeting on 13 December 2004, WT/GC/M/90 (10 February 2005), para. 174 (statement by the representative of Ecuador on the burden which the waivers granted to the EC for preferences under the Cotonou Agreement and the import regime for bananas imposed on Ecuador).

353 On this waiver decision, see Chapter 4 B.II.2.1(b).

354 See General Council, Minutes of the Meeting on 27 July and 1 August 2004, WT/GC/M/87 (4 October 2004), para. 59 (statement by the representative of Tanzania on behalf of LDCs).

355 The lack of a thorough examination of the economic effects of trade preferences justified by waivers, the trade diversion and the trade creation they cause, had already been criticized by Kenneth Dam with reference to the GATT: Dam, *GATT: Law and International Economic Organization*, 53 *et seq.*

356 The Guiding Principles stated that waiver decisions 'should provide for an annual report and, where appropriate for an annual review of the operation of the waiver', L/532, section e.

for this purpose. In the case of the 1955 Agricultural Waiver this was done regularly.[357]

When evaluating the lack of political review with regard to the justification of waiver decisions as well as the effects of action taken under a waiver, one should take into account the different purposes for which waiver decisions are adopted in the WTO. To reiterate, the four main purposes are the following: first, to take account of capacity problems to comply; second, to allow individual WTO members to pursue certain domestic or foreign policy objectives; third, to generally modify WTO rules to adapt them to a new consensus as to the proper balance of interests represented by the legal rules; and fourth, to coordinate WTO law with the law of another international legal regime. Moreover it is important to distinguish review by the highest political organ with a view to termination or modification of the decision from other forms of supervision and review by specialized councils and committees or the judicial organs.

Against this background it is not all that surprising that review of waiver decisions by the Ministerial Conference and the General Council plays a subordinate role. When waiver decisions are adopted to address difficulties which individual members or all developing or least-developed-country members encounter when implementing WTO obligations it is sensible that the supervision of this implementation should be entrusted to the specialized councils and committees. Where a lack of compliance results from limited capacity, the ultimate aim of compliance will rather be promoted by adopting a managerial approach involving assistance than by threatening the termination of a waiver decision. This has been the approach adopted by the Committee on Market Access in relation to the adaptation of members' goods schedules to changes in the Harmonized System. Waivers are adopted to afford members time for the implementation process and at the same time substantial assistance is granted to developing country members to complete the adaptation exercise.[358] Another example for a managerial approach to compliance is evidenced by the work of the Customs Valuation Committee. Members whose obligations under the Customs Valuation Agreement are suspended, are asked to adopt work programmes and submit implementation reports to the Customs Valuation Committee or the Council for Trade in Goods.[359]

---

357 See, for example, Report of the Working Party, United States – Import Restrictions on Agricultural Products, L/6194 (2 July 1987).
358 On the Harmonized System waivers, see Chapter 4 B.I.1.2. and B.II.3.1.
359 See e.g. WT/L/410 (7 August 2001), para. 5. This waiver granted to Thailand to allow it to maintain certain trade-related investment measures requires Thailand to consult

To assist the supervision of schedules' adaptation to HS changes as well as the implementation of the Customs Valuation Agreement, the Secretariat maintains lists of HS waivers as well as extension decisions and reservations under the CVA.[360]

Despite the practice of not reassessing waiver decisions during the formal annual reviews in the General Council, developing countries have expressed the fear that waivers granted for longer periods than one year might be terminated during annual reviews.[361] When the waiver decision that suspends the obligations of least-developed country members under Art. 70.9 TRIPS Agreement with respect to pharmaceutical products was adopted,[362] these fears were explicitly addressed. During the meeting of the General Council at which the waiver decision was adopted, chairman Motta of the TRIPS Council made a statement to the effect that it was understood that the exceptional circumstances would continue to exist for least-developed country members until the expiry date of 2016.[363] At the (pro forma) annual reviews of this waiver in the General Council the respective chairperson usually refers to this statement.[364]

When waivers either limit the WTO's jurisdiction in favour of another international legal regime or generally modify WTO norms to take better account of WTO members' needs and interests, political review might be more desirable than in cases when waiver decisions address capacity problems. The annual review demanded by Article IX:4 WTO Agreement could be a forum in which the effects of the decision as well as potential modifications are discussed. Such a review might, however, also more fruitfully be conducted in the specialized councils. This view is reflected in the TRIPS Waiver. It provides that the functioning of the system set out in the decision shall be reviewed annually by the TRIPS Council and that this review shall be deemed to fulfil the review requirements of Art. IX:4 WTO Agreement.[365]

---

with and submit reports on the phasing out of these measures to the Council for Trade in Goods and specifies that such reports and consultations shall be deemed to fulfil the review requirement in Art. IX:4 WTO Agreement.

360 See e.g. G/VAL/M/37 (30 April 2004) (on reporting under CVA decisions); G/MA/W/23/rev. 2 (27 September 2005) (note by the Secretariat on the situation of schedules of WTO members including waiver decisions).

361 See e.g. TRIPS Council, Minutes of Meeting on 17–19 September 2002, IP/C/M/37 (11 October 2002), para. 4 (statement by the representative of Lesotho).

362 On this waiver, see Chapter 4 B.II.1.2.   363 IP/C/M/36 (18 July 2002), para. 215.

364 See e.g. WT/GC/M/115 (10 October 2008), para. 70.

365 WT/L/540 (2 September 2003), para. 8.

In the literature it was proposed with respect to the political review of waivers that the political organs should be competent to modify and terminate waivers by a simple majority.[366] This proposal is, however, not convincing. While it is desirable that the effects and potential operational problems of rule-making waivers are reviewed with a view to possible improvements, the possibility of a termination or modification by a simple majority would create legal insecurity and prevent members from relying on the new rules created by the waiver.

There remains the group of waivers which are granted to individual members for the pursuit of policy objectives. Important examples are the waivers for the pursuit of foreign policy objectives through trade preference schemes outside the GSP. These waivers are granted for multi-year periods in order to provide some legal predictability and stability in the preference-receiving countries. In these cases stricter scrutiny of the effects of the measures authorized by these waivers might be desirable. Do they really support economic development in the preference-receiving countries? Do they harm other countries in a similar economic situation? Do they discriminate between similarly situated countries? To the extent these questions refer to the objectives of economic development they do fall into the competence of the WTO. Furthermore, they are better dealt with in a political forum than in a judicial process. To address them in the political organs might lead to greater transparency and eventually some pressure on preference-granting countries to design their preference schemes in a way that is more beneficial to the preference-receiving countries.

As to questions of compliance by individual members with the terms and conditions of all types of waiver decisions, these are open to legal determinations which fall within the competence of the judicial organs and should consequently be determined by the judicial and not the political organs.

II Judicial review

In this section on judicial review three distinct issues will be discussed. Firstly, I shall address the question whether the judicial organs have jurisdiction to review the legality of waiver decisions, i.e. to determine whether the political organs have acted within the limits of the law when they

---

366 Harrison, 'Legal and Political Oversight of WTO Waivers', 411, 413 (suggesting that waivers can be terminated by a simple majority vote).

adopted a waiver. Secondly, I shall turn to the judicial determination of compliance by the beneficiary of a waiver with the terms and conditions set out in the waiver decision. And thirdly, I shall examine whether and under what conditions a non-violation complaint may be successfully based on the claim that a measure justified by a waiver decision impairs or nullifies benefits accruing under the WTO Agreements.

1 Judicial review of waiver decisions

The qualification of waiver decisions as secondary law[367] raises the question whether waiver decisions are subject to judicial review, i.e. whether the dispute settlement organs have jurisdiction to examine if the political organs in adopting a waiver decision acted in accordance with the substantive requirements of the waiver power and followed the correct procedure.[368] The question as to the admissibility of a judicial review of waivers has not yet been addressed within the WTO.

The Dispute Settlement Understanding (DSU) does not provide for a direct action for judicial review of the legality of decisions taken by the political organs. It only applies to disputes between members (Art. 1:1 DSU).[369] However, in a dispute between members concerning their rights and obligations under the WTO Agreements the question as to the legality of a waiver decision may arise incidentally.[370] In a dispute about the legality of a measure adopted by the respondent the argument may be made that the measure – even though falling within the scope of a waiver decision – is not justified by the waiver since the waiver decision is invalid and therefore without justificatory effect. Note that the outcome of the member-to-member dispute would only be affected if the dispute settlement organs were to find a waiver to be invalid and thus without effect. A mere finding of illegality without the consequence of invalidity

---

367 See section A.I. above.
368 For such a definition of judicial review, see Lauterpacht, 'Judicial Review of the Acts of International Organisations', 92.
369 Kuijper, 'WTO Institutional Aspects', 2009, 90.
370 Kuijper (*ibid.*) cites as an incidence of incidental legality review the Appellate Body Report in *US – FSC*. In this case, however, the Appellate Body examined how a GATT Council decision that had been adopted in relation to several legal disputes was to be qualified, whether it constituted an authoritative interpretation, binding on all contracting parties, or a decision only binding on the parties to the disputes which had prompted the Council decision. The Appellate Body did not, however, review the decision's legality. See Appellate Body Report, *US – FSC*, WT/DS108/AB/R, adopted 20 March 2000, paras. 104–14.

would not affect the waiver's legal effects. The dispute settlement organs do not have the competence to declare illegal acts by the organization to be invalid.

The admissibility of judicial review affects the institutional balance within an organization. In the EU this question has long been settled: the European Court of Justice may annul legal acts on the basis of certain grounds such as a lack of competence or the violation of an essential procedural requirement.[371] Acts may even be annulled if they were adopted by a unanimous Council decision.[372] In international law judicial review gains in importance if one adopts the view presented earlier in this chapter regarding the qualification of waiver decisions as secondary law. According to this view, legality of international legal acts is an important safeguard for the legitimacy of international governance, in particular where it affects individual rights or the scope for democratic self-government.[373] Frequently, however, there will be no claimant before international tribunals to allege the illegality of a legal act by an international organization: either because the respective act was adopted by consensus or otherwise due to acquiescence by the members of the organization.[374] Consequently, international courts and tribunals only very seldom engage in judicial review.[375] As to waiver decisions, it is similarly unlikely that the legality of a waiver decision will become an issue in dispute settlement proceedings so long as waiver decisions are adopted by consensus. Nonetheless, I shall, in what follows, argue that dispute settlement organs have the competence to engage in a limited judicial review of waiver decisions.

The DSU does not explicitly address the question of incidental legality review.[376] In two cases to date the dispute settlement organs have

---

371 Arts. 263, 264 Treaty on the Functioning of the European Union; Bogdandy and Bast, 'Federal Order of Competences', 275, 279 et seq. (noting the strict judicial review of EC acts by the ECJ and the resulting hierarchization of EC law).

372 Ehlermann, 'How Flexible Is Community Law?', 1274, 1276.

373 See supra section A.I.

374 Klabbers, Introduction to International Institutional Law, 218.

375 On the very few instances in which the ICJ engaged in judicial review of acts of an international organization, ibid., 214 et seq.

376 Bogdandy, 'Law and Politics in the WTO', 609, 630 (suggesting that the Appellate Body may incidentally review waiver decisions). For the view that the dispute settlement organs may not engage in judicial review of waiver decisions, see Harrison, 'Legal and Political Oversight of WTO Waivers', 411, 417; Footer, Institutional and Normative Analysis of the World Trade Organization, 256.

addressed the institutional balance between political organs and dispute settlement organs. In these cases, *India – Quantitative Restrictions* and *Turkey – Textiles*, the issue arose whether the fact that the agreements accorded a competence to the political organs to determine whether the requirements of legal provisions were met, excluded the competence of the judicial organs to also engage in such a determination. To be more specific: in the first case the question was whether the judicial organs could determine the justification of balance-of-payments restrictions according to Art. XVIII:B GATT, even though such a determination falls within the competence of the General Council and the Balance-of-Payments Committee.[377] In the second case the issue was whether the dispute settlement organs could determine whether a customs union met the requirements of Art. XXIV GATT, even though the Committee on Regional Trade Agreements is mandated with such determinations.[378] The Appellate Body held that, if confronted with such questions, panels had the duty to examine them; otherwise they would diminish the procedural rights of the claimant. It did not find that there was, as contended by India, a principle of institutional balance in WTO law which prevented panels from engaging in such examinations.[379]

These constellations differ, however, from the legal review of waiver decisions. In the case of waivers it is clear that Art. IX:3 WTO Agreement accords to the Ministerial Conference the *exclusive* competence to adopt waiver decisions. The question thus is not whether any other organ may also adopt waiver decisions, but whether the judicial organs may determine if the political organs have remained within the competence granted to them by Art. IX:3 WTO Agreement. Under the GATT 1947 this question was touched upon during the *Sugar* dispute between the EEC and the United States concerning import restrictions on sugar and

---

377 Panel Report, *India – Quantitative Restrictions*, WT/DS90/R (6 April 1999); Appellate Body Report, *India – Quantitative Restrictions*, WT/DS90/AB/R, adopted 22 September 1999.

378 Panel Report, *Turkey – Textiles*, WT/DS34/R (31 May 1999); Appellate Body Report, *Turkey – Textiles*, WT/DS34/AB/R, adopted 19 November 1999.

379 Appellate Body Report, *India – Quantitative Restrictions*, WT/DS90/AB/R, adopted 22 September 1999, paras. 80–109. Appellate Body Report, *Turkey – Textiles*, WT/DS34/AB/R, adopted 19 November, para. 60 (referring to its finding in *India – Quantitative Restrictions*); see also Roessler, 'Are the Judicial Organs of the World Trade Organization Overburdened?', 329 (criticizing the decisions, in particular for the reason that the questions whether a balance of payments situation or a regional trade agreement meeting the overall requirements of Art. XXIV GATT exists, due to a lack of normative guidance, are not amenable to judicial review).

sugar containing products. The US argued that the import prohibitions in question were justified by the 1955 Agricultural Waiver. While the EEC did not explicitly argue that the waiver itself was illegal, the US addressed the question of judicial review of waivers and argued that 'the waiver power was supreme, and could only be exercised or reconsidered by the CONTRACTING PARTIES'.[380] The question whether a waiver should be maintained fell, according to the US, within the exclusive competence of the CONTRACTING PARTIES.[381] The panel found the import restrictions on sugar containing products to be justified by the waiver decision, but noted that the CONTRACTING PARTIES when granting the waiver might not have anticipated the restrictions that were at issue in this case. In addressing the issue of judicial review the panel stated that it was only competent to interpret and apply a waiver decision, but that it did not have the mandate to propose changes to GATT provisions and therefore could not address the question of a withdrawal or modification of the waiver. The latter power, so the panel, was implied in the power of the CONTRACTING PARTIES under Art. XXV:5 GATT to grant waivers.[382]

To be sure this statement need not be interpreted to imply that no judicial review is permissible. Indeed review is required in so far as it is necessary to determine that a valid waiver decision exists. A waiver decision is only valid if it was adopted by the competent organ, and if the essential procedural requirements were followed.[383] By contrast, as concerns the substantive requirement that exceptional circumstances exist, the judicial organs should refer to the judgment of the political organs. The requirement of the existence of exceptional circumstances was never defined and has been interpreted by the political organs to encompass a wide range of situations. Since there are no normative standards that could guide legal interpretation the judicial organs should refrain from a determination whether this requirement has been met and defer to the discretion of the political organs.[384]

As to the procedural requirements, legality review should be restricted to essential procedural requirements. This is justified by the limitation of the jurisdiction of the dispute settlement organs to the settlement of

---

380 Panel Report, *US – Sugar Waiver*, BISD 37S/228, adopted 7 November 1990, para. 3.30.
381 *Ibid.*   382 *Ibid.*, para. 5.16.
383 Lauterpacht, 'Judicial Review of the Acts of International Organisations', 92, 93.
384 Even if the dispute settlement organs were to determine whether the exceptional circumstances requirement was met, they could refer to Art. 31:3(b) VCLT and find that the term exceptional circumstances needs to be interpreted in light of the organization's subsequent practice.

disputes between members. As was already noted, a legality review may only take the form of an incidental review in a contentious proceeding. In such a proceeding it is only relevant for the determination whether a waiver decision has legal effects or not. A waiver does not have legal effects if it is invalid. It does, however, have legal effects if it is merely illegal, but not invalid. It is difficult to argue that the violation of procedural requirements such as the requirement that waiver requests should be examined within ninety days leads to an invalidity of a waiver decision. And even the requirements that a waiver decision shall include reasons and a termination date may justify a finding of illegality, but not one of invalidity. Thus, the scope of judicial review of waiver decisions is limited to the question whether the competent organ acted and whether the essential requirements of the decision-making procedure were followed. The latter essentially refer to decision-making by a three-fourths majority vote or consensus.

2 Judicial review of compliance with the terms and conditions of a waiver decision

The violation of terms and conditions of a waiver decision may give rise to a violation complaint. For waivers of GATT obligations this is explicitly stated in paragraph 3 (a) of the Understanding which reads:

> Any Member considering that a benefit accruing to it under GATT 1994 is being nullified or impaired as a result of:
>
> (a) the failure of the Member to whom a waiver was granted to observe the terms and conditions of the waiver . . .
>
> may invoke the provisions of Article XXIII of GATT 1994 as elaborated and applied by the Dispute Settlement Understanding.

Two constellations have to be distinguished. Firstly, violation complaints that are based on an alleged violation of an obligation of the WTO agreements and, secondly, violation complaints based on an alleged violation of the terms of a waiver decision.

2.1 Violation complaints based on the alleged violation of a treaty obligation

In a violation proceeding in which the claimant makes a prima facie showing that a measure of the respondent violates a treaty obligation, the respondent may defend itself by arguing that the measure in question is justified by a waiver decision. Such a justification is successful if the waiver decision indeed suspends the obligation that allegedly was violated with respect to the measure in question.[385] It is not successful if the measure in question does not fall within the scope of a waiver decision. Furthermore, a defence based on a waiver decision may fail even though a measure is encompassed by a waiver decision. This is the case if the suspension by the waiver decision does not take effect because the beneficiary of the waiver failed to meet requirements that are conditions for the waiver to be effective. As was discussed above, most requirements in a waiver decision have to be interpreted as conditions that have to be met if a waiver is to have a justificatory effect.[386]

In *EC – Bananas III* the violation complaints of Ecuador and the US against the EC's allocation of tariff quota shares for bananas were successful because the Appellate Body found that the allocation violated Art. XIII GATT and was not covered by the Lomé Waiver which only suspended Art. I GATT.[387] The panel in this dispute had held that the Lomé Waiver had to be interpreted so as to also suspend Art. XIII GATT for preferential treatment required by the Lomé Convention.[388] The Appellate Body, however, reversed this finding and held that the clear and unambiguous wording of the waiver did not allow for such an interpretation.[389]

To date, no case has been decided in which the dispute settlement organs have found that a measure was not justified under a waiver because the beneficiary failed to meet its terms and conditions.[390]

2.2 Violation complaints based on the alleged violation of the terms of a waiver decision

A waiver decision may include binding terms that are not conditions to the exception created by the waiver, but that create new obligations.[391] Such obligations arguably were established by the TRIPS Waiver decision which

---

385 The respondent carries the burden of proof for the justification of the measure by a waiver decision, see Appellate Body Report, *US – Wool Shirts and Blouses*, WT/DS33/AB/R, adopted 23 May 1997, 12 *et seq.*

386 See *supra* section D.III.2.5.

387 The Fourth ACP–EEC Convention of Lomé, 19 December 1994, L/7604 (19 December 1994).

388 Panel Report, *EC – Bananas III (ECU)*, WT/DS27/R/ECU, paras. 7.106 *et seq.*

389 Appellate Body Report, *EC – Bananas III*, WT/DS27/AB/R, adopted 25 September 1997, paras. 183 *et seq.*

390 The *Sugar* Panel examined the question whether the US had met its reporting requirements, but found that it had: Panel Report, *US – Sugar Waiver*, BISD 37S/228, adopted 7 November 1990, para. 5.13.

391 For this distinction see Jackson, *World Trade and the Law of GATT*, 139.

obliges developed country members to provide upon request technical and financial cooperation to developing countries[392] and obliges all WTO members to take certain measures to prevent the commercial abuse of compulsory licences.[393] With respect to such obligations, the question arises whether their breach may be the subject of a violation complaint based on the violation of the waiver decision. According to Art. 1:1 DSU the 'rules and procedures of this Understanding shall apply to disputes brought pursuant to the consultation and dispute settlement provisions' of the covered agreements. On the basis of this provision one might argue that a waiver decision could only form the basis for a violation complaint if it included a dispute settlement provision.[394] If, however, a waiver decision was interpreted to form part of the agreement whose obligations it suspends, a special dispute settlement provision in the waiver decision would not be required. Following such an interpretation, a complaint that alleges, for example, that benefits are impaired due to a violation of obligations set out in the TRIPS Waiver decision could be based on the dispute settlement provisions in Art. 64:1 TRIPS Agreement and Art. XXIII:1(a) GATT.

3 Non-violation complaints: liability for measures legalized by waiver decisions

In this section it will be argued that while a general cause of action for lawful behaviour is no longer justified in a rules-based legal order such as the WTO, the non-violation complaint may indeed be of specific significance with respect to waiver decisions. This is the case if the non-violation procedure in relation to waivers is interpreted to provide for a judicial cause of action to hold the beneficiary of a waiver liable for damage caused by the measure justified under the waiver. The availability of such a remedy means that waiver decisions can be adopted to increase individual members' regulatory autonomy without externalizing the economic costs caused by the exercise of such freedom.

3.1 Non-violation complaints under the GATT 1947 and in the WTO

Art. XXIII:1 lit. b GATT provides a non-violation cause of action. A non-violation complaint is successful if the dispute settlement organs find that 'any benefit accruing to [the claimant] directly or indirectly under

---

392 WT/L/540 (2 September 2003), para. 4 cl. 2.   393 *Ibid.*, para. 5 cl. 1.
394 Harrison, 'Legal and Political Oversight of WTO Waivers', 411, 419 *et seq.*

this Agreement is being nullified or impaired...as a result of...the application by [the respondent] of any measure, whether or not it conflicts with the provisions of this Agreement'.

Non-violation complaints are not only foreseen with respect to an impairment of benefits accruing under the GATT. Most of the other WTO Agreements incorporate Art. XXIII GATT either with or without modifications.[395] An exception with respect to non-violation complaints is the TRIPS Agreement. Non-violation complaints are, to date, not admissible for the alleged impairment or nullification of benefits under the TRIPS Agreement.[396]

The non-violation complaint is a cause of action for nullification or impairment of benefits '*accruing... under this Agreement*'. In a rules-based system it is not immediately clear how lawful behaviour may impair benefits that accrue under the law. Put differently: it is not immediately clear which benefits will be protected that go beyond the benefits attributable to compliance.[397] The historic origin of non-violation complaints lies in a procedure provided for in bilateral trade agreements concluded by the United States in the 1930s and 1940s. These agreements included provisions according to which one party could demand consultations if the other party's actions adversely affected the balance of benefits under the agreement. In case such consultations proved unsatisfactory the treaty could be terminated.[398]

In the GATT this procedure was transformed into a legal cause of action to determine liability for an impairment of benefits. The main function attributed to non-violation complaints was to protect the competitive opportunities legitimately or reasonably expected from a tariff concession. It was held that such competitive opportunities could be

---

395 Böckenförde, 'Article 26 DSU', 572, 578, paras. 9 *et seq.*
396 Art. 64:2 TRIPS Agreement excluded the admissibility of non-violation and situation complaints under Art. XXIII:1 (b) and (c) GATT for a period of five years. During this time period the TRIPS Council was to examine the scope and modalities for such complaints and submit its recommendations to the Ministerial Conference for approval (Art. 64:3 TRIPS Agreement). To date no consensus could be reached, but it was agreed that no non-violation or situation complaint should be initiated until an agreement is found: see Ministerial Conference, Hong Kong Ministerial Declaration, adopted 18 December 2005, WT/MIN(05)/DEC (22 December 2005), para. 45.
397 Pierre Pescatore called the institution of the non-violation complaint a 'legal fantasy' which should be deleted, a matter to 'be left to the speculations of professors fond of legal paradoxes': Pescatore, 'GATT Dispute Settlement Mechanism', 27, 41.
398 On the origins of the non-violation complaint, see Hudec, *GATT Legal System and World Trade Diplomacy*, 23 *et seq.*

frustrated not only by measures prohibited by the GATT, but also through measures consistent with the GATT, in particular production subsidies. Art. XXIII:1(b) GATT was interpreted to afford redress if legitimate expectations with respect to the competitive opportunities to be derived from tariff concessions were frustrated by measures which could not reasonably be foreseen at the time the tariff concession was negotiated.[399] Unlike the historic provisions in bilateral trade agreements the non-violation complaint is not directly linked to a renegotiation of concessions and the possibility to withdraw from the treaty.[400]

On the basis of the GATT case law on non-violation complaints it is today commonly held that the non-violation cause of action protects competitive opportunities derived from a market access commitment (be it a tariff commitment or a liberalization commitment under the GATS) that can reasonably be expected. These benefits are protected against measures that could not be reasonably foreseen when the commitment was negotiated.[401] Most authors that do not want to do away with

399 See Panel Report, *The Australian Subsidy of Ammonium Sulphate*, adopted 3 April 1955, BISD II, 188. In all four cases in which the CONTRACTING PARTIES found that the legal measures in question impaired benefits accruing under the GATT, these were benefits accruing from tariff concessions. A further Panel Report which held that tariff preferences accorded by the EEC to certain imports of citrus fruit impaired benefits accruing under Article I was never adopted, *EEC – Tariff Treatment on Imports of Citrus Products from Certain Countries in the Mediterranean Region*, L/5778 (20 February 1985). These and other reports on non-violation complaints are discussed in Petersmann, 'Violation-Complaints and Non-Violation Complaints in Public International Trade Law', 175. The same author prepared the survey of all thirteen GATT cases in which Article XXIII:1(b) or (c) GATT was invoked which is included in: GATT Secretariat, Note on Non-Violation Complaints Under GATT Article XXIII:2, MTN.GNG/NG13/W/31 (14 July 1898), 6–21.

400 Upon a finding that a non-violation complaint is justified the respondent shall make a mutually satisfactory adjustment. For dispute settlement in the WTO this is stated in Art. 26:1 (b) DSU. Such an adjustment may be effected by a renegotiation of tariff concessions according to the procedures of Art. XXVIII GATT. If the respondent refuses to make a mutually satisfactory adjustment the claimant may request an authorization to suspend concessions or other obligations (Art. 22 DSU). On the different possible reactions by the respondent to a successful non-violation complaint, see Roessler, 'Concept of Nullification and Impairment', 123, 131.

401 On the requirements for a successful non-violation complaint in the WTO, see Böckenförde, 'Article 26 DSU', 572, 580, paras. 14–27. The fact that non-violation complaints are seen to protect benefits relating to market access have raised doubts about the applicability of non-violation complaints with respect to obligations under the TRIPS Agreement. It is argued that the TRIPS Agreement, while it protects intellectual property rights does not – beyond such protection – aim at the protection of the commercial exploitation of such rights: Roessler and Gappah, 'Re-Appraisal of Non-Violation Complaints', 1371, 1384.

non-violation complaints entirely, more or less agree on these requirements. They have been incorporated into the GATS which provides for
non-violation complaints with respect to benefits that a member 'could
reasonably have expected to accrue to it under a specific commitment'
(Art. XXIII:2 GATS). Where opinions differ is with respect to the place
that non-violation complaints take in the larger framework of public
international law. While some see such action as a special form of liability
for lawful action which disturbs reciprocity of benefits others see it as
based on the legal principle of good faith and the general prohibition of
abus de droit.[402]

In my view, a non-violation cause of action is no longer justified under
WTO law with respect to measures that are not inconsistent with the
legal rules. The legal rules establish the limitations to members' policy
choices to which members subscribe when they become a member of
the WTO. They create the legal order which constitutes the conditions
for domestic trade regulation. While members have to comply with these
rules in good faith, it is not the objective of the law to afford any additional
protection of economic positions beyond those resulting from good faith
compliance.[403] The law does not provide a guarantee that market access is
not impeded by autonomous policy choices which are not prohibited by
legal obligations. Where members hold that the balance of concessions has
tipped in favour of another member they may engage in renegotiations
of commitments.[404]

3.2 Non-violation complaints with respect to measures justified by a waiver

The situation is different, however, when individual members are allowed
to deviate from the general obligations on the basis of a waiver. Depending

---

402 For the former view, Petersmann, 'Violation-Complaints and Non-Violation Com-
plaints in Public International Trade Law', 175 *et seq.*; Bogdandy, 'Non-Violation
Procedure of Article XXIII:2 GATT', 95, 110, 111; Böckenförde, 'Der Non-Violation
Complaint im System der WTO', 43. For the latter view see Cottier and Nadakavukaren
Schefer, 'Non-Violation Complaints in WTO/GATT Dispute Settlement', 143, 180;
Tietje, *Normative Grundstrukturen der Behandlung nichttarifärer Handelshemmnisse,*
360–2; Trebilcock and Howse, *Regulation of International Trade*, 513–14.
403 For similar views see Roessler and Gappah, 'Re-Appraisal of Non-Violation Complaints', 1371–87; Cottier and Nadakavukaren Schefer, 'Non-Violation Complaints in
WTO/GATT Dispute Settlement', 143.
404 A renegotiation of tariff concessions is possible under Art. XXVIII GATT, a renegotiation
of market access in the area of services, under Art. XXI GATS.

on its wording, a waiver decision may be interpreted as a dispensation from the obligation to comply, but not as a dispensation from liability for the damage caused by non-compliance. The International Law Commission's Articles on State Responsibility clarify that consent to the violation of a legal obligation, while precluding wrongfulness, need not preclude any rights to redress concerning the effects of such a measure. Article 27(b) of these Articles states that the invocation of circumstances precluding wrongfulness 'is without prejudice to the question of compensation for any material loss caused by the act in question'.[405]

A non-violation cause of action with respect to measures justified by a waiver decision was envisaged by the CONTRACTING PARTIES under the GATT 1947 when they included in waiver decisions references to Art. XXIII GATT, the dispute settlement provision under the GATT. With respect to some waiver decisions, as for example the Agricultural Waiver, the CONTRACTING PARTIES anticipated that measures justified by the waiver would result in a nullification or impairment of benefits. Consequently, they included references to Art. XXIII GATT in the waiver decision.[406] They did so not only to clarify that members could bring a complaint if a measure violated the terms and conditions of a waiver, but also for nullification and impairment resulting from measures consistent with the waiver decision.[407]

In the WTO the Understanding makes clear for all waivers of obligations under the GATT, whether they include a reference to Article XXIII GATT or not, that members may bring a non-violation complaint with respect to measures consistent with a waiver decision. Paragraph 3 (b) states:

405 International Law Commission, Articles on Responsibility of States for Internationally Wrongful Acts, with commentaries, *Yearbook of the International Law Commission, 2001*, Vol. II, Part Two.

406 Working Party Report, United States Waiver, L/339 (3 March 1955), para. 9. CONTRACTING PARTIES, Waiver Granted to the United States in Connection With Import Restrictions Imposed Under Section 22 of the United States Agricultural Adjustment Act (of 1933), as Amended, Decision of 5 March 1955, BISD 3S (1955), 32, 35.

407 Panel Report, *US – Sugar Waiver*, BISD 37S/228, adopted 7 November 1990, para. 5.20. See also GATT Secretariat, Note on Non-Violation Complaints Under GATT Article XXIII:2, MTN.GNG/NG13/W/31 (14 July 1898), 24, where it is presumed that references to Art. XXIII GATT in waiver decisions are references to Article XXIII:1(b) or (c). Likewise Jackson interprets such references as a recognition that waivers may change the balance of benefits under the agreements: Jackson, Davey and Sykes, *Legal Problems of International Economic Relations*, 416.

> Any Member considering that a benefit accruing to it under GATT 1994 is being nullified or impaired as a result of: . . .
>
> (b) the application of a measure consistent with the terms and conditions of the waiver
>
> may invoke the provisions of Article XXIII of GATT 1994 as elaborated and applied by the Dispute Settlement Understanding.

As to waivers of other than GATT obligations, these have to be interpreted to determine whether they allow for non-violation complaints or not. The TRIPS Waiver, for example, explicitly excludes the admissibility of non-violation complaints.[408] At the end of this section I shall return to the question of admissibility. Before doing so, I shall set out the requirements of a successful non-violation complaint with respect to a measure consistent with a waiver decision.

So far, neither WTO panels nor the Appellate Body have had to examine the merits of a non-violation complaint with respect to a measure justified by a waiver. In the GATT *Sugar* dispute the EEC, inter alia, had made a non-violation claim. The panel in this case held that the EEC had not discharged its burden to demonstrate nullification and impairment of benefits.[409] Apart from addressing burden of proof the panel did not clarify the requirements for a successful non-violation complaint in the waiver constellation.

(a) Requirements for a successful non-violation complaint

Sometimes it is argued that the requirements for a non-violation complaint in the waiver constellation are the same as those established by the case law for non-violation complaints with respect to measures that are in conformity with the legal obligations.[410] Consequently, it is argued that a non-violation complaint with respect to measures justified by a waiver can only be successful if the claimant shows that its reasonable expectations were violated by the adoption of a waiver decision. However, in the waiver constellation the rationale for a requirement of reasonable expectations does not exist. The requirement of reasonable expectations, which the case law established with respect to non-violation complaints,

---

408 WT/L/540 (2 September 2003), para. 10.
409 Panel Report, *US – Sugar Waiver*, BISD 37S/228, adopted 7 November 1990, para. 5.22.
410 This was the opinion of the United States in the *Sugar* case, Panel Report, *US – Sugar Waiver*, BISD 37S/228, adopted 7 November 1990, para. 3.37; see also the statement by the EC in the *Bananas* dispute, Panel Report, *EC – Bananas III*, WT/DS27/R/ECU, 44, para. IV.68 and Harrison, 'Legal and Political Oversight of WTO Waivers', 411, 417.

serves the purpose of determining which benefits – that go beyond the benefits attributable to compliance – shall be protected. Related to tariff concessions the reasonable expectations requirement on the one hand extends the scope of legally protected benefits from the promise not to raise tariffs beyond the bound rate (which is protected by Art. II GATT and whose impairment can thus be alleged in a violation complaint) to the protection of certain competitive opportunities that are expected to result from the concession. On the other hand it limits the legally relevant benefits to those competitive opportunities which could be *reasonably* expected by the complainant.

By contrast, such criteria are not needed to determine the relevant nullification and impairment if the measure is one which is generally prohibited by WTO law, but where unlawfulness is precluded by a waiver. The benefits whose impairment may be alleged are those associated with compliance with the obligation which prohibits the measure. When GATT contracting parties anticipated that US quantitative restrictions that were justified by the Agricultural Waiver might impair benefits, they were talking about benefits protected by Art. XI GATT, namely that imports to the US market would not be restricted by quotas. It is unnecessary to ask whether the benefit that no quotas would be imposed could reasonably be expected since this benefit directly follows from the obligation not to impose quotas. Moreover, since the benefits whose impairment may be alleged are defined by the waived obligation there is no need to restrict the range of benefits to benefits derived from a market access commitment.[411]

To summarize the preceding: provided that a non-violation complaint is admissible, it is justified if a measure which would be unlawful *but for* a waiver decision nullifies or impairs benefits which are protected by the suspended obligation. Two questions still need to be answered: firstly, whether the claimant needs to demonstrate that a measure would be in violation of WTO law without the waiver and, secondly, whether the claimant needs to prove nullification and impairment of benefits.

(b) **Inconsistency of the measure with treaty law**   With respect to the first question it might be argued that the mere existence of a waiver decision should give rise to the presumption that measures falling within the scope of a waiver decision without the waiver would be unlawful. This

---

411   Panel Report, *US – Sugar Waiver*, BISD 37S/228, adopted 7 November 1990, para. 5.21; Bogdandy, 'Non-Violation Procedure of Article XXIII:2, GATT', 95, 107–8.

question was dealt with earlier in this chapter.[412] Here it shall suffice to restate that due to the practice that waivers are often granted for measures whose legality is disputed, inconsistency may not be presumed.[413] Thus, it still needs to be proven, the burden of proof falling, as in a violation proceeding, on the claimant. The matter is different when the waiver decision explicitly states that the measure in question would be illegal without the waiver. Such a statement can be taken as an authoritative interpretation by the General Council which binds the dispute settlement organs.

(c) Nullification or impairment   With respect to the second question, whether the claimant has to prove a nullification or impairment of benefits, the presumption of nullification or impairment in Art. 3:8 DSU immediately comes to mind. Art. 3:8 DSU states:

> In cases where there is an infringement of the obligations assumed under a covered agreement, the action is considered *prima facie* to constitute a case of nullification or impairment.

This means that there is normally a presumption that a breach of the rules has an adverse impact on other Members parties to that covered agreement, and in such cases, it shall be up to the Member against whom the complaint has been brought to rebut the charge. It might be argued that, once it is established that a measure in absence of the waiver would violate a legal provision, nullification or impairment is to be presumed in accordance with this provision.[414]

An argument against the presumption can be based on the wording of Art. 26:1(a) DSU. Art. 26:1(a) DSU provides that if a non-violation complaint concerns a measure that does *not conflict* with the provisions of WTO law, the complaining party shall present a 'detailed justification' in support of the complaint. Arguably a measure justified by a waiver does not conflict within the meaning of Art. 26:1(a) DSU.[415]

---

412 See *supra* B.III.2.   413 *Ibid.*

414 A similar argument was made by Australia in the *Sugar* case. Australia was of the view that the reference in the waiver to Art. XXIII GATT was a recognition that the waiver disturbed the balance of benefits and that complainants need not prove nullification and impairment, Panel Report, *US – Sugar Waiver*, BISD 37S/228, adopted 7 November 1990, para. 4.19.

415 In the *Sugar* case the panel merely stated that the Understanding on Dispute Settlement placed the burden of proof on the claimant in a non-violation procedure. It did not address the fact that the rule on burden of proof merely applies to measures 'not in conflict' with the legal provisions while the non-violation complaint may be brought for any measure 'whether or not it conflicts' with the legal provisions, Panel Report, *US – Sugar Waiver*, BISD 37S/228, adopted 7 November 1990, para. 5.21.

Similarly one can point to the wording of Art. 3:8 DSU, which requires an *infringement* of obligations to trigger the presumption, and argue that a measure cannot infringe an obligation if that obligation was waived with respect to this measure. These arguments based on the wording are weak and a counter-argument could be presented with equal force: even though a waiver has the consequence that the application of the 'waived' legal provision to the measure described in the waiver decision is suspended, it leaves the provisions themselves untouched. Thus, it may be held that the measure is still in conflict with the provision even if it is not illegal since the provision is no longer a standard against which to judge the legality of the measure. A similar argument was made by the EEC in the *Sugar* dispute. The EEC argued that a waiver merely suspended the obligation to bring a certain measure into conformity with the waived obligation, but did not change the fact that the measure was inconsistent with this obligation.[416] Thus, the textual arguments against applying the presumption in Art. 3.8 DSU and in support of an obligation of the claimant to demonstrate nullification or impairment are not cogent.

A better argument can be made on the basis of the rationale for a non-violation cause of action with respect to measures falling within the scope of a waiver as compared with the rationale for violation complaints. Responsibility for a *breach* of the law under WTO dispute settlement provisions is triggered not only by the real trade effects of the unlawful measure in question, but by the mere fact of unlawfulness. By contrast a cause of action with respect to measures justified by a waiver shall ensure liability merely for the negative trade effects against which the law protects individual members.

The presumption of nullification and impairment in Art. 3:8 DSU ensures that responsibility may be invoked for any breach of WTO law.[417] The presumption is justified on the basis that the legal obligations define the conditions of competition among WTO members and that these conditions will be disturbed in case of a violation of legal norms. Petersmann goes so far as to state that 'the violation of a substantive obligation and "nullification or impairment" therefore tend to be synonymous'.[418]

---

416 Panel Report, *US – Sugar Waiver*, BISD 37S/228, adopted 7 November 1990, para. 3.28.
417 With respect to standing the Appellate Body has been very lenient. It stated that no legal interest was required to bring a claim: Appellate Body Report, *EC – Bananas III*, WT/DS27/AB/R, adopted 25 September 1997, para. 133.
418 Petersmann, 'Violation-Complaints and Non-Violation Complaints in Public International Trade Law', 175, 178.

Accordingly, each violation of a substantive norm may give rise to a successful violation complaint with the consequence that the respondent is obliged to bring the measure into conformity with the law. The presumption can be seen as a way to ensure that individual members may enforce the law by bringing violation complaints even if their individual trade interests are not directly affected. This wide interpretation of nullification and impairment allows individual legal actions to more effectively protect *the market* as an institution constituted through the law than by allowing legal actions to succeed only in case of real effects on trade flows.[419] At the same time the presumption approximates WTO law to the general international law on state responsibility where responsibility is triggered by the breach of an obligation and where mere *legal* damage is recognized as giving rise to a right to reparation.[420]

This exposition of the rationale for the presumption of nullification and impairment in violation proceedings makes clear that a different approach to nullification and impairment has to be adopted with respect to non-violation complaints in the waiver constellation. If the organization waives an obligation it waives at the same time the corresponding right to demand compliance. Consequently, inconsistency with the law in itself no longer constitutes impairment. Impairment only exists if the inconsistent measure causes material damage, i.e. if it has economic, trade-distorting effects.[421] Since not every inconsistent measure causes such factual impairment, impairment needs to be demonstrated according to Art. 26:1 DSU for a non-violation complaint to be successful. If, for example, a developing country member brings a non-violation complaint with respect to special trade preferences justified by a waiver suspending Art. I:1 GATT, this member needs to demonstrate that the preferences have resulted in actual trade diversion to its own detriment. The trade that is diverted away from the claimant is the impairment for which the non-violation complaint affords redress.[422] When

---

419 Cf. Stoll, 'Article 3 DSU', 281, 310, para. 73.

420 Articles 1, 2, 31, International Law Commission, Articles on Responsibility of States for Internationally Wrongful Acts, with commentaries, *Yearbook of the International Law Commission, 2001*, Vol. II, Part Two.

421 Cf. Bogdandy, 'Non-Violation Procedure of Article XXIII:2, GATT', 95, 104; for a different view see Tietje, *Normative Grundstrukturen der Behandlung nichttarifärer Handelshemmnisse*, 358, 359.

422 This conceptualization of impairment corresponds to how impairment is determined in proceedings concerning the authorization of a suspension of concessions or other obligations (Art. 22:6 DSU). In an Art. 22:6 DSU proceeding the extent of nullification and impairment is quantified by comparing the actual situation with the counterfactual

The dispute settlement organs have remained unimpressed by these differences. The scarce case law that exists has consistently held that waivers should be viewed as exceptions, with the consequence that they should be interpreted narrowly, or at least 'with care'. Waivers may, however, also take the form of general rule-making instruments that readjust the balance of interests embodied in the legal norms in response to demands by the membership. As such they should not be interpreted narrowly, but rather an openly policy-oriented approach to interpretation should be adopted.

Another significant differentiation, as of yet not reflected in practice, regards non-violation complaints. I propose here that non-violation complaints have a particular potential for waivers as individual exceptions allowing the pursuit of policy choices in deviation from the legal rules. The non-violation procedure allows the institution to waive the duty to comply while maintaining a procedure in which actual trade damage caused by the legalized measure may be assessed and some form of compensation awarded.

Finally, this chapter made the rather counterintuitive observation that the waiver process in the WTO appears rather less legalized and more bilateralized than waiver processes under the GATT. The working party procedure under the GATT ensured that some multilateral review of waiver requests took place, while in the WTO members negotiate their concerns with respect to waiver requests mainly bilaterally or in informal meetings. The working party procedure under the GATT furthermore ensured transparency in that the working party reports documented in detail the reasons for the approval of waiver requests as well as the objections of individual contracting parties. Finally, the political reviews of the operations of waiver decisions under the GATT were more thoroughly conducted. While in the WTO specialized committees frequently supervise progress in compliance by developing country members, the annual reviews of waivers granted to developed country members for special preferences are a mere formality.

I shall come back to the waiver process in Chapter 7, with the suggestion, inter alia, that the working party procedure should be reinstituted. Before I return to the waiver process, however, Chapter 6 will take a step back and evaluate the waiver power in the larger context of international public law and its potential to address the tensions between stability and flexibility which were laid out in Chapter 2.

PART III

The potential of waivers to address the stability/flexibility challenge in international law

The previous part focused on the waiver power of the GATT 1947 and the WTO Agreement, the waiver practice and the rules governing the exercise of the waiver power. Chapter 4 revealed that the political organs exercised the waiver power to address a number of the flexibility challenges identified in Part I. Waiver decisions were adopted to take account of capacity problems to implement legal norms, to accommodate policy preferences, to coordinate WTO law with the law of other international regimes and to adapt legal rules to claims of inadequacy and injustice by the membership. Chapter 6 now attempts to situate the waiver power within the broader framework of legal mechanisms that flexibilize international treaty regimes in order to promote acceptability and effectiveness, as well as legitimacy. I shall compare the waiver power to these mechanisms in order to identify its specific potential. Since the extent and realization of this potential in great part depends on the decision-making process, I shall come back to this process – which was already the subject of the last chapter – in Chapter 7.

To date, apart from the WTO, not many international institutions have the power to waive obligations of members in their external capacity.[1] Nonetheless, the waiver power appears to have certain benefits, if compared to other flexibility devices, which make it attractive beyond the WTO. The findings of the following analysis will therefore not be confined to the specificities of WTO law.

---

1 For the distinction between obligations of members in their internal capacity and obligations in their external capacity, see Chapter 5 A.II.2. While the competence to waive internal obligations counts as an implied power of organizations, suspensions of external obligations by organs of the organization require a specific competence. Such waiver competences are found, for example, in Art. VIII (2), (3) Articles of Agreement of the International Monetary Fund and Art. 47 of the 2001 International Cocoa Agreement. While the IMF's waiver power relates to specific obligations, the waiver power of the International Cocoa Council is similarly as broad as the WTO's waiver power and extends to each obligation of the International Cocoa Agreement, except for the obligation to pay membership contributions.

6

The potential of the waiver as a flexibility device

International law faces the following dilemma. To effectively pursue its objectives, international law requires autonomy from the domestic political processes of individual states. This autonomy is formally achieved by basing the validity of international treaty law on initial state consent and the principle *pacta sunt servanda*.[1] Due to the limited validity criteria of international law,[2] validity and legitimacy do not necessarily coincide in international law. While state consent and ratification are the main requirements to create binding treaty law, they are not sufficient to safeguard its legitimacy. The more international law impacts domestic legislatures, administrations and individuals, the more it requires justification, which goes beyond state consent and ratification, to be considered legitimate. Due to the diversity and pluralism of global society, justification based on shared values is no option. While there may be agreement on broadly formulated principles and values, their application and realization in concrete instances is thoroughly disputed. This leads to the quest for a democratic justification of international law.[3]

---

1 On the attempts by international legal scholarship to explain the basis of the validity of international norms independent from the consent of states, see Bernstorff, *Der Glaube an das universale Recht*, 135 *et seq.*
2 Further validity requirements can be found in the Vienna Convention on the Law of Treaties. These include the requirement that a state's consent to a treaty is not produced by coercion (Art. 51, 52 VCLT) or the requirement that a treaty does not conflict with *jus cogens* (Art. 53 VCLT).
3 Claims for the democratization of international governance take different forms. While some advocate cosmopolitan democracy at the global level, others argue for the realization of certain democratic principles, such as participation, accountability and transparency. For the former suggestion, see Held, *Democracy and the Global Order*; Held, 'Democracy and Globalization', 11; for the latter, see Keohane, 'Contingent Legitimacy of Multilateralism', 56 (coming to the conclusion that so long as global democracy is not feasible international regimes need to be more consistent with certain aspects of democracy such as transparency and accountability); see also Wheatley, *Democratic Legitimacy of International Law*.

Democratic justification today may, however, only be fully realizable at the level of the national (maybe regional) polity.[4] Two requirements result from this finding. Firstly, in light of its legitimacy deficit international law needs to be devised to take account of domestic values and regulatory preferences, as well as restraints that concern individual states' capacity to comply with international law. Secondly, international law's legitimacy deficit should be addressed by making international institutions more accountable, transparent and representative, and thus possibly more democratic.[5]

The waiver may contribute to both quests. As individual exception it permits individual members to deviate from the legal rules either to take account of these members' restrictions in administrative capacity or to allow them to pursue their political choices. As general exception and rule-making instrument it may address legitimacy concerns by limiting one institution's jurisdiction in favour of another's (potentially more legitimate) jurisdiction as well as by adapting legal norms to claims of inadequacy and injustice.[6] At the same time the waiver power takes account of the continuing basic premise of international law's validity, namely the principle of *pacta sunt servanda*.

The following parts will first compare waivers as individual exceptions to other concepts that imbue international treaty regimes with some flexibility to accommodate individual members' needs and preferences, namely reservations, variable geometry, general rules and exceptions and, finally, limitations on law enforcement. Thereafter, the waiver as general exception and rule-making instrument will be compared in particular to treaty amendment and authoritative interpretation. This comparison will concentrate on the waiver's function to coordinate potentially conflicting legal regimes and to readjust the balance of interests represented by legal rules.

---

4 Weiler, 'Geology of International Law', 547, 556. On the democratization of the European Union, see Eriksen, *Unfinished Democratization of Europe*.
5 To introduce such principles into international governance is one of the aims of the 'global administrative law project', Kingsbury, Krisch and Stewart, 'Emergence of Global Administrative Law', 68 *Law & Contemporary Problems* (2005), 1; Krisch, 'Pluralism of Global Administrative Law', 247; see the comments by Marks, 'Naming Global Administrative Law', 995, and Harlow, 'Global Administrative Law', 187.
6 The potential of the waiver process to realize the principles of transparency, representativeness and accountability will be addressed in Chapter 7. To date it evidences great deficiencies in this respect.

A. THE ACCOMMODATION OF INDIVIDUAL NEEDS AND PREFERENCES IN INTERNATIONAL LEGAL REGIMES

Traditionally, reservations to international treaties used to be the instrument of choice to allow states to participate in treaty regimes and at the same time to exclude certain domestic measures and practices from the jurisdiction of such treaties. Reservations, however, cannot take account of changes in preferences and needs over time. Moreover, they may be incompatible with the aims and structure of international legal regimes. Apart from reservations two further general mechanisms take account of domestic needs and preferences at the level of primary obligations. On the one hand, international treaty regimes often evidence what may be called variable geometry, i.e. they allow for varying degrees of commitment by individual contracting parties. On the other hand, treaties contain general provisions which take account of the diversity of members in their regulatory objectives, cultures and administrative capacity. At the level of law enforcement, variations of the subsidiarity principle, such as the principle of exhaustion of local remedies or the doctrine of margin of appreciation, may be interpreted to take account of parties' varying preferences and as protection of their autonomy. Likewise at the level of law enforcement, compliance management instead of strict enforcement allows differentiations according to individual parties' capacities to comply.

In light of the various flexibility devices the question may be posed whether there is a need for additional flexibility. I shall argue that there is. This need arises in particular due to uncertainty as to the future effects and scope of legal rules. It might turn out that with respect to a material aim envisaged by the parties, the application of the negotiated norms in individual cases has a detrimental effect. While the rules may generally be considered adequate, they may in certain instances be over-inclusive in that they cover cases which were not intended to be covered by the legal rule. Finally, there may be such a strong preference within a member against compliance that it may be desirable to grant an individual exception even though there is no agreement as to the general desirability of such an exception.

I Reservations

When thinking about functional equivalents to the waiver as a means to accommodate individual members' needs or preferences reservations to treaties immediately come to mind. A reservation is defined by Art. 2:1 (d) Vienna Convention on the Law of Treaties as

> a unilateral statement, however phrased or named, made by a State, when signing, ratifying, accepting, approving or acceding to a treaty, whereby it purports to exclude or to modify the legal effect of certain provisions of the treaty in their application to that State.

A reservation thus has a very similar effect to a waiver decision in that it excludes or modifies the application of certain provisions of treaty law.

While reservations do so permanently, waivers may have to be – as in the WTO – of limited duration. There are important further differences. For this discussion most relevant are the differences that relate to the function as well as the potential effects of reservations. Firstly, reservations are declared when a state becomes a party to a treaty. Thus reservations can restrict the application of a treaty with respect to existing measures, but they cannot take account of preferences for non-compliance which arise at a future date.[7] Consequently, it is the main function of reservations to enhance the acceptability of treaties at the time a state becomes a party and not necessarily to maintain acceptability over time as policies or cultural preferences may change.[8] Secondly, while waivers require the approval of an organ of the organization and thus are subject to multilateral control, the general rules on reservations make the effect of reservations dependent on acceptance by the other contracting parties individually.[9] As a consequence of this rule, reservations may endanger the realization of a treaty's objectives more than waiver decisions. These points will be elaborated below with reference to the law on reservations. Subsequently, I shall present the law and practice of the GATT 1947 and the WTO with respect to reservations.

1 Reservations to international treaties

If a treaty does not prohibit reservations explicitly or implicitly, as a general rule states may make reservations which are not incompatible

---

7 Reservations which attempt to accommodate future measures which are not yet identifiable, e.g. by stating that treaty provisions shall not apply to conflicting domestic laws, are inadmissible since their content and consequently their compatibility with the treaty's object and purpose cannot be ascertained: see Verdross and Simma, *Universelles Völkerrecht: Theorie und Praxis*, 471.

8 Cf. Giegerich, 'Reservations to Multilateral Treaties', paras. 5 *et seq.*

9 However, if reservations are made to the constituent instrument of an organization, Art. 20:3 VCLT also requires acceptance of the competent organ of that organization.

with the object and purpose of the treaty (Art. 19 VCLT).[10] Unless a special rule applies,[11] a reserving state becomes a party to the treaty upon acceptance of the reservation by other contracting parties (Art. 20:4 (a) VCLT). Acceptance has the effect that the reserving party is only bound by the treaty as modified by the reservation (Art. 21:1 (a) VCLT) and that the accepting parties vis-à-vis the reserving party are also only bound to a reciprocally limited extent (Art. 21:1 (b) VCLT). The reserving state does not become a party in relation to those parties who object to the reservation and in addition express their intention that the treaty shall not enter into force between themselves and the reserving state (Art. 21:3 VCLT).[12] Prior to the codification of this rule in the Vienna Convention on the Law of Treaties, the general rule had been that a reservation had to be accepted unanimously for the reserving state to become a party to the treaty to the extent specified in its reservation.[13]

The rules on reservations demonstrate that with respect to treaties that promote or protect transnational societal interests, reservations are not the most suitable means to accommodate individual states' needs and preferences. Apart from the static nature of reservations which can only take account of existing preferences, reservations often contradict the very principles which these treaties aim to protect.[14] These treaties often constitute a departure from the classic concept of sovereignty by regulating matters and protecting societal concerns which were previously

---

10 On the extent to which the rules on reservations in the Vienna Convention on the Law of Treaties reflect customary international law, see Dahm *et al.*, *Völkerrecht*, vol. I/3, 564 *et seq.*

11 Art. 20 paragraphs 2 and 3 contain special rules for reservations to certain plurilateral treaties and constituent instruments of international organizations. While the former requires the consent of all parties (Art. 20:2 VCLT), the latter requires acceptance of the competent organ of the organization (Art. 20:3 VCLT) for a state to become a party to the treaty to the extent specified by its reservation.

12 The VCLT in this respect codifies the ICJ's pronouncements on the admissibility and effect on reservations in its Advisory Opinion on *Reservations to the Convention on the Prevention and Punishment of the Crime of Genocide*, ICJ Reports 1951, 13, with the one modification that the objecting state, if it does not wish that the treaty take effect between itself and the reserving state, has to express its intent that the reserving state shall not become a party in relation to it (Art. 21:3 VCLT).

13 The ICJ in its Advisory Opinion on *Reservations to the Genocide Convention* had modified this rule explicitly only with respect to the Genocide Convention. On the various positions in the International Law Commission on the question of the admissibility and effect of reservations during its work on the Vienna Convention, see Klabbers, 'On Human Rights Treaties, Contractual Conceptions and Reservations', 149.

14 See e.g. Schöpp-Schilling, 'Reservations to the Convention on the Elimination of All Forms of Discrimination Against Women', 3.

held to fall within a *domaine réservé* of states. By contrast, reservations may be seen as based on the concept of sovereignty in that they allow each contracting party's government to unilaterally determine the reach of international treaty law. This tension is particularly apparent in human rights law. Human rights treaties aim to protect individuals from the illegitimate exercise of governmental power. Reservations may directly compromise this aim by excluding certain governmental measures from the application of treaty norms. If one perceives the need to protect domestic preferences from the perspective of democratic self-government and not the perspective of sovereignty, reservations per se do not ensure the protection of domestic preferences as an expression of self-government. Such preferences would be better protected by a conceptualization of human rights treaties as facilitating political processes domestically.[15]

The normative objections to reservations may partly be addressed by subjecting reservations to institutional control as to their compatibility with the object and purpose of the treaty. Such institutional control in the field of human rights resulted in some restrictions on the admissibility of reservations. Noteworthy in this respect is the decision of the European Court of Human Rights in *Belilos v Switzerland* in which it held a reservation to be void due to its incompatibility with Art. 64 of the European Convention on Human Rights on the admissibility of general reservations. It further found that the invalidity of the reservation did not affect the validity of Switzerland's ratification and that consequently Switzerland remained bound by the European Convention on Human Rights without reservation.[16] Subsequently, the Human Rights Committee under the International Covenant on Civil and Political Rights endorsed the case law of the European Court of Human Rights in its General Comment 24. This comment states, inter alia, that reservations are only admissible if they respect the fundamental rules of the Covenant and that inadmissible reservations will be severable 'in the sense that the Covenant will be operative for the reserving party without benefit of the reservation'.[17]

---

15 For such an approach to human rights, see Klabbers, 'Glorified Esperanto? Rethinking Human Rights', 63; for domestic constitutional law, see Ely, *Democracy and Distrust: A Theory of Judicial Review*.

16 *Belilos v Switzerland* (ECtHR) Series A No. 132, para. 60; subsequently in *Loizidou v Turkey* the European Court of Human Rights found a reservation by Turkey concerning the jurisdiction of the Commission and the Court to be void and consequently Turkey to be fully bound, *Loizidou v Turkey (Preliminary Objections)* (ECtHR) Series A No. 310, para. 95.

17 CCPR/C/21/Rev. 1/Add. 6, 11 November 1994, 7, para. 18.

While the case law of the European Court of Human Rights and General Comment 24 of the Human Rights Committee have given scholars reason to detect an increased restrictiveness of international law on reservations to human rights treaties,[18] their effect on reservations in general should not be overestimated. General Comment 24 was vehemently criticized by state parties to the Covenant, in particular the United States and the United Kingdom[19] and today most international and regional human rights treaties continue to permit reservations. Instances where reservations, which are often far-reaching, were held to be inadmissible have been very few.[20]

It may be noted, however, that where an organ of the institution is entrusted with determining the admissibility of a reservation, the likelihood increases that such an organ will take into account in its determination a common interest in the effectiveness of the treaty with respect to its objectives. By contrast, individual state parties when faced with the question whether to accept a reservation by another state will focus more on how the reservation will affect their own benefits under the treaty.[21]

Indeed, the effect of reservations on the reciprocal 'bargain' among state parties constitutes another reason why reservations may be undesirable as means to account for domestic preferences. The Vienna Convention's rules on reservations provide for reciprocity in the sense that a reservation not only determines the extent of obligation of the reserving state, but reciprocally also the extent of obligation of other contracting parties towards the reserving state. However, the structure of many treaties that promote transnational societal interests does not permit the maintenance of reciprocity in this manner. The Vienna Convention's rules cannot be applied where treaty norms oblige the parties to adopt certain internal measures, or, as Bruno Simma formulates, 'parallel conduct'.[22] If such conduct is required by a treaty it is impossible for a contracting party to differentiate how it complies with the norms with respect to, on the one hand, a reserving state and, on the other hand, a state that has not registered a reservation.

---

18 Frowein, 'Reservations and the International Ordre Public', 411 *et seq.*   19 *Ibid.*
20 For an extensive treatment of practice and doctrinal approaches to reservations to human rights treaties, see the contributions in Ziemele (ed.), *Reservations to Human Rights Treaties and the Vienna Convention Regime.*
21 Klabbers, 'On Human Rights Treaties, Contractual Conceptions and Reservations', 149, 178 *et seq.*
22 Verdross and Simma, *Universelles Völkerrecht: Theorie und Praxis*, §754.

Reciprocity may, however, be an important factor to induce states to become parties to an international agreement and it is seriously endangered by the acceptance of permanent privileged situations created through reservations.[23] Reciprocity is particularly important when an agreement addresses collective action problems as do trade agreements, many environmental agreements, but also some human rights treaties. To clarify the preceding by way of an example: the International Labour Organization's labour conventions oblige states to adopt certain labour standards. One reason for an international agreement on such standards is to prevent individual states from reducing their standards in order to gain a competitive advantage over other states with higher standards. This aim can only be achieved if all states are bound to apply the conventions in the same way.[24]

Where reservations are perceived to endanger the treaty's capacity to effectively address a collective action problem, states are far more willing (and possibly competent) to restrict the admissibility of reservations than they are to do so for normative reasons such as the protection of an *ordre public* of the international community.[25] Therefore, treaties that address collective action problems are in general more restrictive with respect to reservations than human rights treaties which do so to a lesser degree.[26] The negotiating states in these cases have a desire to maintain the integrity of the 'package deal' and the intention to avoid free-riding by states who – if reservations were permitted – could become parties, but restrict their level of commitment.[27] For example the Vienna Convention on the Protection of the Ozone Layer and its Montreal Protocol, the UN Framework Convention on Climate Change and its Kyoto Protocol and the Convention on Biological Diversity and the Cartagena Protocol on

23 On the relevance of reciprocity in international law, see Simma, *Das Reziprozitätselement im Zustandekommen völkerrechtlicher Verträge*; Keohane, 'Reciprocity in International Relations', 1; Parisi and Ghei, 'Role of Reciprocity in International Law', 93.

24 This point was made by the Director General of the ILO in 1972, see Harvard Research on International Law, Vol. III: Law of Treaties 29 *American Journal of International Law* (1935, supplement), 844.

25 Klabbers, 'On Human Rights Treaties, Contractual Conceptions and Reservations', 149, 178 *et seq.*

26 Exceptions are labour conventions or the envisaged conventions to regulate bioethical questions implicated in many fields of research. States have an interest in international rules in this area since they fear competitive disadvantages if other states have looser legal requirements. On the regulation of bioethical questions through international law, see Vöneky *et al.* (eds.), *Chances for and Limits of International Law and Legal Language in the Area of Bioethics.*

27 Kirgis, 'Reservations to Treaties and United States Practice'.

Biosafety exclude reservations entirely.[28] The United Nations Convention on the Law of the Sea provides in its Article 309 that '[n]o reservation or exception may be made unless expressly permitted'.

2 Reservations under the GATT 1947 and in the WTO

The WTO agreements which may also be perceived as an attempt to address collective action problems through international cooperation are similarly restrictive with respect to reservations. The WTO Agreement provides in Art. XVI:5:

> No reservations may be made in respect of any provision of this Agreement. Reservations in respect of any of the provisions of the Multilateral Trade Agreements may only be made to the extent provided for in those Agreements.[29]

Of the Multilateral Trade Agreements neither the GATT nor the GATS explicitly allows for reservations. Even though the GATS does not generally allow for reservations, before the entry into force of the WTO Agreement members had, however, the option to exempt existing measures from the application of the most-favoured-nation obligation in Art. II:1 GATS.[30] They could do so by specifying the respective measures in a list of most-favoured-nation exemptions including the duration for which the measures were to be maintained. The Annex on Article II Exemptions provides that the exemption terminates on the date provided for in the exemption, that in principle exemptions should not exceed ten years and that '[i]n any event they shall be subject to negotiation in subsequent trade liberalization rounds'.[31] The Annex further provides for reviews of MFN exemptions by the Council for Trade in Services of which the first was to take place no more than five years after the entry into force of the WTO Agreement.[32] To date no solution has been found during negotiations as to the fate of the existing exemptions, whether they may be maintained or whether they will terminate. Any new exemptions are not granted

---

28 Art. 18 Vienna Convention on the Protection of the Ozone Layer; Art. 18 Montreal Protocol; Art. 24 UN Framework Convention on Climate Change; Art. 26 Kyoto Protocol; Art. 37 Convention on Biological Diversity; Art. 38 Cartagena Protocol on Biosafety.

29 Art. XVI:5 WTO Agreement states: 'Reservations in respect of a Plurilateral Trade Agreement shall be governed by the provisions of that Agreement' (cl. 3).

30 Art. II:2 GATS and Annex on Article II Exemptions.

31 Annex on Article II Exemptions, paras. 5, 6.

32 Annex on Article II Exemptions, para. 1.

automatically. Instead, members who wish to obtain an exemption need to apply for a waiver in accordance with Art. IX:3 WTO Agreement.[33]

Some of the other Multilateral Trade Agreements do allow for reservations, with the qualification, however, that no reservation may be made with respect to any of the provisions of the respective agreement without the consent of the other members.[34] This requirement of consent corresponds to the Vienna Convention's rule on reservations to plurilateral treaties according to which 'a reservation requires acceptance by all the parties'.[35] It ensures that the balance of rights and obligations is not unilaterally altered by individual members. Due to the unanimity rule, reservations to WTO agreements, where permitted, are subject to even more stringent requirements than waivers. This explains that to date there exist practically no reservations to the WTO agreements.[36]

By contrast, under the GATT 1947 contracting parties' legislation was to a great extent excluded from the applicability of GATT norms. Legislation of the contracting parties which was in force at the time they became parties to the GATT 1947 was exempted from the application of obligations in Part II of the Agreement (so-called 'grandfather rights'). This exemption was included in the protocols by which the contracting parties applied the GATT provisionally.[37] On 7 March 1955 the CONTRACTING PARTIES adopted a unanimous resolution according to which contracting parties who definitely accepted the GATT in accordance with

---

33 Annex on Article II Exemptions, para. 2. On the MFN exemptions under Art. II:2 GATS, see Wolfrum, 'Article II GATS', 71; Wolfrum, 'Annex on Article II Exemptions', 569; Footer and George, 'The General Agreement on Trade in Services', 799, 829 *et seq.* Footer and George point out that for newly acceding states exemptions may be included in the accession protocol (at 830).

34 Art. 18.2 Antidumping Agreement; Art. 21 and Annex III:2 Customs Valuation Agreement; Art. 15.1 TBT Agreement; Art. 32.2 Agreement on Subsidies and Countervailing Measures; Art. 72 TRIPS; the plurilateral agreements contain the following reservation provisions: Art 9.2.1 Agreement on Trade in Civil Aircraft and Art. XXIV:4 Agreement on Government Procurement.

35 Art. 20: 2 VCLT.

36 Broek, 'Article XVI WTO Agreement', 190, para. 47; on the shipbuilding exception which can be considered a reservation by the United States, see below.

37 Para. 1 lit. b Protocol of Provisional Application of the General Agreement of Tariffs and Trade, Signed at Geneva on 30 October 1947, UNTS 55 (1950), 308. Through this protocol the GATT 1947 applied to the original contracting parties as well as to those former territories of Belgium, France, the Netherlands and the United Kingdom which acceded to the GATT under Article XXVI:5(c) GATT. To the other contracting parties the GATT also applied only provisionally by way of protocols, see Jackson, *World Trade and the Law of GATT*, 61.

Art. XXVI GATT could make a valid reservation to maintain their grand-father rights.[38] Other reservations to the GATT 1947 had to be accepted by all other contracting parties which is why already under the GATT 1947 waivers largely replaced reservations as concerns measures beyond those grandfathered by the Protocol of Provisional Application. Only a few states maintained reservations with respect to GATT obligations or obligations included in agreements amending the GATT.[39]

With the entry into force of the WTO Agreement, WTO members were not allowed to maintain their grandfather rights.[40] One such grandfather right was, however, preserved and included in the GATT 1994.[41] It is an exemption from the obligations contained in Part II of the GATT with respect to measures taken under mandatory legislation enacted before a member joined the GATT 1947 which prohibit the use, sale or lease of foreign-built or -reconstructed vessels in commercial application between points in national waters or the exclusive economic zone. The exemption applies only if such legislation was notified prior to 1 January 1995 and only so long as it is not modified in such a way as to decrease its conformity with Part II of the GATT 1994. Although this exemption is phrased in general terms it was included in the GATT 1994 on behalf of the United States.[42] The United States is the only WTO member which has made use of the exemption and due to its formulation will remain the sole member to do so. On 20 December 1994 the US notified legislation, the Merchant Maritime Act of 1920 known as the Jones Act,[43] which inter alia requires that ships for domestic shipping services be built in the United States.[44] The exemption was to be reviewed by the Ministerial Conference at the latest five years after entry into force of the WTO Agreement and thereafter every two years.[45] This construction, namely the modification

---

38 CONTRACTING PARTIES, Resolution of 7 March Expressing the Unanimous Agree-ment of the CONTRACTING PARTIES to the Attaching of a Reservation of Acceptance Pursuant to Article XXVI.
39 Benedek, *Die Rechtsordnung des GATT aus völkerrechtlicher Sicht*, 171.
40 Section 1 lit. b no. ii Introductory Note to GATT 1994.
41 Section 3 Introductory Note to GATT 1994.
42 Jackson, *World Trade and the Law of GATT*, 49.   43 46 U.S.C. (Recodified 2006).
44 The Jones Act has since been modified, but the United States is of the view that these mod-ifications have not decreased conformity with Part II of the GATT, see e.g. WT/GC/W/228 (2 July 1999).
45 Section 3 lit. b Introductory Note to GATT 1994. The first review was initiated in 1999 (WT/GC/M/45 (2 August 1999), para. 9) and ever since reviews have been conducted every two years. The review is conducted on the basis of annual reports which the United States is required to submit (Section 3 lit. c Introductory Note to GATT 1994), questions

of the GATT 1994 to allow the United States to maintain its grandfather right, was necessary precisely because the GATT 1994 does not permit reservations. It is heavily criticized by other members who argue that the exemption in fact constitutes a waiver and therefore should be subject to the rules on waivers.[46]

It was already noted that waivers to a large extent replace reservations within the WTO. When looking at the waiver practice, however, it becomes apparent that the function of reservations and waivers only partly overlaps – at least if one understands reservations as exemptions for certain measures to take effect at the time of becoming a member and for the entire duration of membership. The waiver, which is granted on a regular basis to Cuba and suspends Cuba's obligation under Art. XVI:4 GATT to either become a member of the IMF or to enter into a mutual exchange agreement with the WTO, covers a situation which would be a typical subject of a reservation. It accommodates a situation which already existed when Cuba became a WTO member and where it is uncertain whether it will change in the near future. In fact similar situations under the GATT 1947 were covered by reservations.[47] Other situations which prompted waiver requests arose, however, only after the requesting states had become members of the WTO.[48] Measures, such as special preference schemes, covered by waivers have changed over time and the examination of extension requests have offered an opportunity to reassess whether a waiver should also be granted for the modified measure. Moreover, waivers are often a way to allow for non-compliance for a transitional period until a member is able to comply and do not intend to permanently legalize non-compliance. Examples of such waivers are the decisions which allowed developing country members to continue to use official minimum values to determine customs value or waivers that allowed for a deferral of the implementation of market access commitments for a specified period of time.[49]

and comments by interested WTO members and the United States' responses (see e.g. WT/GC/M/112 (4 March 2008), paras. 161 *et seq*).

46 See e.g. the statement of the Australian representative during a review session, WT/GC/M/45 (2 August 1999), para. 9.

47 On this waiver practice as well as the GATT reservations, see Chapter 4 B.I.1.3.

48 Some waivers suspend, for example, the duty to comply with commitments which acceding members accepted at the time of accession but later had difficulties in complying with, see Chapter 4 B.I.2.1(b).

49 On these waiver decisions, see Chapter 4 B.I.1.1. and B.I.2.1(b).

II Variable geometry

Less harmful to the integrity of a legal regime than reservations is the concept of variable geometry. Treaty regimes which employ this concept oblige all parties to comply with certain general obligations and provide for further-reaching cooperation without requiring all parties to participate.[50]

Variable geometry may take the form that states adopt a framework convention to which further and more concrete obligations are added over time.[51] The main aim of the framework approach, which is often adopted in environmental law, but also in other areas such as human rights, is to agree on basic principles in a framework convention. During future negotiations of the contracting parties consensus may then be built with respect to more concrete and further-reaching commitments which are laid down in protocols or implementing agreements.[52] The instruments enter into force when they are ratified by a quorum of states which means that not all parties to the framework convention need to become members for the instrument to take effect. Thus the framework approach allows contracting parties to progressively develop the treaty regime and to take account of new developments in knowledge and reality.[53] It has the further effect that states may decide to be bound by the basic principles laid out in the framework convention and to participate in conferences of the parties to the framework convention, but not to adopt further obligations contained in additional legal instruments.

In a similar way WTO law allows for variations in the degree of commitment of its members. These variations relate in particular to the extent of market access that each member affords to the other members.[54] While

---

50 The term was originally coined with regard to European integration of different intensity for different member states; on variable geometry in the EU, see e.g. Ehlermann (ed.), *Der rechtliche Rahmen eines Europas in mehreren Geschwindigkeiten und unterschiedlichen Gruppierungen*; Thym, *Ungleichzeitigkeit und Europäisches Verfassungsrecht*.

51 On the notion of framework agreements in international law, Matz-Lück, 'Framework Agreements'. Examples of framework conventions in the field of environmental law are the Vienna Convention for the Protection of the Ozone Layer (adopted 22 March 1985, entered into force 22 September 1988), 1513 UNTS 324 and the United Nations Framework Convention on Climate Change (adopted 9 May 1992, entered into force 21 March 1994), 1771 UNTS 165.

52 On the amendment of international environmental agreements through protocols, Gehring, 'Treaty-Making and Treaty Evolution', 467, 486 *et seq.*

53 Matz-Lück, 'Framework Agreements', paras. 11, 12.

54 Moreover, there are two Plurilateral Trade Agreements annexed to the WTO Agreement and currently in force: the Agreement on Trade in Civil Aircraft and the Agreement on

the Multilateral Trade Agreements lay down general obligations binding all members,[55] they leave WTO members in principle a choice as to the extent of market access which they wish to accord to foreign goods and services. The WTO Agreements do not contain an obligation to either reduce tariffs on goods or to grant market access to services and service suppliers.[56] Tariff concessions and market access commitments with respect to services are negotiated bilaterally during multilateral trade rounds or during accession negotiations. The negotiated commitments are included in members' goods and services schedules which form integral parts of the WTO Agreement.[57] Through the most-favoured-nation obligations in Art. I GATT and Art. II GATS the bilaterally negotiated commitments are extended to all other members.

The flexibility in regard to these specific concessions and commitments is greater in the area of services than in the field of trade in goods. Services schedules specify for each mode of supply[58] in each covered sector the extent of market access as well as any limitations on national treatment.[59] Moreover, before the entry into force of the WTO Agreement, members were allowed to make exemptions to the most-favoured-nation obligation

Government Procurement. A specificity of the WTO Agreement which, however, is of little practical relevance and therefore will not be discussed here, is Art. XIII WTO Agreement. It provides that the '[WTO] Agreement and the Multilateral Trade Agreements . . . shall not apply as between any Member and any other Member if either of the Members, at the time either becomes a Member, does not consent to such application'.

55 With some variation due to differing transitional periods for implementation.

56 However, Art. XIX:1 GATS provides that 'Members shall enter into successive rounds of negotiations . . . with a view to achieving a progressively higher level of liberalization.' By contrast Art. XXVIIIbis:1 GATT merely states that tariffs often constitute serious barriers to trade, that negotiations directed to tariff reductions are of great importance and that therefore the Ministerial Conference may from time to time sponsor tariff negotiations.

57 Article II:7 GATT, Article XX:3 GATS. On the interpretation of market access commitments, see Appellate Body Report, *EC – Computer Equipment*, WT/DS62/AB/R, WT/DS67/AB/R, WT/DS68/AB/R, adopted 22 June 1998; Appellate Body Report, *US – Gambling*, WT/DS285/AB/R, adopted 20 April 2005; Appellate Body Report, *EC – Chicken Cuts*, WT/DS269/AB/R, WT/DS286/AB/R, adopted 27 September 2005.

58 The four modes of supply to which the GATS applies are the cross-border supply of services, consumption of services abroad, the commercial presence of a service supplier from one member in the territory of another member and the supply of services by a service supplier of one member through the presence of natural persons in the territory of any other member (Article 1:2 GATS).

59 On the structure of GATS schedules, see WTO, The General Agreement on Trade in Services (GATS). Objectives, Coverage and Disciplines, www.wto.org/english/tratop_e/serv_e/gatsqa_e.htm (last accessed 11 March 2011).

in Article II:1 GATS.[60] As concerns tariff concessions, members are relatively free to define the products to which concessions shall be granted. While negotiations are usually guided by the World Customs Organization's Harmonized System nomenclature,[61] members are not bound by the Harmonized System's product classifications. They may deviate from a standard product description in order to exclude certain products from the commitment. The freedom of members to define the scope of their tariff commitments needs to be taken into account when interpreting what it means for products to be like in the sense of the most-favoured-nation obligation in Art. I:1 GATT.[62] The Agreement on Agriculture adds a further level of variable commitments. The agreement's obligations to reduce domestic support measures are dependent on the level of support which was previously granted by each member. Furthermore, the agreement allows members to maintain certain export subsidies which they list in their GATT schedules. These subsidies, with the exception of export subsidies granted by least-developed country members, are subject to reduction commitments. Export subsidies which are not specified in the schedule are prohibited.[63]

While WTO law in principle allows for the mentioned variations in individual members' market access commitments as well as with respect to the obligation to reduce subsidies for agricultural products, this freedom in part has been counteracted by the considerable pressure exercised by the existing WTO membership on states that wished to accede to the WTO to agree to far-reaching liberalization commitments.[64]

The GATT and GATS not only provide formally for flexibility in the undertaking of market access commitments, they also allow for their modification and withdrawal. Even though modifications of schedules, strictly speaking, constitute treaty amendments, the amendment procedure in Art. X WTO Agreement does not need to be followed to make changes to individual members' commitments. Members may withdraw or modify their concessions following the procedures in Article XXVIII GATT and Article XXI GATS respectively as well as those laid down in secondary law adopted by the organization.[65] According

---

60 See *supra* A.I.2.   61 On the Harmonized System see Chapter 4 B.II.3.1.

62 Hudec, '"Like Products": The Difference in Meaning in GATT Articles I and III', 101.

63 McMahon, 'The Agreement on Agriculture', 187, 207 *et seq.*

64 Charnovitz, 'Mapping the Law of WTO Accession', 855.

65 The relevant legal provisions are Article XXVIII GATT, Procedures for Modification and Rectification of Schedules of Tariff Concessions, Decision of 26 March 1980, L/4962, BISD 27S/25, Understanding on the Interpretation of Art. XXVIII of the General Agreement on

to these procedures a member that wishes to withdraw or modify a commitment shall enter into negotiations with other members with a view to reaching agreement on compensatory adjustment. Concerning tariff concessions negotiations shall be conducted with those members with whom the concession was initially negotiated as well as with those that have a specific interest in the concession.[66] If a member intends to modify or withdraw services commitments, negotiations shall be conducted on request with any member whose benefits under the GATS may be affected by the proposed modification or withdrawal.[67] If commitments are withdrawn or modified without compensation being made, other members may reciprocate by withdrawing substantially equivalent concessions.[68]

Thus, where members wish to raise bound tariffs or restrict access for services contrary to a specific commitment, the GATT and the GATS allow them to do so if certain procedures are followed. This might be a time-consuming and costly option since other members either need to be compensated or will be allowed to retaliate. However, it has the advantage for the modifying or withdrawing member that no consent is required, and that the decision to withdraw or modify may be made unilaterally. There is furthermore no duty to give a justification why commitments are withdrawn or modified and no obligation to revert at any point in time to the original commitment. Thus, after the Appellate Body had found in the *Gambling* dispute that the United States had violated its market access commitment with respect to cross-border gambling services,[69] the United States chose to initiate the procedure for

---

Tariffs and Trade 1994; Article XXI GATS, Procedures for the Implementation of Article XXI of the General Agreement on Trade in Services (GATS) (Modification of Schedules), adopted by the Council for Trade in Services on 19 July 1999, S/L/97 (20 October 1999).

66 Members who may participate in Art. XXVIII GATT negotiations are members who have an initial negotiation right or a principal supplying interest. Members with a substantial interest have a right to be consulted. On principal supplying interest see the Understanding on the Interpretation of Art. XXVIII of the General Agreement on Tariffs and Trade 1994.

67 Article XXI:2 GATS.

68 The modified schedules enter into force through certification: see Procedures for Modification and Rectification of Schedules of Tariff Concessions, Decision of 26 March 1980, L/4962, BISD 27S/25.

69 Appellate Body Report, *US – Gambling*, WT/DS285/AB/R, adopted 20 April 2005. An arbitrator had subsequently determined that Antigua might request authorization from the DSB to suspend obligations under the TRIPS Agreement at a level not exceeding US$ 21 million annually, Decision by the Arbitrator, *US – Gambling (Article 22.6)*, WT/DS285/ARB (21 December 2007).

the withdrawal of this commitment under Article XXI GATS.[70] Withdrawal allows the United States to maintain its ban on Internet gambling even if it discriminates between domestic and foreign services providers in a way that cannot be justified under the general provisions of the GATS.

The flexibility of WTO rules as concerns market access commitments can be explained by the WTO objectives and the role of WTO law as conceptualized in Chapter 3. The main objective of the WTO is not to liberalize trade, but to coordinate members' activities that affect trade so as to, on the one hand, avoid protectionism and, on the other hand, to maintain members' regulatory freedom in both domestic and international policies to protect economic and non-economic public interests that potentially have a negative effect on trade. This objective is pursued through the establishment of a legal regime which lays down general and binding legal rules. At the same time the WTO provides a forum for the negotiation of market access commitments among members in their bilateral relationships. The results are contracts among members secured by WTO law which may, however, be renegotiated or even be modified unilaterally.

Yet, members who wish to be freed from specific market access commitments do not always follow the route of modification and withdrawal. In the past, when members merely sought a deferral of implementation because the economic costs of compliance were considered too high, they requested waivers.[71] Through the adoption of a waiver the duty to comply with commitments may be suspended for a specified period of time and the requesting member will not necessarily be asked to compensate. Contrary to the procedures foreseen in Articles XXVIII GATT and XXI GATS members that request waivers are required to give reasons for their request.[72]

All in all the concept of variable geometry is valuable to address different levels of capacity and preference for international cooperation. With respect to the WTO it is frequently proposed that the WTO should allow for further variable geometry and depart from its single undertaking approach according to which all members must participate in all of the

---

70 Dispute Settlement Body, Minutes of the Meeting on 22 May 2007, statement of the representative of the United States, WT/DSB/M/232 (25 June 2007), para. 57.
71 See the waiver decisions discussed in Chapter 4 B.I.2.1(b).
72 On the requirements that waiver requests have to meet, see Chapter 5 C.I.

Multilateral Trade Agreements, whether they expect to benefit from such participation or not.[73]

III General rules and exceptions and the need for additional exit options

The tension between the demand for responsiveness to changes in domestic preferences on the one hand and for effectiveness on the other seems to be best addressed by general rules and exceptions. They may pay deference to domestic regulatory choices and cultural preferences and take account of differences in capacity to comply. They have the further advantage that they do not privilege sovereign interests per se (as reservations potentially do), but exercise some control by prescribing legal requirements which domestic measures have to meet. Since each state party may base a claim on a general rule or avail itself of a general exception (as long as the legal requirements are met) the principle of equality of states is upheld and individual states are not being privileged.[74]

Generally, one can distinguish between: firstly, general rules and exceptions that take account of regulatory choices or cultural preferences which may differ from party to party; secondly, special rules for developing country parties which are either less demanding or allow for longer time periods for implementation; and thirdly, escape clauses which permit a party temporarily not to meet certain obligations owing to difficulties with compliance as a result of special circumstances.

After a short exposition of these three ways in which generally applicable treaty law may account for differences in needs and preferences, I shall address the question as to any additional potential of a waiver power in this regard.

1 General rules

Generally applicable rules and exceptions have the advantage that they maintain the formal equality of states in that states are equally bound by the treaties' obligations and at the same time are equally entitled to

73 Howse, 'For a Citizen's Task Force on the Future of the World Trade Organization', 877, 880; Pauwelyn, 'Transformation of World Trade', 1, 61.

74 While formally individual states are not privileged, certain states may profit more from an agreement than others. A good example of this is the TRIPS Agreement which disproportionately benefits industrialized members over developing country members: see Chapter 3 C.II.

the justification of non-compliance provided for by the exceptions. In addition – and contrary to reservations – they accommodate the fact that contracting parties' preferences are not fixed, but may change over time. Increasingly, legal rules pierce the state's veil in that they make justification of state measures dependent on internal conditions or procedures being met. Article 11 para. 2 of the European Convention on Human Rights, for example, allows for restrictions on the right to assembly if such restrictions are 'prescribed by law and are necessary in a democratic society in the interests of national security or public safety, for the prevention of disorder or crime, for the protection of health or morals or for the protection of the rights and freedoms of others'. Another example is the WTO's SPS Agreement which allows states to depart from international standards in the adoption of health measures if such measures are based on a scientific risk assessment that meets certain rationality requirements.[75]

In the WTO a number of legal rules take account of the diversity of regulatory preferences among WTO members, and the types of risks their societies wish to address, as well as the levels of risk against which they intend to protect persons, animals or the environment. These are in particular the general exceptions in Art. XX GATT and Art. XIV GATS which allow members to take measures for the pursuit of public interests that contradict the general rules, in particular the prohibition of quantitative restrictions and the most-favoured-nation and national treatment obligations. Furthermore the rules of the SPS Agreement and the TBT Agreement take account of differences in societies' acceptance and management of risk. The justifications of measures necessary for regional integration (Art. XXIV GATT and Art. V GATS) may also be named here, as well as the exceptions in the TRIPS Agreement which allow for deviation from the general rules, e.g. on the exclusion of certain products from patentability, exceptions to the rights conferred by a patent or the granting of compulsory licences under certain conditions.[76]

2 Special and differential treatment

Special and differential treatment rules constitute a departure from the principle of formal equality of states.[77] However, they do not privilege specific states, but apply to all states falling into abstractly designated

75 Art. 3.3 SPS Agreement. For an interpretation of the SPS Agreement as strengthening domestic democratic processes, see Howse, 'Democracy, Science, and Free Trade', 2329.
76 Cf. Articles 27, 30, 31 TRIPS Agreement.
77 Cullet, *Differential Treatment in International Environmental Law*.

groups, usually of developing or least-developed countries. They acknowledge the different situation of developing countries as concerns their capacity to comply with international standards. Sometimes these rules also acknowledge a differentiated responsibility, for example as concerns developing countries' contribution to climate change.[78]

The capacity problems which developing country members and least-developed country members may encounter with respect to compliance with WTO norms are addressed in a variety of ways, including modifications in the rules on dispute settlement if a developing country is a party to a dispute or (non-binding) promises with respect to technical assistance.[79] Differentiation with respect to the substantive obligations mainly took the form that developing country members were (and partly still are) granted transitional periods for implementation which exceeded implementation periods of developed country members. Upon the expiry of transitional periods, the substantive obligations to a large extent correspond to those of developed country members.[80]

3 Escape clauses

While general legal rules that apply to all parties or to abstractly defined groups of parties may take account of the general diversity in state parties' needs and preferences, so-called escape clauses allow for temporary deviations in exceptional circumstances.[81] Where escape clauses do not require prior authorization by an organ of an international institution[82]

---

78 Thus, under the Kyoto Protocol developing countries were not obliged to reduce CO_2 emissions. Generally on the principle of common but differentiated responsibility in international environmental law, see Beyerlin, 'Different Types of Norms in International Environmental Law', 425, 441 *et seq.*

79 On special and differential treatment of developing countries under WTO law, see Jessen, *WTO-Recht und 'Entwicklungsländer'*.

80 Some exceptions for developing country members are provided for in Art. XXVIII GATT which, inter alia due to the cumbersome procedures it prescribes, is, however, hardly used. For a criticism of the limited value of special and differential treatment provisions in the WTO Agreements, see Trachtman, 'Legal Aspects of a Poverty Agenda at the WTO', 3.

81 Special Rapporteur A. Pellet, Fifth Report on Reservations to Treaties, para. 138; on the relationship between escape clauses in treaties and necessity under general international law, see Binder, 'Non-Performance of Treaty Obligations in Cases of Necessity', 3.

82 Escape clauses that make the justification of non-compliance dependent on prior authorization may be conceptualized as waiver powers: Special Rapporteur A. Pellet, Fifth Report on Reservations to Treaties, para. 138. The waiver power in its function as escape clause will be discussed below in section A. III.4.1(a).

these exceptional circumstances are abstractly defined. For example, Art. 4 of the International Covenant on Civil and Political Rights allows for derogations from obligations under the Covenant '[i]n time of public emergency which threatens the life of the nation and the existence of which is officially proclaimed'.[83]

In the WTO agreements the safeguard provisions for the GATT (Art. XIX GATT, the Agreement on Safeguards) and the Agreement on Agriculture (Art. 5 Agreement on Agriculture) which allow members to adopt temporary measures to protect domestic industries from injury caused by foreign imports, constitute escape clauses.[84] Moreover, Art. XXI GATT and Art. XIVbis GATS provide for a justification of measures to protect essential security interests or to implement obligations under the UN Charter for the maintenance of international peace and security. They too may be considered escape clauses that justify non-compliance in exceptional circumstances.[85]

4 The need for additional exit options

Given the potential of generally applicable rules, exceptions and escape clauses to take account of variations in preferences and needs among parties to an international legal regime, the additional value of a general waiver power may be doubted. General rules and exceptions can not only protect parties' autonomy to make regulatory choices, but can also take into account differences in parties' capacities to comply. They do so without reference to the concept of sovereignty or by singling out individual parties whose obligations will be loosened. Instead they abstractly define relevant societal preferences or situations which may justify a deviation from legal rules, as well as conditions which justify differential treatment.[86]

---

83 Art. 4 ICCPR requires the notification of measures taken under this clause to the other state parties. Huesa Vinaixa, 'Convention de Vienne de 1969, Article 57', 2006, 2015, 2030 para. 18 (noting that safeguard clauses usually involve some institutional control).
84 The GATS does not include a comparable safeguards clause, but merely, in Art. X GATS, a promise to negotiate one.
85 See Binder, 'Non-Performance of Treaty Obligations in Cases of Necessity', 3.
86 They thus meet the principle of generality which may be seen as a necessary characteristic of public law: see Kingsbury, 'Concept of "Law" in Global Administrative Law', 23, 31, 50 et seq.

In this light it may not only be asked whether a general waiver power is unnecessary, but also whether it is undesirable from a normative perspective. One could argue that the waiver power undermines the principle of equality of states since a waiver request may lead to the adoption of a waiver decision in one case, while in a comparable situation the waiver request by another party may be denied. Furthermore, waivers may be granted where there is no legitimate need for a waiver, in the sense that it does not safeguard a public interest, but instead serves special interests of government officials or specific societal groups with a forceful lobby.

From an empirical perspective it appears that indeed only few international institutions, mainly international economic institutions, have formal waiver powers, and that even fewer of these powers are comparable in breadth to the WTO's waiver power in that they allow for the suspension of any treaty obligation.[87] This observation might support – if not the claim that waivers are undesirable – the claim that waiver powers are generally not perceived by parties to be necessary.

In what follows I argue that there may be a need for a waiver power to allow for non-compliance in individual situations in which insistence on compliance is not desirable, but which could not be predefined by general legal rules at the time of treaty negotiations. I shall concentrate in this section on this need for additional exit options. In Chapter 7 I shall then address the question as to the procedure and process that is required to ensure that the waiver power adequately meets this demand.

4.1 The potential of waivers in light of the uncertainty concerning the operation of legal rules

A general waiver power may take account of the uncertainty as regards the operation of legal rules in the future. This uncertainty may relate to the effects of compliance in individual situations as well as to the scope of obligation.

(a) **Uncertainty as to the effects of compliance**   After a treaty enters into force, situations may arise in which compliance would be excessively burdensome for individual parties. Such situations are usually covered by escape clauses. Escape clauses in the form of general legal rules, such as for example the safeguards clause of Art. XIX GATT, abstractly define the situations which trigger the justification for escape. Thus, Art. XIX GATT inter alia sets out the requirements that a product is imported

---

87 See *supra* fn. 1.

in increased quantities and that such imports cause or threaten serious injury to domestic producers. Such a formulation of legal requirements is necessary, for if a legal rule merely stated that a party is excused from compliance if compliance is excessively burdensome, there would be a danger of abuse. Such danger could not be contained by legal dispute settlement, since judicial organs would not have any legal standard on the basis of which to determine whether the escape clause was rightly applied or not. However, when a treaty is negotiated, it may be difficult or impossible to foresee compliance with which norms and under which circumstances may pose particular difficulties for individual parties.

Joel Trachtman recently noted the uncertainty about the effects that compliance with the rules that are currently being negotiated during the Doha Development Round will have on economic development and poverty alleviation in developing countries. He argues that in light of this uncertainty developing countries should be excused from compliance where it appears in the future that compliance would be detrimental to development or to poverty alleviation.[88] Uncertainty in this constellation exists in many respects. Thus, it may not be clear which rules will turn out to have detrimental effects for economic development. Moreover, it is not clear what will be adequate policy measures to further development and alleviate poverty in a given future situation and context.[89] An abstractly phrased rule would be unsuitable to take account of this uncertainty and at the same time to prevent abuse of its application. By contrast, an exit option which depends on an authorization by the institution does not require any determinations at the time of treaty negotiations, for example, as to the factual circumstances under which compliance would be detrimental to poverty alleviation. At the same time the authorization requirement can ensure that such an exit option is not abused.

In the WTO the waiver power entrusts the General Council, which decides by consensus, with the decision whether an exit option in the form of a waiver shall be granted. It may be doubted whether this process is indeed suitable; firstly, to determine whether compliance is excessively burdensome, for example, due to its detrimental effects on development or poverty alleviation; and secondly, to ensure, when such a finding is made, that a waiver is indeed granted and not vetoed for considerations

---

88 Trachtman, 'Ensuring a Development-Friendly WTO'.
89 Rodrik, *One Economics, Many Recipes* (demonstrating the contingency of effective development policy).

unrelated to economic development and poverty alleviation. I shall come back to these questions in Chapter 7.

In the past the GATT and WTO waiver power in several instances was used to allow for escape where compliance was found to be excessively burdensome. Indeed this was the function originally attributed to the waiver power by its drafters.[90] From the WTO practice one may name in particular the waivers of specific commitments as examples of waivers functioning as escape clauses in light of uncertainty.[91] Moreover, the extension of transitional periods is often justified on the basis that the need for further delays in implementation has become apparent over time.[92]

(b) Uncertainty as to the scope of obligation   As concerns the scope of legal obligations, the operation of the law may reveal that certain rules are over-inclusive in that they cover situations which should not be covered. The generalization and abstraction from specific situations which is the purpose of legal rules will almost always lead to the fact that some situations will be covered that need not be covered or should not be covered to further the objective of a given rule.[93] Legal rules are over-inclusive, not only because it would be too time-consuming and too costly to negotiate all potential instances of application, but also because generalization and abstraction are needed to enable rules to perform their function to stabilize expectations and thus to achieve predictability and security. While over-inclusiveness necessarily results from the choice of the legal form, it might still be desirable to allow for exceptions from compliance in specific situations. This is particularly the case in international relations. In international relations the application of a norm to a situation not covered by its rationality will often be of greater significance than in a domestic legal system where legal rules are applied in a far greater number of cases so that a single instance of undesired application does not have much weight. The waiver power allows an institution to address instances of over-inclusiveness by suspending the application of legal norms where parties agree that compliance would not

---

90 See Chapter 5 B.III.1.1; for a conceptualization of waivers as escape clauses, see also Special Rapporteur A. Pellet, Fifth Report on Reservations to Treaties, para. 138.

91 On these waivers see Chapter 4 B.I.2.1(b).

92 For the extension of transitional periods by waiver decisions see Chapter 4 B.I.1.1 and B.I.2.1(a).

93 Koskenniemi, *From Apology to Utopia*, 591 *et seq.* A determination of over-inclusiveness presupposes of course a certain understanding of the objective of a legal norm.

further a treaty objective or would be detrimental to its pursuit. Since the waiver decision formally suspends a treaty obligation in such a situation, non-application does not negatively affect the norm's validity.

The UK Margins of Preferences Waiver may be seen as mitigating the over-inclusiveness of Art. I:4 GATT, the prohibition to increase margins of preferences.[94] The waiver allowed the UK to raise tariffs on unbound items as long as this did not result in a diversion of trade in favour of products benefiting from Commonwealth preferences. In support of its waiver request the United Kingdom argued that the envisaged tariffs would not violate the objectives of the GATT since they would not increase the value of preferences. To prevent increases in tariff preferences, arguably, had been the rationale for the inclusion of Art. I:4 GATT into the General Agreement.

Similarly, the waivers granted to the United States for preferences to South Pacific Island states may be conceptualized as a response to the over-inclusiveness of the prohibition of preferences by Art. I:1 GATT, or – if you will – the under-inclusiveness of its exception in Art. I:2 GATT for historic preferences.[95] The US preferences had not been covered by the exception in Art. I:2 GATT for the mere reason that at the time the exception was drafted the same preferences had been granted by Japan. Only in 1948 did the United States take over from Japan the administration of these Pacific Islands under a trusteeship agreement with the United Nations and therewith the responsibility to continue the trade preferences formerly granted by Japan.[96]

Finally, collective HS waivers address situations in which the strict application of Art. II GATT (the obligation to comply with tariff reduction commitments), would make it impossible for members to comply with their obligations under the Harmonized System Convention to implement changes to the Harmonized System and their obligation under Art. II GATT at the same time. Such a situation is undesirable given that the implementation of Harmonized System changes is a shared interest of the WTO membership.[97]

4.2 Waivers as exception for domestic preferences

Additional exit options to allow for non-compliance based on strong domestic preferences may ensure the continued acceptance by individual

---

94 Chapter 4 B.I.2.2.a.   95 Chapter 4 B.I.3.3.a.
96 Chapter 4 B.I.3.3.a.   97 Chapter 4 B.II.3.1.

members of an international legal regime[98] and may serve to mitigate the limitations that the regime imposes on democratic self-government. Even though I shall elaborate on the last point, the former is equally important. For example, the 1955 Agricultural Waiver that allowed US protectionist measures, indeed played a crucial role in maintaining congressional support for the international trading regime.[99]

As was noted previously, legal rules strike a balance and constitute a compromise between competing preferences. How this balance is struck is not a matter of scientific truth, but a political decision which requires justification. This justification according to traditional international law doctrine is based on the consent of states. It is complemented by the benefits of order and stability, and other values which the legal order promises to realize. However, in light of the democratic deficit of international law, i.e. its limited ability to reflect domestic democratic choice as well as to react to changes in transnational societal needs and preferences, this justification appears lacking.[100] While limitations on the enforcement of international law (which will be discussed in the next section) constitute an important safeguard for self-government, the waiver power might also serve to mitigate the legitimacy deficit of international law.[101]

With respect to WTO law it is increasingly demanded that it should be more responsive to WTO members' preferences concerning, for example, economic development priorities or the protection of certain values which are broadly shared within a society. When such preferences are generalizable they will usually result in a demand for a renegotiation of the rules in order to reflect such preferences. However, they are often context-dependent and potentially irrational and thus do not lend themselves to generalization. Consequently, it is not likely that they can be accounted for by generally and abstractly phrased legal rules.

Take, for example, the fear of yet unknown and unproven risks to health or biodiversity posed by genetically modified organisms (GMOs). The SPS Agreement requires that measures to protect against such risks either be

---

98 On the need for exit options to ensure the acceptability of international legal regimes, see Chapter 2 B.I.

99 On this waiver, see Chapter 4 B.I.2.2(a).

100 Howse and Nicolaïdis, 'Democracy Without Sovereignty', 163, 164. (making the argument that it is impossible to protect and promote democratic politics through a stable division of competences between local and national democratic institutions and global institutions).

101 Cf. Pauwelyn, 'Transformation of World Trade', 1, 56 (denoting exit options including waivers as important 'democratic safety valves').

based on international standards or a scientific risk assessment (Art. 3:2, 3:3 SPS Agreement). Where there is no scientific evidence to support the existence of a risk, members may 'provisionally' adopt measures, but 'shall seek to obtain the additional information necessary for a more objective assessment of risk and review the . . . measure accordingly within a reasonable period of time' (Art. 5:7 SPS Agreement). Arguably, this variation of the precautionary principle is insufficient to protect against anticipated dangers which may only materialize in the distant future.[102] The potential dangers, which in several European countries motivate strong opposition to GMOs, are largely, however, of such a nature. At the same time, the desire to protect against these dangers, for example with a ban on GMOs, need not be interpreted as calling into doubt the general principles of the SPS Agreement. The wish to ban GMOs does not necessarily implicate the claim that the SPS Agreement should include a broader precautionary principle. A society that decides to take a broad precautionary approach in one specific instance may nonetheless be opposed to the inclusion into the SPS Agreement of a general authorization for precautionary measures absent scientific evidence for the reason that such a rule does not lend itself to a rational application.[103] However, even if not resulting in demands for a change of the legal rules, preferences for certain measures may be so strong and broadly shared within a society that it would not only endanger the acceptance of an international legal regime, but would also mitigate its legitimacy if the law cannot respond to such preferences.[104]

Different scholarly proposals address this potential divergence between matters of general principle and societal preference in specific situations and contexts. While some argue for a solution at the level of adjudication and law enforcement[105] others propose to include special safeguard

---

102 Perdikis, Kerr and Hobbs, 'Reforming the WTO to Defuse Potential Trade Conflicts in Genetically Modified Goods', 379, 384.

103 Bhagwati, *In Defense of Globalization*, 152; Sunstein, *Laws of Fear: Beyond the Precautionary Principle*; rationality of international law may be all the more important given its democratic deficit.

104 Obviously there is always the option to defect which may be more or less costly given the defecting states' power as well as the extent to which other parties are affected.

105 Atik, 'Identifying Antidemocratic Outcomes', 229, 234, 261 (proposing a specific standard of review test when a measure reflects a deeply embedded value, that enjoys clear support of the population and if the member imposing the measure bears the greater part of the cost of the trade distortion caused by the measure); Bhagwati, *In Defense of Globalization*, 152 (suggesting that WTO members who adopt measures dictated by public opinion but inconsistent with WTO law should not be retaliated against, but instead should make a tort payment to the injured industry).

provisions into the WTO Agreements in order to justify measures based on strong societal preferences.[106] In this section I shall focus on the latter proposal and shall come back to the role of law enforcement as concerns the preferences of individual members in the next section.

The proposals for special safeguard clauses that I discuss here coincide in the view that additional exit options should not permit measures that serve special interests, but measures that enjoy broad public support. Thus, Dani Rodrik proposes that deviations from the general rules will be justified for policy measures that were the subject of an investigative process in which all relevant parties were heard, including consumer and public interest groups, importers, exporters and civil society organizations and which evidenced broad support for these measures.[107] Pascal Lamy, by contrast, remains relatively vague and merely states that the measures to be justified by his proposed safeguard clause need to be based on collective preferences, which he defines as 'the end result of choices made by human communities that apply to the community as a whole'. He further states that collective preferences require 'institutions capable of forging collective preferences'.[108] While both Rodrik and Lamy, explicitly[109] or implicitly,[110] refer to democratic structures Nicholas Perdikis et al. in their proposal on exceptions for trade barriers based on consumer concern merely require the demonstration of a sufficient level (in quantity

---

106 Perdikis, Kerr and Hobbs, 'Reforming the WTO to Defuse Potential Trade Conflicts in Genetically Modified Goods', 379 (proposing a new WTO Agreement that would allow for trade barriers responding to consumer preferences); Lamy, *Emergence of Collective Preferences in International Trade* (arguing that WTO law should allow for temporary non-protectionist least trade restrictive measures that give effect to collective preferences); Rodrik, *One Economics, Many Recipes*, 230 *et seq.* (proposing an Agreement on Developmental and Social Safeguards to allow for temporary deviation from the rules to pursue developmental policies or to protect social values).

107 *Ibid.*, 231.   108 Lamy, *Emergence of Collective Preferences in International Trade*, 2.

109 Dani Rodrik is explicit in stating that '[n]ondemocratic countries cannot count on the same trade privileges as democratic ones': Rodrik, *One Economics, Many Recipes*, 229. At the same time Rodrik points out that the inclusive investigations he proposes as a requirement for a special safeguard to apply in practice rarely happen even in industrialized countries (232).

110 Pascal Lamy writes: 'democratic societies are organised in such a way as to allow the emergence of "collective" preferences, which synthesise the preferences of individuals through political debate and institutions. These preferences then become standards which apply to everyone and provide a framework for relations between individuals': Lamy, *Emergence of Collective Preferences in International Trade*, 2. He does not address whether collective preferences as he understands them may also be forged in non-democratic societies.

and quality) of such consumer concern.[111] It may be argued, however, that in the absence of democratic structures it may not be possible to determine whether a sufficient level of consumer concern is reached.[112]

Since the proposals aim to ensure a certain responsiveness of the regime to strong domestic preferences without predetermining the content of such preferences,[113] they merely establish requirements related to the formal quality of the preference, not, however, its material content. They require that the preference is a collective preference (Lamy), that it was tested in an inclusive investigation (Rodrik), and that it is broadly shared by consumers (Perdikis et al.). With respect to the measures that can be justified by the proposed safeguards the proposals state negative requirements relating to the qualities of the measures. The proposed negative requirements include requirements that the measure may not be more trade restrictive than necessary, that it is temporary, that it is not protectionist or that it does not aim at the imposition of preferences on other societies.[114] The proposals do not, however, impose any additional positive requirements that determine the applicability of the safeguard clause, as does Art. XIX GATT with the requirements of an import surge and of injury to domestic producers.

This lack of additional positive requirements raises doubts as to whether the inclusion of such safeguards into an international legal regime is feasible or even desirable. It is true that international law increasingly takes an interest in democratic structures at the national level.[115] Nonetheless, it seems unlikely that members, including non-democratic members, would agree on a safeguard clause that would make deliberative and inclusive policy-making processes a precondition for an escape clause to apply.

---

111 Perdikis, Kerr and Hobbs, 'Reforming the WTO to Defuse Potential Trade Conflicts in Genetically Modified Goods', 379, 395 *et seq.*

112 Perdikis et al. propose the establishment of a 'professional, social science-based institution . . . to develop harmonized international procedures for evaluating the existence and intensity of consumer concerns': *ibid.*, 379, 397.

113 As was explained above such predetermination would not be desirable or not feasible given the contextuality and potential irrationality of the preferences.

114 According to Rodrik's proposal, if there is a strong preference within a WTO member for import restrictions in order to protect domestic food safety, labour or environmental standards such restrictions may be justified. They would, however, not be justified if they aim to impose these standards on other members: Rodrik, *One Economics, Many Recipes*, 232.

115 Charnovitz, 'Emergence of Democratic Participation in Global Governance', 45, 50; d'Aspremont, *L'Etat non démocratique en droit international*; Petersen, *Demokratie als teleologisches Prinzip.*

Furthermore, the dispute settlement organs appear ill-suited to apply such standards.[116]

In the absence of special safeguards for democratic preferences the waiver power, which on its face is indifferent to domestic policy-making processes, could be used to respond to domestic democratic preferences. Indeed, some characteristics of the waiver power reveal its potential for being used as a 'democratic preferences safeguard'. If the examination of waiver requests is conducted in a transparent, representative and principled way, it may test whether a measure is indeed based on strong domestic support. At the same time such a process may reveal support for the measure in question in other members' societies and thus increase the chances that consensus may be achieved. Moreover, consensus becomes more likely given the possibility, if other members' export interests are strongly affected, to negotiate compensation or to maintain the option of members bringing a non-violation complaint in case of real trade damage.[117]

To be sure, whether the examination process may provide a good test of the quality of the preferences in question and lead to a consensus on waivers to legalize measures based on strong domestic preferences largely depends on how this process is framed and who participates. These questions will be addressed in Chapter 7.

IV Limitations on law enforcement

Account of domestic preferences and needs may not only be taken at the level of primary obligations, but also at the enforcement stage. Consideration of the individual situations of states at the enforcement stage may either be motivated by concern for domestic self-government or by the realization that capacity problems and not a lack of willingness to comply are the reasons for non-compliance. On the one hand, various rules that may be interpreted as specifications of a subsidiarity principle protect domestic self-government;[118] on the other hand, compliance

---

116 For such criticism directed at Pascal Lamy's proposal for a collective preferences exception, see Charnovitz, 'Analysis of Pascal Lamy's Proposal on Collective Preferences', 449, 456 *et seq.*

117 Lamy's proposal for a collective preferences safeguard foresees compensation: Lamy, *Emergence of Collective Preferences in International Trade*. On the admissibility and legal requirements of non-violation complaints alleging nullification and impairment by measures covered by a waiver decision, see Chapter 5 F.II.3.

118 Jackson, 'Sovereignty-Modern: A New Approach to an Outdated Concept', 782; Jackson, *Sovereignty: The WTO and Changing Fundamentals of International Law*; Howse

management instead of strict law enforcement takes account of variations in states' capacities to comply with their international legal obligations. I shall show below how the waiver power in a highly legalized regime with a strong enforcement system may allow for more flexible compliance management.

1 Subsidiarity

In light of the difficulty of devising 'democratic safeguard clauses' as part of treaty law subsidiarity in law enforcement plays an important role in safeguarding domestic self-government.[119] The rules on jurisdiction of international tribunals as well as on the standard of judicial review may be seen as concretizations of the subsidiarity principle in international law aiming at the protection of domestic self-government.[120] The legal rule that local remedies be exhausted before protection can be sought at the international level, as contained in a number of human rights treaties,[121] gives preference to adjudication of claims at the national level and sees international adjudication as a subsidiary means if judicial protection is not, or is insufficiently, granted at the national level. Similarly, the complementary jurisdiction of the International Criminal Court can be seen as a specific application of the subsidiarity principle protecting domestic self-government.[122]

Once jurisdiction is established, the exercise by international courts of their adjudicatory function, in particular the standard of review they employ, can also be guided by subsidiarity concerns. Subsidiarity concerns explain why the European Court of Human Rights frequently accords a margin of appreciation to the parties of the European Convention on

and Nicolaïdis, 'Enhancing WTO Legitimacy', 73; Broude and Shany (eds.), *Shifting Allocation of Authority in International Law.*

119 Howse and Nicolaïdis, 'Democracy Without Sovereignty', 146 (stating the impossiblility of protecting and promoting democratic politics through a stable division of competences between local and national democratic institutions and global institutions).

120 For a conception of these doctrines as giving effect to a subsidiarity principle in international law, see Feichtner, 'Subsidiarity'; Shany, 'Toward a General Margin of Appreciation Doctrine in International Law?', 907.

121 For example Arts. 13, 35 (1) European Convention on Human Rights, Art. 46 (1) (a) American Convention on Human Rights, Art. 56 (5) African Charter on Human and Peoples' Rights, or Art. 2 Optional Protocol to the International Covenant on Civil and Political Rights.

122 Benzing, 'Complementarity Regime of the International Criminal Court', 591.

Human Rights. The Court does so where it deems that there is no consensus among the parties on the scope of the right in question[123] or on conceptions of morals or the requirements of the rights of others, in the sense of Art. 10:2 ECHR, that may justify interferences with the right to freedom of expression.[124] Moreover, the European Court of Human Rights defers to national determinations where it holds national authorities to be in a better position to evaluate certain issues, such as the presence and scope of an emergency in the sense of Art. 15 ECHR and the nature and scope of derogations necessary to avert it.[125]

In the WTO, if a dispute between members arises, the parties to the dispute shall attempt to settle it through consultations. If consultations are unsuccessful a member may request the establishment of a panel. A panel will be established unless the Dispute Settlement Body opposes the request by consensus. To date, the dispute settlement organs have not been very responsive to attempts to restrict their jurisdiction. Demands for judicial restraint in favour of another international regime's adjudicative body[126] or in favour of the WTO's political organs have so far been unsuccessful.[127]

As concerns the standard of review, the dispute settlement organs could pay more deference to members' choices than they currently do, in particular when applying Art. XX GATT or the provisions of the SPS Agreements to measures that pursue public policy interests.[128] For example, the

---

123 See, for example, *Sheffield and Horsham v United Kingdom* (1999) 27 EHRR 163, paras. 55–9.

124 See, for example, *Handyside v United Kingdom*, (1979–80) 1 EHRR 737, para. 48; *Wingrove v United Kingdom* (1997) 24 EHRR 1, para. 58.

125 See, for example, *Ireland v United Kingdom* (1979–80) 2 EHRR 25, para. 207; see Letsas, 'Two Concepts of the Margin of Appreciation', 705, 720 *et seq.*

126 *EC – Chicken Cuts* concerned the customs classification of chicken products by the EC. The World Customs Organization had taken the position that the settlement procedures provided for in the HS Convention should have been followed by the parties to the dispute before the panel took a decision on a violation of WTO law: see Panel Report, *EC – Chicken Cuts*, WT/DS269/R, WT/DS/286/R (30 May 2005), para. 7.53. On this dispute and the question where it should have been adjudicated, see Horn and Howse, 'European Communities: Customs Classification of Frozen Boneless Chicken Cuts', 9, 32 *et seq.*; Appellate Body Report, *Mexico – Taxes on Soft Drinks*, WT/DS308/AB/R, adopted 24 March 2006, paras. 44 *et seq.* (confirming the panel's finding that it had no competence to decline its jurisdiction in favour of a NAFTA arbitration panel).

127 Appellate Body Report, *India – Quantitative Restrictions*, WT/DS90/AB/R, adopted 22 September 1999, paras. 80–109. Appellate Body Report, *Turkey – Textiles*, WT/DS34/AB/R, adopted 19 November 1999, para. 60; on these decisions, see Chapter 5 F.II.1.

128 See, for example, Charnovitz, 'Analysis of Pascal Lamy's Proposal on Collective Preferences', 449, 467 *et seq.*; Howse, 'Moving the WTO Forward', 223, 229 (reading the

Appellate Body repeatedly stresses that members under Art. XX GATT as well as the SPS Agreement are free to determine the level of risk that is acceptable to their societies.[129] Nonetheless, it did not accept members' zero risk policies in a couple of cases in which the public interests pursued were not of vital importance, but the trade effects were great.[130] A more deferent interpretation of the legal rules would be important not only to maintain acceptance for the system, but also in order to increase the WTO's legitimacy.[131]

2 Compliance management

While the above mentioned concretizations of the subsidiarity principle are mainly concerned with the legitimacy of international adjudication, compliance management aims at increasing effectiveness of international legal regimes. It follows from the recognition that states frequently lack the capacity to comply with legal obligations, in particular those of regulatory treaties. International environmental regimes especially do not provide for contentious dispute settlement procedures. They place a stronger focus on compliance assistance than on the determination of state responsibility which may then trigger enforcement measures.[132]

In international legal regimes with compulsory contentious dispute settlement, such as the WTO, a waiver power provides an option to withdraw a dispute from the jurisdiction of the dispute settlement organs in order to allow for a more flexible procedure to achieve compliance.

Appellate Body Report in *EC – Hormones* as according an extra margin of deference to representative governments).

129 See, for example, Appellate Body Report, *Australia – Salmon*, WT/DS18/AB/R, adopted 6 November 1998, para. 125.

130 Appellate Body Report, *Korea – Various Measures on Beef*, WT/DS161/AB/R, WT/DS169/AB/R, adopted 10 January 2001, para. 162 (stating a balancing test); Appellate Body Report, *Japan – Apples*, WT/DS245/AB/R, adopted 10 December 2003. On the latter decision, see Neven and Weiler, '*Japan – Measures Affecting the Importation of Apples (AB-2003–4): One Bad Apple?*', 280 (arguing that the Appellate Body in fact did not accept a zero risk policy in this case). On the question whether the Appellate Body does or should engage in balancing when applying the general exceptions, see also Regan, 'Meaning of "Necessary" in GATT Article XX and GATS Article XIV', 347. Eeckhout, 'Scales of Trade', 3.

131 Charnovitz, 'Analysis of Pascal Lamy's Proposal on Collective Preferences', 449, 467 *et seq.*

132 Klabbers, 'Compliance Procedures', 995. For a critical view of the concept of compliance, see Koskenniemi, 'Breach of Treaty or Non-Compliance?', 123; generally on the concept, Kingsbury, 'Concept of Compliance as a Function of Competing Conceptions of International Law', 345.

There are no limitations on the waiver power as to the time when it is exercised. A waiver may thus be granted after the illegality of a measure was established in dispute settlement proceedings.

A waiver decision can multilateralize a dispute where many members' interests are involved and acknowledge the difficulties which the non-compliant member has to bring its measures into conformity with WTO law. The *Bananas III* dispute is a case in point. The Appellate Body authoritatively established the illegality of the EC's import regime for bananas which the EC had insisted was justified by the Lomé Waiver.[133] This determination of illegality was important since it established legal clarity and the EC's duty to comply. Beyond the establishment of state responsibility the formal dispute settlement proceedings were, however, of limited use in promoting compliance by the EC. This was mainly due to the fact that compliance not only required a change in domestic EC legislation. A solution had to be found which was not only in compliance with WTO law, but also acceptable to ACP states benefiting from the EC's illegal tariff quotas for bananas. In this situation the claimants and the EC concluded understandings to settle the dispute preliminarily. Since the tariff quotas agreed upon in these understandings were, however, not in conformity with WTO law, they required legalization by a waiver decision. The Bananas Waiver which was consequently adopted allowed for a period of time in which the EC's tariff regime was immune from claims of illegality and the EC could negotiate a solution which was consistent with the WTO Agreements.[134]

Waivers may also be granted where non-compliance is not due to a lack of political, but of administrative capacity.[135] Formal dispute settlement proceedings in such cases too would not be helpful to promote compliance. Again they may be important to authoritatively establish a duty to comply. The waiver process, the framing of the waiver decision, as well as subsequent reviews then have the additional benefit that they allow for members to engage in compliance management as known in international environmental regimes. Thus, members may, for example, be asked to establish phase-out plans and to regularly report on their implementation of these plans. Multilateral reviews not only allow members to discuss and monitor progress in compliance, but also to offer

---

133 Chapter 4 B.I.3.3(b).
134 In this case the waiver expired before the dispute was settled, see Chapter 4 B.I.3.3(b).
135 Chapter 4 B.I.1.

assistance in the form of transmission of knowledge or technical and financial support.[136]

V Conclusion

The claim that international law should take account of domestic values and regulatory preferences as well as capacity restraints raises a certain tension which has been more or less apparent throughout this section. It is the tension between the principle of sovereign equality of states and the recognition that international law can no longer be ignorant of domestic processes and their democratic credentials.[137]

Legal doctrine increasingly disaggregates the state when addressing the legitimacy of multi-level governance. This is evidenced, for example, by the shift from a discourse on sovereignty to a discourse on subsidiarity. While previously the doctrinal concept of sovereignty was frequently invoked to shield certain state domains, certain *national* interests, from the reach of international law, sovereignty today is increasingly displaced by a notion of subsidiarity. Subsidiarity is less concerned with protecting 'the state', but seeks to guide the allocation of authority in order to protect autonomy and self-government.[138] The state in this concept is important not qua statehood, but since the national polity enables self-government.

The shift in focus from sovereignty to autonomy and legitimate governance means that decision-making processes and their democratic qualities will assume an increasingly important role when determining the boundaries between domestic and international governance. Such an approach bears, however, certain dangers, in particular of the exclusion of non-democratic states from international society and governance and

---

136 The supervision of the transposition of Harmonized System changes into members' schedules which is regularly accompanied by the granting of waivers provides a good example for such compliance management: see Feichtner, 'Administration of the Vocabulary of International Trade', 1481; on the practice of granting Harmonized System waivers, see Chapter 4 B.I.1.2 and B.II.3.1. For the view that the information exchange on and discussion of members' trade policies in the political organs of the WTO may constitute a form of technical assistance, cf. Lang and Scott, 'Hidden World of WTO Governance', 575, 581.

137 Traditionally international law used to be ignorant as to the internal political organization of states, see e.g. Oppenheim, *International Law. A Treatise*, 403.

138 Jackson, 'Sovereignty-Modern: A New Approach to an Outdated Concept', 782; Howse and Nicolaïdis, 'Enhancing WTO Legitimacy', 73; Shany, 'Toward a General Margin of Appreciation Doctrine in International Law', 907; Broude and Shany (eds.), *Shifting Allocation of Authority in International Law*.

the hegemony of powerful liberal democracies.[139] The tension with international law's foundational principle of equality of states is apparent and legal doctrine must attempt to find a careful balance.

Subsidiarity is not only suggested as a guiding principle for the vertical division of authority between international and domestic governance, but also horizontally in relation to the competences of international institutions.[140] As will be seen in the next section, the waiver may be used to implement a principle of horizontal subsidiarity by restricting an international institution's jurisdiction in favour of another regime with greater legitimacy as concerns the measures legalized by the waiver.

B. THE ACCOMMODATION OF COLLECTIVE NEEDS AND PREFERENCES: WAIVERS COMPARED TO INTERPRETATION AND AMENDMENT

The previous section inquired into the potential of the waiver as an individual exception to accommodate needs and preferences of individual states or their constituencies. This section now will compare the waiver as a general exception and rule-making instrument in particular to treaty amendment and interpretation. As was shown in Chapter 5, waiver decisions may constitute general exceptions. As such they allow (potentially) all members or groups of members not to comply with certain rules. In practice such waivers have taken account of capacity restraints,[141] facilitated inter-regime cooperation,[142] and have paid deference to another potentially conflicting legal regime with respect to trade measures mandated by that regime.[143] Furthermore, collective waivers may modify obligations. They do so by conditioning the suspension of obligations on compliance with abstractly phrased requirements. In the past such waivers responded to claims that WTO rules take insufficient account of development concerns and other public interests.[144] The following analysis will concentrate on the waiver's function as general exception to defer to the jurisdiction of a potentially conflicting legal regime, and as rule-making instrument to readjust the compromises of interests represented by legal rules.[145]

---

139 See, for example, José Alvarez's critique of Anne-Marie Slaughter's liberal theory of international law: Alvarez, 'Do Liberal States Behave Better?', 183.
140 Howse and Nicolaïdis, 'Enhancing WTO Legitimacy', 73.
141 Art. 70.9 TRIPS Agreement Waiver, Chapter 4 B.II.1.2, 2.2.
142 Collective HS Waivers, Chapter 4 B.II.3.1.   143 Kimberley Waiver, Chapter 4 B.II.3.2.
144 1971 GSP Waiver, 1999 Preferences Waiver, TRIPS Waiver, Chapter 4 B.II.2.1.
145 The following sections are based on Feichtner, 'Waiver Power of the WTO', 615.

I The need for political solutions to norm and interest conflicts

As was already pointed out in Part I the formation of issue-specific legal regimes at the international level leads to what is denoted as the fragmented state of the international legal order. However, while the various international legal regimes for the protection of public goods and transnational societal interests such as the environment, human rights or trade are institutionally separate, often mirroring a similar separation of government agencies domestically, their subject matters are interconnected and the interests pursued by each regime potentially conflict.

In a polity, be it the state or a supranational polity such as the European Union, legally framed processes of political deliberation provide for a legitimate balancing and reconciliation of conflicting interests – the outcome being *the* public interest. On the international level, a global legislature which could legitimately engage in such balancing is not in sight. Moreover, functional differentiation has led to the situation that there are few forums in which debates across regime boundaries can take place. Political organs of international organizations or conferences of the parties to an international treaty often have a limited mandate that restricts discussions to issues within the ambit of the specific regime.

As a consequence values which are pursued and protected in one regime are neglected in another, leading to ever more situations of potential conflict. With respect to the World Trade Organization these dangers of fragmentation have materialized in the following ways: on the one hand, international regimes that foresee measures which affect trade are faced with claims that such measures are inconsistent with WTO law; on the other hand, the narrow focus of WTO law on trade and intellectual property protection neglects the negative effects which this law – in particular the TRIPS Agreement – has on other internationally protected interests and values such as the human right to health care or indigenous traditional knowledge. Since the WTO has – due to mandatory dispute settlement – a relatively strong enforcement mechanism, in case of conflict WTO law is likely to prevail.[146]

Legal scholarship, which perceives the fragmentation of international law as problematic,[147] frequently focuses on legal doctrine and the legal

---

146 Holger Hestermeyer refers to this as the 'factual hierarchy of regimes': Hestermeyer, *Human Rights and the WTO: The Case of Patents and Access to Medicines*, 193 *et seq.*; see also Trachtman, *Economic Structure of Economic Law*, 201.

147 While Eyal Benvenisti and George W. Downs cite American authors (with the exception of Martti Koskenniemi and Päivi Leino) to support their thesis that few legal theorists view fragmentation as a serious problem (Benvenisti and Downs, 'Empire's New

tools that general international law provides to address potential norm conflict. Conflict norms are employed, as are rules of interpretation, and frequently evidence is given of a hierarchization of international legal norms.[148]

From a doctrinal perspective the solution to conflict often appears as a matter of the technical application of the rules on interpretation, as embodied in Articles 31 and 32 of the Vienna Convention on the Law of Treaties,[149] or of conflict rules of general international law. I attempt to clarify this point by reference to the most prominent proposal by Joost Pauwelyn on the application of conflict norms to solve norm conflicts between obligations of WTO law and other international legal obligations.[150] With respect to the relationship between WTO norms and norms of subsequent human rights or environmental law treaties Pauwelyn argues that – absent any express provisions on the relationship – the latter shall take precedence over conflicting WTO norms according to the *lex posterior* rule as embodied in Art. 30 VCLT.[151] This shall be the case as between states both of which are not only parties to the WTO, but also to the subsequent treaty. This result is achieved by conceptualizing WTO norms as being of a bilateral structure which allows WTO members *inter se* to contract out of these norms without affecting the rights of third states.[152] However, not only subsequent obligations, but also obligations preceding WTO law can, according to Pauwelyn, prevail over WTO obligations in case of conflict. Multilateral human rights or environmental treaties are conceptualized by Pauwelyn as 'continuing

Clothes', 598, 600–4), legal scholarship in Europe draws a different picture. Here Ph.D. theses on the effects of fragmentation and avenues to achieve coherence abound. To name just a few: Böckenförde, *Grüne Gentechnik und Welthandel*; Hestermeyer, *Human Rights and the WTO: The Case of Patents and Access to Medicines*; Matz, *Wege zur Koordinierung völkerrechtlicher Verträge*; Pauwelyn, *Conflict of Norms in Public International Law*; S. Vöneky, *Die Fortgeltung des Umweltvölkerrechts in internationalen bewaffneten Konflikten*.

148 These works focus by and large on the doctrinal tools to address norm conflict which were also presented in: International Law Commission, *Fragmentation of International Law* (13 April 2006).

149 For a critical view and argumentation that treaty interpretation is highly political, see Klabbers, 'On Rationalism and Politics', 405.

150 Pauwelyn, 'Role of Public International Law in the WTO', 535.

151 For the prevalence of the KPCS over the WTO treaty, see Pauwelyn, 'WTO Compassion or Superiority Complex?', 1177, 1193 *et seq.*

152 Pauwelyn, 'Role of Public International Law in the WTO', 535, 545. On the conceptualization of most WTO norms as bilateral, see Pauwelyn, 'Typology of Multilateral Treaty Obligations', 907.

treaties' which makes it, in his view, inappropriate to apply the later in time rule if obligations in such treaties conflict with WTO obligations.[153] Rather, the relationship between WTO law and conflicting norms in such multilateral treaties will be determined by reference to the intentions of the parties. Where the intentions are not explicit, the implicit intentions have 'to be deduced from general principles of law or logic'.[154] Applied, for example, to trade restrictions in multilateral environmental agreements that precede the WTO, logic, according to Pauwelyn, supports the conclusion that the respective obligation of the environmental treaty prevails over conflicting prohibitions on trade restrictions in the GATT.[155]

While Pauwelyn's theory might be welcomed since it will in many instances lead to a prevalence of human rights or environmental law obligations over WTO obligations, it is highly questionable whether this outcome can really be justified as an application of legal logic. To claim that logic can be used to give expression to states' implicit intentions presupposes that states aim at coherence in their foreign relations. This, however, often appears not be the case. States may pursue conflicting aims in different venues and do so purposefully to satisfy different domestic constituencies. When it is acknowledged, however, that norm conflicts cannot always be reconciled in a way which gives expression to the intentions of states, but that the application of legal principles to norm conflict as well as interpretation entail a choice between conflicting interests, the reconciliation of competing norms becomes less a question of legal logic than one of policy.[156]

The recognition of the political dimension of legal doctrine shall not, however, discredit doctrinal approaches which adhere to the ideal of international law as a coherent system of norms. As is convincingly argued by Eyal Benvenisti and George Downs the conceptualization by legal scholars and legal practitioners of international law as a coherent legal system is important because it may serve to restrict strong actors' opportunities for venue shifting.[157] This is very well demonstrated by Pauwelyn's thesis that WTO dispute settlement organs should apply conflicting (and prevailing) non-WTO international law norms. If WTO dispute settlement

---

153 Pauwelyn, 'Role of Public International Law in the WTO', 535, 545–6.
154 *Ibid.*, 546.   155 *Ibid.*, 546–7.
156 For a discussion of treaty conflict on the premise that treaty conflicts are often a result of value clashes, see Klabbers, *Treaty Conflict and the European Union*, 1–112.
157 Benvenisti and Downs, 'Empire's New Clothes', 598, 630–1; see also Benvenisti, 'Conception of International Law as a Legal System', 393.

bodies followed his line of argument members could not evade their commitments under non-WTO law simply by claiming that within the WTO their other commitments were of no relevance.

Doctrinal approaches to norm conflict are often complemented by institutional proposals for coordination, information exchange and institutional linkage to avoid or mitigate norm conflict.[158] These approaches firstly advocate better coordination and cooperation of different government departments at the national level. Secondly, it is proposed that institutional linkages at the international level should be strengthened. The most common suggestions in this regard relate to information exchange between international institutions, especially through the granting of observer status and cooperation between secretariats.[159] In case conflicts materialize, information from other institutions will help adjudicators to find an adequate solution to such conflict. Thus, it is argued that dispute settlement panels in the WTO should seek advice from other international organizations on the basis of Art. 13 DSU. Another suggestion goes further and aims at the integration of 'external' perspectives into sectoral regimes. Accordingly, it is proposed with respect to WTO dispute settlement that experts from non-economic fields, such as human rights, environmental protection or culture, should be included in dispute settlement panels.[160]

However, just as the interest and value clashes which underlie many norm conflicts cannot be solved by applying legal logic, neither can they be solved through coordination. It has already been noted that states often deliberately cause conflicts and tensions between regimes, for example

---

158 See e.g. Matz, *Wege zur Koordinierung völkerrechtlicher Verträge*, 340–89; Shany, *Competing Jurisdictions of International Courts and Tribunals*; Graber, 'New UNESCO Convention on Cultural Diversity', 553, 571 *et seq.* (proposing to include non-trade experts such as, for example, cultural experts in WTO panels which adjudicate on cases where cultural interests are at stake); Hestermeyer, *Human Rights and the WTO: The Case of Patents and Access to Medicines*, 287–8 (on institutional solutions to conflicts between the TRIPS Agreement and human rights).

159 See suggestions in European Communities, Submission to the Committee on Trade and Environment, dated 22 March 2004, The Relationship between WTO Rules and MEAs in the Context of the Global Governance System, TN/TE/W/39 (24 March 2004). For existing forms of information exchange between UNEP/MEAs and the WTO, see Note by the Secretariat to the Committee on Trade and Environment, TN/T/S/2/Rev. 2 (16 January 2007).

160 Hestermeyer, *Human Rights and the WTO: The Case of Patents and Access to Medicines*, 288; Graber, 'New UNESCO Convention on Cultural Diversity', 553, 571; for such suggestions to enhance the sensitivity for environmental concerns within the WTO, see Perez, *Ecological Sensitivity and Global Legal Pluralism*, 96 *et seq.*

by initiating negotiations in one institutional setting in order to pursue certain aims which they see frustrated in another.[161] Examples for this behaviour abound. One is the initiation of negotiations on the Convention on the Protection and Promotion of the Diversity of Cultural Expression in UNESCO. The initiating states believed that they would be able to pursue their aim of cultural protection more successfully within UNESCO than they had been within the WTO.[162] Another instance of venue shifting occurred in the early 1960s. When developing countries realized that the powerful countries within the GATT, in particular the US, were not willing to allow exceptions to the most-favoured-nation obligation for further trade preferences for developing countries, they shifted their efforts to negotiate a Generalized System of Preferences to the UN, which led to the formation of the United Nations Conference on Trade and Development.[163] Finally, to take up the example of the tension between patent protection demanded by the TRIPS Agreement and access to essential medicines, it is not plausible to argue that the TRIPS Agreement would look any different had the negotiators for the United States and the European Communities been better informed about the state of international human rights law.

In light of the interest conflicts which lead to the fragmentation of international law and with regard to the inadequacy of doctrinal and institutional approaches to address these conflicts, it is important to pay attention to opportunities in international relations for political debates which are not limited by the perspectives, rationales and objectives of one sectoral regime and thus have the potential to bridge fragmentation.[164]

Within the WTO the waiver power has the potential to open the WTO for an inclusive political debate which goes beyond trade objectives and takes into account perspectives from other international institutions. Since the waiver power provides for a law-making procedure this debate need not remain mere talk without any effect on the law of the WTO, but can result in binding law-making. In this respect the waiver may be compared to treaty amendments and authoritative interpretations. However,

---

161 Helfer, 'Regime Shifting', 1; Benvenisti and Downs, 'Empire's New Clothes', 598, 614–19.
162 On the failure of the EC and Canada to introduce a cultural exception doctrine into WTO law, see Graber, 'New UNESCO Convention on Cultural Diversity', 553, 554 et seq.
163 Cf. Hudec, *Developing Countries in the GATT Legal System*, 39 et seq.
164 Supporting the importance of international organizations as 'public realms in which international issues can be debated and, perhaps, decided' is Klabbers, 'Two Concepts of International Organization', 277–93, at 282.

it also differs in important respects. These differences will be addressed in the following sections, before Chapter 7 addresses the question whether the politics of the waiver process may indeed allow for transparent and representative debate on questions transcending regime boundaries.

The next sections discuss, firstly, the waiver as general exception which excepts measures mandated by other international legal regimes from the application of WTO norms. Secondly, I address the waiver as rule-making instrument that may readjust the compromises between competing interests as embodied by the legal norms.

II The waiver as deference to another international legal regime

I have argued that the waiver power may provide an important mechanism to justify measures supported by a strong domestic preference. Similarly, the waiver power may be used to justify measures which are mandated by another international legal regime. In this case the waiver does not constitute deference to a domestic preference, but to a transnational preference as expressed by the other legal regime. It constitutes a way to avoid potential conflict between two regimes by restricting the jurisdiction of one regime in favour of another.

The WTO's waiver power was used in this way to address potential norm conflicts between the trade bans mandated by the Kimberley Process Certification Scheme (KPCS) and norms of the GATT.[165] The Kimberley Waiver suspends Articles I, XI, and XIII GATT and thus ensures conformity with WTO law of trade bans foreseen by the KPCS. The waiver has the effect that in case of a conflict about the conformity with WTO law of trade bans that are adopted to implement the KPCS the WTO's dispute settlement organs will merely inquire whether these trade bans are indeed trade bans mandated by the KPCS. If they are, their conformity with the suspended GATT norms will not be examined. Such a waiver can be interpreted as deference by the WTO to the greater competence and legitimacy of the KPCS in measures to protect human security against threats posed by the trade in conflict diamonds.

The Kimberley Waiver was, however, not only applauded, but also severely criticized as an inadequate solution to clarify the relationship between the norms of the Kimberley Process Certification Scheme and WTO norms. Scholars argued that it constituted a missed opportunity to

---

165 On the KPCS and the Kimberley Waiver see Chapter 4 B.II.3.2.

deal with the interface head on, either by adopting an authoritative interpretation or letting the dispute settlement organs – in case of conflict –
decide questions as to the conformity of measures implementing the
KPCS with WTO law.[166] Pauwelyn expressed the opinion that the adoption of the waiver was a sign of the WTO's 'superiority complex'. This was,
in his view, evidenced by the fact that the WTO not only felt the need to
address potential conflict by way of a waiver (instead of acknowledging
that the KPCS could add to or override WTO law), but that by adopting
a waiver it also gave rise to a presumption of illegality of the trade bans
provided for in the KPCS.[167]

In my view, these critiques misinterpret the waiver decision when they
see it as a verdict by the WTO that the trade bans provided for by the
KPCS with respect to non-participants are not justified under the general
exceptions. Moreover, they ignore the fact that the decision can be read
as an acknowledgement of the greater competence and legitimacy of the
KPCS with respect to issues of human security.

First, it should be noted that a waiver decision need not give rise to a
presumption of illegality of the measures for which it was granted. In the
past several waivers were adopted even though there was no consensus
on the illegality of the measures for which the waivers were requested.[168]
Rather than verdicts of illegality these waivers were a means to ensure
legal security in the light of uncertainty due to divergent views on the
legality of certain measures. In the case of the Kimberley Waiver it was
emphasized by the General Council that it represented no consensus of
the WTO membership that the trade bans mandated by the Kimberley
Process Certification Scheme were not justified under the general exceptions in Art. XX of GATT or the security exception in Art. XXI GATT. The
waiver decision makes this very clear by stating in its preamble: '[n]oting
that this Decision does not prejudge the consistency of domestic measures taken consistent with the Kimberley Process Certification Scheme
with provisions of the WTO Agreement, including any relevant WTO
exceptions, and that the waiver is granted for reasons of legal certainty'.[169]
Thus, due to its clear wording and in light of the GATT and WTO waiver

---

166 For such criticism see Nadakavukaren Schefer, 'Stopping Trade in Conflict Diamonds',
    391, 447 *et seq.* and Pauwelyn, 'WTO Compassion or Superiority Complex?', 1177, 1198
    et seq.
167 Pauwelyn, *ibid.*, 1198 *et seq.*   168 For this practice see Chapter 5 B.III.2.
169 WT/L/518 (27 May 2003), preamble, recital 4; WT/L/676 (19 December 2006), preamble,
    recital 5.

practice, the waiver decision should not be interpreted as implying the illegality of the measures for which it was adopted.

Secondly, the waiver decision can be interpreted as giving expression to the view that panels and the Appellate Body should not – when a dispute arises – inquire into the legality of the measures under WTO law. Thus, the emphasis lies less on the question whether the measures provided for by the KPCS can or cannot be justified under WTO law, but rather on the question of which institution should decide whether the measures are or are not desirable and adequate. A waiver decision has the important advantage that – even though it is a decision by the WTO – it can answer this question in favour of another international institution. As regards the KPCS the General Council by adopting the Kimberley Waiver decided in favour of the Kimberley Process. Thus, in the event of a dispute about the legality of trade bans vis-à-vis non-participants in the KPCS, neither panels nor the Appellate Body will engage in an interpretation of the applicable GATT exceptions and their application to the measures at hand. Instead, they will merely examine whether the measures at issue are covered by the waiver decision, that is whether they are measures 'necessary to prohibit the export of rough diamonds to [and import from] non Participants in the Kimberley Process Certification Scheme *consistent with the Kimberley Scheme*'.[170]

This deference has two advantages: most importantly, the waiver recognizes the specific competence of the Kimberley Process with respect to questions about the adequacy of the measures and procedures on implementation. Moreover, as a further benefit, it maintains the consistency of legal doctrine on the interpretation of Art. XX GATT at a time when a coherent doctrine with respect to the application of Art. XX GATT to internationally mandated trade measures has yet to be developed. I shall clarify these two points by reference to the questions that dispute settlement organs would have to address if asked to determine the legality under WTO law of trade bans vis-à-vis non-participants of the KPCS.

The trade bans would most likely be justified under Art. XX(a) GATT, the public morals exception.[171] To be justified under Art. XX GATT,

---

170 WT/L/518 (27 May 2003), at para. 1; WT/L/676 (19 December 2006), preamble, at para. 1 (emphasis added).

171 Pauwelyn argues that the trade bans would also be justified under the security exceptions in Art. XXI(b) and (c) GATT: see Pauwelyn, 'WTO Compassion or Superiority Complex?', 1177, 1184 *et seq.* I find this interpretation doubtful. The trade bans do not appear necessary to protect the security interests of the member imposing the ban which speaks against a justification under Art. XXI(b). Secondly, neither the KPCS nor UN

measures have to pursue one of the objectives acknowledged in Art. XX GATT, they may not be more trade restrictive than necessary to achieve the desired level of protection, and the application of the measure may not discriminate between WTO members in which the same conditions prevail. There are good reasons why the least-restrictive measure analysis should also inquire whether the perceived risk is addressed in a consistent way.[172] If this is not the case, for example because measures are taken with respect to some products which pose a risk but not with respect to others which pose the same risk, this lack of consistency can call into doubt the claim that the measure is indeed necessary to achieve the desired level of protection.[173]

In light of these requirements the compatibility with WTO law of the trade bans mandated by the KPCS is not beyond doubt. First, the KPCS is inconsistent in the sense that it is limited to trade in rough diamonds and does not extend to processed diamonds. Thus a non-participant is not hindered in exporting processed diamonds which may, like rough diamonds, stem from illegitimate sources. Another inconsistency lies in the fact that the KPCS addresses only cross-border trade but is silent on diamond trade within the participating states. These weaknesses of the system are vehemently criticized by NGOs which are active in the fight against conflict diamonds.[174] A more provocative question would be whether it is not greatly inconsistent to claim that the protection of public morals requires trade bans on rough diamonds, while every day and often knowingly consumers in developed countries through their consumption choices contribute to massive human rights violations. In this context it should be mentioned that – after NGOs had raised awareness of the problem of conflict diamonds – it was the diamond industry which, for fear of profit losses, was the driving force behind the Kimberley Process.[175] These comments should not be misunderstood. While they are not meant

resolutions give rise to a binding obligation to implement such bans which mandates against a justification under Art. XXI(c) GATT. In general sceptical of a justification of the trade bans under GATT exceptions is Gray, 'Conflict Diamonds and the WTO', 451.

172 For an explicit consistency requirement in the WTO Agreements, see Art. 5.5 SPS Agreement.

173 For an in-depth discussion of the Appellate Body's recent interpretation of Art. XX GATT in *Brazil – Measures Affecting Imports of Retreaded Tyres* (DS322) see the contributions of Bown and Trachtman and of Weiler in 8 *World Trade Review* (2009) 85 and 137.

174 On this criticism and with further references see Nadakavukaren Schefer, 'Stopping Trade in Conflict Diamonds', 391, 414–16.

175 On the role of the diamond industry in the Kimberley Process, see Woody, 'Diamonds on the Souls of her Shoes', 335, 342–4.

to call into doubt the desirability of the KPCS to promote human security in Africa, they are rather meant to point at the problem of presenting a coherent argument that the trade bans are necessary to protect public morals in – for instance – the US or the EU.

Secondly, the ban on imports of rough diamonds from non-participants applies to all rough diamonds no matter by whom they were mined and by whom they are being traded, and there is no possibility for non-participants to demonstrate that the diamonds which are exported from their territory are 'clean'. Thus non-participants might argue that they are being discriminated against if their products are subjected to a trade ban even though they are able to demonstrate that they control their diamond trade to make sure that no blood diamonds are being exported. Furthermore, in order to determine whether the application of the trade ban constitutes arbitrary or unjustifiable discrimination it may become necessary for dispute settlement organs to inquire into how non-participant status is determined. In general, states become participants by adopting the Interlaken Declaration. However, participants who do not implement the minimum requirements set out in the KPCS can be considered non-participants, with the consequence that the complete trade ban applies to them. Whether the minimum requirements are met is assessed by the Participation Committee.[176] Thus for dispute settlement organs properly to assess the application of the trade ban it would be necessary to inquire into the practice of the Participation Committee with respect to the determination of non-participant status.

Two insights may be drawn from this rough sketch of the issues raised by the application of Art. XX GATT to a domestic measure which implements a trade ban vis-à-vis non-participants in the KPCS. Firstly, the doctrine on the application of the general exceptions in Art. XX GATT to trade measures as developed for domestic measures raises difficulties with respect to measures that are the outcome of multilateral international negotiations. Due to the difficulties in negotiating multilateral solutions to global problems, such measures will often address only very narrowly defined issues and include many compromises. International legal regimes will often mandate measures which do not meet the standards of consistency and non-discrimination that are legitimately set for measures

---

176 See Chair's Notice, End of Toleration Period in the Kimberley Process, 31 July 2003, available at: www.kimberleyprocess.com/documents/basic_core_documents_en.html (last accessed 11 March 2011).

which are the outcome of a domestic legislative process. As of now, however, no coherent doctrine has been developed on the interpretation and application of Art. XX GATT with respect to measures which were agreed in international negotiations. Secondly, and more importantly, the above was meant to demonstrate that a determination whether the trade bans are justified under Art. XX GATT would require dispute settlement organs to look not only at the measure as implemented by domestic legislation, but also at the institutional law and practice of the KPCS, in particular the determination of participant status.

Against this background the waiver solution appears preferable both to potential dispute settlement on the legality of trade bans and to an authoritative interpretation which determines their legality. The waiver decision maintains the coherence of legal doctrine on the interpretation of Art. XX GATT. It achieves this by a political decision that the trade bans cannot be challenged as illegal. By contrast, an authoritative interpretation purports to lay down an interpretation in a specific case without clarifying how this interpretation can be reconciled with the existing legal doctrine. As compared to judicial interpretation, the waiver solution has the advantage that it limits the WTO's jurisdiction in favour of other international institutions. The Kimberley Waiver acknowledges that the KPCS, as well as the UN with which the KPCS closely cooperates, has greater expertise, and is more representative of and accountable to the affected constituencies as far as the prevention of conflict diamonds remaining the fuel of cruel conflicts is concerned. Due to this greater expertise, representativeness and accountability, these institutions have greater legitimacy to answer questions on the adequacy of measures to prevent trade in conflict diamonds as well as their application and enforcement. In a non-hierarchical and fragmented international legal order such self-restraint of one international institution in favour of other institutions which are more competent, representative, and accountable should be welcomed as enhancing the legitimacy of international governance.[177]

As an exercise of such restraint the Kimberley Waiver can serve as an important precedent and acknowledgement that the WTO may cede its jurisdiction, and not insist on the applicability of its law, in favour of other regimes.[178] The precedential effect of the Kimberley Waiver is particularly

---

177 See Howse and Nicolaïdis, 'Enhancing WTO Legitimacy', 73, 86 *et seq.* (arguing for a corresponding principle of horizontal subsidiarity); cf. also Trachtman, 'Constitutions of the WTO', 623, 634 *et seq.* (speaking of functional subsidiarity).

178 Cf. Aaronson and Zimmermann, *Trade Imbalance: The Struggle for Human Rights Concerns in Trade Policy-Making*, 43, citing the Canadian Trade Minister for the view that

important, if one considers that during negotiations on international instruments that may have an effect on trade negotiators frequently point to the potential inconsistency of the instrument with WTO law in order to 'water down' the content of the negotiated texts.[179] The Kimberley Waiver now provides negotiators with an argument that WTO law can show some flexibility in avoiding potential norm conflict through the adoption of a waiver.

I wish to add a last note on the feasibility of further waivers for measures mandated by another international legal regime. The adoption of further waivers obviously depends on whether consensus can be achieved among the WTO membership. However, consensus will be more easily achieved on a waiver decision than on an authoritative interpretation. Firstly, discussions with respect to an authoritative interpretation will likely extend beyond the specific trade measures at issue. For fear that the interpretation under discussion might have implications also for the application of WTO law to further measures mandated by other international legal regimes, members will be more likely to veto an authoritative interpretation than a waiver decision. Secondly, for members who are of the opinion that the trade measures in question indeed violate WTO law, it will be easier to consent to a waiver decision than to agree to an interpretation which constitutes a positive statement as to the legality of these measures.[180]

III Norm change through waivers

While the Kimberley Waiver is an example of the use of a waiver decision to determine the relationship between WTO law and other international norms, the power to suspend legal rules may also be used to modify legal rules. This can be done, as was seen in Chapter 5, by coupling the suspension with abstractly worded terms and conditions. The waiver power may thus lead to the modification of existing rules. It may not, however,

the adoption of the Kimberley Waiver shows the WTO's flexibility with regard to human security and development.

179 See Pauwelyn, 'WTO Compassion or Superiority Complex?', 1177, 1200 *et seq.*

180 Where the commercial interests of a member are affected that member may be compensated. Similarly, Pascal Lamy in his proposal for an exception in WTO law for collective preferences suggested that such an exception should be coupled with compensation for affected members: Lamy, *Emergence of Collective Preferences in International Trade*, 11 *et seq.* See also the discussion of non-violation complaints with respect to measures justified by a waiver decision in Chapter 5 F.II.3.

be used to impose new and independent obligations on members.[181] The waiver power therefore possesses a particular potential to address claims that legal rules are overly restrictive.

The GATT and WTO waiver power was used in several instances as a rule-making power. As such it addressed claims that the legal rules took insufficient account of the developmental needs of developing and least-developed countries by allowing for trade preferences in deviation of the most-favoured-nation principle.[182] It was also used with the adoption of the TRIPS Waiver to readjust the compromise between the interest in protecting patents for pharmaceutical products on the one hand and the interest in making essential medicines more accessible on the other hand in favour of the latter.[183] These waivers can be – and in the past have been – a first step towards a more permanent norm change by way of treaty amendment.

There are several advantages of a waiver decision as an interim solution before a more permanent treaty amendment is adopted and enters into force. Firstly, the waiver competence enables members to achieve such norm change more quickly than through treaty amendment, since the formal and often time-consuming requirements which exist with respect to the entry into force of an amendment need not be met for a waiver to take effect.[184] Thus, the TRIPS Waiver, with its adoption by the General Council, put in place new rules with immediate effect. The amendment will replace these rules once it enters into force without any interruption of the legal regime established by the waiver.[185]

Secondly, the intermediate waiver solution has the further advantage that the term of a rule-making waiver can serve as a test period during which modifications can be undertaken before a final solution is adopted by an amendment decision. The annual review of waivers which is provided for in Art. IX:4 WTO Agreement provides a forum in which the rules set out in a waiver could be evaluated and modifications discussed.[186]

Finally, a waiver can modify and make new rules for only a part of the WTO membership while leaving intact the existing rules for members

---

181 Chapter 5 D.III.3.   182 Chapter 4 B.II.2.1.   183 Chapter 4 B.II.2.2.
184 Nonetheless domestic legislation may be required so that the rules laid down in a waiver take effect domestically. Moreover, the debates on waivers sometimes take a long time, the TRIPS Waiver being but one example: see Chapter 4 B.II.2.2.
185 According to Art. X:3 WTO Agreement the amendment will take effect upon acceptance by two-thirds of the members for those members only.
186 So far no meaningful political reviews of waiver decisions have taken place in the General Council. On the political review of waivers, see Chapter 5 F.I.

which do not wish to be subjected to the changed rules. It can thus be used to achieve what has been termed 'variable geometry'.[187] In a way the TRIPS Waiver is an expression of such variable geometry by leaving it up to the WTO members whether they wish to make use of the decision or not. Several developed members have indicated that they will not use the decision in order to import pharmaceuticals produced under a compulsory licence in another member.[188] Another example of such variability is provided by the waiver which was granted in 1966 to allow Australia to grant general tariff preferences to products from developing countries and territories.[189] The decision was granted while discussions on a Generalized System of Preferences were still continuing in UNCTAD. The waiver can be seen as a precursor to the general exception to the most-favoured-nation obligation which was enacted in 1971 through the adoption of the waiver decision which legalized the Generalized System of Preferences.[190]

C. CONCLUSION

This chapter attempted to clarify the advantages of a waiver power as compared to other flexibility devices common in international treaty regimes. As individual exceptions waivers have three advantages in particular. Firstly, a waiver power may take account of the uncertainty in relation to the operation of legal rules at the time of their negotiation. It may be used to justify non-compliance where it appears that compliance would be unduly burdensome, for example, in that it negatively affects individual states' development prospects. By contrast, structural problems or a systemic inadequacy of the rules as concerns development should rather be addressed through a general change in the rules, e.g. the introduction of longer transitional periods, than on a case-by-case basis. Secondly, the waiver power may be used to mitigate the tension between international and domestic governance, by granting exceptions

---

187 For the view that the WTO should allow for more variable geometry see Howse, 'For a Citizen's Task Force on the Future of the World Trade Organization', 877, 880; Pauwelyn, 'Transformation of World Trade', 1, 61.

188 WT/L/540 (2 September 2003), footnote 3 to para. 1(b).

189 CONTRACTING PARTIES, Tariff Preferences for Less-Developed Countries, Decision of 28 March 1966, BISD 14S/23.

190 Chapter 4 B.II.2.1(a).

in instances in which strong domestic preferences mitigate against compliance. And thirdly, in a highly legalized regime, such as the WTO, a waiver may – by withdrawing certain measures from the jurisdiction of dispute settlement organs – provide opportunities for more flexible compliance management.

As general exception the waiver may address the challenge of fragmentation. It may reverse the 'factual hierarchy' which otherwise exists between the WTO with its strong dispute settlement system and other international legal regimes. By adopting a waiver the WTO may restrict its own jurisdiction in favour of the jurisdiction of another institution. As a rule-making instrument it is more flexible than the amendment power and allows for some deviation from the single undertaking approach that dominates WTO rules negotiations.

This may all sound very well. I also pointed out throughout this chapter, however, that the waiver process, in particular its representativeness and transparency, is crucial to fully answer the question as to the benefits of a waiver power. The politics of this process will be the subject of the next chapter.

7

The politics of the waiver process

It is the claim of this study that an institutional waiver power may play an important role in flexibilizing international law and to thus address concerns as to its legitimacy and effectiveness. A waiver power may be used to address a number of such concerns. Firstly, through the exercise of a waiver power an international institution may take account of strong domestic policy preferences in individual situations. Secondly, the temporary suspension of obligations may mitigate the economic burden of compliance. Thirdly, international legal regimes can be linked and coordinated through the waiver power. And fourthly, legal norms may be adapted through the waiver process to the collective needs and preferences of the membership.

As was seen in Chapter 4 the waiver power of the GATT 1947 and the WTO Agreement was indeed exercised to take account of these constellations. However, limitations of the waiver practice also became apparent.[1] Even though WTO law's potentially negative effects on development in poor countries constitute one of the major legitimacy deficits of the WTO, the waiver power was exercised rather reluctantly to relieve individual developing country members of their legal obligations. In the WTO capacity problems and claims by individual members that compliance with specific WTO obligations impeded their pursuit of important public policy objectives were only addressed through waivers either where the agreements already provided for differential treatment by way of transitional periods or where members sought relief from special commitments assumed when becoming members of the WTO.[2]

By contrast, waivers are adopted relatively frequently to legalize special preference arrangements beyond developed country members' GSP legislation. As concerns these waivers, it is doubtful whether they can

---

1 See discussion in Chapter 4 C.   2 See Chapter 4 B.I.1.1, B.I.2.1(a), B.I.2.1(b).

be conceptualized as enhancing either the effectiveness or the legitimacy of WTO law. In particular, it is questionable whether the special preference arrangements contribute to economic development in the preference-receiving countries or rather establish further impediments to development.[3]

Finally, the instances in which waivers generally modified WTO rules in order to adapt them to claims of inadequacy or injustice of the legal norms have been few, and only in one case to date has the waiver been used to restrict the WTO's jurisdiction in favour of another international legal regime.[4] Not only has the waiver power seldom been used in this way. The few waiver decisions that did address the widespread discontents as to the potentially negative effects of WTO norms on economic development and non-economic interests and values are being criticized: on the one hand for the long negotiating processes,[5] on the other hand for the inadequacy of their content.[6]

The circumstance that the waiver power has only been put to limited use in relation to the flexibility demands identified in Chapters 2 and 3 may be explained by the differing interests among WTO members and their differing views with respect to the WTO's objectives. This said, it may once again be questioned who exactly we mean, when we speak about *members* and *their* differing interests and views: governments, industry, consumers, citizens? If the waiver power is to contribute to making international governance more responsive, on the one hand, to domestic democratic preferences and, on the other hand, to transnationally shared societal

---

3 Hudec, *Developing Countries in the GATT Legal System*; Dunoff, 'Dysfunction, Diversion, and the Debate over Preferences', 45, 50 *et seq.* (noting that much of the literature on the economic effects of preferences is deeply sceptical about their value to promote development (at 51)); Hoekman and Özden, 'Trade Preferences and Differential Treatment of Developing Countries'.

4 For a discussion of these waivers, in particular the 1999 Preferences Waiver, the 2003 TRIPS Waiver and the 2003 Kimberley Waiver, see Chapter 4 B.II.2.1(a), B.II.2.2, B.II.3.2.

5 Kuijper, 'Sutherland Report and the WTO's Institutional Law', 191, 194 (referring to the 1999 Preferences Waiver and noting 'the callousness with which a crucial waiver for dirt-poor countries can be held hostage for years in the Council for Trade in Goods and at lower levels'); the TRIPS Waiver was only adopted on 30 August 2003, while paragraph 6 of the Doha Declaration on the TRIPS Agreement and Public Health had instructed the TRIPS Council 'to find an expeditious solution to this problem [of the restrictions on compulsory licensing] and to report to the General Council before the end of 2002', see Chapter 4 B.II.2.2.

6 Médecins sans Frontières, for example, hold that the TRIPS Waiver's improvements on access to essential medicines for the poor are negligible. Médecins sans Frontières, *An Unsolved Problem: The August 30th Decision*.

interests, it is crucial that the waiver process is not only representative of the views of WTO members' executive officials or special interests which influence such officials, but of the views of domestic constituencies as well as the diversity of transnational societal interests as represented, inter alia, by other international institutions, as well as non-governmental organizations.

Before I turn to discuss in more detail the potential of the waiver procedure to allow for transparent and representative debate, I shall briefly return to actual WTO practice. Chapter 5 analysed the decision-making process in legal terms. This analysis revealed that one cannot speak of *the* waiver process since waiver processes differ widely from waiver to waiver. Broadly speaking, three types of processes may be distinguished: processes of administration, processes of diplomatic bargaining and processes of transnational political debate. In the following, I support this thesis by reference to examples from the waiver practice.

I then come back to the claim that transparent and representative processes are required to ensure responsiveness to domestic as well as transnational societal needs and preferences. The literature on these themes is vast and proposals range from visions of world government,[7] over more modest federalist models,[8] to claims that the state is the only place where legitimate government is realizable.[9] I do not attempt to engage with these studies and proposals here. My approach is much more modest. Proceeding from the status quo I shall inquire into the potential for transparent and representative debate on waiver requests under the procedures as they exist right now or with slight modifications.[10]

A. THE WAIVER PROCESS: BARGAINING, ADMINISTRATION, DEBATE

WTO treaty and secondary law establish one legal procedure for the examination of waiver requests and the adoption of waiver decisions. In short,

---

7 See e.g. Held, *Democracy and the Global Order*.
8 See e.g. Habermas, 'Hat die Konstitutionalisierung des Völkerrechts noch eine Chance?', 113 *et seq.*; contributions in Nicolaïdis and Howse (eds.), *The Federal Vision*.
9 See e.g. Rabkin, *Case for Sovereignty*.
10 I shall therefore also dodge the question whether there should be a return to majority voting. For a discussion of different scholarly proposals whether or not to adopt a practice of majority voting in the WTO, see Pauwelyn, 'The Transformation of World Trade', 1, 24 *et seq.*

a member that wishes to benefit from a waiver decision needs to submit a reasoned request. This request is examined by the competent council who shall consider the request within ninety days and submit a report to the Ministerial Conference or the General Council, acting on behalf of the Ministerial Conference. The General Council or Ministerial Conference decide by consensus. The waiver decision has to include reasons as well, i.e. it has to state the circumstances justifying the waiver. It shall further specify the terms and conditions governing the application of the waiver.[11]

Even though the law sets out one legal procedure, the processes leading to the adoption of waiver decisions differ widely. While, for instance, some waiver requests are exclusively examined and discussed by trade experts in committees even below the level of the specialized councils, others are highly politicized and eventually decided at the highest political level by the Ministerial Conference.

The waiver processes that can be observed in practice approximate to three types: processes of bargaining, processes of administration and processes of transnational political debate. While most WTO waiver processes fall within the first category, processes leading to the adoption of collective Harmonized System Waivers may be conceptualized as administration, while the process which led to the adoption of the TRIPS Waiver, while not free of elements of bargaining, can be characterized as a transnational political debate. Before I substantiate this thesis by reference to actual WTO waiver processes, I shall briefly explain what I understand by bargaining, administration and transnational politics and how I perceive the role of these law-making *modi* in international governance.

I Three types of international law-making: bargaining, administration and transnational politics

1 Bargaining

One traditional way of international law-making is bargaining. Sovereign states, often represented by diplomats, negotiate to promote their respective 'national interests', interests that are ascribed to the state as a whole, such as national security or economic well-being. Frequently, such negotiations take place in secrecy and detached from domestic public discourse. Hans Morgenthau described this process as follows:

---

11 These procedural requirements are analysed in more detail in Chapter 5.

> It is a common characteristic of negotiations that they are started by each side with maximum demands, which are whittled down in a process of persuasion, bargaining, and pressures until both sides meet on a level below the one from which they started.[12]

The outcome of such bargaining processes is largely impacted by each party's bargaining power, which is often a function of economic or military power.[13] Bargaining in the national interest may be seen as an adequate process for the creation of transactional law which, in the words of Joseph Weiler and Iulia Motoc, 'is premised on an understanding of a world order composed of equally sovereign states pursuing their respective national interest through an enlightened use of law to guarantee bargains struck'.[14]

2 Administration

With increased interdependence and the resulting regulation of transnationally shared societal concerns at the international level, diplomatic bargaining has been complemented by other forms of international law-making. One may make out two trends in particular: on the one hand a turn to administrative processes and, on the other, a trend towards transnational politics.

The regulation of specific societal sectors such as trade or of societal problems such as environmental degradation requires knowledge and raises the need for expertise in order to ensure rationality and effectiveness of such regulation. Consequently, sector-specific experts have become important actors in law-making processes not only on the national and regional, but also on the international and transnational level. Transgovernmental networks emerge which engage in policy-making outside formal international institutions.[15] However, experts also become increasingly important in law-making processes within international organizations.[16] The experts acting in international institutions are

---

12 Morgenthau, *Politics Among Nations*, 519 *et seq.*
13 To be sure, this antagonistic view of inter-national bargaining is exaggerated. As international relations scholars have convincingly shown, bargaining processes may also be influenced by generalized principles of conduct: Ruggie, 'Multilateralism: The Anatomy of an Institution', 3, 11.
14 Weiler and Motoc, 'Taking Democracy Seriously', 47, 63; see also Ruggie, 'Reconstituting the Global Public Domain', 499, 505. On the contractual conception of WTO law, see Chapter 3 B.I.
15 Slaughter, 'Governing the Global Economy Through Government Networks', 177; Slaughter, *A New World Order*.
16 Alvarez, *International Organizations as Law-Makers*, 304 *et seq.*

international civil servants[17] or domestic officials from ministries or specialized government agencies who regularly meet within the political organs of the institution. These government officials no longer represent 'the *national* interest', but rather sectoral interests and expertise. Where they engage in policy-making and regulation to address narrowly defined 'technical questions' such activity may be qualified as administration. Administrative policy-making is frequently being justified on the grounds that it provides rational and efficient solutions to specific problems which are defined in technical terms and require prompt solutions.[18]

3 Transnational politics

As the distributional effects of international law-making processes become apparent, along with the limitations which they impose on self-government,[19] another development occurs: a re-politicization which is driven by domestic constituencies represented by parliaments, as well as non-governmental organizations that promote specific societal interests. These actors increasingly seek to partake in the shaping of policies made at the international level.[20]

The normative claim for international law-making which is more representative of societal diversity and pluralism of preferences rests on the following argumentation: the state as the principal form of political organization has lost some of its regulatory capacity due to the increasing disembeddedness of social processes.[21] Thus, for example, multinational

---

17 Economic Organizations such as the OECD, for example, have chief economists and the UNEP recently decided to appoint a chief scientist.

18 See e.g. Winter, 'Transnational Administrative Comitology'. The technical nature of many of these problems may be doubted in particular when the solutions to these issues have distributional implications. For a critique of the limited effectiveness of transnational regulatory networks, see Verdier, 'Transnational Regulatory Networks and their Limits', 113.

19 On the impact of non-binding instruments which are frequently the outcome of such expert law-making on domestic legislatures and administrations, see Friedrich, 'Nonbinding Instruments' (manuscript on file with the author). See also Tietje, *Internationalisiertes Verwaltungshandeln*; Walter, 'Constitutionalizing (Inter)National Governance', 170.

20 Participation of non-governmental actors in international law-making is not, however, a recent phenomenon. It can be traced back to international conferences of the early twentieth century, see Charnovitz, 'Nongovernmental Organizations and International Law', 348; Charnovitz, 'Emergence of Democratic Participation in Global Governance', 45.

21 See, for example, Kratochwil, 'Politics, Norms, and Peaceful Change', 193; Ruggie, 'Globalization and the Embedded Liberalism Compromise', 79.

corporations may influence, either through labour relocation or book-keeping operations, where value is added or taxes are paid making it increasingly difficult for individual states to adopt policies of redistribution and to provide for social welfare. Another example is provided by the phenomenon of global warning. Due to the disembeddedness of the economy and the transboundary effects of greenhouse gas emissions, states alone cannot adopt effective climate change policies. Therefore increased international cooperation is required so that states can implement social policies domestically or to achieve an effective protection of the global commons. International policy-making that addresses such questions involves, however, important value judgments, for example, concerning the question of the responsibility for harm caused by climate change or what kind of distribution of the world's resources constitutes a fair distribution. Just answers to these questions require political processes and debates in which all affected interests are represented.[22]

States, through their governments, will continue to play an indispensable role in international law-making processes that aim at more representativeness since they constitute the primary form of political organization in which representative policy-making is possible.[23] To remedy the representation deficit caused by the disproportionate influence of the executive (and often of specialized government agencies) in international law-making, domestic parliaments should be more involved and better cooperation should take place between specialized governmental agencies.[24] While parliamentary involvement and interagency cooperation address some of the legitimacy deficits of international law-making for democracies,[25] these remedies do not result in better representation for that part of the world's population which is not represented by any state, either because they live in failed states or under dictatorships.

It should be recognized that international institutions as well as non-governmental organizations, even if they do not represent these persons, may play an important part in informing law-making processes as concerns the distributional effects of policies, in particular for the global poor, and in making policy proposals that take into account perspectives which

22 Fraser, *Scales of Justice*, 12 *et seq.*
23 Sassen, 'Participation of States and Citizens in Global Governance', 5.
24 On the role of existing parliamentary assemblies in international economic governance, see Krajewski, 'Legitimizing Global Economic Governance'.
25 For the view that developing countries' governments frequently represent the interests of a capitalist class and not of the poor, see Chimni, 'Prolegomena to a Class Approach to International Law', 57.

otherwise would not be represented.[26] Such participation of international institutions and NGOs may improve representativeness. There is, however, also the danger that certain imbalances in representation might be increased through their participation. Thus caution is in order: more in relation to claims for direct participation and less as concerns attributing to them a role in offering information and advice and in observing and reporting about the process.[27]

Furthermore, transparency becomes indispensable to ensure that domestic constituencies and parliaments, other international institutions and NGOs, who do not directly participate in formal international law-making procedures, may nonetheless take an active part in the political process through a public debate which critiques and controls formal law-making processes.[28]

Finally, and before turning to the WTO, I wish to add a note on the *modus* of transnational politics. Within a state, where regular elections are held, laws are adopted by majority vote and parties represent different conceptions of societal ordering, politics can be understood as allowing antagonistic battles between competing conceptions of a good life and a just order of society. Some hold that politics indeed needs to be antagonistic to offer citizens real choices and to provide them with opportunities for identification.[29] By contrast, at the international level representative transnational politics are usually conceptualized as aiming at processes of deliberation and persuasion in which the better arguments prevail and consensus may be found.[30] This model is offered as a remedy to the legitimacy deficit of international governance. By contrast, the antagonistic model in which consensus is not desirable and in which

---

26 Dunoff, 'Public Participation in the Trade Regime', 961, 970; generally on the role of NGOs in improving the legitimacy of international governance: Charnovitz, 'Nongovernmental Organizations and International Law', 348; Esty, 'Non-Governmental Organizations at the World Trade Organization', 123; Perez, *Ecological Sensitivity and Global Legal Pluralism*, 100 *et seq.*; Bast, 'Das Demokratiedefizit fragmentierter Internationalisierung', 185 (on the additional need for multiperspectivity in light of sectoral fragmentation); Lindblom, *Non-Governmental Organisations in International Law* (for a study of NGO participation in international governance based on a Habermasian understanding of deliberative politics); Bernstorff, 'Zivilgesellschaftliche Partizipation in Internationalen Organisationen', 277 (making the argument that NGOs may play an important role in connecting international law-making processes with domestic public discourses).

27 On different forms of NGO participation in international institutions, see Rebasti, 'Beyond Consultative Status', 21.

28 Peters, 'Transparency, Secrecy, and Security', 183, 187.   29 Mouffe, *On the Political*.

30 See e.g. Risse, '"Let's Argue!": Communicative Action in World Politics', 1; Niesen and Herborth (eds.), *Anarchie der kommunikativen Freiheit*.

political confrontations are decided by vote cannot (yet) be transposed to the international level. This is, inter alia, the case because this model's claim to legitimacy depends on the existence of political institutions such as political parties and periodic elections.

II Waiver processes in the WTO

In the WTO the predominant mode of political law-making is bargaining. Government representatives are the primary actors; the participation of NGOs and other international institutions is largely seen as unnecessary or undesirable.[31] A statement on the WTO's official website is telling in this respect:

> If the claim that 'governments do not represent the interests of citizens' were true, then it is something that citizens need to correct at home. It is not something that an inter-governmental body like WTO can deal with.[32]

However, even though bargaining is the prevailing mode, administration takes place as well, and one may even detect a trend towards more representative forms of political debate on the reconciliation of competing transnational societal, as opposed to national, interests.

1 Special preferences waivers: bargaining for consensus

The processes that led to the adoption of waiver decisions to legalize special preference arrangements of the EC and the United States provide good examples of bargaining processes on waiver requests.[33]

The United States and the EC justified their requests for waivers to legalize special preferences for products from certain developing countries on the grounds that special preferences – in addition to the preferences granted under the requesting members' Generalized System of Preferences legislation – were needed to further the economic development of the preference-receiving states. In addition, waiver requests are sometimes supported by other policy objectives such as peace and stability in the region or the prevention of illicit drug trafficking and consumption. All of these objectives are recognized as legitimate policy objectives, either

---

31 On the rather limited possibilities that exist for NGO participation, see Bonzon, 'Institutionalizing Public Participation in WTO Decision Making', 751; Ripinsky and van den Bossche, *NGO Involvement in International Organizations*, 189 *et seq.*
32 WTO, *WTO Policy Issues for Parliamentarians*.
33 On these waiver decisions, see Chapter 4 B.I.3.3(b).

by the WTO itself, as in the case of economic development, or other international regimes, an example being the objective to reduce illicit drug production and trafficking.[34]

These justifications by the EC and the United States of their waiver requests are, however, hardly a subject of discussion during the examination process. The publicly available minutes do not give evidence of an in-depth examination of whether the proposed measures, i.e. the trade preferences, are indeed likely to contribute to the alleged objectives.[35] Instead, the examination process is characterized by attempts of individual states or groups of states to safeguard their commercial interests. The success of these attempts largely depends on the respective members' bargaining power. Bargaining takes place outside formal meetings and is marked by lack of transparency in the outcome of bilateral consultations.[36]

To illustrate this finding by way of example: special preferences potentially affect the commercial interests of other members that export products which are in a competitive relationship with the products that benefit from the preferences. Usually the export interests of other developing countries are affected most by special preferences. Thailand and the Philippines feared, for example, that the EC preferences for ACP states under the Cotonou Agreement would negatively impact their own exports of canned tuna to the EC market.[37] The EC preferences for bananas from ACP states are resented by Latin American banana exporters to the EC. The case of preferences for bananas furthermore demonstrates that opposition to preferences may not only be triggered by local producers in export-competing developing countries, but also by large multinational corporations. Among the main exporters of Latin American bananas to the EC market that compete with ACP banana exporters are US corporations such as Chiquita or Dole. These corporations' export

---

34 On the justifications given by the EC and the US for their requests, see Chapter 4 B.I.3.3(b).

35 For an exceptionally detailed statement concerning the undesirability of special preferences as concerns economic development, see Council for Trade in Goods, Minutes of the Meeting on 18 April 2001, G/C/M/48 (6 June 2001), 6 *et seq.* (statement by the Representative of Paraguay).

36 The character of these negotiation processes was pointedly formulated by the representative of Kenya commenting on the process leading to the adoption of the Cotonou and Bananas Waiver: 'the process had been characterized by intense negotiations in a spirit of give and take' (Ministerial Conference, Summary Record of the Ninth Meeting on 14 November 2001, WT/MIN(01)/SR/9 (10 January 2001), 3).

37 Council for Trade in Goods, Minutes of the Meeting of 14 November 2001, G/C/M/57 (6 December 2001), para. 3 (statement of the representative of the European Communities).

interests were represented by the United States who also was a claimant in the *EC – Bananas III* dispute and at first was strongly opposed to the adoption of a waiver that would legalize preferences for ACP bananas.[38] Paraguay is neither a beneficiary of the EC's ACP preferences, nor of preferences granted under the United States special preferences legislation and consequently was opposed to the EC's request in relation to the Cotonou Agreement, as well as to the United States' requests concerning the CBERA, ATPA and AGOA Waivers.[39]

The reasons for members' opposition to special preferences waivers are hardly discussed openly in formal meetings of the Council for Trade in Goods where the requests are examined. This might be explained by the thesis that for objections to have argumentative weight they need to be generalizable and thus formulated as matters of principle or in terms of public interest.[40] Such arguments are, however, either not available to the opposing members or would be detrimental to their own interests. When it was still a new practice to request waivers for special preference arrangements opposition to special preferences could be formulated as a matter of principle. Thus, with request to the first waiver requests for special preferences the argument was made that such waivers would undermine the fundamental most-favoured-nation principle. Today, however, in light of the extensive practice of granting waivers of Art. I GATT for special trade preferences, this argument no longer bears any weight.[41] Moreover, most members will not have an interest in a principled assessment of the economic advantages and disadvantages of the special preference scheme in question since they either grant special preferences themselves or benefit from special preferences under another arrangement whose desirability in terms of economic policy could also be called into doubt.

Instead of debating whether the preference schemes further the WTO's objective of economic development, members who believe that their

---

38 For a discussion whether in light of the rather attenuated effect of these preferences on the trade interests of the United States the US nonetheless had a right to bring a legal claim that these preferences violated WTO law, see Appellate Body Report, *EC – Bananas III*, WT/DS27/AB/R, adopted 25 September 1997, 60 *et seq.*

39 See Council for Trade in Goods, Minutes of the Meeting of 14 November 2001, G/C/M/57 (6 December 2001), para. 3 (statement of the representative of the European Communities). On the US waiver requests for preferences under CBERA, AGOA and ATPA see Chapter 4 B.I.3.3(b).

40 Oeter, 'Chancen und Defizite internationaler Verrechtlichung', 46, 51.

41 Sutherland *et al., The Future of the WTO,* 19 *et seq.* (noting the erosion of the most-favoured-nation principle, inter alia through trade preferences).

industries' interests might be negatively affected attempt to bargain with the preference-granting member and to exchange their veto for certain other benefits. In such bargaining processes substantively unrelated issues are frequently linked by members in order to enhance their bargaining power.

Thus, the Latin American members who opposed the preferences for ACP bananas linked the resolution of the bananas dispute to the broader issue of tariff preferences under the Cotonou Agreement. They insisted that the request for a waiver of Art. I GATT for tariff preferences under the Cotonou Agreement could not be examined independently from the question how to treat the new EC banana import regime.[42] They then blocked any substantive examination of both the Cotonou Waiver request and the separate waiver request concerning the EC's import regime for bananas, on the ground that information on the banana regime was not complete. They did so even though the issue of the new import regime for bananas could have easily been separated from the question of a waiver for the Cotonou tariff preferences (for which all necessary information was provided).[43] As a response to this obstruction of the examination process, the ACP countries themselves reverted to issue linkage. They threatened not to proceed with the multilateral trade negotiations at the upcoming Doha Ministerial, should the Latin American members continue to block the examination of the waiver request.[44]

These waiver processes further indicate the relevance of differences in economic power. As a result of the US-backed opposition to the Bananas Waiver, the EC gave in to several demands of the opponents of preferences for ACP bananas. Thus it agreed to a time frame by which it would convert its banana import regime to a tariff only regime which would maintain overall market access for MFN banana exporters. This promise was coupled with an arbitration procedure to determine whether this promise was indeed kept.[45] By contrast, Thailand and the Philippines eventually gave up their opposition to the Cotonou Waiver for the mere assurance by the EC that it would enter into full consultations. These consultations were to be conducted on the question of the extent to which the legitimate interests of the Philippines and Thailand were being

---

42 Council for Trade in Goods, Minutes of the Meeting of 7 July and 16 October 2002, G/C/M/44 (30 October 2000), 18 (statement of the chairman).

43 *Ibid.*

44 ICTSD, EC-ACP Cotonou Waiver Finally Granted, *Bridges Weekly* Vol. 5, No. 39 (15 November 2001).

45 See Chapter 4 B.I.3.3(b).

unduly impaired as a result of the implementation of the preferential tariff treatment of canned tuna originating in ACP states.[46]

The special preferences waivers are not the only waivers that are the outcome of bargaining processes. Thus it is alleged that members made their consent to waivers extending the transition period under the TRIMs Agreement dependent on the granting of tariff concessions by the beneficiaries.[47] In general, developing country members have complained that their waiver requests were subject to a lot of 'horse-trading'.[48]

2 Harmonized System waivers: administration in the WTO

By contrast, the process of the transposition of HS changes into members' goods schedules can be conceptualized as a rare instance of administration within the WTO. As was discussed in Chapter 4 the collective HS waivers form an important part of this process.[49]

The process almost exclusively takes place within a lower organ of trade experts, namely the Committee on Market Access and the WTO Secretariat and chairpersons play a substantial role. The characteristics of this process which mainly aims at effectiveness can be explained by the relative harmony of members' interests as well as the largely technical nature of the transposition exercise.

The questions as to which products shall fall under which subject heading of the Harmonized System nomenclature may implicate important economic and other interests and may thus be contentious. These issues are, however, addressed in the World Customs Organization. Once changes to the Harmonized System are adopted, their implementation then is indeed a rather technical matter. As concerns the adaptation of goods schedules to these changes, WTO members' interests coincide. It is in the membership's interest that schedules conform to the Harmonized

---

46 Council for Trade in Goods, Minutes of the Meeting of 14 November 2001, G/C/M/57 (6 December 2001), para. 3 (statement of the representative of the European Communities). In the aftermath of the adoption of the waiver decisions these consultations led to mediation with the result that the 24 per cent EC tariff on canned tuna was reduced to 12 per cent. Nilaratna Xuto, Thailand: Conciliating a Dispute on Tuna Exports to the EC, www.wto.org/english/res_e/booksp_e/casestudies_e/case40_e.htm.
47 Sterlini, 'Agreement on Trade-Related Investment Measures', 437, 456.
48 See TRIPS Council, Minutes of the Meeting on 17–19 September 2002, IP/C/M/37 (11 October 2002), para. 79 (statement of the representative of the Philippines).
49 Chapter 4 B.II.3.1.

System.[50] Members' interests can collide, if the adaptation of schedules affects the value of concessions. On the question of which concessions will be affected by the transposition of HS changes members are, however, in the same position of uncertainty. Thus, there is again a common and shared interest to devise and implement procedures in a manner that all members are able to detect when their economic interests are affected. Once safeguards are instituted that enable members to distinguish between schedule adaptation which affects their economic interests and schedule adaptation which does not, and thus between mere technical changes and others, there is little reluctance to entrust the organization, i.e. the Secretariat, with wide-ranging tasks with respect to the technicalities of schedule adaptation. By contrast, instances in which the economic value of concessions is indeed affected through the adaptation exercise are addressed outside multilateral structures in bilateral negotiations between members.[51]

The role of collective HS waivers in the process of schedules adaptation is to ensure legality in instances in which members are not able to comply at the same time with their obligations under the HS Convention to implement HS changes domestically and with their obligation under Art. II GATT to extend the agreed upon concessions to other members. Since the main objective of these waivers is less the reconciliation of competing interests, but instead the effectiveness of the transposition exercise, the process mainly takes place within the body of customs experts, namely the Committee on Market Access. Even though the HS waivers are adopted by the General Council this adoption is a mere formality. Draft waiver decisions are exclusively discussed in formal and informal meetings of the Committee on Market Access.[52]

---

50 On the relevance of the Harmonized System in WTO law, see Feichtner, 'Administration of the Vocabulary of International Trade', 1481, 1486 *et seq.*

51 It should be noted, however, that the capacity of developing members to benefit from these safeguards is much more limited than that of developed countries since they will often not have the resources available to review all documentation and attend all informal meetings. I have described elsewhere in detail the WTO procedures on adaptation of goods schedules to HS changes as well as the WTO's practice in this respect, see *ibid.*, 1481.

52 For the agreement in the Committee on Market Access to forward the draft of the collective waiver for introduction of HS2007 changes to schedules of tariff concessions to the Council for Trade in Goods, see Committee on Market Access, Minutes of the Meeting of 16 October 2006, G/MA/M/42/Add. 1 (14 November 2006), para. 5. For the agreement in the Council for Trade in Goods to refer this waiver to the General Council for adoption, see Council for Trade in Goods, Minutes of the Meeting of 20 November 2006, G/C/M/86 (3 January 2007), para. 3.9. For the adoption of the HS2007 Waiver by the General Council, see General Council, Minutes of the Meeting of 14–16 December

The chairpersons and Secretariat initiate and coordinate this process and give substantive input. Thus, after the WCO Council had adopted the amendments to the Harmonized System that were to enter into force on 1 January 2007, the chairman of the Committee on Market Access called upon the committee to start considering the adaptation process. This process should preferably have been concluded before 1 January 2007 in order to avoid the need for waivers. The chairman thus proposed that the transposition exercise for developing countries be conducted by the Secretariat as for the HS2002 changes and asked the Secretariat to come up with proposals for this process.[53] When it became clear that schedules would not be adapted by 1 January 2007 the chairman noted that the Committee needed to consider a waiver. He proposed to use the collective HS2002 Waiver decision as a basis and to request the Secretariat to prepare a first draft.[54] The draft waiver decision which the Secretariat consequently prepared with assistance of its Legal Division was accepted by the Committee members without substantive modifications.[55]

The described characteristics of the HS waiver processes which allow for their conceptualization as administration, in particular the technicality of the questions involved, the routine which is established through the periodic repetition of schedules adaptation and the high degree of expertise involved (by Secretariat, chairman and specialized government officials), are exceptional and not shared by any other waiver processes in the WTO. The non-political nature of the HS waiver processes is in particularly stark contrast to the highly politicized TRIPS Waiver process.

3 The TRIPS Waiver: political debate on norm change

The process leading to the adoption of the TRIPS Waiver approximates to what was termed above transnational politics in that it was relatively representative as concerns the range of affected socio-economic interests

2006, WT/GC/M/106 (1 March 2007), para. 145 (since two additional members had asked to be included in the Annex the General Council adopted the draft decision with this addition, para. 144).

53 Committee on Market Access, Minutes of the Meeting of 30 March 2005, G/MA/M/39 (13 May 2005), para. 4.43 (statement of the chairman).

54 Committee on Market Access, Minutes of the Meeting of 4 April 2006, G/MA/M/41 (15 May 2006), para. 3.12 (statement of the chairman).

55 The draft prepared by the Secretariat is included in document G/MA/W/82 (21 September 2006) and the draft submitted to the General Council for adoption in G/C/W/566/Rev.1 (23 November 2006).

as well as the actors involved who included other international institutions and non-governmental organizations.

The process had been prompted by the concern that the TRIPS Agreement unduly impeded access to affordable medicines.[56] While this is mainly a concern of developing countries it is not limited to developing countries. Populations in developed countries may also be confronted with health crises, such as bird or swine flu, which require the import of medicines produced under compulsory licences. Underlying the issue of access to affordable medicines is the broader question as to the desirable extent of intellectual property protection given the competing public interests, on the one hand, to spur research and development through the protection of intellectual property and, on the other hand, to make publicly accessible the benefits from intellectual achievements.[57]

The great public attention with respect to the likely effect that the TRIPS Agreement would have on the costs and consequently accessibility of essential drugs for the global poor influenced discussions within the WTO. It contributed to the fact that the question how access to affordable medicines should be reconciled with protection of pharmaceutical patents to spur further research and development was openly addressed within the WTO.[58]

Not only in debates outside the WTO but also within the WTO, the issue was framed as a conflict between competing public interests: the interest in spurring research and development through the protection of patents and the interest in public health.[59] This conflict was addressed in a relatively open and transparent exchange of arguments which centred on the contentious substantive issues such as the scope of diseases, the eligible members and the mode of implementation of paragraph 6 of the Doha Declaration on the TRIPS Agreement and Public Health.[60]

The discussions were informed by the direct and indirect participation of other international institutions and non-governmental organizations

---

56 See Chapter 4 B.II.2.2.

57 Shaffer, 'Recognizing Public Goods in WTO Dispute Settlement', 459.

58 On the process which eventually led to the adoption of the TRIPS Waiver, see Matthews, 'WTO Decision on Implementation of Paragraph 6 of the Doha Declaration', 73; Sell, 'Quest for Global Governance in Intellectual Property and Public Health', 363; Abbott, 'WTO Medicines Decision', 317; Drezner, *All Politics Is Global*, 176 *et seq.*

59 See e.g. Ministerial Conference, Doha Declaration on the TRIPS Agreement and Public Health, adopted on 14 November 2001, WT/MIN(01)/DEC/2 (20 November 2001).

60 On the content of the Doha Declaration on the TRIPS Agreement and Public Health, see Chapter 4 B.II.2.2.

who introduced multiple perspectives on the various issues under discussion. For example, in formal meetings of the TRIPS Council one member's delegation referred to an expert opinion from an NGO.[61] One of the observing international organizations, the World Health Organization, even introduced a very specific proposal regarding the most suitable mechanism to implement paragraph 6,[62] and UNAIDS provided information on the impact of AIDS on African countries.[63] Transparency of the discourse allowed public opinion to scrutinize the arguments put forward. Thus the US position on the scope of diseases which prevented a consensus on the Motta Draft in December 2002 could be exposed as untenable on public policy grounds and mainly motivated by the protection of special interests of the pharmaceutical industry. After the veto of the draft waiver decision of chairman Motta by the US delegation this position was very outspokenly scandalized by a statement of the observer of the Holy See who reported that 'Pope John Paul II, in his message on the theme of peace, had stressed that the promises made to the poor must be respected and the implementation of those promises was a moral problem'.[64]

These observations show that in waiver processes that concern the proper reconciliation of competing public interests debate may be possible which takes into account not only economic, but also a variety of other transnational societal interests, and which is informed and scrutinized by government representatives, as well as by other international institutions and international civil society.[65]

---

61 See statement by the Norwegian Representative in the meeting of the TRIPS Council held on 5–7 March 2002, who drew attention to a report on para. 6 written by Professor Frederick Abbott for the Quaker United Nations Office in Geneva and which had been distributed to the delegates, IP/C/M/35 (22 March 2002), para. 125.

62 See statement of the representative of the WHO in the meeting of the TRIPS Council held on 17–19 September 2002, which endorsed the provision of a limited exception under Art. 30 TRIPS Agreement as the solution most consistent with a basic public health principle, IP/C/M/37 (11 October 2002), para. 5.

63 See statement of the representative of UNAIDS in the meeting of the TRIPS Council, held on 25–27 June 2002, IP/C/M/36 (18 July 2002), paras. 124 *et seq.*

64 TRIPS Council, Minutes of the meeting on 25–27, 29 November 2002 and 20 December 2002, IP/C/M/38 (5 February 2003), para. 47.

65 Robert Howse observed that the TRIPS debate was evidence of a greater openness of the WTO: Howse, 'From Politics to Technocracy – and Back Again', 94, 117. The fact that other international institutions and NGOs played a significant role in the process, does not, however, necessitate the conclusion that their influence was decisive for the adoption of the waiver decision: see Drezner, *All Politics Is Global*, 176 *et seq.*; for a more positive account of civil society influence on the TRIPS Waiver, see Sell, 'Quest for Global Governance in Intellectual Property and Public Health', 363.

B. THE POTENTIAL OF THE WAIVER PROCESS IN INCREASING THE LEGITIMACY AND EFFECTIVENESS OF WTO LAW

The TRIPS Waiver process so far has been an exception as concerns the extent of involvement of other international institutions in the process, the input given by NGOs, as well as the public debate which accompanied discussions within the WTO. Similarly, as was noted and explained above, the processes that led to the adoption of Harmonized System waivers are not the rule. Most waiver requests do not concern technical matters, best examined by trade experts, but do indeed require political decisions.

To date, these decisions are mostly prepared in informal meetings and influenced mainly by considerations as to what each member might gain or lose if a waiver decision were adopted. Whose interests matter in determining what counts as a loss and what counts as a benefit depend on which actors have the greatest influence on the governmental department that decides whether to veto a waiver or whether to give its consent. Often, organized export interests will have a disproportionately large influence in the process as compared with other societal interests.

Nonetheless, in my view, several characteristics of the waiver procedure, as it stands today, bear a particular potential to structure the political process in a way that is more responsive to the flexibility needs identified in this study. These characteristics – which I shall discuss below – are of particular significance in relation to the following functions of the waiver power that I hold to be its most important functions: firstly, its function to take account of individual members' needs and preferences, in particular if they concern development or poverty alleviation or measures that are backed by strong public support; secondly, its function to restrict the WTO's jurisdiction with respect to certain measures in favour of another international institution that mandates these measures; and thirdly, its function to modify the law to take account of claims as to the general injustice of certain norms in particular due to their effects on developing countries.

I The right to request a waiver

Art. IX:3 WTO Agreement affords each WTO member the right to submit a waiver request. This procedural right enables WTO members, developed and developing members alike, to put a matter on the agenda of the competent council or committee as long as it is phrased as a request for the suspension of an obligation and indicates the reasons why a waiver is requested. The ability to place an issue on the agenda by making use of a procedural right that is specifically provided for in the WTO Agreement is of particular importance to developing country members. These members might otherwise have difficulties in making their concerns heard and in having them discussed in formal meetings.[66]

II Timely consideration of waiver requests

Since Art. IX:3 (b) WTO Agreement sets out a time frame for the consideration of waiver requests which is not to exceed ninety days, it may ensure that discussion of the request is not unduly delayed.[67] The rules of procedure of the specialized councils for the Multilateral Trade Agreements provide that matters on which no consensus is reached shall be transferred to the General Council.[68] This procedural rule serves as a safeguard that a matter remains on the agenda. If no consensus is achieved in the competent council that initially deals with the waiver request, the issue is transferred to the General Council. Referral from the specialized body of trade experts to the General Council helps the request to gain visibility and further politicizes the matter.

III Separation and specification of issues

Of particular importance concerning requests for collective waivers is the fact that the waiver process allows for a deviation from the single undertaking principle which generally guides law-making in multilateral trade negotiation rounds. According to this principle negotiations are to result in a package deal to be adopted as a whole. This means that members who might benefit from some agreements, but not from others, will not have the choice to merely accept those agreements that they hold to be

---

66 On the difficulties of weak states in convening negotiations on treaty amendments see Benvenisti and Downs, 'Empire's New Clothes', 598, 612.

67 This requirement in practice does not always lead to a timely consideration. Thus the consideration of the EC's request for a waiver for trade preferences granted under the Cotonou Agreement was substantially delayed, since members opposing the waiver argued that the request did not meet the procedural requirements: see Statement of the Chairman in the Meeting of the Council for Trade in Goods on 7 July and 16 October 2000, G/C/M/44 (30 October 2000), 18.

68 See General Council, Rules of Procedure for Meetings of the Council for Trade in Goods, adopted on 31 July 1995, WT/L/79 (7 August 1995), Rule 33.

beneficial.[69] By contrast, the waiver procedure allows for a separation of certain issues from the 'package' negotiated at the multilateral rounds.

The request of a waiver to suspend a specific obligation either completely or with respect to certain measures can serve to concretize an issue and to separate it from general rules negotiations. This separation and concretization have the advantage that the debate becomes more focused and potentially more transparent. The focus on one specific issue will enable developing countries to concentrate their resources on the issue at hand – something which, due to their limited means, is difficult during the multilateral negotiation rounds in which many issues are discussed in parallel.

Furthermore, the specification of an issue in a waiver request makes it easier for external actors to inform, scrutinize and potentially scandalize the process. The isolation of issues from multilateral trade negotiations will enable the concentration of the discourse on specific questions, and thus facilitate scrutiny. For example, if members' representatives are asked to explain how their opposition to a waiver request is reconcilable with their commitments under other international legal regimes, they will have to address this question in concrete terms.

This point is supported by the debates on the implementation of paragraph 6 of the Doha Declaration on the TRIPS Agreement and Public Health. As was mentioned above, the tension between the protection of intellectual property rights and the human right to health may be presented as a conflict between two public interests: the interest to spur research and development and the interest in public health.[70] There are, however, instances in which the argument that patent protection is indispensable to spurring research is not much more than a cover for the pharmaceutical industry's interest in profit maximization. To give an example: the first research on AIDS medication, for which pharmaceutical companies later obtained patent rights, was conducted by public institutions and mainly publicly funded, and not spurred by the prospect of patent protection.[71]

---

69 For criticism of the single undertaking principle, see Howse, 'For a Citizen's Task Force on the Future of the World Trade Organization', 877, 880; see also Sutherland *et al.*, *The Future of the WTO*, 61 *et seq.*

70 See e.g. Doha Declaration on the TRIPS Agreement and Public Health, adopted on 14 November 2001, WT/MIN(01)/DEC/1 (20 November 2001), para. 3.

71 See Hestermeyer, *Human Rights and the WTO: The Case of Patents and Access to Medicines*, 2 *et seq.*

The presentation of special interests of a small and powerful constituency such as the pharmaceutical industry as public interests becomes
more difficult the more specifically the debate is framed. Thus, while
it may be hard to deny a causal link between patent protection and
research and development in general, there are good reasons why loosen-
ing this protection in certain areas is possible without impeding necessary
research, for example where such research is mainly publicly funded. The
concentration of the debate in the TRIPS Council on the specific question
of patent protection for essential medicines arguably forced participants
to focus their arguments on these reasons and made it more difficult
for them to revert to generalizations on the link between patent protection and innovation. While it cannot be ignored that the outcome of the
negotiations on the implementation of paragraph 6 was also to a large
extent influenced by special interests of the pharmaceutical industry,[72]
this influence was arguably weaker than in the negotiation of the TRIPS
Agreement during the Uruguay Round.[73]

IV Openness of the process to non-legal and non-economic arguments

Another feature of the waiver process which is of particular relevance for
rule-making waivers that address claims of injustice and collective waivers
that pay deference to another international legal regime is its openness to a
wide range of different arguments. It is a necessary – albeit not sufficient –
condition for an inclusive and representative debate on the reconciliation
of competing interests that non-legal as well as non-economic arguments
are admitted and may carry weight in the process. When the debate
centres on the question whether WTO norms are to be suspended –
either to legalize measures mandated by another international regime or
for abstractly defined measures – the scope of admissible arguments is not
limited to arguments on the question as to what extent a certain decision
would further WTO objectives, or to legal arguments as to how a certain
norm of WTO law should be interpreted. By contrast, in discussions
on treaty amendments or the adoption of authoritative interpretations
arguments will be more successful if phrased as legal arguments – in the

---

72 Fleck, 'No Deal in Sight on Cheap Drugs for Poor Countries', 307.
73 On the role of the pharmaceutical industry during the Uruguay Round, see Sell, 'Industry
Strategies for Intellectual Property and Trade', 79.

event of a debate on interpretation – or remain within the (purportedly economic) rationality of the WTO.

It is true that the objectives of the WTO are not fixed and that they should already now be interpreted as including manifold public interests. Nonetheless, it is probable that during an amendment process delegates will attempt to disqualify arguments on the basis that they do not fall within the proper competence of the WTO. This was, for example, the case in the debate on the inclusion of labour rights protection within the WTO.[74]

The range of admissible arguments is even more restricted in debates on the adoption of an authoritative interpretation according to Art. IX:2 WTO Agreement. In an exercise of interpretation successful arguments will have to present the favoured outcome as a possible legal interpretation. This is underlined by Art. IX:2 cl. 3 of the WTO Agreement which states: '[t]his paragraph shall not be used in a manner that would undermine the amendment provisions in Article X'. Thus, in a debate on an authoritative interpretation delegates will try to justify their position by referring to the wording of the provision being interpreted as well as to the provision's and the Agreement's overall object and purpose. Thus, despite the observation that the boundaries of possible interpretations are wide,[75] the mere fact that arguments have to be formally phrased as legal arguments as to the proper interpretation of a particular provision of WTO law weakens non-legal arguments which refer, for example, to the desirability of trade measures mandated by another legal regime from a human rights or environmental perspective.

Since debates on amendments as well as on authoritative interpretations are conducted merely from a WTO perspective, it will be difficult to introduce into this debate perspectives and rationalities from other institutions without runnung the risk that they will be disqualified as falling outside the logic of the amendment or interpretation process. By contrast, during a debate on the question whether WTO norms should be temporarily suspended – either in favour of norms from another

---

74 The view that labour standards do not fall within the objectives of the WTO is expressed in para. 4 of the Singapore Ministerial Declaration, adopted on 13 December 1996 (WT/MIN(96)/DEC (18 December 1996)) which reads in part: '[t]he International Labour Organization (ILO) is the competent body to set and deal with these standards, and we affirm our support for its work in promoting them'.

75 For the proposition that interpretations adopted under Art. IX:2 WTO Agreement may modify legal rules, see Ehlermann and Ehring, 'Authoritative Interpretation under Article IX:2', 803, 808 et seq.

legal regime or for abstractly described measures – arguments can be presented which both go beyond legal argumentation and are unrelated to trade interests. Ethical and non-economic arguments are admitted, as well as arguments referring to the greater competence or legitimacy of another international legal regime with regard to the issue in question. This is particularly true for debates on the possible coordination of WTO law with other international legal norms by way of exception. Since such a waiver decision restricts the reach of WTO law in favour of another international legal regime it would be difficult to exclude arguments which refer to the other regime's objectives and rationality.

To make sure that the whole breadth of perspectives and arguments on the proper solution to a conflict is represented, the (potential) openness of the waiver process with respect to the admissible arguments should be matched by the openness of the process for actors representing different public interests and constituencies. As was already noted, other international institutions should be represented as observers (and commentators), and delegates should coordinate with all affected government departments or even be accompanied to the meetings at the WTO by officials from non-trade departments.

In order to enable other actors who are not admitted to the waiver procedure as participants or observers nonetheless to play a part in the decision-making process, the latter should be more transparent and conducted in formal meetings. If transparency is ensured, civil society actors can play an important role in informing, scrutinizing, and critiquing the waiver process.[76]

V The requirements of a reasoned request and a reasoned decision

Finally, the reason-giving requirements which are a part of the waiver procedure as set out in WTO law may have a particular significance as regards individual waiver requests. In Chapter 6 I identified two functions of special relevance to ensure the responsiveness of the law to individual needs and preferences. Firstly, I argued that the waiver power may be used to suspend norms if it should turn out that compliance will be detrimental to development or impede poverty alleviation.[77] Secondly, I presented the waiver as an instrument to allow members to temporarily maintain

---

76 On the role of NGOs in providing non-politicized information to the WTO, see Perez, *Ecological Sensitivity and Global Legal Pluralism*, 100.

77 Chapter 6 A.III.4.1(a).

measures inconsistent with the agreements if they are based on a strong democratic preference.[78] Regarding the waiver process I also indicated, however, that a number of questions need to be raised: does the political nature of the process allow for a determination whether compliance is detrimental to economic development? If such a determination is made, how is it ensured that a waiver is not vetoed for reasons unrelated to the requesting member's economic situation? Can the waiver process ensure that a measure, arguably backed by strong domestic support, is not in fact the outcome of effective lobbying of special interests? And, finally, I noted a potential equality problem: waivers may be granted to some members, but not to others even though the requests are comparable.

To be sure, the waiver process is deficient in that it cannot clear these doubts.[79] Nonetheless, the reason-giving requirements mitigate them to a certain extent. They could do so even more if the WTO returned to the working party procedure as was common practice under the GATT 1947.[80]

A waiver request needs to state the reasons why the waiver is being requested, i.e. the policy objectives that are pursued and the reasons why this cannot be done in a manner consistent with the law.[81] In case a waiver request concerns measures based on development policy or particular poverty alleviation programmes, the requesting member could include in its request the opinions of economic experts, either from its own government, from NGOs or other international institutions.

Such a reasoned request constitutes the basis for the further examination process in which the given reasons may be tested. As was indicated above when discussing the process concerning waiver requests for special preferences, members themselves might not have an interest in a principled discussion. Transparency and the inclusion into the process of other perspectives, in particular from other institutions, would therefore increase the likelihood that a principled discussion which tests the reasons given for the request will indeed take place.

---

78 Chapter 6 A.III.4.2.
79 At the same time, alternative processes that would fare better on these counts are currently not available and might not be for a long time.
80 On the practice of establishing working parties to examine waiver requests, see Chapter 5 C.II.
81 Understanding in Respect of Waivers of Obligations under the General Agreement on Tariffs and Trade 1994, para. 1. On the legal requirement of a reasoned request, see Chapter 5 C.I.

Given the large number of WTO members and the fact that not all members will have an interest in each individual waiver request, a discussion which centres on the reasons for the request could be conducted more efficiently if the WTO reverted to the practice of establishing working parties as was common under the GATT 1947. Such working parties would be mandated to examine the waiver requests. They would be required to submit a report, summarizing their findings, to the competent organ. Such an additional reporting requirement forces opposing members to formulate their objections and to do so in an acceptable way. Objections based on reasons unrelated to the request will not generally be acceptable.

While a transparent, reasoned and representative debate about a waiver request may serve to test whether the measure in question really serves the objectives which the requesting member purports to pursue, its value is not immediately clear in a case in which a waiver request is justified on the basis of a strong domestic preference against compliance. However, a transparent examination process may even play a role in testing whether the preference is indeed broadly supported by public opinion or rather backed by narrow special interests. This argument was convincingly made by Kenneth Dam with respect to the United States' request for a waiver of Art. I:1 GATT to allow the economic integration of the Canadian and United States car industry.[82] A principled examination of the waiver request would have revealed, according to Dam, that the measures in question benefited the car industry, but that they did not reduce prices for the benefit of consumers. He goes on to state:

> One may…suspect that if the GATT waiver exercise had been more serious and more penetrating, and if, to take the suggestion one step further, there had been an independent body to examine from an overall point of view the implications of the agreement, there might have been more vocal and effective criticism of the preferential arrangement within the US and Canada.[83]

Following this argument, an open and transparent debate of a waiver request may even have a democracy-enhancing effect domestically.

Finally, the reason-giving request constitutes a safeguard against arbitrariness in the waiver practice. Art. IX:4 WTO Agreement requires that a waiver decision 'state the exceptional circumstances justifying the decision'. Currently waiver decisions are not very elaborate in this respect. Such reason-giving is important, however, in that it provides guidance to future

82 On this waiver Chapter 4 B.I.2.2(b).
83 Dam. *The GATT: Law and International Economic Organization*, 50, 51.

waiver examinations. It will strengthen the precedential effects of waiver processes in that it creates a justificatory burden for future processes.[84] Even though there is no legal obligation to decide like waiver requests alike there will exist an expectation among the membership that the institution will not deviate from a given waiver practice unless there are reasons to do so. This protection against arbitrariness would be strengthened if the GATT practice were adopted, according to which working parties drafted reports that included the reasons why the working party supported or did not support a waiver. The GATT working party reports were adopted by the CONTRACTING PARTIES. They not only provided guidance on the interpretation of the respective waiver decision, they also constituted important references for future waiver processes.

84 On precedent in international law-making, see Jacob, 'Precedents'.

8

Conclusion

I set out in this study with large questions concerning the deficits in legitimacy and effectiveness of public international law and the WTO in particular. While sensitive to the deficits of WTO law when I began working on this topic, I am now convinced that it contributes to serious injustices. The redistributional consequences of the TRIPS Agreement to the detriment of the global poor and in favour of large pharmaceutical companies are but the most evident example.

Nonetheless, this study is based on the premise that international law and governance is needed more urgently than ever and that the WTO may play an important role in containing a bilateralism which might have even more detrimental consequences for the distribution of wealth in this world. It further rests on the argument that the legal form is indispensable to ensure that such governance may at least strive towards more representativeness and, consequently, global justice.

Given the aim to make international governance based on law more legitimate, the waiver power bears two relevant characteristics. Firstly, it allows for the modification of law in a legal procedure and thus does not endanger the validity of law. Secondly, it provides for a political process without substantive limitations. Its exercise may thus exceed the boundaries of WTO law, for example by restricting the WTO's jurisdiction in favour of another international legal regime. Furthermore, the fact that it is a political organ that decides potentially leads to more representativeness.

Given the large questions at the beginning of this study the eventual answer as to the waiver's potential to address the identified effectiveness and legitimacy challenges may appear disappointing. If the waiver process were more representative, it could perform this function better. This sounds like a truism.

Nonetheless, it should not be forgotten that the two recent movements in the otherwise deadlocked WTO, which were hailed as a new responsiveness of the WTO to social concerns, were realized through waiver decisions: namely the TRIPS Waiver and the Kimberley Waiver. Furthermore a fair number of other waiver requests, even if not similarly spectacular, mitigated the economic burdens of compliance for individual developing countries and allowed them to pursue policy choices in deviation from the law. Moreover, the Harmonized System waivers, even though of a very technical nature, provide a good example that effective administration across regimes that is framed by formal legal procedures is possible.

And even with respect to the waiver process which is largely determined by members' bargaining power this study has made one important finding. The analysis of the waiver practice reveals that better procedures, in the sense of allowing for a more principled debate less dominated by commercial interest, are not unknown to the international trade regime. While the WTO is lauded for being highly legalized, the GATT in fact followed a more transparent and more multilateral procedure when examining waiver requests. Returning to this procedure would be one, not entirely unrealistic, step towards more transparency and representativeness in the waiver process. A little step, admittedly, towards a more legitimate WTO.

BIBLIOGRAPHY

Aaronson, S. A., Zimmermann, J. M., *Trade Imbalance: The Struggle for Human Rights Concerns in Trade Policy-Making*, Cambridge University Press 2007

Abbott, F. M., 'The WTO Medicines Decision', 99 *American Journal of International Law* (2005), 317

Abbott, F. M., 'Intellectual Property Provisions of Bilateral and Regional Trade Agreements in Light of US Federal Law', *ICTSD Issue Paper* No. 12, February 2006, www.unctad.org/en/docs/iteipc20064_en.pdf

Abbott, K. W., 'Modern Relations Theory: A Prospectus for International Lawyers', 14 *Yale Journal of International Law* (1989), 335

Abbott, K. W., 'GATT as a Public Institution: The Uruguay Round and Beyond', 18 *Brooklyn Journal of International Law* (1992), 31

Abbott, K. W., Keohane, R. O., Moravcsik, A., Slaughter, A.-M., Snidal, D., 'The Concept of Legalization', 54 *International Organization* (2000), 401

Ago, R., 'Second Report on State Responsibility: The Origin of International Responsibility', UN Doc. A/CN.4/233 (20 April 1970)

Alvarez, J. E., 'Do Liberal States Behave Better? A Critique of Slaughter's Liberal Theory', 12 *European Journal of International Law* (2001), 183

Alvarez, J. E., *International Organizations as Law-Makers*, Oxford University Press 2005

Arendt, H., *The Human Condition*, University of Chicago Press 1958

Aspremont, J. d', 'Abuse of the Legal Personality of International Organizations and the Responsibility of Member States', 4 *International Organizations Law Review* (2007), 91

Aspremont, J. d', *L'Etat non démocratique en droit international: étude critique du droit international positif et de la pratique contemporaine*, Paris: Pedone 2008

Aston, J. D., *Sekundärgesetzgebung internationaler Organisationen zwischen mitgliedstaatlicher Souveränität und Gemeinschaftsdisziplin*, Berlin: Dunker & Humblot 2005

Atik, J., 'Identifying Antidemocratic Outcomes. Authenticity, Self-Sacrifice and International Trade', 19 *University of Pennsylvania Journal of International Economic Law* (1998), 229

Aust, A., *Modern Treaty Law and Practice*, Cambridge University Press 2nd edn 2007

Bagwell, K., Mavroidis, P. C., Staiger, R. W., 'It's a Question of Market Access', 96 *American Journal of International Law* (2002), 56

Barak, A., *Purposive Interpretation in Law*, Princeton University Press 2005

Bartels, L., 'The WTO Enabling Clause and Positive Conditionality in the European Community's GSP Program', 6 *Journal of International Economic Law* (2003), 507

Bartels, L., *Human Rights Conditionality in the EU's International Agreements*, Oxford University Press 2005

Bartels, L., 'The Trade and Development Policy of the European Union', 18 *European Journal of International Law* (2007), 715

Bartels, L., Häberli, C., 'Binding Tariff Preferences for Developing Countries Under Article II GATT', 13 *Journal of International Economic Law* (2010), 969

Bartosch, U., *Weltinnenpolitik: Zur Theorie des Friedens von Carl Friedrich von Weizsäcker*, Berlin: Duncker & Humblot 1994

Bast, J., *Grundbegriffe der Handlungsformen der EU: Entwickelt am Beschluss als praxisgenerierter Handlungsform des Unions- und Gemeinschaftsrechts*, Berlin, Heidelberg, New York: Springer 2006

Bast, J., 'Das Demokratiedefizit fragmentierter Internationalisierung', in: H. Brunkhorst (ed.), *Demokratie in der Weltgesellschaft*, Baden-Baden: Nomos 2009, 185

Benedek, W., *Die Rechtsordnung des GATT aus völkerrechtlicher Sicht*, Berlin, Heidelberg, New York: Springer 1990

Benvenisti, E., 'Exit and Voice in the Age of Globalization', 98 *Michigan Law Review* (1999), 167

Benvenisti, E., 'The Conception of International Law as a Legal System', 50 *German Yearbook of International Law* (2007), 393

Benvenisti, E., Downs, G. W., 'The Empire's New Clothes: Political Economy and the Fragmentation of International Law', 60 *Stanford Law Review* (2007), 595

Benzing, M., 'The Complementarity Regime of the International Criminal Court: International Criminal Justice between State Sovereignty and the Fight against Impunity', 7 *Max Planck Yearbook of United Nations Law* (2003), 591

Benzing, M., 'International Organizations or Institutions, Secondary Law' (March 2007), in: R. Wolfrum (ed.), *Max Planck Encyclopedia of International Law*, Oxford University Press 2008-2011, www.mpepil.com

Bernstorff, J. von, *Der Glaube an das universale Recht: Zur Völkerrechtstheorie Hans Kelsens und seiner Schüler*, Baden-Baden: Nomos 2001

Bernstorff, J. von, 'Procedures of Decision-Making and the Role of Law in International Organizations', in: A. v. Bogdandy *et al.* (eds.), *The Exercise of Public Authority by International Institutions: Advancing International Institutional Law*, Berlin, Heidelberg, New York: Springer 2009, 777

Bernstorff, J. von, 'Zivilgesellschaftliche Partizipation in Internationalen Organ-isationen: Form globaler Demokratie oder Baustein westlicher Experten-herrschaft?', in: H. Brunkhorst (ed.), *Demokratie in der Weltgesellschaft*, Baden-Baden: Nomos 2009, 277

Bernstorff, J. von, *The Public International Law Theory of Hans Kelsen: Believing in Universal Law*, Cambridge University Press 2010

Beyerlin, U., 'Different Types of Norms in International Environmental Law. Policies, Principles, and Rules', in: D. Bodansky, J. Brunnée, E. Hey (eds.), *The Oxford Handbook of International Environmental Law*, Oxford University Press 2007, 425

Bhagwati, J., *In Defense of Globalization*, Oxford University Press 2004

Bilder, R. B., *Managing the Risks of International Agreement*, Madison: University of Wisconsin Press 1981

Binder, C., 'Non-Performance of Treaty Obligations in Cases of Necessity', 13 *Austrian Review of International and European Law* (2008), 3

Blokker, N., 'International Organizations and their Members', 1 *International Organizations Law Review* (2004), 139

Blokker, N., 'International Organizations or Institutions, Decision-Making Bodies' (January 2008), in: R. Wolfrum (ed.), *Max Planck Encyclopedia of International Law*, Oxford University Press 2008–2011, www.mpepil.com

Böckenförde, M., *Grüne Gentechnik und Welthandel*, Berlin, Heidelberg, New York: Springer 2004

Böckenförde, M., 'Der Non-Violation Complaint im System der WTO: Neue Per-spektiven im Konflikt um Handel und Umwelt?', 43 *Archiv des Völkerrechts* (2005), 43

Böckenförde, M., 'Article 26 DSU', in: R. Wolfrum, P.-T. Stoll, K. Kaiser (eds.), *WTO: Institutions and Dispute Settlement*, Leiden: Nijhoff 2006, 572

Bogdandy, A. von, 'Eine Ordnung für das GATT', *Recht der internationalen Wirtschaft* (1991), 55

Bogdandy, A. von, 'The Non-Violation Procedure of Article XXIII:2, GATT: Its Operational Rationale', 26 *Journal of World Trade* (1992), 95

Bogdandy, A. von, *Gubernative Rechtsetzung: Eine Neubestimmung der Rechts-etzung und des Regierungssystems unter dem Grundgesetz in der Perspektive gemeineuropäischer Dogmatik*, Tübingen: Mohr Siebeck 2000

Bogdandy, A. von, 'Law and Politics in the WTO', 5 *Max Planck United Nations Yearbook* (2001), 609

Bogdandy, A. von, 'Legitimacy of International Economic Governance: Interpret-ative Approaches to WTO Law and the Prospects of its Proceduralization', in: S. Griller (ed.), *International Economic Governance and Non-Economic Concerns: New Challenges for the International Legal Order*, Vienna, New York: Springer 2003, 103

Bogdandy, A. von, 'Lawmaking by International Organizations: Some Thoughts on Non-Binding Instruments and Democratic Legitimacy', in: R. Wolfrum,

V. Röben (eds.), *Developments of International Law in Treaty Making*, Berlin, Heidelberg, New York: Springer 2005, 171

Bogdandy, A. von, 'Legal Effects of World Trade Organization Decisions within European Union Law: A Contribution to the Theory of the Legal Acts of International Organizations and the Action for Damages under Article 288(2) EC', 39 *Journal of World Trade* (2005), 45

Bogdandy, A. von, 'Preamble WTO Agreement', in: R. Wolfrum, P.-T. Stoll, K. Kaiser, *WTO: Institutions and Dispute Settlement*, Leiden: Nijhoff 2006, 1

Bogdandy, A. von, 'Pluralism, Direct Effect, and the Ultimate Say', 6 *International Journal of Constitutional Law* (2008), 397

Bogdandy, A. von, 'Wissenschaft vom Verfassungsrecht: Vergleich', in: A v. Bogdandy, P. Cruz Villalón, P. M. Huber (eds.), *Handbuch Ius Publicum Europaeum. Offene Staatlichkeit. Wissenschaft vom Verfassungsrecht*, Vol. II, Heidelberg: C. F. Müller 2008, 807

Bogdandy, A. von, Bast, J., 'The Federal Order of Competences', in: A. v. Bogdandy, J. Bast (eds.), *Principles of European Constitutional Law*, Oxford: Hart Publishing 2nd edn 2010, 275

Bogdandy, A. von, Dann, P., Goldmann, M., 'Developing the Publicness of Public International Law: Towards a Legal Framework for Global Governance Activities', 9 *German Law Journal* (2008), 1375

Bogdandy, A. von, Goldmann, M., 'The Exercise of International Public Authority Through National Policy Assessment: The OECD's PISA Policy as a Paradigm for a New International Standard Instrument', 5 *International Organizations Law Review* (2008), 241

Bogdandy, A. von, Stelzer, R., 'Article II WTO Agreement', in: R. Wolfrum, P.-T. Stoll, K. Kaiser, *WTO: Institutions and Dispute Settlement*, Leiden: Nijhoff 2006, 20

Bogdandy, A. von, Venzke, I., *In Whose Name? An Investigation of International Courts' Public Authority and its Democratic Justification*, 2010, http://ssrn.com/abstract=1593543

Bogdandy, A. von, Wolfrum R., von Bernstorff, J., Dann, P., Goldmann, M. (eds.), *The Exercise of Public Authority by International Institutions: Advancing International Institutional Law*, Berlin, Heidelberg, New York: Springer 2009

Bonzon, Y., 'Institutionalizing Public Participation in WTO Decision Making', 11 *Journal of International Economic Law* (2008), 751

Bora, B., 'Trade-Related Investment Measures', in: B. M. Hoekman, A. Mattoo, P. English (eds.), *Development, Trade, and the WTO*, Washington DC: World Bank 2002, 171

Borchert, I., 'Trade Diversion under Selective Preferential Market Access', 42 *Canadian Journal of Economics* (2009), 1390

Bossche, P. van den, *The Law and Policy of the World Trade Organization*, Cambridge University Press 2005

Bown, C. P., Trachtman, J. P., 'Brazil – Measures Affecting Imports of Retreaded Tyres: A Balancing Act', 8 *World Trade Review* (2009), 85

Braithwaite, J., Drahos, P., *Global Business Regulation*, Cambridge University Press 2000

Broek, N. van den, 'Article XVI WTO Agreement', in: R. Wolfrum, P.-T. Stoll, K. Kaiser, *WTO: Institutions and Dispute Settlement*, Leiden: Nijhoff 2006, 190

Brölmann, C., 'Law-Making Treaties: Form and Function in International Law', 74 *Nordic Journal of International Law* (2005), 383

Bronckers, M. C., 'Better Rules for a New Millennium: A Warning against Undemocratic Developments in the WTO', 2 *Journal of International Economic Law* (1999), 547

Broude, T., Shany, Y. (eds.), *The Shifting Allocation of Authority in International Law*, Oxford: Hart Publishing 2008

Brunnée, J., 'COPing with Consent: Law-Making under Multilateral Environmental Agreements', 15 *Leiden Journal of International Law* (2002), 1

Bustamante, R., 'The Need for a GATT Doctrine of Locus Standi: Why the United States Cannot Stand the European Community's Bananas Import Regime', 6 *Minnesota Journal of Global Trade* (1997), 533

Caldwell, D. J., 'International Environmental Agreements and the GATT: An Analysis of the Potential Conflict and the Role of a GATT "Waiver" Resolution', 18 *Maryland Journal of International Law and Trade* (1994), 173

Calliess, C., 'Gemeinwohl in der EU', in: W. Brugger (ed.), *Gemeinwohl in Deutschland, Europa und der Welt*, Baden-Baden: Nomos 2002, 174

Carmody, C., 'WTO Obligations as Collective', 17 *European Journal of International Law* (2006), 419

Cass, D. Z., *The Constitutionalization of the World Trade Organization: Legitimacy, Democracy, and Community in the International Trading System*, Oxford University Press 2005

Chang, H. J., *Kicking Away the Ladder: Development Strategy in Historical Perspective*, London, New York, Delhi: Anthem Press 2002

Charnovitz, S., 'The Legal Status of the Doha Declarations', 5 *Journal of International Economic Law* (2002), 207

Charnovitz, S., 'The Emergence of Democratic Participation in Global Governance (Paris, 1919)', 10 *Indiana Journal of Global Legal Studies* (2003), 45

Charnovitz, S., 'Recent Developments and Scholarship on WTO Enforcement Remedies', in: J. Lacarte, J. Granados (eds.), *Inter-Governmental Trade Dispute Settlement. Multilateral and Regional Approaches*, London: Cameron May 2004, 151

Charnovitz, S., 'The Appellate Body's GSP Decision', 3 *World Trade Review* (2004), 239

Charnovitz, S., 'An Analysis of Pascal Lamy's Proposal on Collective Preferences', 8 *Journal of International Economic Law* (2005), 449

Charnovitz, S., 'Nongovernmental Organizations and International Law', 100 *American Journal of International Law* (2006), 348

Charnovitz, S., 'Mapping the Law of WTO Accession', in: M. E. Janow, V. Donaldson, A. Yanovich (eds.), *The WTO: Governance, Dispute Settlement, and Developing Countries*, New York: Juris 2008, 855

Chayes, A., Handler Chayes, A., *The New Sovereignty: Compliance with International Regulatory Agreements*, Harvard University Press 1995

Chimni, B. S., 'The World Trade Organization, Democracy and Development: A View from the South', 40 *Journal of World Trade* (2006), 5

Chimni, B. S., 'Prolegomena to a Class Approach to International Law', 21 *European Journal of International Law* (2010), 57

Cooper Dreyfuss, R., Lowenfeld, A. F., 'Two Achievements of the Uruguay Round: Putting TRIPS and Dispute Settlement Together', 37 *Virginia Journal of International Law* (1997), 275

Correa, C. M., *Implications of the Doha Declaration on the TRIPS Agreement and Public Health*, Geneva: WHO 2002

Cosbey, A., *A Sustainable Development Roadmap for the WTO*, 2009, 1, www.iisd. org/publications/pub.aspx?pno=1196

Cottier, T., 'A Theory of Direct Effect in Global Law', in: A. v. Bogdandy, P. C. Mavroidis, Y. Mény (eds.), *European Integration and International Coordination: Studies in Honour of Claus-Dieter Ehlermann*, The Hague, London, New York: Kluwer Law International 2002, 106

Cottier, T., 'International Trade Law: The Impact of Justiciability and Separation of Powers in EC Law', *NCCR Trade Working Paper* No. 18/09, http://phase1. nccr-trade.org/index.php%3Foption=com_content&task=view&id=1589& Itemid=199.html

Cottier, T., Nadakavukaren Schefer, K., 'Non-Violation Complaints in WTO/GATT Dispute Settlement: Past, Present and Future', in: E.-U. Petersmann (ed.), *International Trade Law and the GATT/WTO Dispute Settlement System*, The Hague, London, New York: Kluwer Law International 1997, 143

Crawford, J., Marks, S., 'The Global Democracy Deficit: An Essay in International Law and its Limits', in: J. Crawford (ed.), *International Law as an Open System*, London: Cameron May Publishers 2002, 137

Croome, J., *Reshaping the World Trading System: A History of the Uruguay Round*, The Hague, London, New York: Kluwer Law International 2nd edn 1999

Cullet, P., *Differential Treatment in International Environmental Law*, Aldershot: Ashgate 2003

Curzon, G., *Multilateral Commercial Diplomacy: The General Agreement on Tariffs and Trade and its Impact on National Commercial Policies and Techniques*, London: Joseph 1965

Dahm, G., Delbrück, J., Wolfrum, R., *Völkerrecht*, Vol. I/3, Berlin: de Gruyter 2nd edn 2002

Dam, K. W., 'Regional Economic Arrangements and the GATT: The Legacy of a Misconception', 30 *University of Chicago Law Review* (1963), 615

Dam, K. W., *The GATT: Law and International Economic Organization*, University of Chicago Press 1970

Delbrück, J., 'Prospects for a "World (Internal) Law?" Legal Developments in a Changing International System', 9 *Indiana Journal of Global Legal Studies* (2002), 401

Downs, G. W., Rocke, D. M., *Optimal Imperfection? Domestic Uncertainty and Institutions in International Relations*, Princeton University Press 1995

Drezner, D. W., *All Politics Is Global: Explaining International Regulatory Regimes*, Princeton University Press 2007

Dunoff, J. L., 'Public Participation in the Trade Regime', 56 *Rutgers Law Review* (2004), 961

Dunoff, J. L., 'Dysfunction, Diversion, and the Debate over Preferences: (How) Do Preferential Trade Policies Work?', in: C. Thomas, J. P. Trachtman (eds.), *Developing Countries in the WTO Legal System*, Oxford University Press 2009, 45

Dutfield, G., 'TRIPS-Related Aspects of Traditional Knowledge', 33 *Case Western Reserve Journal of International Law* (2001), 133

Eeckhout, P., 'The Scales of Trade: Reflections on the Growth and Functions of the WTO Adjudicative Branch', 13 *Journal of International Economic Law* (2010), 3

Ehlermann, C.-D., 'How Flexible Is Community Law?', 82 *Michigan Law Review* (1984), 1274

Ehlermann, C.-D. (ed.), *Der rechtliche Rahmen eines Europas in mehreren Geschwindigkeiten und unterschiedlichen Gruppierungen. Multi-Speed Europe: The Legal Framework of Variable Geometry*, Köln: Bundesanzeiger Verlag 1999

Ehlermann, C.-D., Ehring, L., 'Decision-Making in the World Trade Organization', 8 *Journal of International Economic Law* (2005), 51

Ehlermann, C.-D., Ehring, L., 'The Authoritative Interpretation under Article IX:2 of the Agreement Establishing the World Trade Organization', 8 *Journal of International Economic Law* (2005), 803

Elfring, K., 'Article 70', in: P.-T. Stoll, J. Busche, K. Arend (eds.), *WTO: Trade-Related Aspects of Intellectual Property Rights*, Leiden: Nijhoff 2008, 842

Ely, J. H., *Democracy and Distrust: A Theory of Judicial Review*, Harvard University Press 1980

Eriksen, E. O., *The Unfinished Democratization of Europe*, Oxford University Press 2009

Esty, D. C., 'Non-Governmental Organizations at the World Trade Organization', 1 *Journal of International Economic Law* (1998), 123

Feichtner, I., 'Community Interest' (February 2007), in: R. Wolfrum (ed.), *Max Planck Encyclopedia of International Law*, Oxford University Press 2008–2011, www.mpepil.com

Feichtner, I., 'Subsidiarity' (October 2007), in: R. Wolfrum (ed.), *The Max Planck Encyclopedia of International Law*, Oxford University Press 2008–2011, www.mpepil.com

Feichtner, I., 'The Administration of the Vocabulary of International Trade: The Adaptation of WTO Schedules to Changes in the Harmonized System', 9 *German Law Journal* (2008), 1481

Feichtner, I., 'The Waiver Power of the WTO: Opening the WTO for Political Debate on the Reconciliation of Competing Interests', 20 *European Journal of International Law* (2009), 615

Feichtner, I., 'Introductory Note GATT 1994', in: R. Wolfrum, T.-P. Stoll, H. P. Hestermeyer (eds.), *WTO: Trade in Goods*, Leiden: Nijhoff 2011, 25

Fennelly, N., 'Legal Interpretation at the European Court of Justice', 20 *Fordham International Law Journal* (1997), 656

Finger, J. M., 'Trade and Development: Systemic Lessons from WTO Experience with Implementation, Trade Facilitation, and Aid for Trade', in: C. Thomas, J. P. Trachtman (eds.), *Developing Countries in the WTO Legal System*, Oxford University Press 2009, 75

Finger, J. M., Winters, L. A., 'What Can the WTO Do for Developing Countries', in: K. Anderson, B. M. Hoekman (eds.), *The Global Trading System, Vol. 3: Exceptions to the Core Rules*, New York, London: I. B. Tauris Publishers 2002, 71

Fischer-Lescano, A., Liste, P., 'Völkerrechtspolitik: Zur Trennung und Verknüpfung von Politik und Recht der Weltgesellschaft', 12 *Zeitschrift für Internationale Beziehungen* (2005), 209

Fitzmaurice, G., Report on the Law of Treaties, 368th meeting, (1956/I) *Yearbook of the International Law Commission*, 218

Fleck, F., 'No Deal in Sight on Cheap Drugs for Poor Countries', 81 *Bulletin WHO* (2003), 307

Footer, M. E., 'The Role of Consensus in GATT/WTO Decision-Making', 17 *Northwestern Journal of International Law and Business* (1996), 653

Footer, M. E., *An Institutional and Normative Analysis of the World Trade Organization*, Leiden: Nijhoff 2006

Footer, M. E., George, C., 'The General Agreement on Trade in Services', in: P. F. J. Macrory, A. E. Appleton, M. G. Plummer (eds.), *The World Trade Organization. Legal, Economic and Political Analysis*, Vol. I, New York: Springer 2005, 799

Forrester, I., Odara, O. E., 'The Agreement on Customs Valuation', in: P. F. J. Macrory, A. E. Appleton, M. G. Plummer (eds.), *The World Trade Organization. Legal, Economic and Political Analysis*, Vol. I, New York: Springer 2005, 531

Fraser, N., *Scales of Justice: Reimagining Political Space in a Globalizing World*, Columbia University Press 2009

Friedeberg, A. S., *The United Nation Conference on Trade and Development of 1964: The Theory of the Peripheral Economy at the Center of International Political Discussions*, University of Rotterdam Press 1969

Friedmann, W., *The Changing Structure of International Law*, Columbia University Press 1964

Friedrich, J., 'Nonbinding Instruments: The Functions and Limits of Nonbinding Instruments in International Environmental Law (manuscript on file with the author)

Frowein, J. A., 'Reservations and the International Ordre Public', in: J. Makerczyk (ed.), *Theory of International Law at the Threshold of the 21st Century: Essays in Honor of Krysztof Skubiszewski*, The Hague, London, Boston: Kluwer Law International 1996, 411.

Frowein, J. A., 'Konstitutionalisierung des Völkerrechts', in: *Völkerrecht und Internationales Privatrecht in einem sich globalisierenden internationalen System: Auswirkungen der Entstaatlichung transnationaler Rechtsbeziehungen*, 39 *Berichte der Deutschen Gesellschaft für Völkerrecht* (2000), 427

Gardbaum, S., 'Human Rights as International Constitutional Rights', 19 *European Journal of International Law* (2008), 749

Gardner, R. N., *Sterling–Dollar Diplomacy: Anglo-American Collaboration in the Reconstruction of Multilateral Trade*, Oxford: Clarendon Press 1956

Gehring, T., 'Treaty-Making and Treaty Evolution', in: D. Bodansky, J. Brunnée, E. Hey (eds.), *The Oxford Handbook of International Environmental Law*, Oxford University Press 2007, 467

Giegerich, T., 'Reservations to Multilateral Treaties' (October 2010), in: R. Wolfrum (ed.), *Max Planck Encyclopedia of International Law*, Oxford University Press 2008–2011, www.mpepil.com

Goldmann, M., 'Inside Relative Normativity: From Sources to Standard Instruments for the Exercise of International Public Authority', in: A. v. Bogdandy et al. (eds.), *The Exercise of Public Authority by International Institutions: Advancing International Institutional Law*, Berlin, Heidelberg, New York: Springer 2009, 661

Goldsmith, J. L., Posner, E. A., *The Limits of International Law*, Oxford University Press 2005

Goldstein, J. L., Martin, L., 'Legalization, Trade Liberalization, and Domestic Politics', 54 *International Organization* (2000), 603

Govaere, I., Ullrich, H. (eds.), *Intellectual Property, Public Policy, and International Trade*, Bern: P.I.E. Peter Lang 2007

Graber, B., 'The New UNESCO Convention on Cultural Diversity: A Counterbalance to the WTO', 9 *Journal of International Economic Law* (2006), 553

Gray, K. R., 'Conflict Diamonds and the WTO: Not the Best Opportunity to Be Missed for the Trade–Human Rights Interface', in: T. Cottier, J. Pauwelyn,

E. Bürgi (eds.), *Human Rights and International Trade*, Oxford University Press 2005, 451

Gros Espiell, H., 'GATT: Accommodating Generalized Preferences', 8 *Journal of World Trade* (1974), 341

Guzman, A. T., 'Global Governance and the WTO', 45 *Harvard International Law Journal* (2004) 303

Haberler, G., *et al.*, *Trends in International Trade: Report by a Panel of Experts*, Geneva: GATT 1958

Habermas, J., *Der gespaltene Westen*, Frankfurt: Suhrkamp 2004

Hahn, M., *Die einseitige Aussetzung von GATT-Verpflichtungen als Repressalie*, Berlin, Heidelberg, New York: Springer 1995

Harlow, C., 'Global Administrative Law: The Quest for Principles and Values', 17 *European Journal of International Law* (2006), 187

Harrison, J., 'Legal and Political Oversight of WTO Waivers', 11 *Journal of International Economic Law* (2008), 411

Hart, L. A., *The Concept of Law*, Oxford: Clarendon Press 1961

Held, D., *Democracy and the Global Order. From the Modern State to Cosmopolitan Governance*, Stanford University Press 1995

Held, D., 'Democracy and Globalization', in: D. Archibugi, D. Held, M. Köhler (eds.), *Re-Imagining Political Community: Studues in Cosmopolitan Democracy*, Cambridge: Polity Press 1998, 11

Helfer, L. R., 'Overlegalizing Human Rights: International Relations Theory and the Commonwealth Caribbean Backlash Against Human Rights Regime', 102 *Columbia Law Review* (2002), 1832.

Helfer, L. R., 'Constitutional Analogies in the International Legal System', 37 *Loyola of Los Angeles Law Review* (2003), 193

Helfer, L. R., 'Regime Shifting: The TRIPS Agreement and New Dynamics of International Intellectual Property Lawmaking', 29 *Yale Journal of International Law* (2004), 1

Hestermeyer, H. P., 'Flexible Entscheidungsfindung in der WTO', 53 *Gewerblicher Rechtsschutz und Urheberrecht* (2004), 194

Hestermeyer, H. P., *Human Rights and the WTO: The Case of Patents and Access to Medicines*, Oxford University Press 2007

Hestermeyer, H. P., 'Canadian-Made Drugs for Rwanda: The First Application of the WTO Waiver on Patents and Medicines', 11 *ASIL Insights*, Issue 28 (10 December 2007)

Hippler Bello, J., 'The WTO Dispute Settlement Understanding: Less Is More', 90 *American Journal of International Law* (1996), 416

Hodu, Y. N., 'Third Party Rights and the Concept of Legal Interest in World Trade Organization Dispute Settlement: Extending Participatory Rights to Enforcement Rights', 38 *Journal of World Trade* (2004), 757

Hoekman, B. M., Kostecki, M. M., *The Political Economy of the World Trading System: The WTO and Beyond*, Oxford University Press 2nd edn 2001

Hoekman, B. M., Özden, C., *Trade Preferences and Differential Treatment of Developing Countries: A Selective Survey*, World Bank Policy Research Working Paper Series 3566 (2005), http://ideas.repec.org/p/wbk/wbrwps/3566.html

Hoffmann, Lord L., 'The Universality of Human Rights', Judicial Studies Board Annual Lecture, 19 March 2009, www.judiciary.gov.uk/Resources/JCO/Documents/Speeches/Hoffmann_2009_JSB_Annual_Lecture_Universality_of_Human_Rights.pdf

Hohfeld, W. N., 'Fundamental Legal Conceptions as Applied in Judicial Reasoning' (Part 2), 26 *Yale Law Journal* (1917), 710

Horn, H., Howse, R., 'European Communities – Customs Classification of Frozen Boneless Chicken Cuts', 7 *World Trade Review* (2008), 9

Howse, R., 'Adjudicative Legitimacy and Treaty Interpretation in International Trade Law: The Early Years of WTO Jurisprudence', in: J. H. H. Weiler (ed.), *The EU, the WTO and the NAFTA*, Oxford University Press 2000

Howse, R., 'Democracy, Science, and Free Trade: Risk Regulation on Trial at the World Trade Organization', 98 *Michigan Law Review* (2000), 2329

Howse, R., 'The Canadian Generic Medicines Panel: A Dangerous Precedent in Dangerous Times', 3 *Journal of World Intellectual Property* (2000), 493

Howse, R., 'The Legitimacy of the World Trade Organization', in: J.-M. Coicaud, V. Heiskanen (eds.), *The Legitimacy of International Organizations*, New York: UNU Press 2001, 355

Howse, R., 'From Politics to Technocracy – and Back Again: The Fate of the Multilateral Trading Regime', 96 *The American Journal of International Law* (2002), 94

Howse, R., 'Human Rights in the WTO: Whose Rights, What Humanity? Comment on Petersmann', *Jean Monnet Working Paper* No. 12 (2002), 6, http://centers.law.nyu.edu/jeanmonnet/papers/02/021201-01.pdf

Howse, R., 'India's WTO Challenge to Drug Enforcement Conditions in the European Community Generalized System of Preferences: A Little Known Case with Major Repercussions for "Political" Conditionality in US Trade Policy', 4 *Chicago Journal of International Law* (2003), 385

Howse, R., 'For a Citizen's Task Force on the Future of the World Trade Organization', 56 *Rutgers Law Review* (2004), 877

Howse, R., 'Moving the WTO Forward: One Case at a Time', 42 *Cornell International Law Journal* (2009), 223

Howse, R., Nicolaïdis, K., 'Legitimacy and Global Governance: Why Constitutionalizing the WTO Is a Step Too Far', in: B. Porter, P. Sauvé, A. Subramanian, A. B. Zampetti (eds.), *Efficiency, Equity, Legitimacy: The Multilateral Trading System at the Millennium*, Washington DC: Brookings Institution Press 2001, 227

Howse, R., Nicolaïdis, K., 'Enhancing WTO Legitimacy: Constitutionalization or Global Subsidiarity?', 16 *Governance* (2003), 73

Howse, R., Nicolaïdis, K., 'Democracy without Sovereignty: The Global Vocation of Political Ethics', in: T. Broude, Y. Shany, *The Shifting Allocation of Authority in International Law*, Oxford: Hart Publishing 2009, 163

Howse, R., Regan, D., 'The Product/Process Distinction: An Illusory Basis for Disciplining "Unilateralism" in Trade Policy', 11 *European Journal of International Law* (2000), 249

Howse, R., Teitel, R., 'Beyond the Divide: The Covenant on Economic, Social and Cultural Rights and the World Trade Organization', *Friedrich-Ebert-Stiftung Occasional Paper*, No. 30 (2007)

Hudec, R. E., 'The GATT Legal System: A Diplomat's Jurisprudence', 4 *Journal of World Trade Law* (1970), 615

Hudec, R. E., 'GATT or GABB? The Future Design of the General Agreement on Tariffs and Trade', 80 *Yale Law Journal* (1971), 1299

Hudec, R. E., *The GATT Legal System and World Trade Diplomacy*, New York: Praeger 1975

Hudec, R. E., *Developing Countries in the GATT Legal System*, Aldershot: Gower for the Trade Policy Research Centre 1987

Hudec, R. E., 'The Structure of South-South Trade Preferences in the 1988 GSTP Agreement: Learning to Say MFMFN', in: J. Whalley (ed.), *Developing Countries and the Global Trading System: Thematic Studies from a Ford Foundation Project*, London: Macmillan 1989, 210

Hudec, R. E., *The GATT Legal System and World Trade Diplomacy*, Salem: Butterworth Legal Publishers 2nd edn 1990

Hudec, R. E., 'GATT/WTO Constraints on National Regulation. Requiem for an "Aims and Effects" Test', 32 *International Lawyer* (1998), 619

Hudec, R. E., '"Like Products": The Difference in Meaning in GATT Articles I and III', in: T. Cottier, P. Mavroidis (eds.), *Regulatory Barriers and the Principle of Non-Discrimination in World Trade Law*, University of Michigan Press 2000, 101

Huesa Vinaixa, R., 'Convention de Vienne de 1969, Article 57', in: O. Corten, P. Klein (eds.), *Les Conventions de Vienne sur le droit des traités*, Vol. III, Brussels: Bruylant 2006, 2015

ICTSD, 'EC–ACP Cotonou Waiver Finally Granted', 5 *Bridges Weekly* No. 39 (15 November 2001)

ICTSD, 'Members Strike Deal on TRIPS and Public Health. Civil Society Unimpressed', 9 *Bridges Weekly Trade News Digest* (7 December 2005)

ICTSD, 'Truce Declared in Beef Hormones Dispute', 13 *News and Analysis* No. 2 (June 2009), http://ictsd.org/i/news/bridges/48574/

Ignatieff, M. (ed.), *American Exceptionalism and Human Rights*, Princeton University Press 2005

International Law Commission, Articles on Responsibility of States for Internationally Wrongful Acts, with commentaries, *Yearbook of the International Law Commission* (2001) Vol. II, Part Two

International Law Commission, *Fragmentation of International Law. Difficulties Arising from the Diversification and Expansion of International Law*, Report of the Study Group of the International Law Commission, finalized by Martti Koskenniemi, UN Doc. A/CN.4/L.682 (13 April 2006)

Irwin, D. A., Weiler, J. H. H., 'Measures Affecting the Cross-Border Supply of Gambling and Betting Services (DS 285)', 7 *World Trade Review* (2008), 71

Jackson, J. H., *World Trade and the Law of GATT*, Indianapolis: Bobbs-Merrill 1969

Jackson, J. H., *The World Trading System. Law and Policy of International Economic Relations*, Cambridge, MA: MIT Press 2nd edn 1997

Jackson, J. H., 'The WTO Dispute Settlement Understanding: Misunderstanding on the Nature of Legal Obligation', 90 *American Journal of International Law* (1997), 60

Jackson, J. H., *The Jurisprudence of GATT and the WTO*, Cambridge University Press 2000

Jackson, J. H., 'Sovereignty-Modern: A New Approach to an Outdated Concept', 97 *American Journal of International Law* (2003), 782

Jackson, J. H., 'International Law Status of WTO Dispute Settlement Reports', 98 *American Journal of International Law* (2004), 109

Jackson, J. H., *Sovereignty, the WTO and Changing Fundamentals of International Law*, Cambridge University Press 2006

Jackson, J. H., 'History of GATT', in: R. Wolfrum, T.-P. Stoll, H. P. Hestermeyer (eds.), *WTO: Trade in Goods*, Leiden: Nijhoff 2011, 1

Jackson, J. H., Davey, W. J., Sykes, A. O., *Legal Problems of International Economic Relations*, St. Paul: West Publishing 1st edn 1977

Jackson, J. H., Davey, W. J., Sykes, A. O., *Legal Problems of International Economic Relations*, St. Paul: West Publishing 4th edn 2002

Jacob, M., 'Precedents: Lawmaking through International Adjudication', 12 *German Law Journal* (2011), 1005

Jawara, F., Kwa, A., *Behind the Scenes at the WTO. The Real World of International Trade Negotiations*, London, New York: Zed Books 2nd edn 2003

Jessen, H., *WTO-Recht und 'Entwicklungsländer'. 'Special and Differential Treatment for Developing Countries' im multidimensionalen Wandel des Wirtschaftsvölkerrechts*, Berliner Wissenschafts-Verlag 2006

Joerges, C., Neyer, J., 'Politics, Risk Management, World Trade Organization Governance and the Limits of Legalisation', 30 *Science and Public Policy* (2003), 219

Kaiser, K., 'Coordination of International Organizations: Intellectual Property Law as an Example', in: R. A. Miller, R. M. Bratspies (eds.), *Progress in International Law*, Leiden: Nijhoff 2008, 315

Kelsen, H., *Reine Rechtslehre*, Leipzig: Deuticke 1934

Kennedy, D., 'Laws and Developments', in: A. Perry-Kessaris, J. Hatchard (eds.), *Law and Development: Facing Complexity in the 21st Century*, London: Cavendish Publishing 2003, 17

Kennedy, M., 'When Will the Protocol Amending the TRIPS Agreement Enter into Force?', 13 *Journal of International Economic Law* (2010), 459

Keohane, R. O., 'Reciprocity in International Relations', 40 *International Organization* (1986), 1

Keohane, R. O., 'The Contingent Legitimacy of Multilateralism', in: E. Newman, R. Thakur, J. Tirman, *Multilateralism Under Challenge? Power, International Order and Structural Change*, New York: UNU Press 2006, 56

Keohane, R. O., Macedo, S., Moravcsik, A., 'Democracy-Enhancing Multilateralism', 63 *International Organization* (2009), 1

Keohane, R. O., Nye Jr, J. S., 'The Club Model of Multilateral Cooperation and Problems of Democratic Legitimacy', in: R. B. Porter, P. Sauvé, A. Subramanian, A. B. Zampetti (eds.), *Efficiency, Equity, Legitimacy. The Multilateral Trading System at the Millennium*, Washington DC: Brookings Institution Press 2001, 264

Kessie, E., 'The Legal Status of Special and Differential Treatment Provisions under the WTO Agreements', in: G. A. Bermann, P. C. Mavroidis (eds.), *WTO Law and Developing Countries*, Cambridge University Press 2007, 12

Kingsbury, B., 'The Concept of Compliance as a Function of Competing Conceptions of International Law', 19 *Michigan Journal of International Law* (1998), 345

Kingsbury, B., 'The Concept of "Law" in Global Administrative Law', 20 *European Journal of International Law* (2009), 23

Kingsbury, B., Krisch, N., Stewart, R. B., 'The Emergence of Global Administrative Law', 68 *Law and Contemporary Problems* (2005), 15

Kirgis, F. L., 'Reservations to Treaties and United States Practice', *ASIL Insights*, May 2003

Klabbers, J., 'Glorified Esperanto? Rethinking Human Rights', 13 *Finnish Yearbook of International Law* (2002), 63

Klabbers, J., 'On Human Rights Treaties, Contractual Conceptions and Reservations', in: I. Ziemele (ed.), *Reservations to Human Rights Treaties and the Vienna Convention Regime: Conflict, Harmony or Reconciliation*, Leiden: Nijhoff 2004

Klabbers, J., 'On Rationalism in Politics: Interpretation of Treaties and the World Trade Organization', 74 *Nordic Journal of International Law* (2005), 405

Klabbers, J., 'Two Concepts of International Organization', 2 *International Organizations Law Review* (2005), 277

Klabbers, J., 'Compliance Procedures', in: D. Bodansky, J. Brunnée, E. Hey (eds.), *The Oxford Handbook of International Environmental Law*, Oxford University Press 2007, 995

Klabbers, J., *An Introduction to International Institutional Law*, Cambridge University Press 2nd edn 2009

Klabbers, J., 'Goldmann Variations', in: A. v. Bogdandy *et al.* (eds.), *Exercise of Public Authority by International Institutions: Advancing International Institutional Law*, Berlin, Heidelberg, New York: Springer 2009, 713

Klabbers, J., *Treaty Conflict and the European Union*, Cambridge University Press 2009

Klein, P., 'International Organizations or Institutions, Decision-Making' (March 2007), in: R. Wolfrum (ed.), *Max Planck Encyclopedia of International Law*, Oxford University Press 2008–2011, www.mpepil.com

Kornhauser, L., 'An Introduction to the Economic Analysis of Contract Remedies', 57 *University of Colorado Law Review* (1986), 683

Kornhauser, L., 'Economic Analysis of Law' (revised May 2006), in: E. N. Zalta (ed.), *The Stanford Encyclopedia of Philosophy*, http://plato.stanford.edu/entries/legal-econanalysis/

Koskenniemi, M., 'Breach of Treaty or Non-Compliance? Reflexions on the Enforcement of the Montreal Protocol', 3 *Yearbook of International Environmental Law* (1992), 123

Koskenniemi, M., *The Gentle Civilizer of Nations*, Cambridge University Press 2002

Koskenniemi, M., *From Apology to Utopia*, Cambridge University Press 2nd edn 2005

Koskenniemi, M., 'What Is International Law For?', in: M. D. Evans (ed.), *International Law*, Oxford University Press 2nd edn 2006, 57

Koskenniemi, M., 'The Fate of Public International Law: Between Technique and Politics', 70 *Modern Law Review* (2007), 1

Krajewski, M., 'Democratic Legitimacy and Constitutional Perspectives of WTO Law', 35 *Journal of World Trade* (2001), 167

Krajewski, M., *Verfassungsperspektiven und Legitimation des Rechts der Welthandelsorganisation (WTO)*, Berlin: Duncker & Humblot 2001

Krajewski, M., 'Legitimizing Global Economic Governance Through Transnational Parliamentarization: The Parliamentary Dimensions of the WTO and the World Bank', *TranState Working Paper*, No. 136/10, www.sfb597.uni-bremen.de/pages/pubApBeschreibung.php?SPRACHE=de&ID=177

Krasner, S. D., 'Structural Causes and Regime Consequences: Regimes as Intervening Variables', 36 *International Organisation* (1982), 185

Kratochwil, F., 'The Limits of Contract', 5 *European Journal of International Law* (1994), 456

Kratochwil, F., 'Politics, Norms, and Peaceful Change: Two Moves to Institutions', 24 *Review of International Studies* (1998), 193

Kreide, R., 'The Ambivalence of Juridification: On Legitimate Governance in the International Context', 2 *Global Justice: Theory Practice Rhetoric* (2009), 18

Krisch, N., 'International Law in Times of Hegemony', 16 *European Journal of International Law* (2005), 369

Krisch, N., 'The Pluralism of Global Administrative Law', 17 *European Journal of International Law* (2006), 247

Krishnamurti, R., 'Tariff Preferences in Favour of the Developing Countries', 1 *Journal of World Trade Law* (1967), 643

Kuijper, P. J., 'Some Institutional Issues Presently Before the WTO', in: D. L. M. Kennedy, J. D. Southwick (eds.), *The Political Economy of International Trade Law: Essays in Honor of Robert E. Hudec*, Cambridge University Press 2002, 81

Kuijper, P. J., 'The Sutherland Report and the WTO's Institutional Law: Do Parallels With Other Organizations Help?', 2 *International Organizations Law Review* (2005), 191

Kuijper, P. J., 'WTO Institutional Aspects', in: D. Bethlehem, D. McRae, R. Neufeld, I. van Damme (eds.), *The Oxford Handbook of International Trade Law*, Oxford University Press 2009, 79

Kumm, M., 'The Legitimacy of International Law: A Constitutionalist Framework of Analysis', 15 *European Journal of International Law* (2004), 907

Lamy, P., *The Emergence of Collective Preferences in International Trade: Implications for Regulating Globalisation*, 15 September 2004, http://trade.ec.europa.eu/doclib/docs/2004/september/tradoc_118929.pdf

Lang, A., Scott, J., 'The Hidden World of WTO Governance', 20 *European Journal of International Law* (2009), 575

Lauterpacht, E., 'Judicial Review of the Acts of International Organisations', in: L. Boisson de Chazournes (ed.), *International Law, the International Court of Justice and Nuclear Weapons*, Cambridge University Press 1999, 92

Lee, Y.-S., *Reclaiming Development in the World Trading System*, Cambridge University Press 2006

Letsas, G., 'Two Concepts of the Margin of Appreciation', 26 *Oxford Journal of Legal Studies* (2006), 705

Lindblom, A.-K., *Non-Governmental Organisations in International Law*, Cambridge University Press 2005

Long, O., *Law and its Limitations in the GATT Multilateral Trade System*, Dordrecht: Nijhoff 1985

Lowenfeld, A. F., *International Economic Law*, Oxford University Press 2002

Luhmann, N., *A Sociological Theory of Law* (1980), translated by Elizabeth King and Martin Albrow and edited by Martin Albrow, Boston: Routledge & Kegan Paul 1985, 264

Marceau, G., 'Conflicts of Norms and Conflicts of Jurisdictions: The Relationship Between the WTO Agreement and MEAs and Other Treaties', 35 *Journal of World Trade* (2001), 1081

Marinberg, D., 'GATT/WTO Waivers: "Exceptional Circumstances" as Applied to the Lomé Waiver', 19 *Boston University International Law Journal* (2001), 129

Marks, S., 'Naming Global Administrative Law', 37 *New York University Journal of International Law and Politics* (2006), 995

Matthews, D., 'WTO Decision on Implementation of Paragraph 6 of the Doha Declaration on the TRIPS Agreement and Public Health: A Solution to the Access to Essential Medicines Problem?', 7 *Journal of International Economic Law* (2004), 73

Matz, N., *Wege zur Koordinierung völkerrechtlicher Verträge*, Berlin, Heidelberg, New York: Springer 2005

Matz-Lück, N., 'Framework Agreements' (May 2006), in: R. Wolfrum (ed.), *Max Planck Encyclopedia of International Law*, Oxford University Press 2008–2011, www.mpepil.com

Mavroidis, P. C., 'Remedies in the WTO Legal System: Between a Rock and a Hard Place', 11 *European Journal of International Law* (2000), 763

Mavroidis, P. C., 'Judicial Supremacy, Judicial Restraint, and the Issue of Consistency of Preferential Trade Agreements with the WTO: The Apple in the Picture', in: D. L. M. Kennedy, J. D. Southwick (eds.), *The Political Economy of International Trade Law: Essays in Honor of Robert E. Hudec*, Cambridge University Press 2002, 583

Mbengue, M. M., 'Preamble' (September 2006), in: R. Wolfrum (ed.), *Max Planck Encyclopedia of International Law*, Oxford University Press 2008–2011, www.mpepil.com

McGinnis, J. O., Movesian, M. L., 'The World Trade Constitution', 114 *Harvard Law Review* (2000), 511

McGinnis, J. O., Movesian, M. L., 'Against Global Governance in the WTO', 45 *Harvard International Law Journal* (2004), 353

McGinnis, J. O., Somin, I., 'Should International Law Be Part of our Law?', 59 *Stanford Law Review* (2007), 1175

McMahon, J. A., 'The Agreement on Agriculture', in: P. F. J. Macrory, A. E. Appleton, M. G. Plummer (eds.), *The World Trade Organization. Legal, Economic and Political Analysis*, Vol. I, New York: Springer 2005, 187

Médecins sans Frontières, *An Unsolved Problem: The August 30th Decision*, www.msfaccess.org/main/access-patents/introduction-to-access-and-patents/trips/an-unsolved-problem-the-august-30th-decision/

Metzger, S. D., 'The United States–Canada Automotive Products Agreement of 1965', 1 *Journal of World Trade Law* (1967), 103

Morgenthau, H. J., *Politics Among Nations: The Struggle for Power and Peace*, New York: Alfred A. Knopf 2nd edn 1954

Mouffe, C., *On the Political*, London, New York: Routledge 2005

Nadakavukaren Schefer, K., 'Stopping Trade in Conflict Diamonds: Exploring the Trade and Human Rights Interface with the WTO Waiver for the Kimberley Process', in: T. Cottier, J. Pauwelyn, E. Bürgi (eds.), *Human Rights and International Trade*, Oxford University Press 2005, 391

Neven, D. J., Weiler, J. H. H., '*Japan – Measures Affecting the Importation of Apples* (AB-2003-4): One Bad Apple? (DS245/AB/R). A Comment', in: H. Horn, P. C. Mavroidis (eds.), *The WTO Case Law of 2003*, Philadelphia: American Law Institute 2006, 280

Nicolaïdis, K., Howse, R. (eds.), *The Federal Vision. Legitimacy and Levels of Governance in the US and EU*, Oxford University Press 2002

Niesen, P., Herborth, B. (eds.), *Anarchie der kommunikativen Freiheit: Jürgen Habermas und die Theorie der Internationalen Politik*, Frankfurt: Suhrkamp 2007

Nye, J. S., 'Book Review of *The United Nations Conference on Trade and Development of 1964* by A. S. Friedeberg (1969)', 5 *Journal of World Trade Law* (1971), 230

Odell, J. S., 'Chairing a WTO Negotiation', 8 *Journal of International Economic Law* (2005), 425

Oeter, S., 'Chancen und Defizite internationaler Verrechtlichung: Was das Recht jenseits des Nationalstaats leisten kann', in: B. Zangl, M. Zürn (eds.), *Make Law, Not War: Internationale und transnationale Verrechtlichung als Baustein für Global Governance*, Bonn: J. H. W. Dietz 2004, 46

Onyejekwe, K., 'International Law of Trade Preferences: Emanations from the European Union and the United States', 26 *St Mary's Law Journal* (1994), 425

Oppenheim, L. F., *International Law: A Treatise*, London: Longmans, Green & Co. 1905, 403

Ostry, S., 'The Uruguay Round North–South Grand Bargain: Implications for Future Negotiations', in: D. L. M. Kennedy, J. D. Southwick (eds.), *The Political Economy of International Trade Law. Essays in Honor of Robert E. Hudec*, Cambridge University Press 2002, 285

Oxfam, 'All Costs, No Benefits: How TRIPS-plus Intellectual Property Rules in the US–Jordan FTA Affect Access to Medicines', *Briefing Paper*, March 2007, www.oxfam.org/sites/www.oxfam.org/files/all%20costs,%20no%20benefits.pdf

Özden, C., Reinhardt, E., 'The Perversity of Preferences: The Generalized System of Preferences and Developing Country Trade Policies, 1976–2000', *World Bank Policy Research Working Paper Series* 2955 (2003)

Parisi, F., Ghei, N., 'The Role of Reciprocity in International Law', 36 *Cornell International Law Journal* (2003), 93

Pauwelyn, J., 'The Role of Public International Law in the WTO: How Far Can We Go?', 95 *American Journal of International Law* (2001), 535

Pauwelyn, J., 'The Nature of WTO Obligations', *Jean Monnet Working Paper* No. 1 (2002), http://centers.law.nyu.edu/jeanmonnet/papers/02/020101.html

Pauwelyn, J., 'A Typology of Multilateral Treaty Obligations: Are WTO Obligations Bilateral or Collective in Nature?', 14 *European Journal of International Law* (2003)

Pauwelyn, J., *Conflict of Norms in Public International Law: How WTO Law Relates to Other Rules of International Law*, Cambridge University Press 2003

Pauwelyn, J., 'WTO Compassion or Superiority Complex? What to Make of the WTO Waiver for "Conflict Diamonds"', 24 *Michigan Journal of International Law* (2003), 1177

Pauwelyn, J., 'The Transformation of World Trade', 104 *Michigan Law Review* (2005), 1

Pauwelyn, J., *Optimal Protection of International Law: Navigating Between European Absolutism and American Voluntarism*, Cambridge University Press 2008

Pellet, A., 'Fifth Report on Reservations to Treaties' (2000), UN Doc. A/CN.4/508/Add. 1

Perdikis, N., Kerr, W. A., Hobbs, J. E., 'Reforming the WTO to Defuse Potential Trade Conflicts in Genetically Modified Goods', 24 *World Economy* 2002

Perez, O., *Ecological Sensitivity and Global Legal Pluralism: Rethinking the Trade and Environment Conflict*, Oxford: Hart Publishing 2004

Pescatore, P., 'The GATT Dispute Settlement Mechanism: Its Present Situation and its Prospects', 10 *Journal of International Arbitration* (1993), 27

Peters, A., 'Compensatory Constitutionalism: The Function and Potential of Fundamental International Norms and Structures', 19 *Leiden Journal of International Law* (2006), 579

Peters, A., 'Transparency, Secrecy, and Security: Liaisons Dangereuses', in: J. Iliopoulos-Strangas, O. Diggelmann, H. Bauer (eds.), *Rule of Law, Freedom and Security in Europe*, Brussels: Bruylant 2010, 183

Petersen, N., 'Demokratie als teleologisches Prinzip: Zur Legitimität von Staatsgewalt im Völkerrecht', Berlin, Heidelberg, New York: Springer 2009

Petersmann, E.-U., *Constitutional Functions and Constitutional Problems of International Economic Law*, Fribourg: University Press 1991

Petersmann, E.-U., 'Violation-Complaints and Non-Violation Complaints in Public International Trade Law', 43 *German Yearbook of International Law* (1991), 175

Petersmann, E.-U., 'Time for Integrating Human Rights into the Law of Worldwide Organizations: Lessons from European Integration Law for Global Integration Law', *Jean Monnet Working Paper* 7 (2001), 35, http://centers.law.nyu.edu/jeanmonnet/papers/01/012301.html

Petersmann, E.-U., 'From "Member-Driven Governance" to Constitutionally Limited "Multi-Level Trade Governance" in the WTO', in: G. Sacerdoti, A. Yanovich, J. Bohanes (eds.), *The WTO at Ten: The Contribution of the Dispute Settlement System*, Cambridge University Press 2006, 86

Pogge, T., 'Montréal Statement on the Human Right to Essential Medicines', 16 *Cambridge Quarterly of Healthcare Ethics* (2007), 97

Posner, E. A., *The Perils of International Legalism*, University of Chicago Press 2009

Pound, R., *Interpretations of Legal History*, Cambridge University Press 1923

Prebisch, R., *Towards a New Trade Policy for Development*, UN Doc. E/Conf.46/141, Vol. II, 5

Price, T. M., 'The Kimberley Process: Conflict Diamonds, WTO Obligations, and the Universality Debate', 12 *Minnesota Journal of Global Trade* (2003), 1

Qin, J. Y., '"WTO-Plus" Obligations and their Implications for the World Trade Organization Legal System: An Appraisal of the China Accession Protocol', 37 *Journal of World Trade* (2003), 483

Qureshi, A. H., *Interpreting WTO Agreements: Problems and Perspectives*, Cambridge University Press 2006

Rabkin, J. A., *The Case for Sovereignty: Why the World Should Welcome American Independence*, Washington DC: AEI Press 2004

Raftopoulos, E., *The Inadequacy of the Contractual Analogy in the Law of Treaties*, Athens: Hellenic Institute of International and Foreign Law 1990

Raustiala, K., Victor, D., 'The Regime Complex for Plant Genetic Resources', 58 *International Organization* (2004), 277

Raz, J., *The Concept of a Legal System*, Oxford: Clarendon 2nd edn 1980

Rebasti, E., 'Beyond Consultative Status: Which Legal Framework for an Enhanced Interaction Between NGOs and Intergovernmental Organizations?', in: P.-M. Dupuy, L. Vierucci (eds.), *NGOs in International Law. Efficiency in Flexibility?*, Cheltenham: Edward Elgar 2008, 21

Regan, D. H., 'The Meaning of "Necessary" in GATT Article XX and GATS Article XIV: The Myth of Cost–Benefit Balancing', 6 *World Trade Review* (2007), 347

Rege, V., 'Customs Valuation and Customs Reform', in: B. M. Hoekman, A. Mattoo, P. English (eds.), *Development, Trade, and the WTO*, Washington DC: World Bank 2002, 128

Ricardo, D., *Works*, Vol. 1, edited by P. Straffa, Cambridge University Press 1955

Riphagen, W., 'State Responsibility: New Theories of Obligation in Interstate Relations', in: R. S. J. Macdonald, D. M. Johnston (eds.), *The Structure and Process of International Law: Essays in Legal Philosophy, Doctrine and Theory*, The Hague: Nijhoff 1983, 583

Ripinsky, S., van den Bossche, P., *NGO Involvement in International Organizations: A Legal Analysis*, London: British Institute of International and Comparative Law 2007

Risse, T., '"Let's Argue!": Communicative Action in World Politics', 54 *International Organization* (2000), 1

Röben, V., 'Institutional Developments under Modern International Environmental Agreements', 4 *Max Planck Yearbook of United Nations Law* (2002), 363

Rodrik, D., *The Global Governance of Trade as if Development Really Mattered*, New York: UNDP 2001

Rodrik, D., *One Economics, Many Recipes: Globalization, Institutions, and Economic Growth*, Princeton University Press 2007

Roessler, F., 'The Concept of Nullification and Impairment in the Legal System of the World Trade Organization', in: E.-U. Petersmann (ed.), *International Trade Law and the GATT/WTO Dispute Settlement System*, The Hague, London, New York: Kluwer Law International 1997, 123

Roessler, F., 'Are the Judicial Organs of the World Trade Organization Overburdened', in: R. B. Porter, P. Sauvé, A. Subramanian, A. B. Zampetti (eds.), *Efficiency, Equity, Legitimacy. The Multilateral Trading System at the Millennium*, Washington DC: Brookings Institution Press 2001, 329

Roessler, F., Gappah, P., 'A Re-Appraisal of Non-Violation Complaints Under the WTO Dispute Settlement Procedures', in: P. F. J. Macrory, A. E. Appleton, M. G. Plummer (eds.), *The World Trade Organization: Legal, Economic and Political Analysis*, Vol. I, New York: Springer 2005, 1371

Rosendorff, B. P., Milner, H. V., 'The Optimal Design of International Trade Institutions. Uncertainty and Escape', 55 *International Organization* (2001), 829

Rötting, M., *Das verfassungsrechtliche Beitrittsverfahren zur Europäischen Union*, Berlin, Heidelberg, New York 2009

Ruggie, J. G., 'International Regimes, Transactions, and Change: Embedded Liberalism in the Postwar Economic Order', 36 *International Organization* (1982), 379

Ruggie, J. G., 'Multilateralism: The Anatomy of an Institution', in: J. G. Ruggie (ed.), *Multilateralism Matters. The Theory and Praxis of an Institutional Form*, New York: Columbia University Press 1993, 3

Ruggie, J. G., 'Globalization and the Embedded Liberalism Compromise: The End of an Era?', in: W. Streeck (ed.), *Internationale Wirtschaft, Nationale Demokratie: Herausforderungen für die Demokratietheorie*, Frankfurt: Campus Verlag 1998

Ruggie, J. G., 'Reconstituting the Global Public Domain: Issues, Actors and Practices', 10 *European Journal of International Relations* (2004), 499

Ruggie, J. G., 'Business and Human Rights: The Evolving International Agenda', 101 *American Journal of International Law* (2007), 819

Ruse-Khan, H., 'The Role of Chairman's Statements in the WTO', 41 *Journal of World Trade* (2007), 475

Salomon, M. E., *Global Responsibility for Human Rights: World Poverty and the Development of International Law*, Oxford University Press 2007

Sarooshi, D., *International Organizations and their Exercise of Sovereign Powers*, Oxford University Press 2005

Sassen, S., 'The Participation of States and Citizens in Global Governance', 10 *Indiana Journal of Global Legal Studies* (2003), 5

Scharpf, F. W., 'Democratic Policy in Europe', 2 *European Law Journal* (1996), 136

Schermers, H. G., Blokker, N., *International Institutional Law*, Boston: Nijhoff 4th edn 2003

Schöpp-Schilling, H. B., 'Reservations to the Convention on the Elimination of All Forms of Discrimination Against Women: An Unresolved Issue or (No) New Developments', in: I. Ziemele (ed.), *Reservations to Human Rights Treaties and the Vienna Convention Regime*, Leiden: Nijhoff 2004, 3

Schropp, S. A. B., *Trade Policy Flexibility and Enforcement in the WTO: A Law and Economics Analysis*, Cambridge University Press 2009

Schropp, S. A. B., Palmeter, D., 'Commentary on the Appellate Body Report in EC – Bananas III (Article 21.5): Waiver-Thin, or Lock, Stock and Metric Ton?', 9 *World Trade Review* (2010), 7

Schwartz, W. F., Sykes, A. O., 'The Economic Structure of Renegotiation and Dispute Resolution in the World Trade Organization', 31 *Journal of Legal Studies* (2001), S179

Scott, R. E., Stephan, P. B., *The Limits of Leviathan: Contract Theory and the Enforcement of International Law*, Cambridge University Press 2006

Sell, S., 'Industry Strategies for Intellectual Property and Trade: The Quest for TRIPS, and Post-TRIPS Strategies', 10 *Cardozo Journal of International and Comparative Law* (2002), 79

Sell, S., 'The Quest for Global Governance in Intellectual Property and Public Health: Structural, Discursive, and Institutional Dimensions', 77 *Temple Law Review* (2004), 363

Shaffer, G. C., 'Recognizing Public Goods in WTO Dispute Settlement: Who Participates? Who Decides?', 7 *Journal of International Economic Law* (2004), 459

Shany, Y., *The Competing Jurisdictions of International Courts and Tribunals*, Oxford University Press 2003

Shany, Y., 'Toward a General Margin of Appreciation Doctrine in International Law?', 16 *European Journal of International Law* (2005), 907

Shin, Y., 'Implementation of the WTO Customs Valuation Agreement in Developing Countries: Issues and Recommendations', 33 *Journal of World Trade* (1999), 125

Simma, B., *Das Reziprozitätselement im Zustandekommen völkerrechtlicher Verträge*, Berlin: Duncker & Humblot 1972

Simma, B., 'From Bilateralism to Community Interest in International Law', 250 *Receuil des Cours* (1994), 217

Simma, B., Brunner, S., Kaul, H.-P., 'Article 27', in: B. Simma (ed.), *The Charter of the United* Nations, Oxford University Press 2002, 476

Slaughter, A.-M., 'Governing the Global Economy through Government Networks', in: M. Byers (ed.), *The Role of Law in International Politics: Essays in International Relations and International Law*, Oxford University Press 2000, 177

Slaughter, A.-M., 'Global Government Networks, Global Information Agencies, and Disaggregated Democracy', 24 *Michigan Journal of International Law* (2003), 1041

Slaughter, A.-M., *A New World Order*, Princeton University Press 2004

Smillie, I., *Blood on the Stone: Greed, Corruption and War in the Global Diamond Trade*, London, New York, Delhi: Anthem Press 2010

Steger, D. P., 'WTO Dispute Settlement: What Do You Win When You Win?', in: D. Steger (ed.), *Peace Through Trade: Building the World Trade Organization*, Cameron May Publishers 2004, 243

Steinberg, R. H., 'In the Shadow of Law or Power?', 56 *International Organization* (2002), 339

Sterlini, M. L. de, 'The Agreement on Trade-Related Investment Measures', in: P. F. J. Macrory, A. E. Appleton, M. G. Plummer, *The World Trade Organization: Legal, Economic and Political Analysis*, Vol. I, New York: Springer 2005, 437

Stewart, T. P. (ed.), *The GATT Uruguay Round: A Negotiating History (1986–1992)*, Vol. II, Deventer: Kluwer 1993

Stiglitz, J. E., *Globalization and its Discontents*, New York: W. W. Norton & Co. 2002

Stiglitz, J. E., Charlton, A., *Fair Trade for All: How Trade Can Promote Development*, Oxford University Press revised edn 2007

Stoll, P.-T., 'Article 3 DSU', in: R. Wolfrum, P.-T. Stoll, K. Kaiser (eds.), *WTO: Institutions and Dispute Settlement*, Leiden: Nijhoff 2006, 281

Sunstein, C., *Laws of Fear: Beyond the Precautionary Principle*, Cambridge University Press 2005

Supachai, P., 'Introduction to Part IV GATT', in: R. Wolfrum, P.-T. Stoll, H. Hestermeyer, *WTO: Trade in Goods*, Leiden: Nijhoff 2011, 766.

Sutherland, P., *et al.*, *The Future of the WTO: Report by the Consultative Board to the Director-General Supachai Panitchapkdi*, Geneva: WTO 2004

Suy, E., *Les Actes juridiques unilatéraux en droit international public*, Paris: Librairie Générale de Droit et de Jurisprudence 1962

Sykes, A. O., 'Protectionism as a "Safeguard": A Positive Analysis of the GATT "Escape Clause" with Normative Speculations', 58 *The University of Chicago Law Review* (1991), 255

Thym, D., *Ungleichzeitigkeit und Europäisches Verfassungsrecht: Die Einbettung der verstärkten Zusammenarbeit, des Schengener Rechts und anderer Formen von Ungleichzeitigkeit in den einheitlichen rechtlichen institutionellen Rahmen der Europäischen Union*, Berlin: Duncker & Humblot 2004

Tietje, C., *Normative Grundstrukturen der Behandlung nichttarifärer Handelshemmnisse in der WTO/GATT-Rechtsordnung*, 1998

Tietje, C., 'The Changing Legal Structure of International Treaties as an Aspect of an Emerging Global Governance Architecture', 42 *German Yearbook of International Law* (1999), 26

Tietje, C., *Internationalisiertes Verwaltungshandeln*, Berlin: Duncker & Humblot 2001

Tomuschat, C., 'Der Verfassungsstaat im Geflecht der internationalen Beziehungen', 36 *Veröffentlichungen der Vereinigung der Deutschen Staatsrechtslehrer* (1978), 7

Tomuschat, C., 'International Law: Ensuring the Survival of Mankind on the Eve of a New Century', 281 *Recueil des Cours* (1999), 9

Trachtman, J. P., 'Bananas, Direct Effect and Compliance', 10 *European Journal of International Law* (1999), 655

Trachtman, J. P., 'The Domain of WTO Dispute Resolution', 40 *Harvard International Law Journal* (1999), 333

Trachtman, J. P., 'Legal Aspects of a Poverty Agenda at the WTO: Trade Law and "Global Apartheid"', 6 *Journal of International Economic Law* (2003), 3

Trachtman, J. P., 'Review of *Conflict of Norms in Public International Law: How WTO Law Relates to Other Rules of International Law* by Joost Pauwelyn', 98 *American Journal of International Law* (2004), 855

Trachtman, J. P., 'The Constitutions of the WTO', 17 *European Journal of International Law* (2006), 623

Trachtman, J. P., 'The WTO Cathedral', 43 *Stanford Journal of International Law* (2007), 127

Trachtman, J. P., 'Ensuring a Development-Friendly WTO', 12 *ICTSD News and Analysis* No. 1, February 2008

Trachtman, J. P., *The Economic Structure of International Law*, Harvard University Press 2008

Trebilcock, M. J., Howse, R., *The Regulation of International Trade*, London: Routledge 3rd edn 2005

Uerpmann, R., *Das öffentliche Interesse*, Tübingen: Mohr Siebeck 1999

UNCTAD, WTO, *Trade-Related Investment Measures and Other Performance Requirements*, Part II, Evidence on the Use, the Policy Objectives, and the Impact of Trade-Related Investment Measures and Other Performance Requirements, WTO Doc. G/C/W/307 Add. 1 (8 February 2002)

UNDP, *Human Development Report 2005: International Cooperation at a Crossroads*, New York: UNDP 2005

UNEP, WTO, *Trade and Climate Change*, Geneva: WTO 2009

Van Damme, I., *Treaty Interpretation by the WTO Appellate Body*, Oxford University Press 2009

Verdier, P. H., 'Transnational Regulatory Networks and their Limits', 34 *Yale Journal of International Law* (2009), 113

Verdross, A., Simma, B., *Universelles Völkerrecht: Theorie und Praxis*, Berlin: Duncker & Humblot 3rd edn 1984

Viner, J., 'Conflicts of Principle in Drafting a Trade Charter', 25 *Foreign Affairs* (1947), 613

Vöneky, S., *Die Fortgeltung des Umweltvölkerrechts in internationalen bewaffneten Konflikten*, Berlin, Heidelberg, New York: Springer 2001

Vöneky, S., Hagedorn, C., Clados, M., von Achenbach, J. (eds.), *Chances for and Limits of International Law and Legal Language in the Area of Bioethics*, Berlin, Heidelberg, New York: Springer 2009

Vranes, E., 'From Bananas I to the 2001 Bananas Settlement: A Factual and Procedural Analysis of the WTO Proceedings', in: F. Breuss, S. Griller, E. Vranes (eds.), *The Banana Dispute: An Economic and Legal Analysis*, Vienna: Springer 2003, 1

Walter, C., 'Constitutionalizing (Inter)National Governance: Possibilities for and Limits to the Development of an International Constitutional Law', 44 *German Yearbook of International Law* (2001), 170

Weiler, J. H. H., 'Alternatives to Withdrawal from an International Organization: The Case of the European Economic Community', 20 *Israel Law Review* (1985), 282

Weiler, J. H. H., *The European Community in Change: Exit, Voice and Loyalty*, Saarbrücken: Europa-Institut der Universität des Saarlandes 1987

Weiler, J. H. H., 'The Rule of Lawyers and the Ethos of Diplomats', 35 *Journal of World Trade* (2001), 191

Weiler, J. H. H., 'The Geology of International Law: Governance, Democracy and Legitimacy', 64 *Heidelberg Journal of International Law* (2004), 547

Weiler, J. H. H., '*Brazil – Measures Affecting Imports of Retreaded Tyres* (DS322)', 8 *World Trade Review* (2009), 137

Weiler, J. H. H., 'The Interpretation of Treaties: A Re-Examination', 21 *European Journal of International Law* (2010), 507

Weiler, J. H. H., Motoc, I., 'Taking Democracy Seriously: The Normative Challenge to the International System', in: S. Griller (ed.), *International Economic Governance and Non-Economic Concerns*, Vienna: Springer 2003, 47

Weizsäcker, C. F. von, 'Bedingungen des Friedens', in: C.F. von Weizsäcker *et al.*, *Vier Ansprachen anlässlich der Verleihung des Friedenspreises des Deutschen Buchhandels*, Frankfurter Börsenverein 1963

Wheatley, S., *The Democratic Legitimacy of International Law*, Oxford: Hart Publishing 2010

Wilcox, C., *A Charter for World Trade*, New York: Macmillan 1949

Williams, P. J., *A Handbook on Accession to the WTO*, Cambridge University Press 2008

Winter, G., 'Transnational Administrative Comitology: The Global Harmonization of Chemicals Classification and Labelling', in: O. Dilling, M. Herberg, G. Winter (eds.), *Transnational Administrative Rule-Making: Performance, Legal Effects, and Legitimacy*, Oxford: Hart Publishing 2011, 111

Wolfrum, R., 'Article IX WTO Agreement', in: R. Wolfrum, P.-T. Stoll, K. Kaiser (eds.), *WTO. Institutions and Dispute Settlement*, Leiden: Nijhoff 2006, 106.

Wolfrum, R., 'Annex on Article II Exemptions', in: R. Wolfrum, P.-T. Stoll, C. Feinäugle, *WTO: Trade in Services*, Leiden: Nijhoff 2008, 569

Wolfrum, R., 'Article II GATS', in: R. Wolfrum, P.-T. Stoll, C. Feinäugle, *WTO: Trade in Services*, Leiden: Nijhoff 2008, 71

Woody, K., 'Diamonds on the Souls of her Shoes: The Kimberley Process and the Morality Exception to WTO Restrictions', 22 *Connecticut Journal of International Law* (2007), 335

WTO, *Analytical Index of the GATT*, Volumes I and II, Geneva: WTO 1995 (6th edn 2001)

WTO, *Understanding the WTO*, www.wto.org/english/thewto_e/whatis_e/tif_e/understanding_e.pdf

WTO, *WTO Policy Issues for Parliamentarians: A Guide to Current Trade Issues for Legislators*, Geneva: WTO 2001, www.wto.org/english/res_e/booksp_e/parliamentarians_e.pdf

WTO, *Analytical Index: Guide to WTO Law and Practice*, Geneva: WTO 2nd edn 2004, www.wto.org/english/res_e/booksp_e/analytic_index_e/analytic_index_e.htm

WTO, *Annual Report 2004*, Geneva: WTO 2005, www.wto.org/english/res_e/reser_e/annual_report_e.htm

Yi-Chong, X., Weller, P., *The Governance of World Trade: International Civil Servants and the GATT/WTO*, Cheltenham: Edward Elgar 2004

Young, M. A., 'Fragmentation or Interaction: The WTO, Fisheries Subsidies and International Law', 8 *World Trade Review* (2009), 477

Yu, D., 'The Harmonized System: Amendments and their Impact on WTO Members' Schedules', *WTO Staff Working Paper* ERSD-2008-02, at 12, 13, www.wto.org/english/res_e/reser_e/ersd200802_e.htm

Yusuf, A., *Legal Aspects of Trade Preferences for Developing States: A Study in the Influence of Development Needs on the Evolution of International Law*, Geneva: Nijhoff 1982

Zangl, B., Zürn, M. 'Verrechtlichung jenseits des Staates', in: B. Zangl, M. Zürn (eds.), *Make Law, Not War: Internationale und transnationale Verrechtlichung als Baustein für Global Governance*, Bonn: J. H. W. Dietz 2004

Ziemele, I., (ed.), *Reservations to Human Rights Treaties and the Vienna Convention Regime*, Leiden: Nijhoff 2004

INDEX